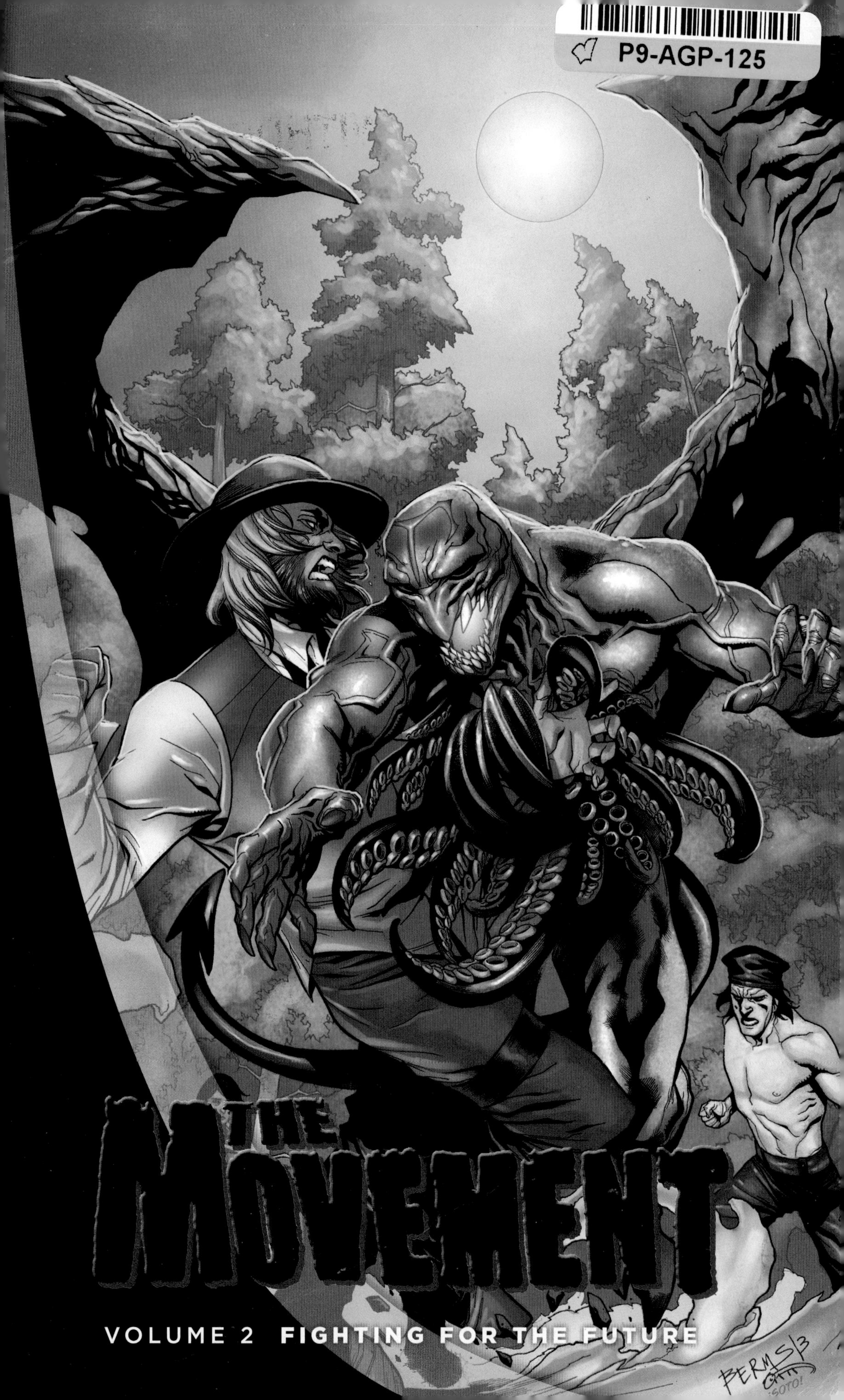
THE
MOVEMENT
VOLUME 2 FIGHTING FOR THE FUTURE

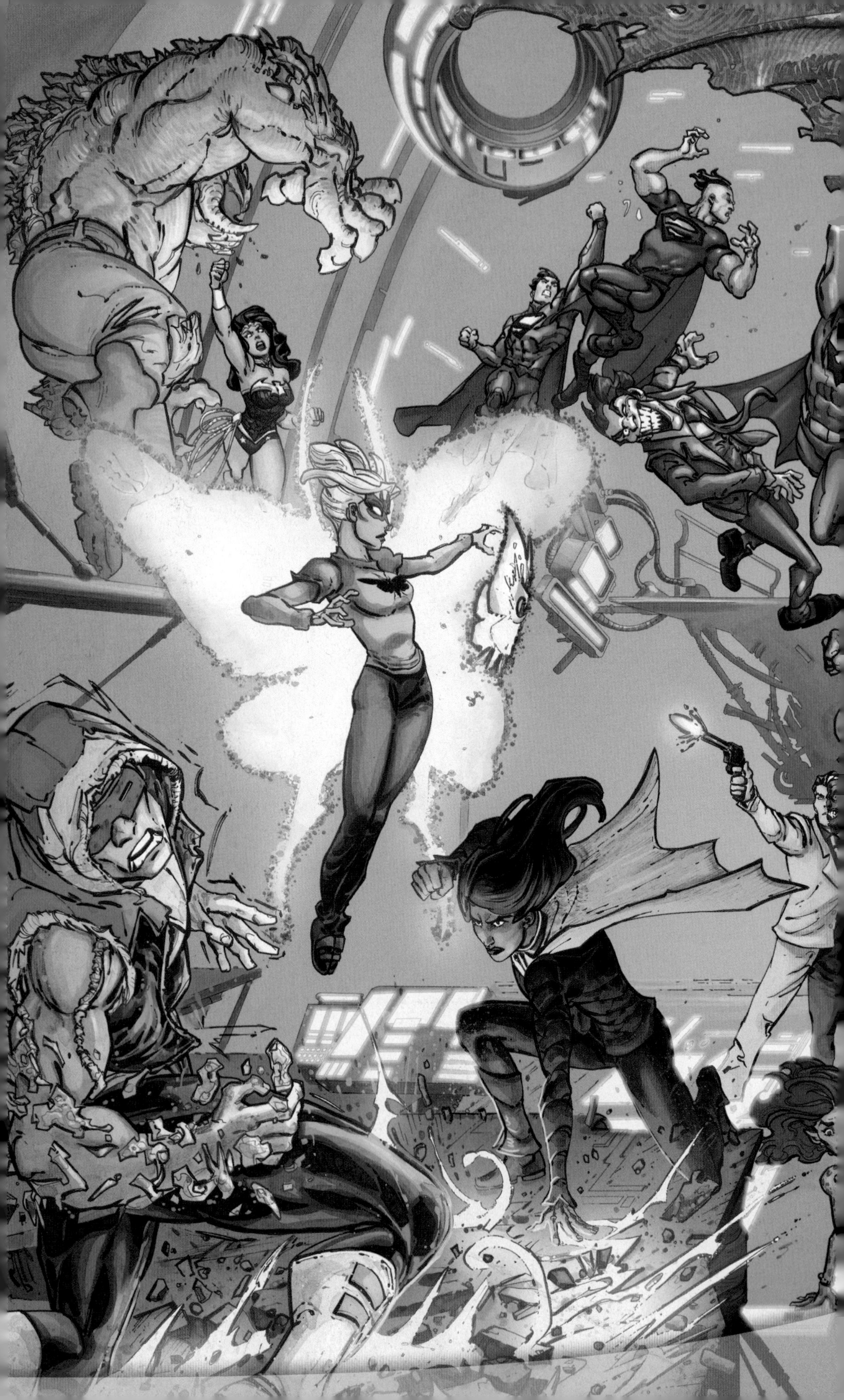

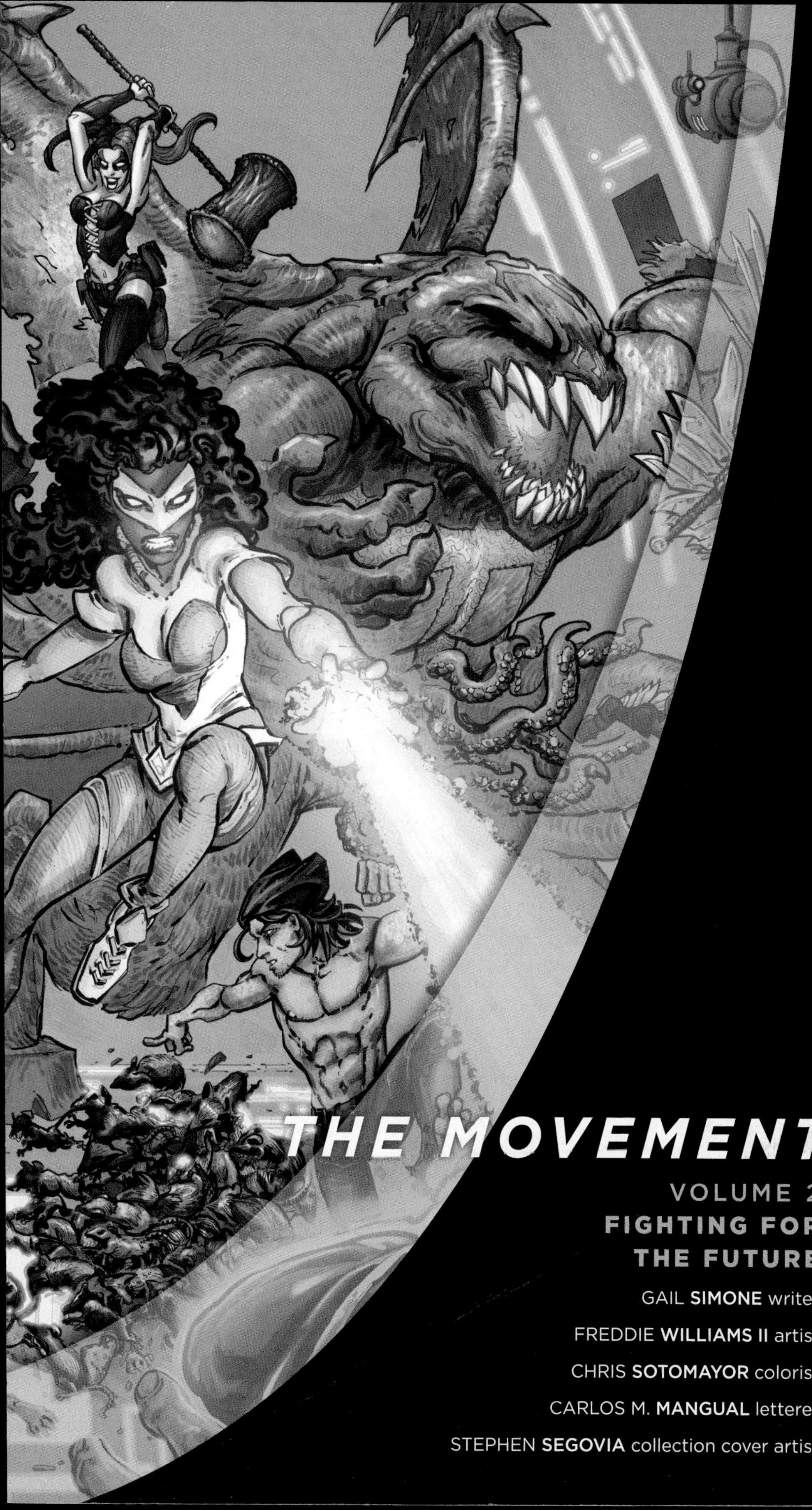

THE MOVEMENT

VOLUME 2
FIGHTING FOR THE FUTURE

GAIL **SIMONE** writer

FREDDIE **WILLIAMS II** artist

CHRIS **SOTOMAYOR** colorist

CARLOS M. **MANGUAL** letterer

STEPHEN **SEGOVIA** collection cover artist

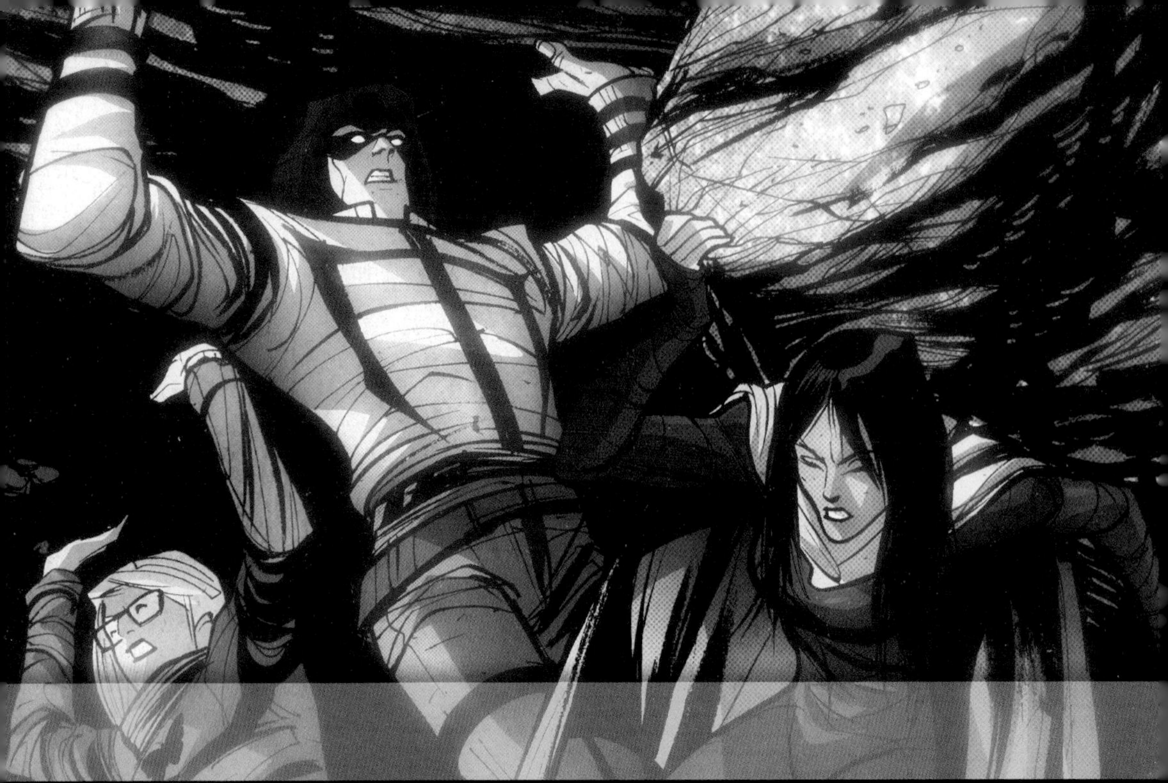

JOEY CAVALIERI Editor - Original Series KYLE ANDRUKIEWICZ Assistant Editor - Original Series LIZ ERICKSON Editor
ROBBIN BROSTERMAN Design Director - Books ROBBIE BIEDERMAN Publication Design

BOB HARRAS Senior VP - Editor-in-Chief, DC Comics

DIANE NELSON President DAN DIDIO and JIM LEE Co-Publishers
GEOFF JOHNS Chief Creative Officer AMIT DESAI Senior VP - Marketing and Franchise Management
AMY GENKINS Senior VP - Business and Legal Affairs NAIRI GARDINER Senior VP - Finance
JEFF BOISON VP - Publishing Planning MARK CHIARELLO VP - Art Direction and Design
JOHN CUNNINGHAM VP - Marketing TERRI CUNNINGHAM VP - Editorial Administration
LARRY GANEM VP - Talent Relations and Services ALISON GILL Senior VP - Manufacturing and Operations
HANK KANALZ Senior VP - Vertigo and Integrated Publishing JAY KOGAN VP - Business and Legal Affairs, Publishing
JACK MAHAN VP - Business Affairs, Talent NICK NAPOLITANO VP - Manufacturing Administration SUE POHJA VP - Book Sales
FRED RUIZ VP - Manufacturing Operations COURTNEY SIMMONS Senior VP - Publicity BOB WAYNE Senior VP - Sales

THE MOVEMENT VOLUME 2: FIGHTING FOR THE FUTURE

DC Comics, 1700 Broadway, New York, NY 10019
A Warner Bros. Entertainment Company.
Printed by RR Donnelley, Salem, VA, USA. 10/31/14. First Printing.
ISBN: 978-1-4012-4952-6

Library of Congress Cataloging-in-Publication Data

Simone, Gail, author.
The Movement. Volume 2, Fighting for the future / Gail Simone, writer ; Freddie Williams II, artist.
pages cm. — (The New 52!)
ISBN 978-1-4012-4952-6 (paperback)
1. Social movements--Comic books, strips, etc. 2. Graphic novels. I. Williams, Freddie E., 1977- illustrator. II. Title. III. Title: Fighting for the future.

PN6728.M685S57 2014
741.5'973—dc23

2014027357

SUSTAINABLE FORESTRY INITIATIVE
Certified Chain of Custody
20% Certified Forest Content,
80% Certified Sourcing
www.sfiprogram.org
SFI-01042
APPLIES TO TEXT STOCK ONLY

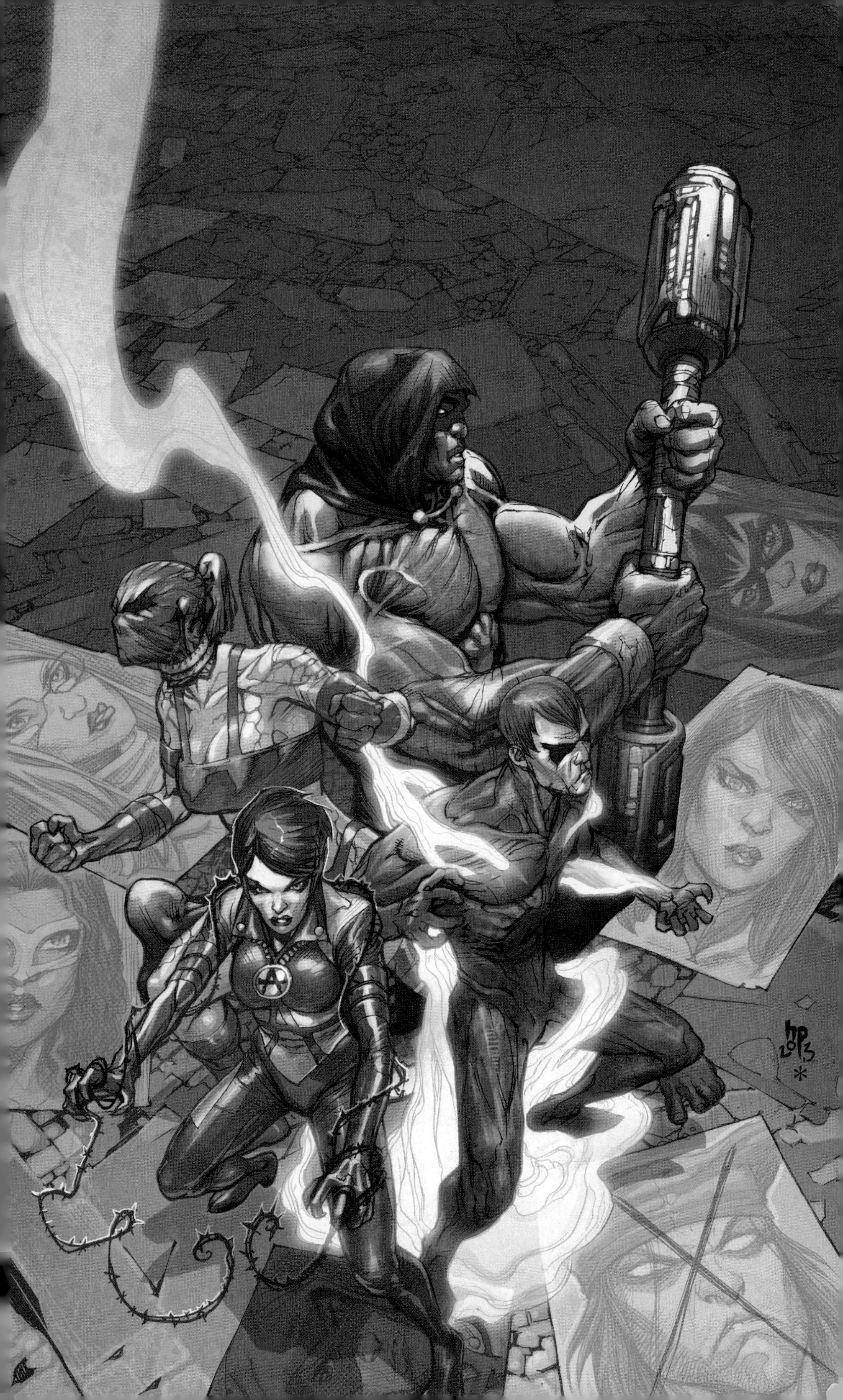

Cover Art by Howard Porter & Hi-Fi

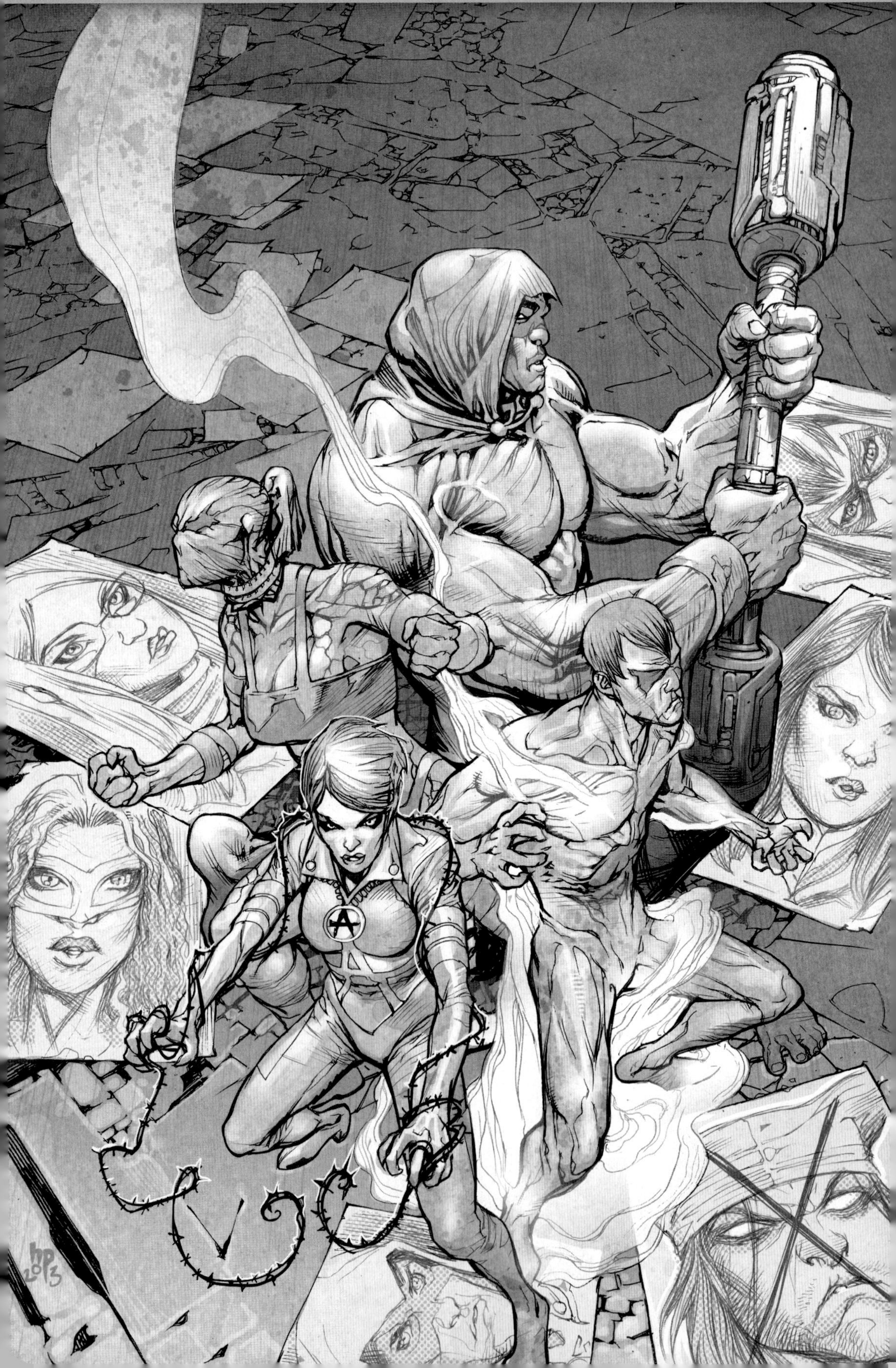
hp
2013

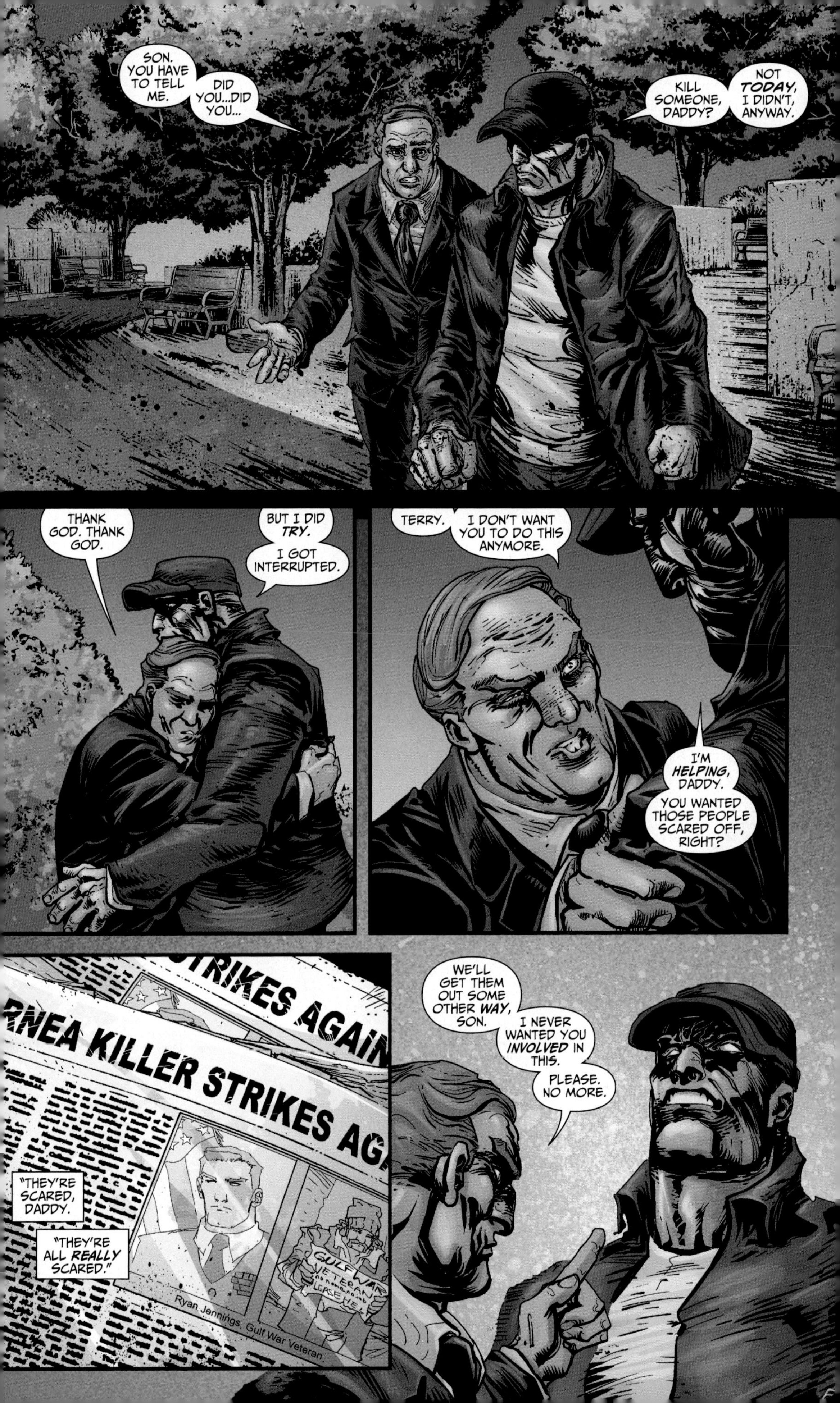
SON. YOU HAVE TO TELL ME.
DID YOU...DID YOU...
KILL SOMEONE, DADDY?
NOT *TODAY*, I DIDN'T, ANYWAY.
THANK GOD. THANK GOD.
BUT I DID *TRY.*
I GOT INTERRUPTED.
TERRY.
I DON'T WANT YOU TO DO THIS ANYMORE.
I'M *HELPING*, DADDY.
YOU WANTED THOSE PEOPLE SCARED OFF, RIGHT?
TRIKES AGAIN
RNEA KILLER STRIKES AG
GULF WAR VETERAN
Ryan Jennings, Gulf War Veteran
"THEY'RE SCARED, DADDY.
"THEY'RE ALL *REALLY* SCARED."
WE'LL GET THEM OUT SOME OTHER *WAY*, SON.
I NEVER WANTED YOU *INVOLVED* IN THIS.
PLEASE. NO MORE.

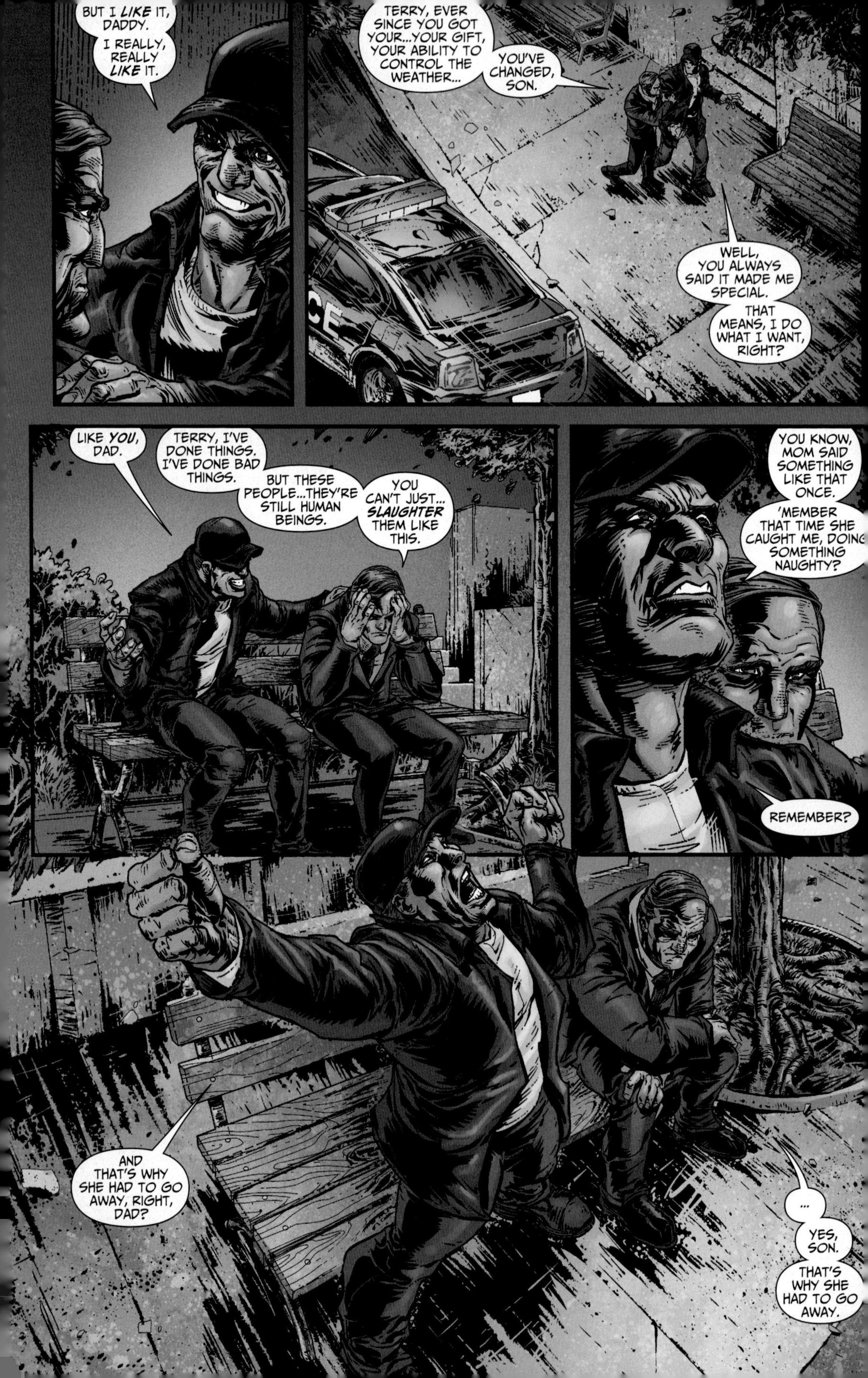
BUT I *LIKE* IT, DADDY.
I REALLY, REALLY *LIKE* IT.
TERRY, EVER SINCE YOU GOT YOUR...YOUR GIFT, YOUR ABILITY TO CONTROL THE WEATHER...
YOU'VE CHANGED, SON.
WELL, YOU ALWAYS SAID IT MADE ME SPECIAL.
THAT MEANS, I DO WHAT I WANT, RIGHT?
LIKE *YOU*, DAD.
TERRY, I'VE DONE THINGS. I'VE DONE BAD THINGS.
BUT THESE PEOPLE...THEY'RE STILL HUMAN BEINGS.
YOU CAN'T JUST... *SLAUGHTER* THEM LIKE THIS.
YOU KNOW, MOM SAID SOMETHING LIKE THAT ONCE.
'MEMBER THAT TIME SHE CAUGHT ME, DOING SOMETHING NAUGHTY?
REMEMBER?
AND THAT'S WHY SHE HAD TO GO AWAY, RIGHT, DAD?
...
YES, SON.
THAT'S WHY SHE HAD TO GO AWAY.

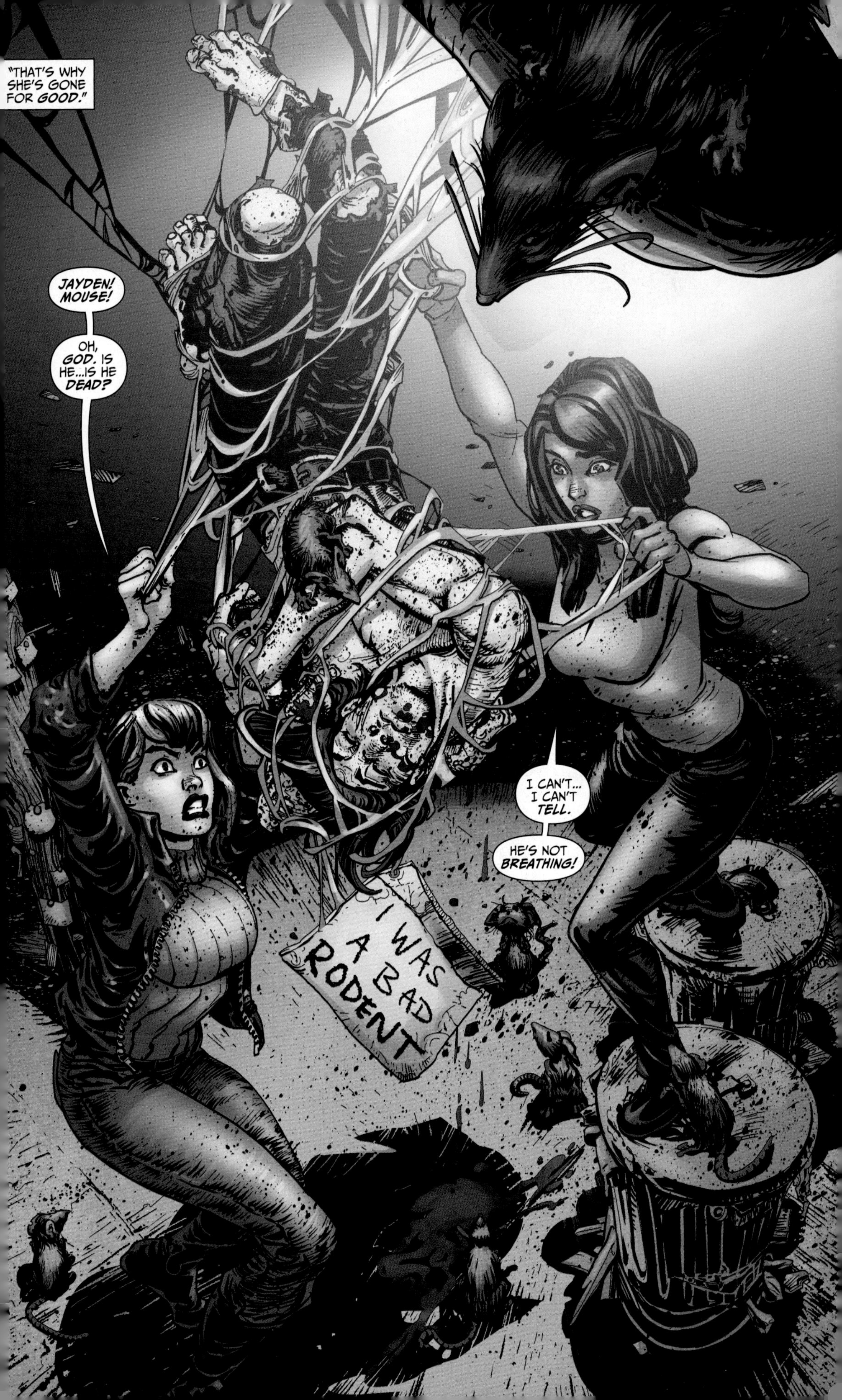
"THAT'S WHY SHE'S GONE FOR GOOD."
JAYDEN! MOUSE!
OH, GOD. IS HE...IS HE DEAD?
I CAN'T... I CAN'T TELL.
HE'S NOT BREATHING!
I WAS A BAD RODENT

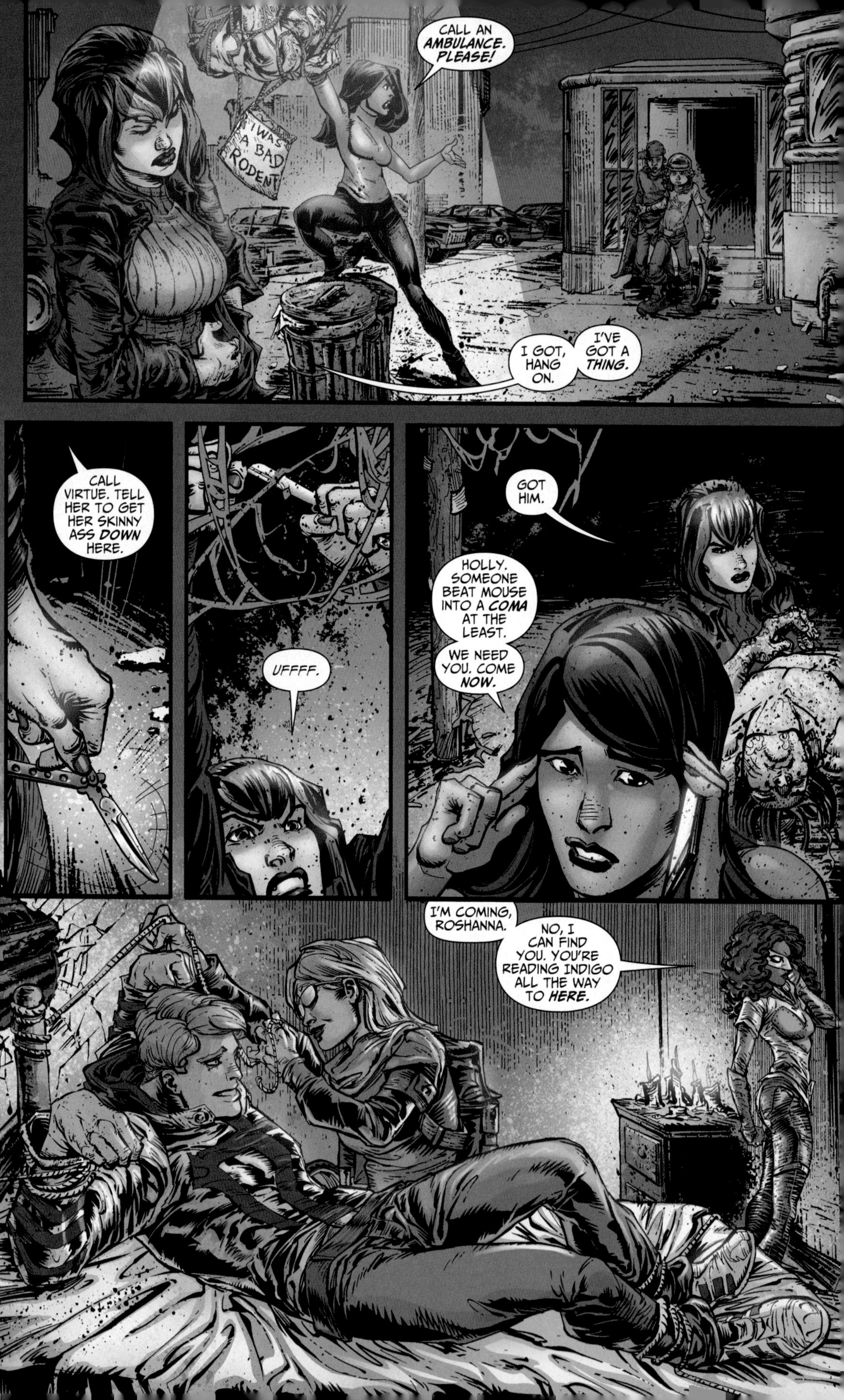
I WAS A BAD RODENT
CALL AN AMBULANCE. PLEASE!
I GOT, HANG ON.
I'VE GOT A THING.
CALL VIRTUE. TELL HER TO GET HER SKINNY ASS DOWN HERE.
UFFFF.
GOT HIM.
HOLLY. SOMEONE BEAT MOUSE INTO A COMA AT THE LEAST.
WE NEED YOU. COME NOW.
I'M COMING, ROSHANNA.
NO, I CAN FIND YOU. YOU'RE READING INDIGO ALL THE WAY TO HERE.

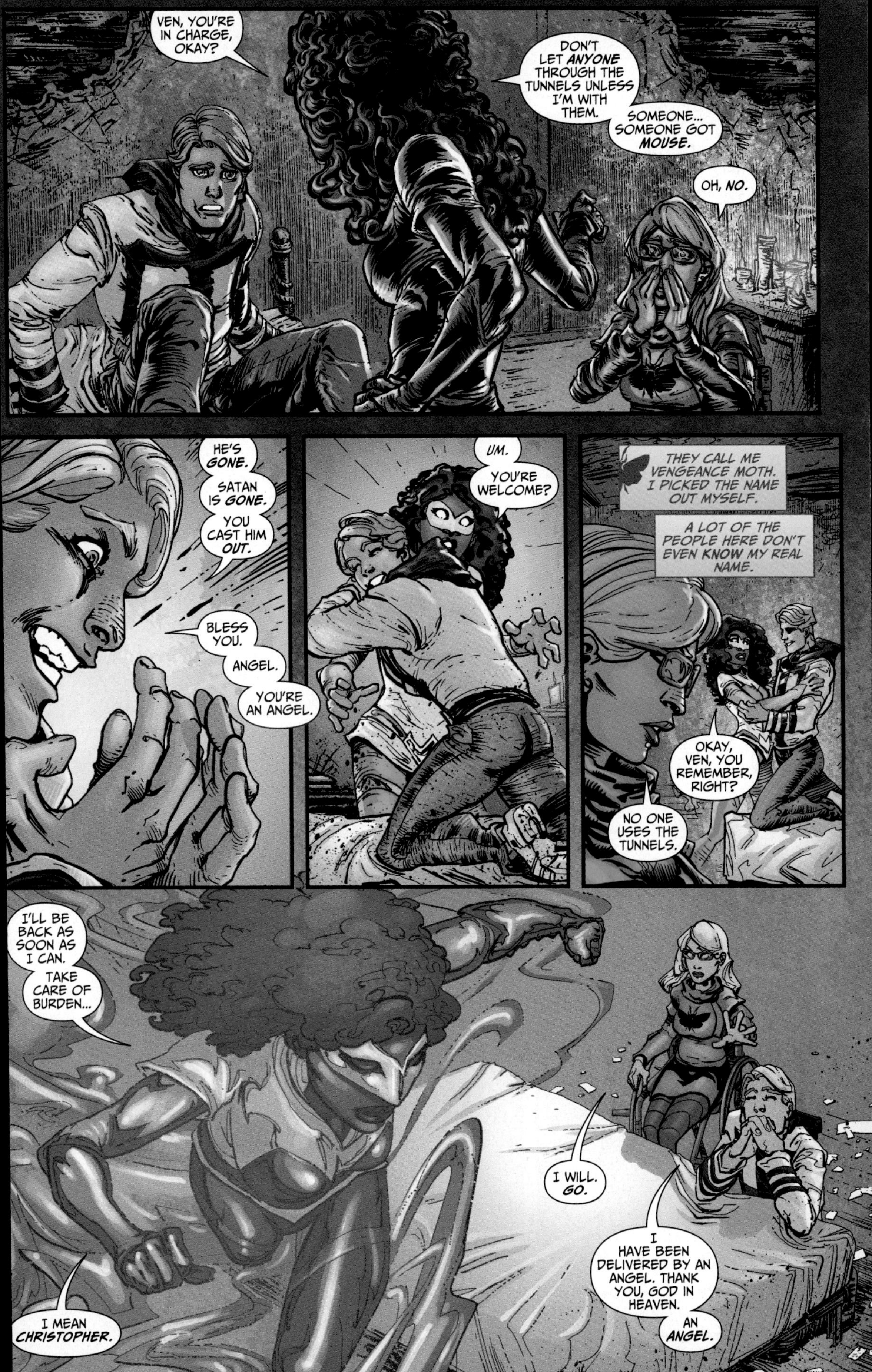
VEN, YOU'RE IN CHARGE, OKAY?
DON'T LET ANYONE THROUGH THE TUNNELS UNLESS I'M WITH THEM.
SOMEONE... SOMEONE GOT MOUSE.
OH, NO.
HE'S GONE.
SATAN IS GONE.
YOU CAST HIM OUT.
BLESS YOU.
ANGEL.
YOU'RE AN ANGEL.
UM.
YOU'RE WELCOME?
THEY CALL ME VENGEANCE MOTH. I PICKED THE NAME OUT MYSELF.
A LOT OF THE PEOPLE HERE DON'T EVEN KNOW MY REAL NAME.
OKAY, VEN, YOU REMEMBER, RIGHT?
NO ONE USES THE TUNNELS.
I'LL BE BACK AS SOON AS I CAN.
TAKE CARE OF BURDEN...
I MEAN CHRISTOPHER.
I WILL. GO.
I HAVE BEEN DELIVERED BY AN ANGEL. THANK YOU, GOD IN HEAVEN.
AN ANGEL.

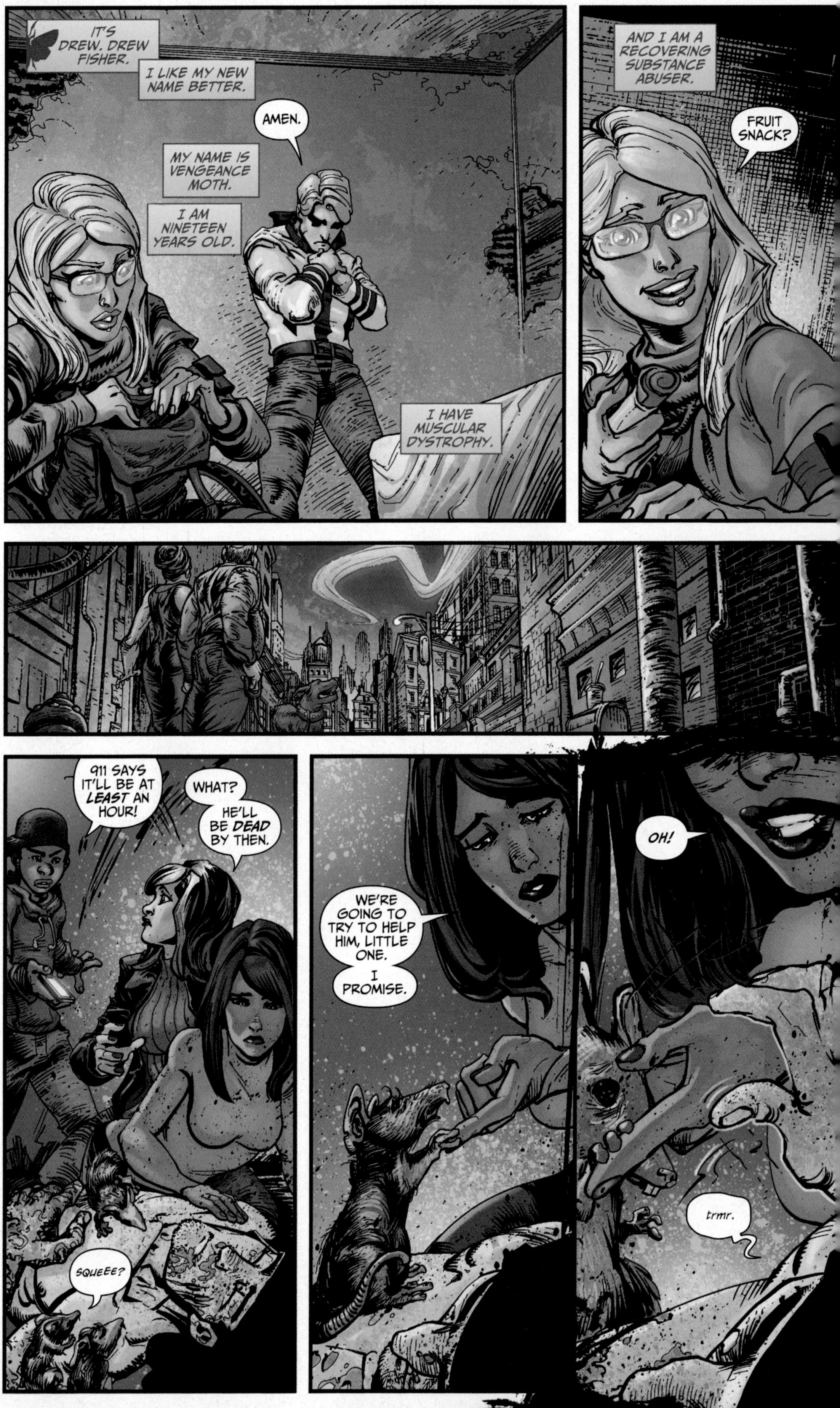
IT'S DREW. DREW FISHER.
I LIKE MY NEW NAME BETTER.
AMEN.
MY NAME IS VENGEANCE MOTH.
I AM NINETEEN YEARS OLD.
I HAVE MUSCULAR DYSTROPHY.
AND I AM A RECOVERING SUBSTANCE ABUSER.
FRUIT SNACK?
911 SAYS IT'LL BE AT LEAST AN HOUR!
WHAT?
HE'LL BE DEAD BY THEN.
SQUEEE?
WE'RE GOING TO TRY TO HELP HIM, LITTLE ONE.
I PROMISE.
OH!
trmr.

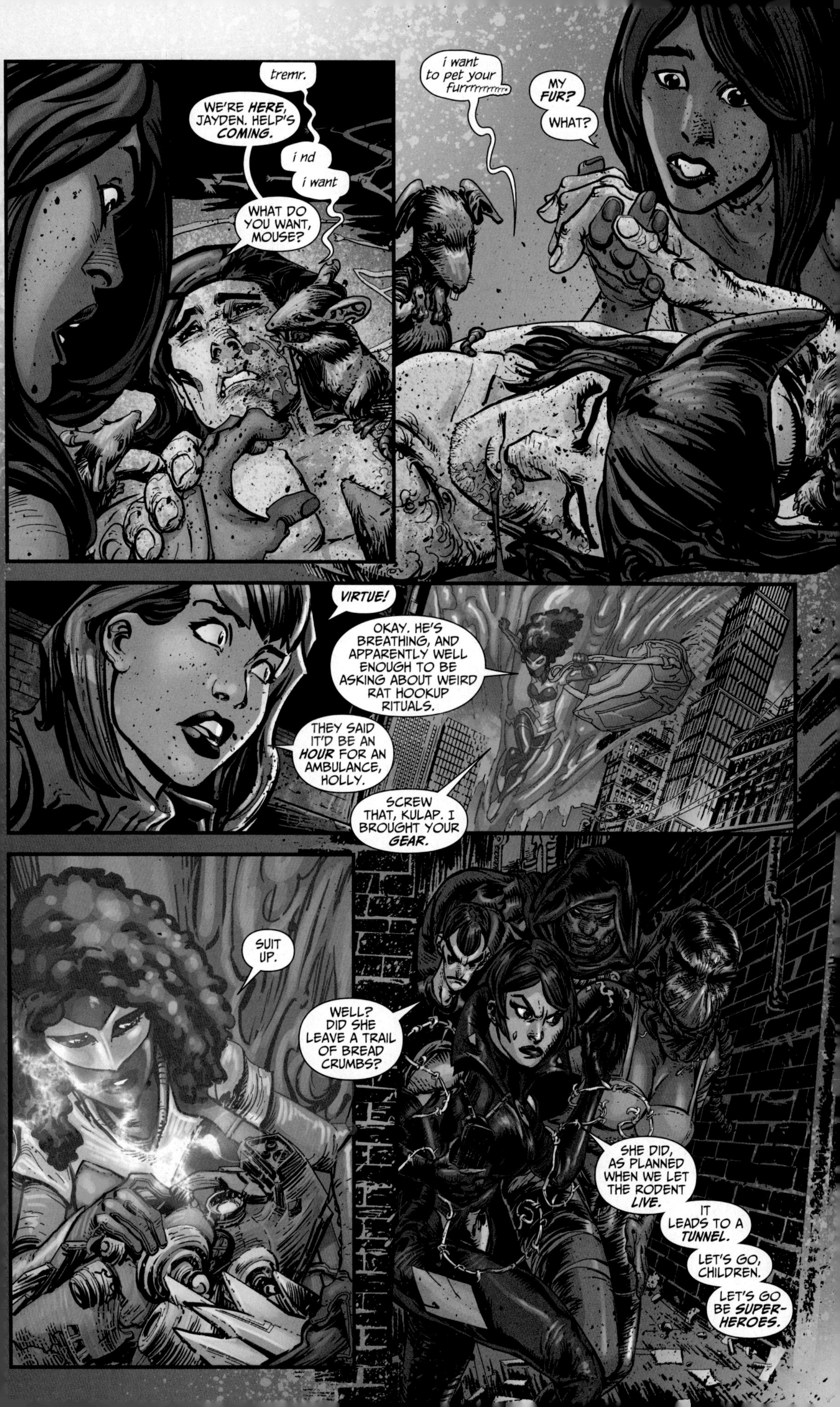
tremr.
WE'RE HERE, JAYDEN. HELP'S COMING.
i nd
i want
WHAT DO YOU WANT, MOUSE?
i want to pet your furrrrrrrrrr
MY FUR?
WHAT?
VIRTUE!
OKAY. HE'S BREATHING, AND APPARENTLY WELL ENOUGH TO BE ASKING ABOUT WEIRD RAT HOOKUP RITUALS.
THEY SAID IT'D BE AN HOUR FOR AN AMBULANCE, HOLLY.
SCREW THAT, KULAP. I BROUGHT YOUR GEAR.
SUIT UP.
WELL? DID SHE LEAVE A TRAIL OF BREAD CRUMBS?
SHE DID, AS PLANNED WHEN WE LET THE RODENT LIVE.
IT LEADS TO A TUNNEL.
LET'S GO, CHILDREN.
LET'S GO BE SUPER-HEROES.

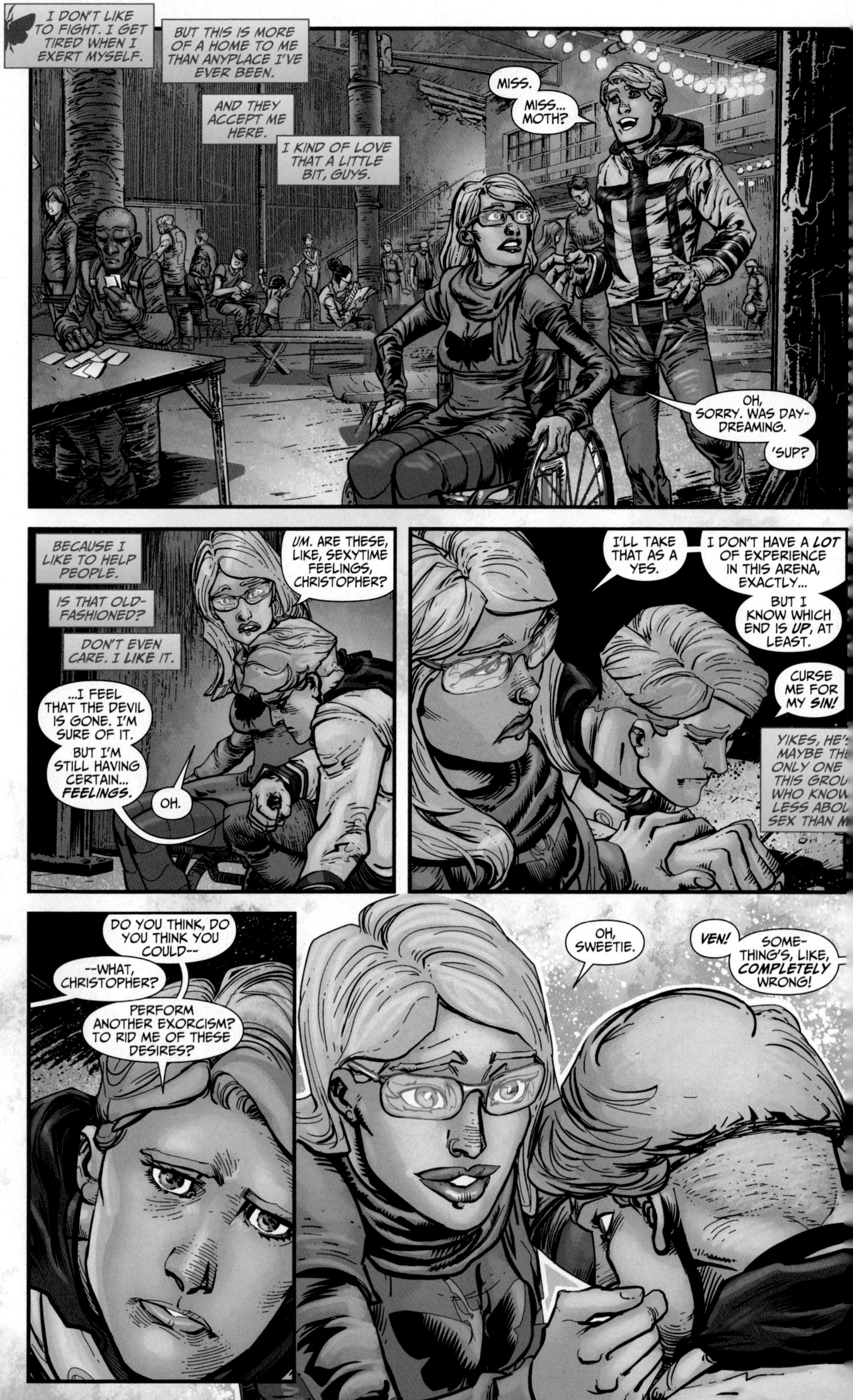

I DON'T LIKE TO FIGHT. I GET TIRED WHEN I EXERT MYSELF.
BUT THIS IS MORE OF A HOME TO ME THAN ANYPLACE I'VE EVER BEEN.
AND THEY ACCEPT ME HERE.
I KIND OF LOVE THAT A LITTLE BIT, GUYS.
MISS.
MISS... MOTH?
OH, SORRY. WAS DAY-DREAMING.
'SUP?
BECAUSE I LIKE TO HELP PEOPLE.
IS THAT OLD-FASHIONED?
DON'T EVEN CARE. I LIKE IT.
...I FEEL THAT THE DEVIL IS GONE. I'M SURE OF IT.
BUT I'M STILL HAVING CERTAIN... FEELINGS.
OH.
UM. ARE THESE, LIKE, SEXYTIME FEELINGS, CHRISTOPHER?
I'LL TAKE THAT AS A YES.
I DON'T HAVE A LOT OF EXPERIENCE IN THIS ARENA, EXACTLY...
BUT I KNOW WHICH END IS UP, AT LEAST.
CURSE ME FOR MY SIN!
DO YOU THINK, DO YOU THINK YOU COULD--
--WHAT, CHRISTOPHER?
PERFORM ANOTHER EXORCISM? TO RID ME OF THESE DESIRES?
OH, SWEETIE.
VEN!
SOME-THING'S, LIKE, COMPLETELY WRONG!

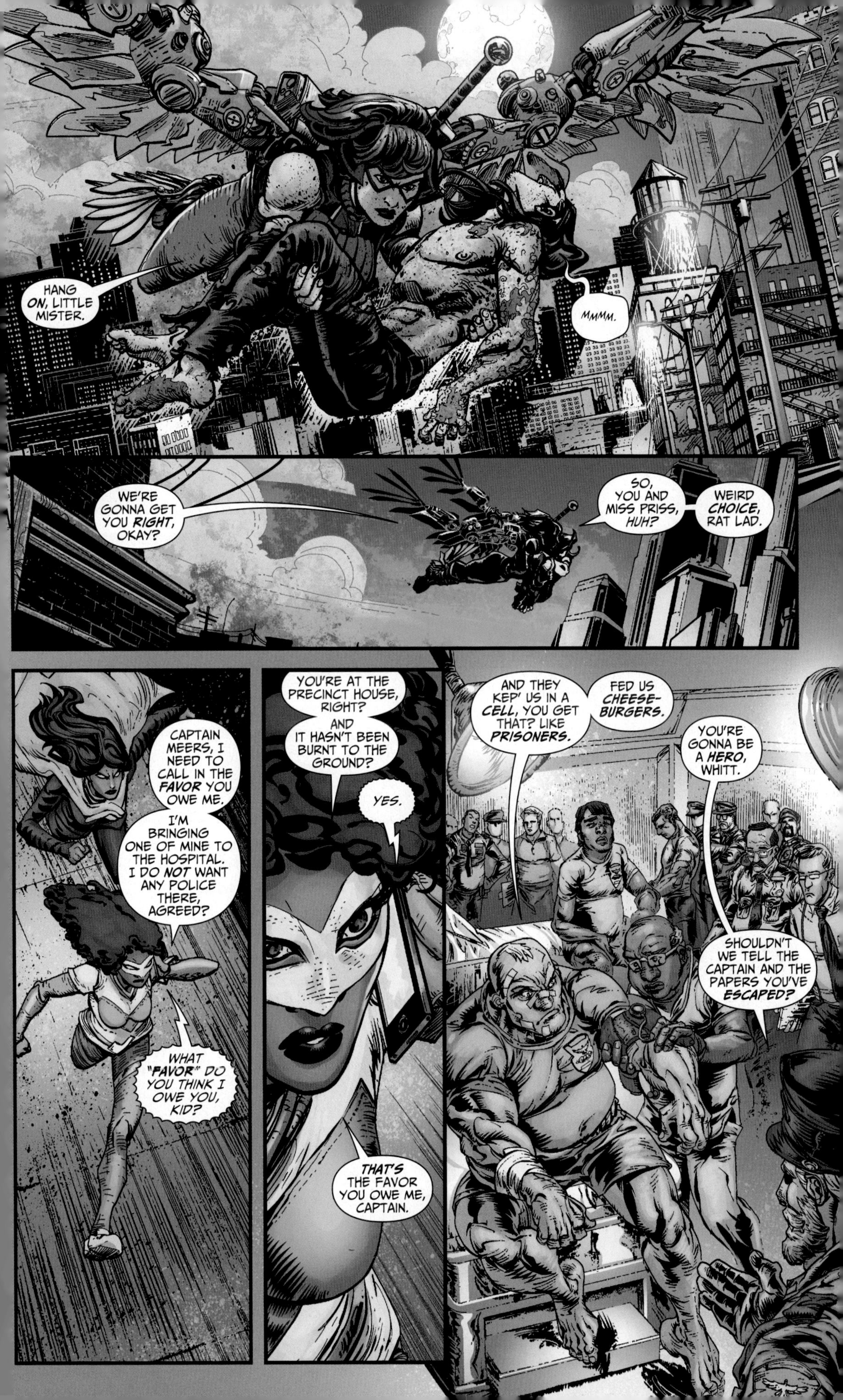
HANG ON, LITTLE MISTER.
MMMM.
WE'RE GONNA GET YOU RIGHT, OKAY?
SO, YOU AND MISS PRISS, HUH?
WEIRD CHOICE, RAT LAD.
CAPTAIN MEERS, I NEED TO CALL IN THE FAVOR YOU OWE ME.
I'M BRINGING ONE OF MINE TO THE HOSPITAL. I DO NOT WANT ANY POLICE THERE, AGREED?
WHAT "FAVOR" DO YOU THINK I OWE YOU, KID?
YOU'RE AT THE PRECINCT HOUSE, RIGHT?
AND IT HASN'T BEEN BURNT TO THE GROUND?
YES.
THAT'S THE FAVOR YOU OWE ME, CAPTAIN.
AND THEY KEP' US IN A CELL, YOU GET THAT? LIKE PRISONERS.
FED US CHEESE-BURGERS.
YOU'RE GONNA BE A HERO, WHITT.
SHOULDN'T WE TELL THE CAPTAIN AND THE PAPERS YOU'VE ESCAPED?

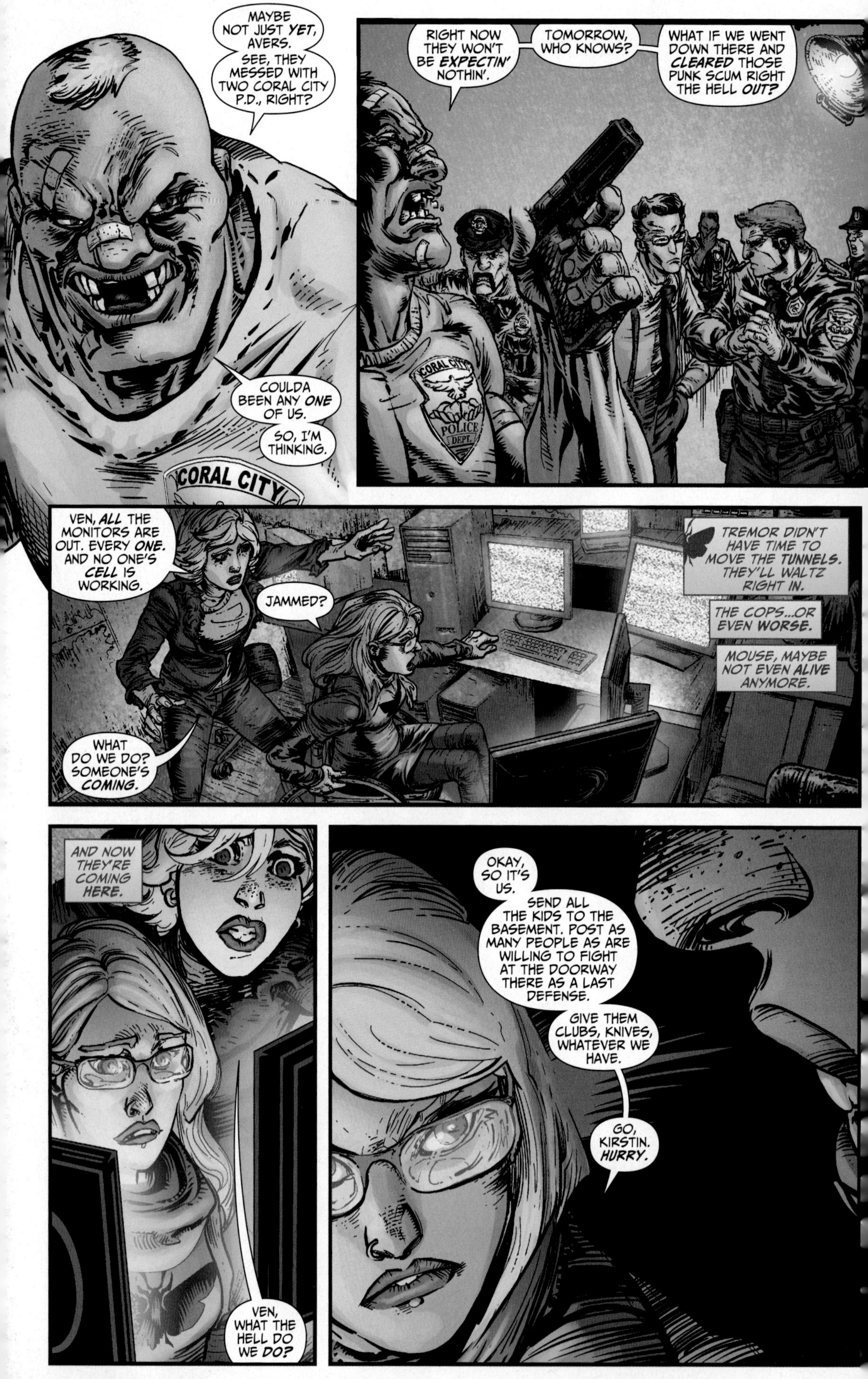
MAYBE NOT JUST YET, AVERS. SEE, THEY MESSED WITH TWO CORAL CITY P.D., RIGHT?
COULDA BEEN ANY ONE OF US.
SO, I'M THINKING.
CORAL CITY
RIGHT NOW THEY WON'T BE EXPECTIN' NOTHIN'.
TOMORROW, WHO KNOWS?
WHAT IF WE WENT DOWN THERE AND CLEARED THOSE PUNK SCUM RIGHT THE HELL OUT?
CORAL CITY POLICE DEPT.
VEN, ALL THE MONITORS ARE OUT. EVERY ONE. AND NO ONE'S CELL IS WORKING.
JAMMED?
TREMOR DIDN'T HAVE TIME TO MOVE THE TUNNELS. THEY'LL WALTZ RIGHT IN.
THE COPS...OR EVEN WORSE.
MOUSE, MAYBE NOT EVEN ALIVE ANYMORE.
WHAT DO WE DO? SOMEONE'S COMING.
AND NOW THEY'RE COMING HERE.
VEN, WHAT THE HELL DO WE DO?
OKAY, SO IT'S US.
SEND ALL THE KIDS TO THE BASEMENT. POST AS MANY PEOPLE AS ARE WILLING TO FIGHT AT THE DOORWAY THERE AS A LAST DEFENSE.
GIVE THEM CLUBS, KNIVES, WHATEVER WE HAVE.
GO, KIRSTIN. HURRY.

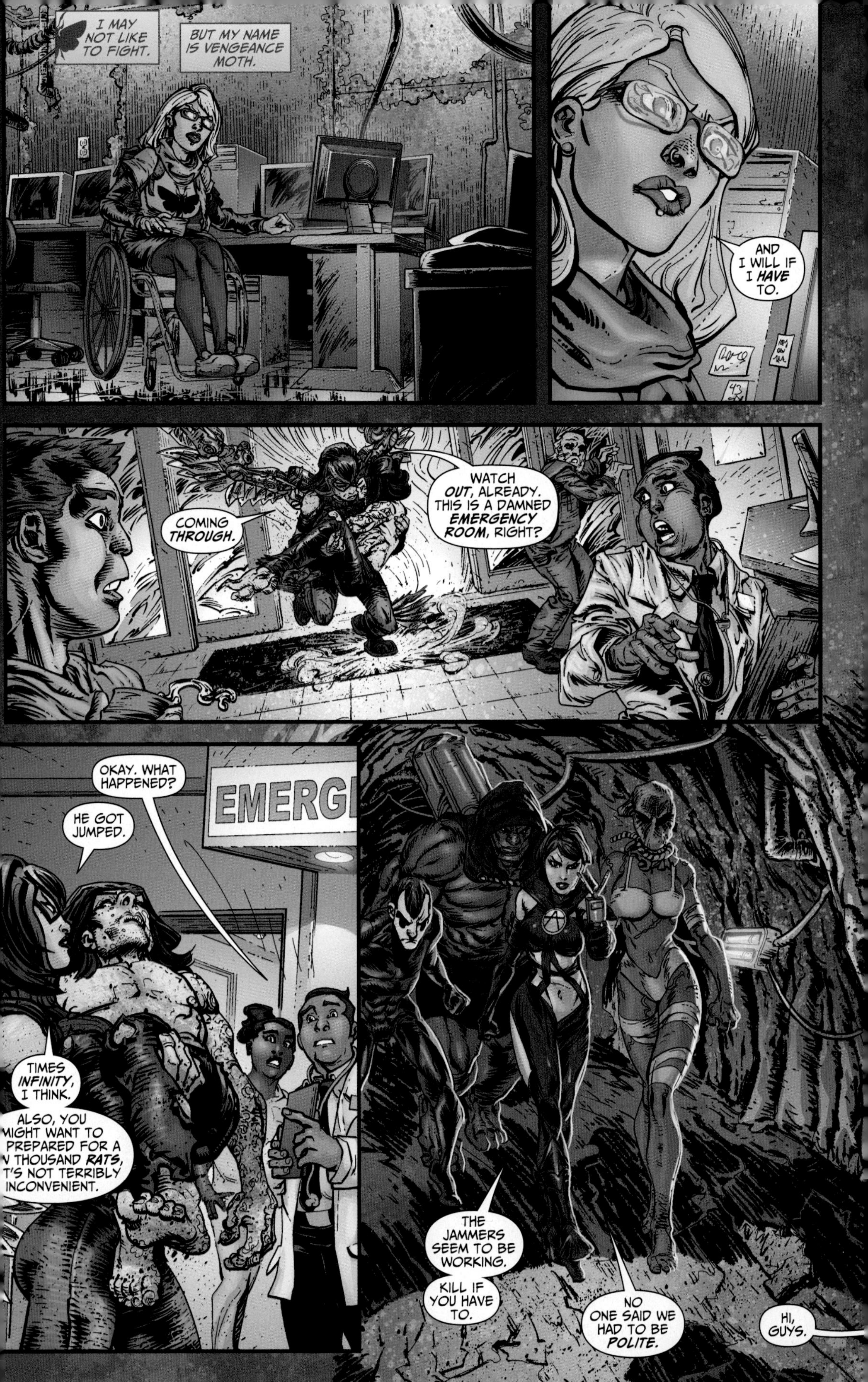

I MAY NOT LIKE TO FIGHT.
BUT MY NAME IS VENGEANCE MOTH.
AND I WILL IF I *HAVE* TO.
COMING *THROUGH*.
WATCH *OUT*, ALREADY. THIS IS A DAMNED *EMERGENCY ROOM*, RIGHT?
EMERG
OKAY. WHAT HAPPENED?
HE GOT JUMPED.
TIMES *INFINITY*, I THINK.
ALSO, YOU MIGHT WANT TO PREPARED FOR A N THOUSAND *RATS*, T'S NOT TERRIBLY INCONVENIENT.
THE JAMMERS SEEM TO BE WORKING.
KILL IF YOU HAVE TO.
NO ONE SAID WE HAD TO BE *POLITE*.
HI, GUYS.

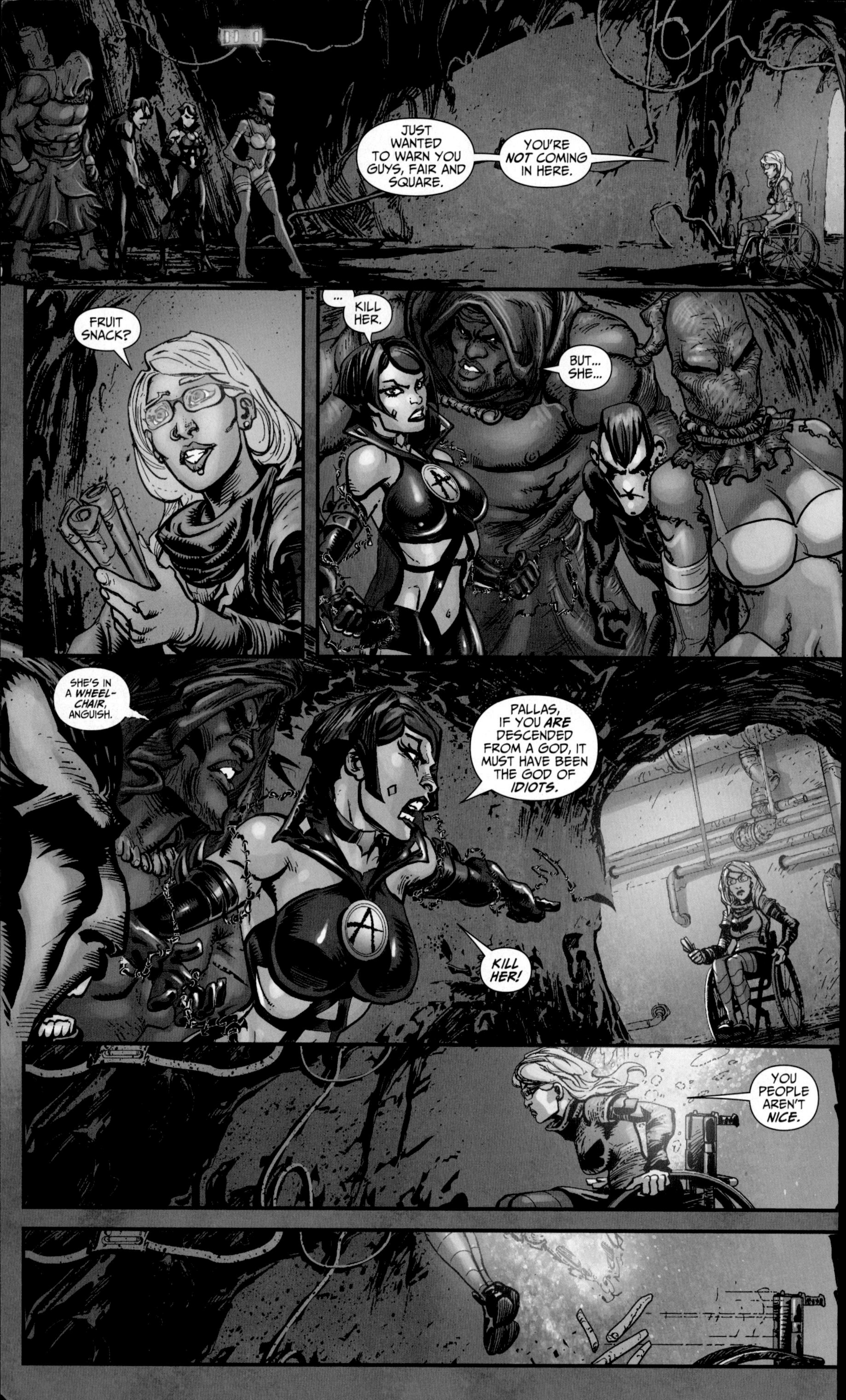
JUST WANTED TO WARN YOU GUYS, FAIR AND SQUARE.
YOU'RE *NOT* COMING IN HERE.
FRUIT SNACK?
...KILL HER.
BUT... SHE...
SHE'S IN A *WHEEL-CHAIR*, ANGUISH.
PALLAS, IF YOU *ARE* DESCENDED FROM A GOD, IT MUST HAVE BEEN THE GOD OF *IDIOTS*.
KILL HER!
YOU PEOPLE AREN'T *NICE*.

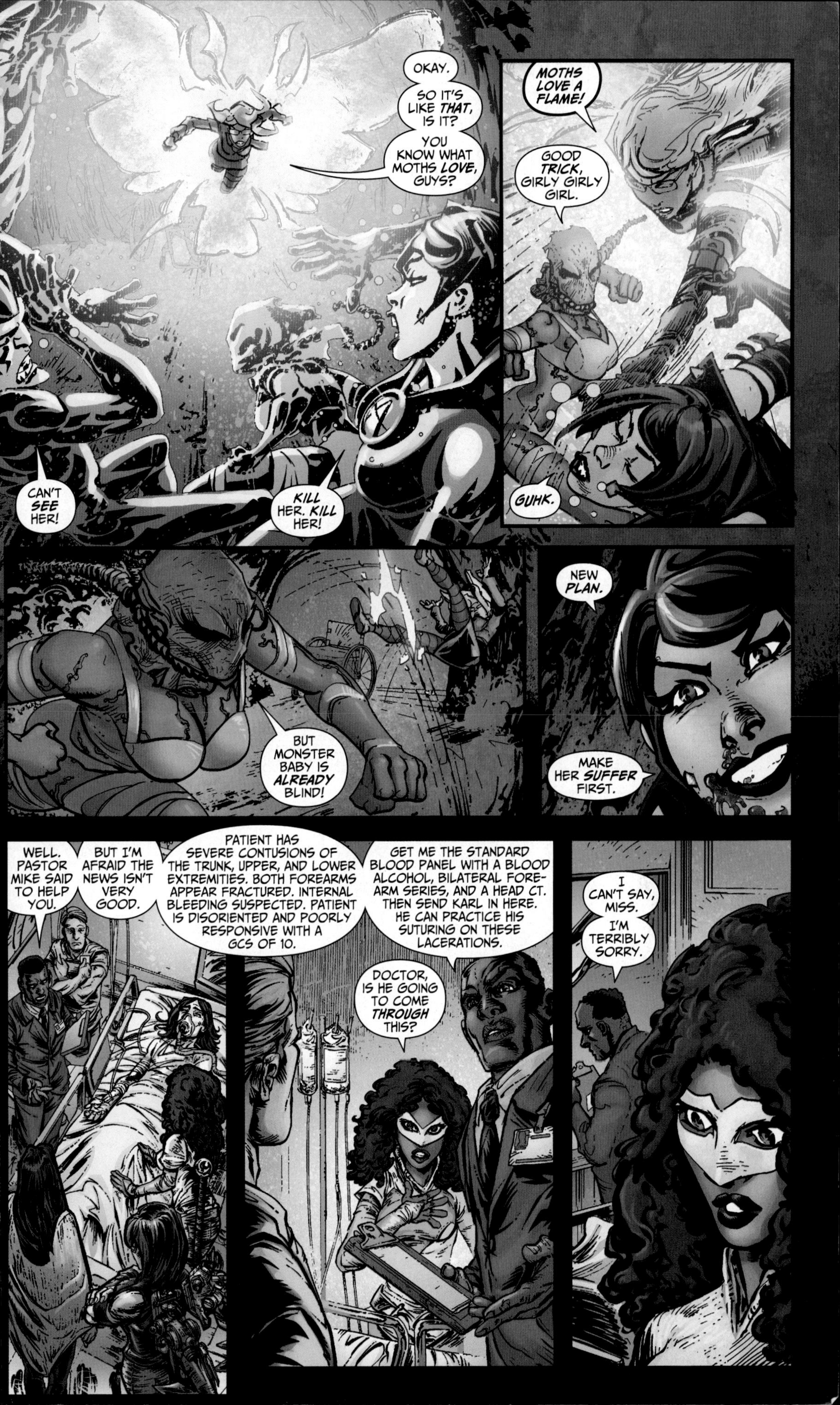
OKAY.
SO IT'S LIKE *THAT*, IS IT?
YOU KNOW WHAT MOTHS *LOVE*, GUYS?
CAN'T *SEE* HER!
KILL HER. *KILL* HER!
MOTHS LOVE A FLAME!
GOOD *TRICK*, GIRLY GIRLY GIRL.
GUHK.
BUT MONSTER BABY IS *ALREADY* BLIND!
NEW *PLAN*.
MAKE HER *SUFFER* FIRST.
WELL. PASTOR MIKE SAID TO HELP YOU.
BUT I'M AFRAID THE NEWS ISN'T VERY GOOD.
PATIENT HAS SEVERE CONTUSIONS OF THE TRUNK, UPPER, AND LOWER EXTREMITIES. BOTH FOREARMS APPEAR FRACTURED. INTERNAL BLEEDING SUSPECTED. PATIENT IS DISORIENTED AND POORLY RESPONSIVE WITH A GCS OF 10.
GET ME THE STANDARD BLOOD PANEL WITH A BLOOD ALCOHOL, BILATERAL FORE-ARM SERIES, AND A HEAD CT. THEN SEND KARL IN HERE. HE CAN PRACTICE HIS SUTURING ON THESE LACERATIONS.
DOCTOR, IS HE GOING TO COME *THROUGH* THIS?
I CAN'T SAY, MISS.
I'M TERRIBLY SORRY.

YOU ALL SAW.
THEY BEAT ME RAW AND THEN PUT ME ON TRIAL.
YOU THINK THEY WON'T DO WORSE TO ALL OF YOU IF WE DON'T LEARN THEM NOT TO SCREW WITH C.C.P.D.?
GRAB WHAT GEAR YOU GOT. BATONS, SPRAY, GUNS AND ARMOR.
BETTER TO STRIKE HARD AND APOLOGIZE LATER THAN WAIT FOR THESE LITTLE CRAPSTAINS TO TAKE US DOWN ONE ON ONE.
WHO'S UP FOR A LITTLE SKULL CRACKING?
YEE?
I'M SORRY, JOE.
I'M NOT GOING TO LET YOU DO THIS.
YEE. YOU'RE A FINE OFFICER.
BUT NEED I REMIND YOU THAT YOU'RE IN CANNON'S POCKET AS DEEP AS ANY OF US?
YOU GOING TO STAND ALONE AGAINST YOUR BROTHERS, YEE?
THAT ALWAYS WORKED BEFORE, JOE. NOT THIS TIME.
I OWE THE CAPTAIN THIS.
YEE. WHAT DO YOU WEIGH, A BUCK TWENTY?
DON'T MAKE ME HURT YOU.
STINTON, HOLD MY CAP, WILL YOU?
THERE'S SOMETHING I'VE ALWAYS WANTED TO TELL YOU, JOE.

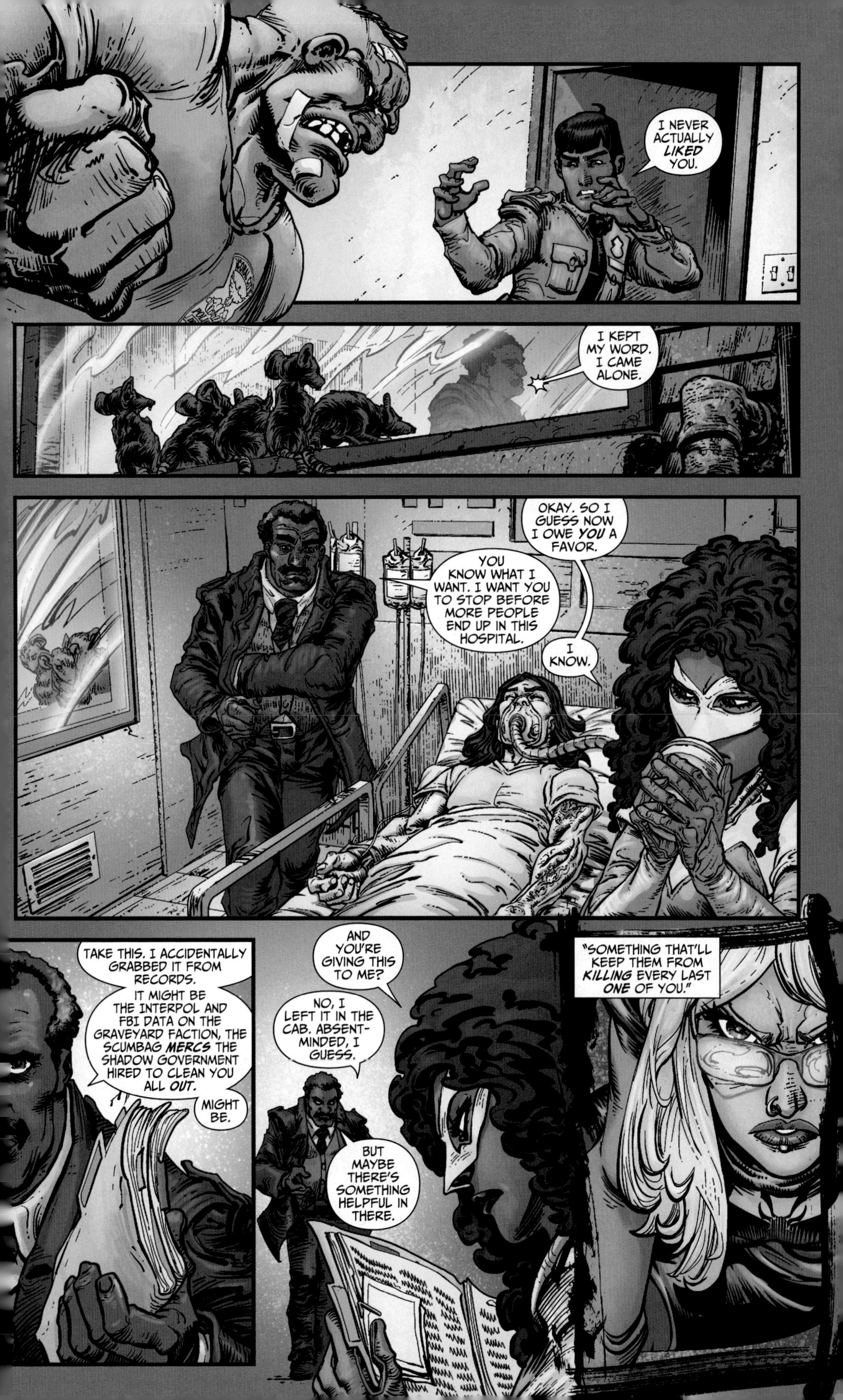

I NEVER ACTUALLY LIKED YOU.
I KEPT MY WORD. I CAME ALONE.
OKAY. SO I GUESS NOW I OWE YOU A FAVOR.
YOU KNOW WHAT I WANT. I WANT YOU TO STOP BEFORE MORE PEOPLE END UP IN THIS HOSPITAL.
I KNOW.
TAKE THIS. I ACCIDENTALLY GRABBED IT FROM RECORDS.
IT MIGHT BE THE INTERPOL AND FBI DATA ON THE GRAVEYARD FACTION, THE SCUMBAG MERCS THE SHADOW GOVERNMENT HIRED TO CLEAN YOU ALL OUT.
MIGHT BE.
AND YOU'RE GIVING THIS TO ME?
NO, I LEFT IT IN THE CAB. ABSENT-MINDED, I GUESS.
BUT MAYBE THERE'S SOMETHING HELPFUL IN THERE.
"SOMETHING THAT'LL KEEP THEM FROM KILLING EVERY LAST ONE OF YOU."

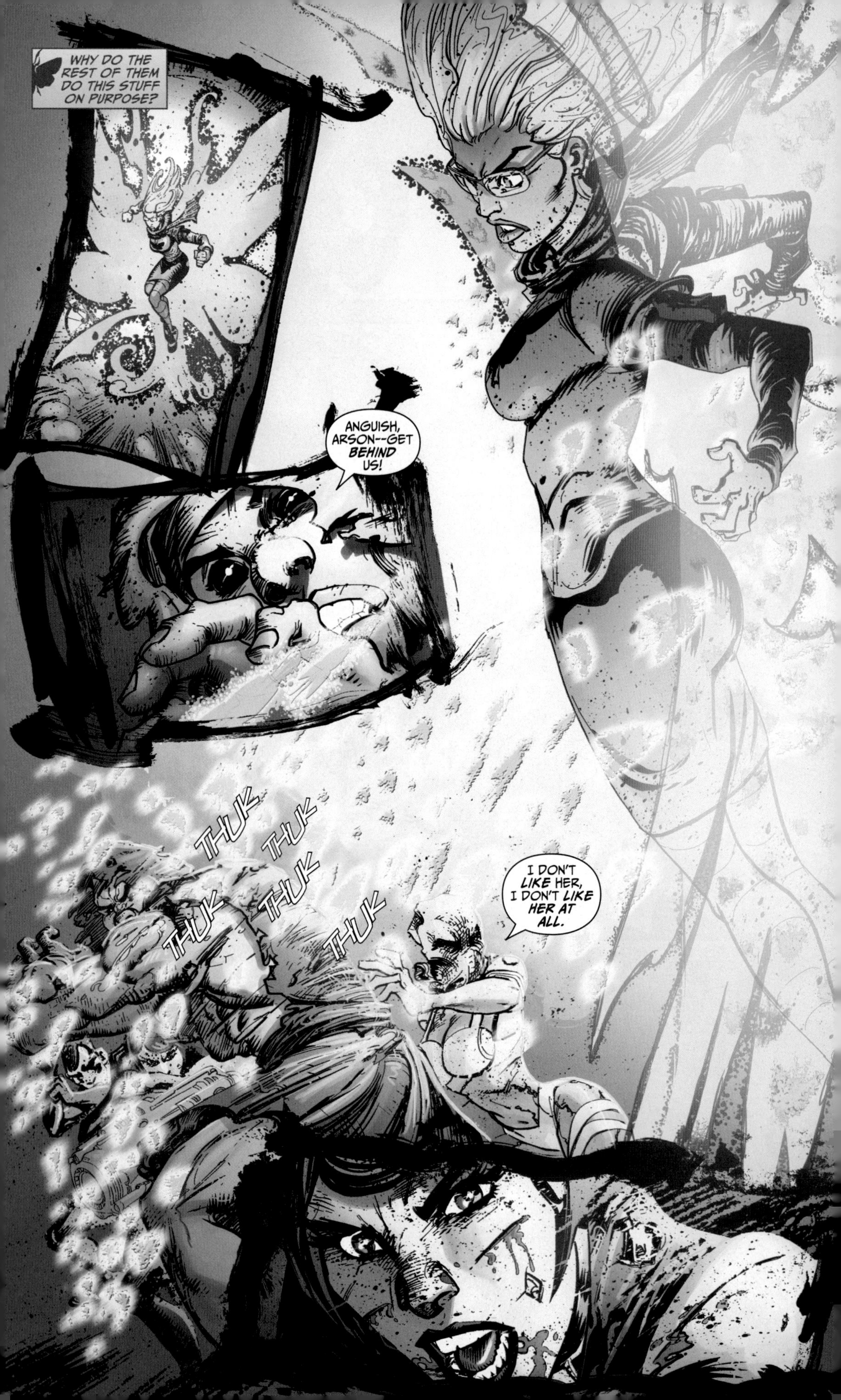
WHY DO THE REST OF THEM DO THIS STUFF ON PURPOSE?
ANGUISH, ARSON--GET BEHIND US!
THUK THUK THUK THUK THUK
I DON'T LIKE HER, I DON'T LIKE HER AT ALL.

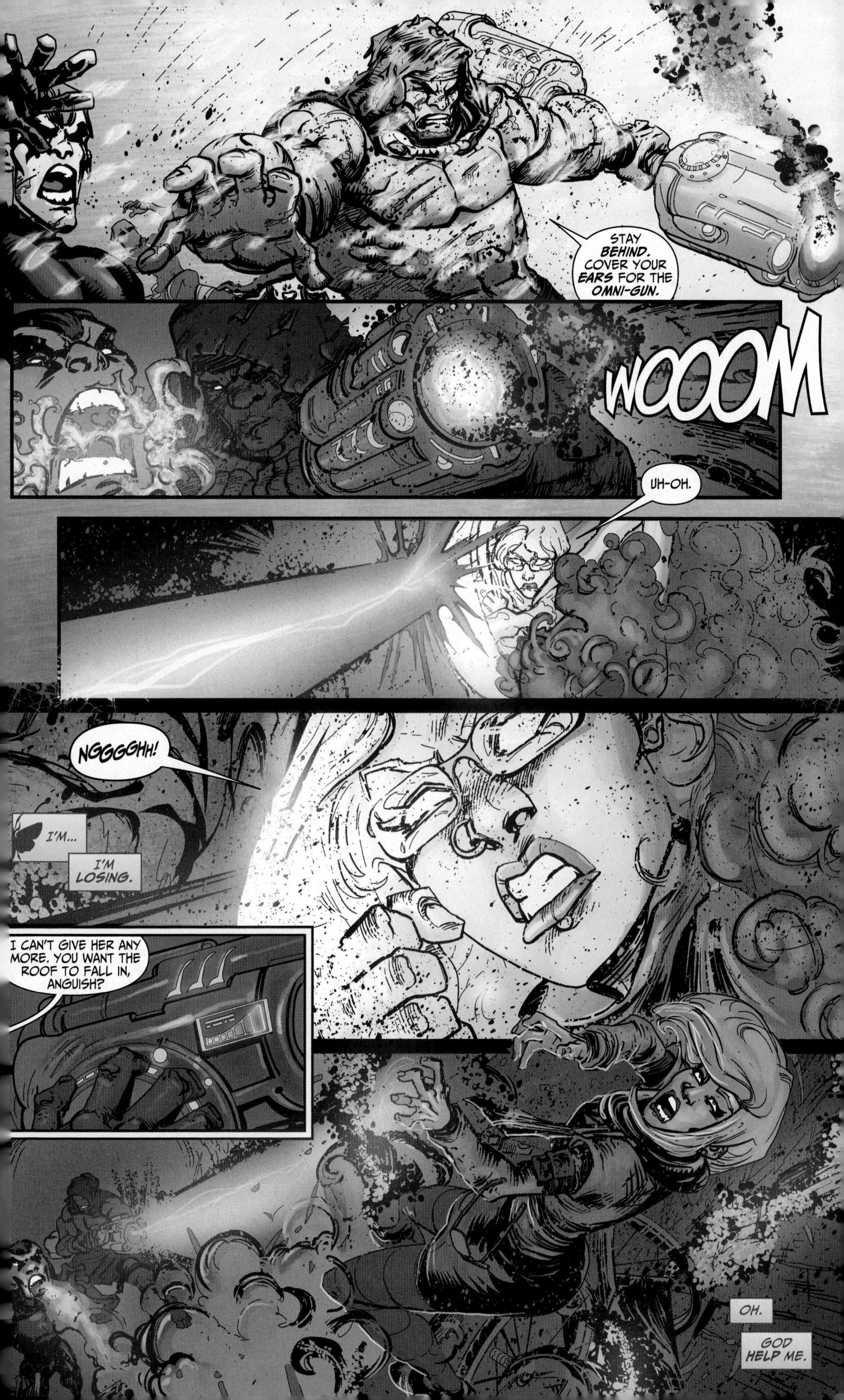

STAY BEHIND. COVER YOUR EARS FOR THE OMNI-GUN.
WOOOM
UH-OH.
NGGGGHH!
I'M...
I'M LOSING.
I CAN'T GIVE HER ANY MORE. YOU WANT THE ROOF TO FALL IN, ANGUISH?
OH.
GOD HELP ME.

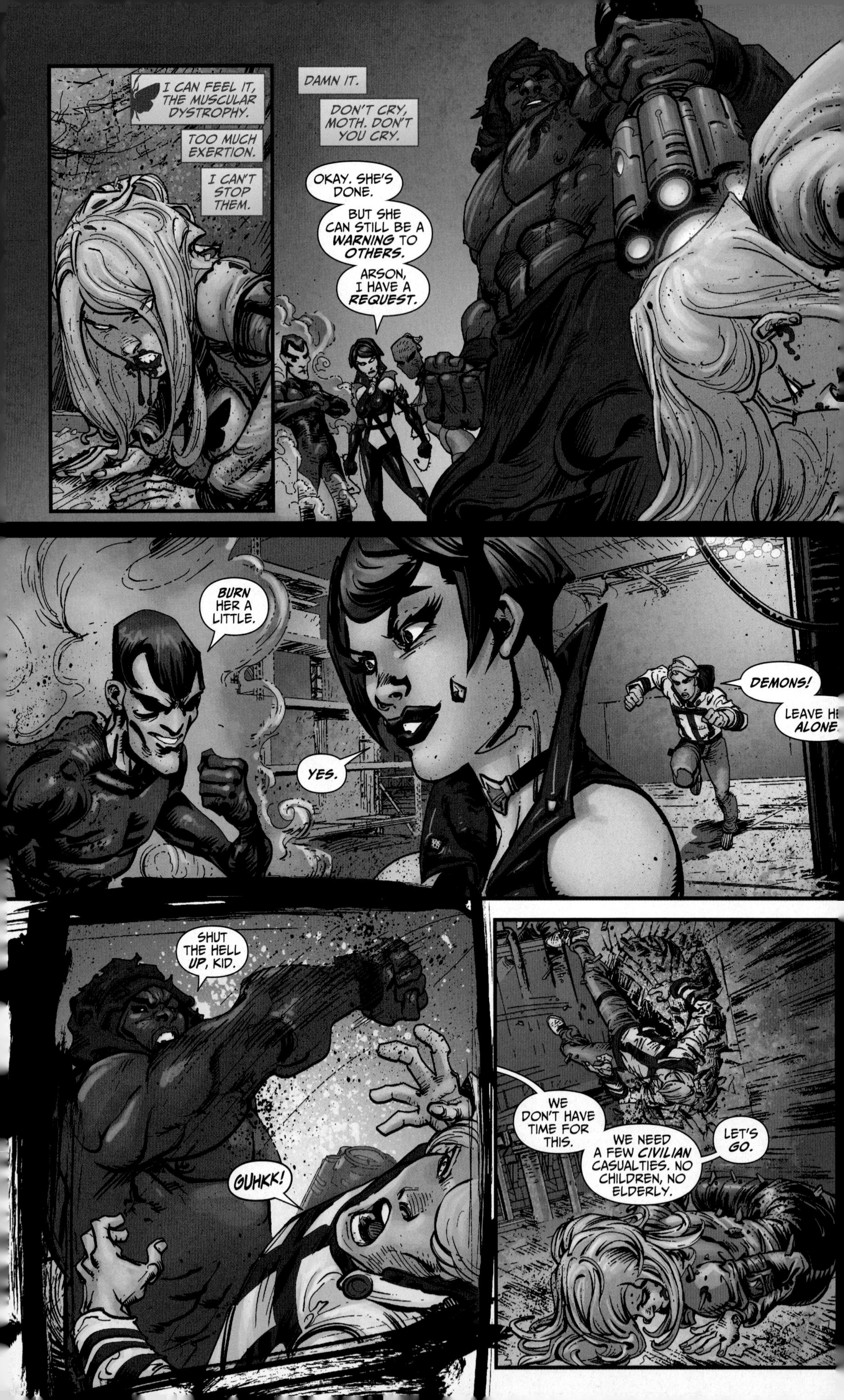
I CAN FEEL IT, THE MUSCULAR DYSTROPHY.
TOO MUCH EXERTION.
I CAN'T STOP THEM.
DAMN IT.
DON'T CRY, MOTH. DON'T YOU CRY.
OKAY. SHE'S DONE.
BUT SHE CAN STILL BE A WARNING TO OTHERS.
ARSON, I HAVE A REQUEST.
BURN HER A LITTLE.
YES.
DEMONS!
LEAVE HE
ALONE
SHUT THE HELL UP, KID.
GUHKK!
WE DON'T HAVE TIME FOR THIS.
WE NEED A FEW CIVILIAN CASUALTIES. NO CHILDREN, NO ELDERLY.
LET'S GO.

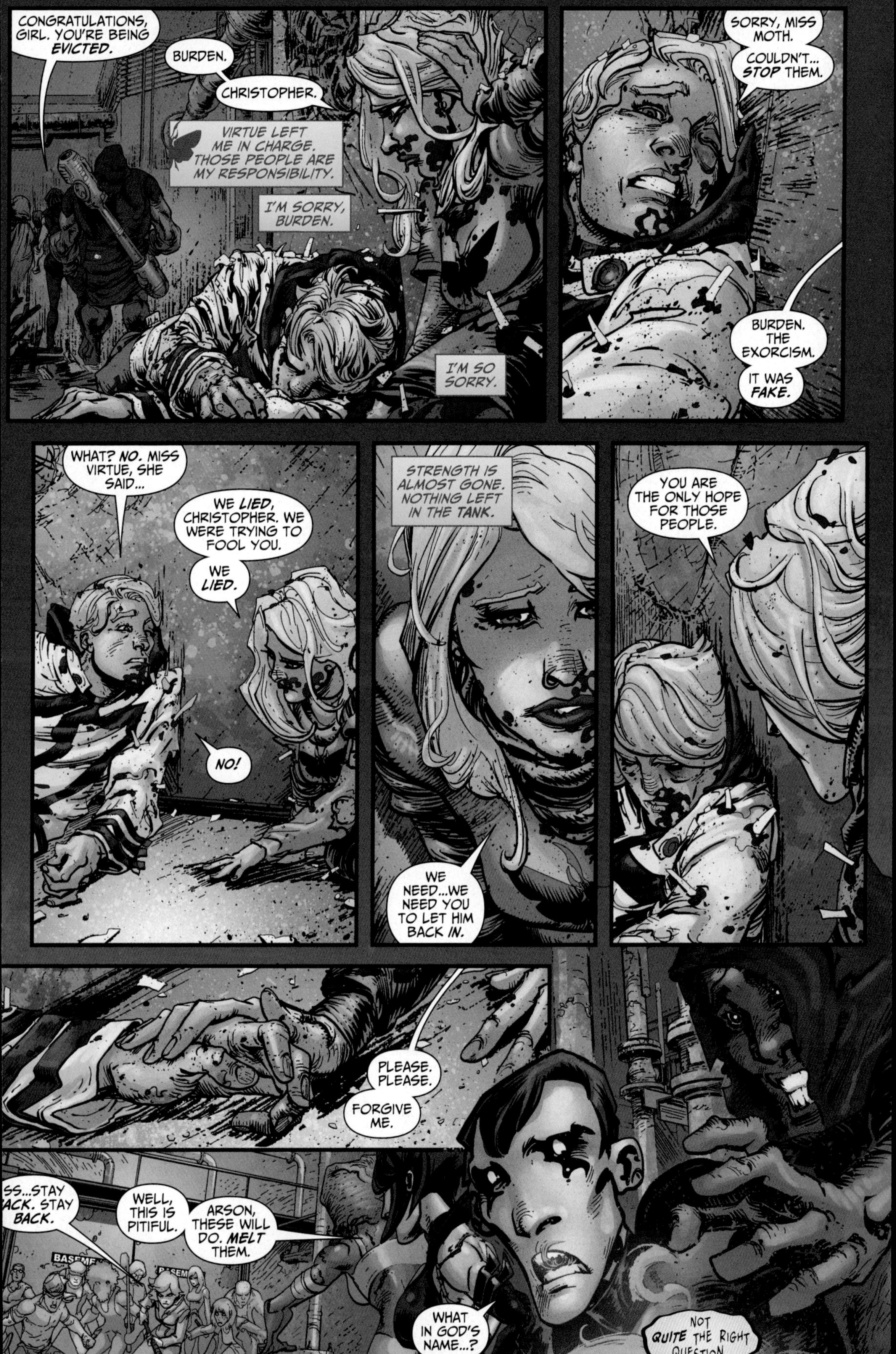
CONGRATULATIONS, GIRL. YOU'RE BEING EVICTED.
BURDEN.
CHRISTOPHER.
VIRTUE LEFT ME IN CHARGE. THOSE PEOPLE ARE MY RESPONSIBILITY.
I'M SORRY, BURDEN.
I'M SO SORRY.
SORRY, MISS MOTH.
COULDN'T... STOP THEM.
BURDEN. THE EXORCISM.
IT WAS FAKE.
WHAT? NO. MISS VIRTUE, SHE SAID...
WE LIED, CHRISTOPHER. WE WERE TRYING TO FOOL YOU.
WE LIED.
NO!
STRENGTH IS ALMOST GONE. NOTHING LEFT IN THE TANK.
WE NEED...WE NEED YOU TO LET HIM BACK IN.
YOU ARE THE ONLY HOPE FOR THOSE PEOPLE.
PLEASE. PLEASE.
FORGIVE ME.
SS...STAY ACK. STAY BACK.
WELL, THIS IS PITIFUL.
ARSON, THESE WILL DO. MELT THEM.
WHAT IN GOD'S NAME...?
NOT QUITE THE RIGHT QUESTION.
HELLO, SINNERS.

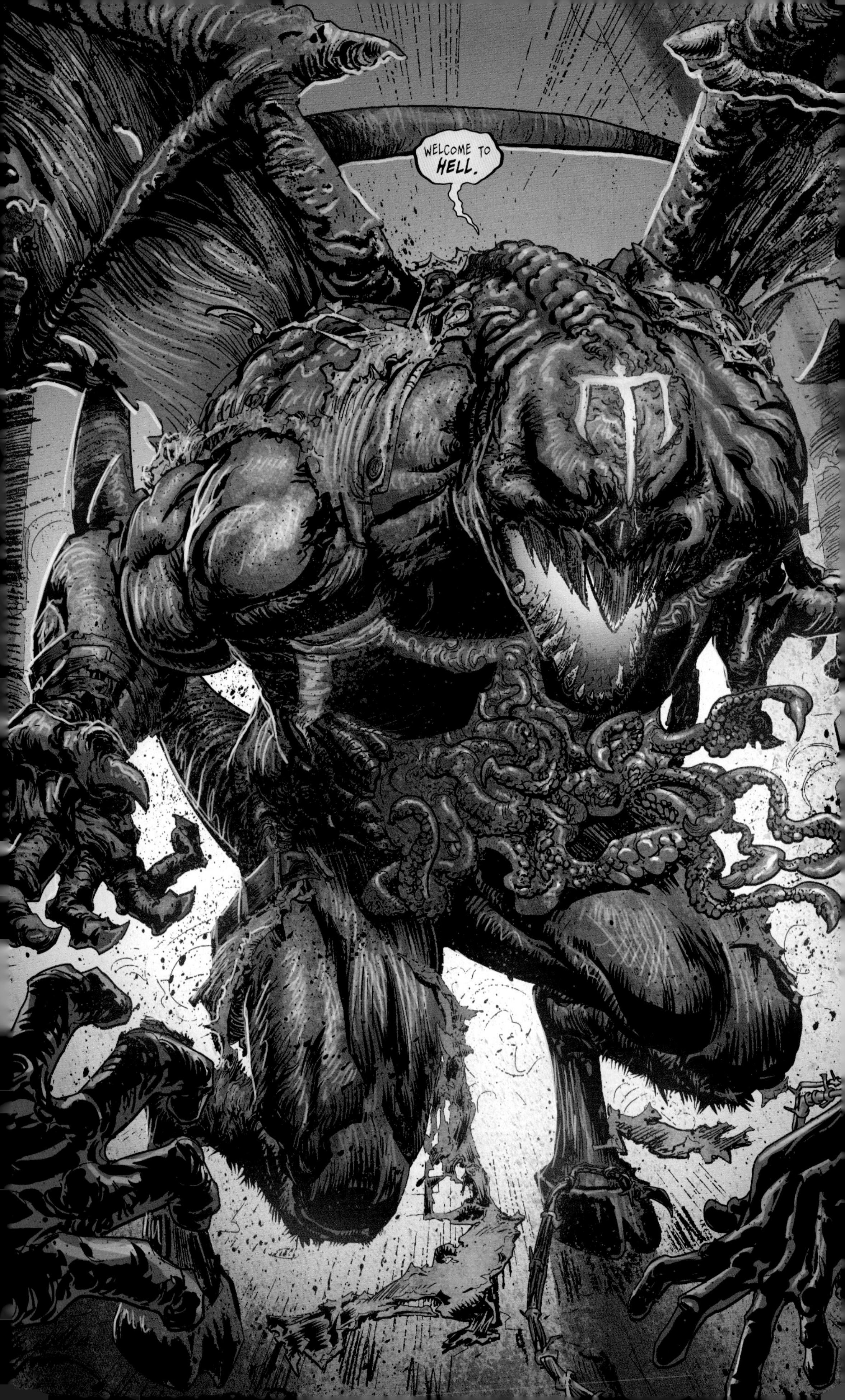
WELCOME TO HELL.

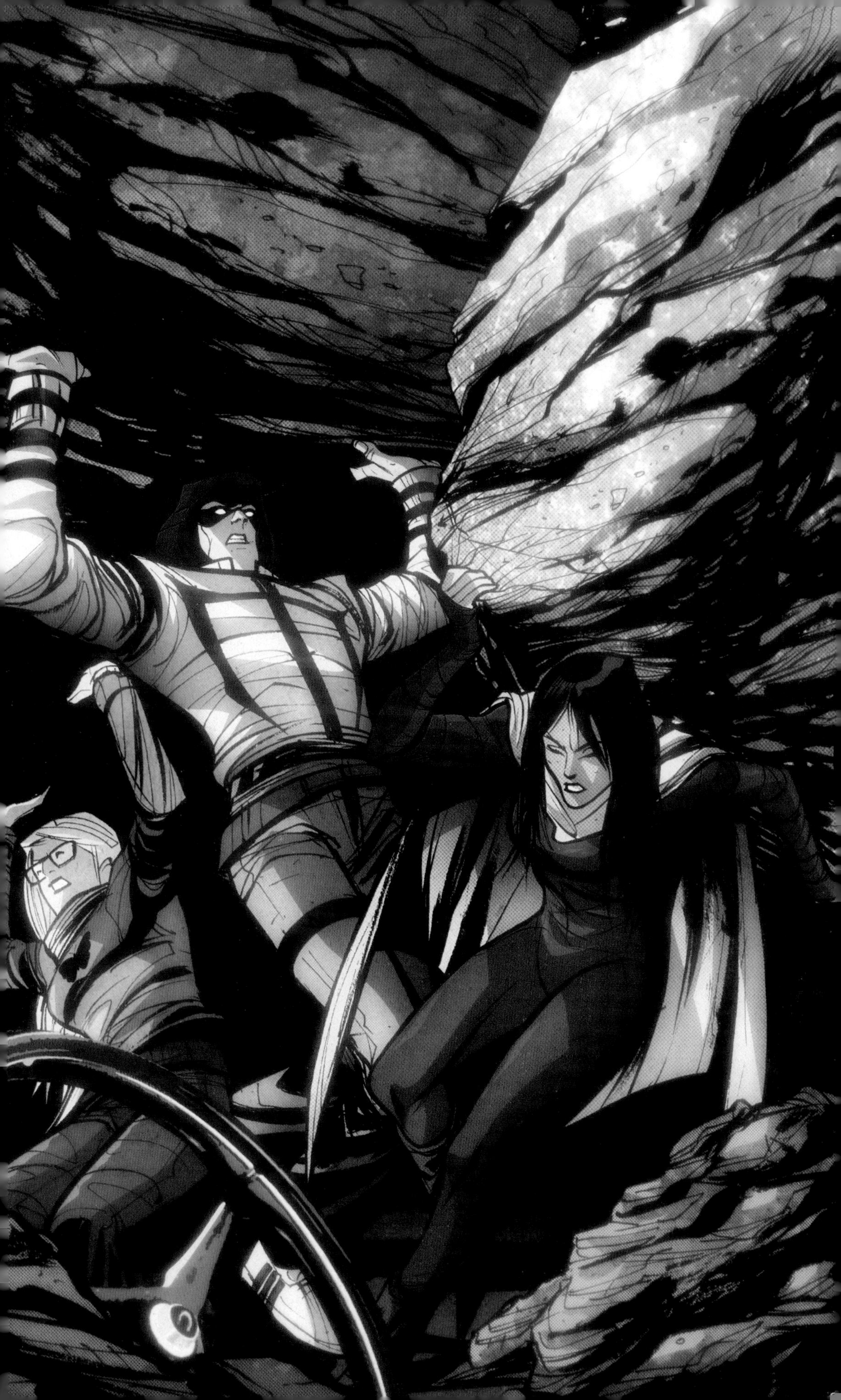

Cover Art by Juan Doe & Hi-Fi

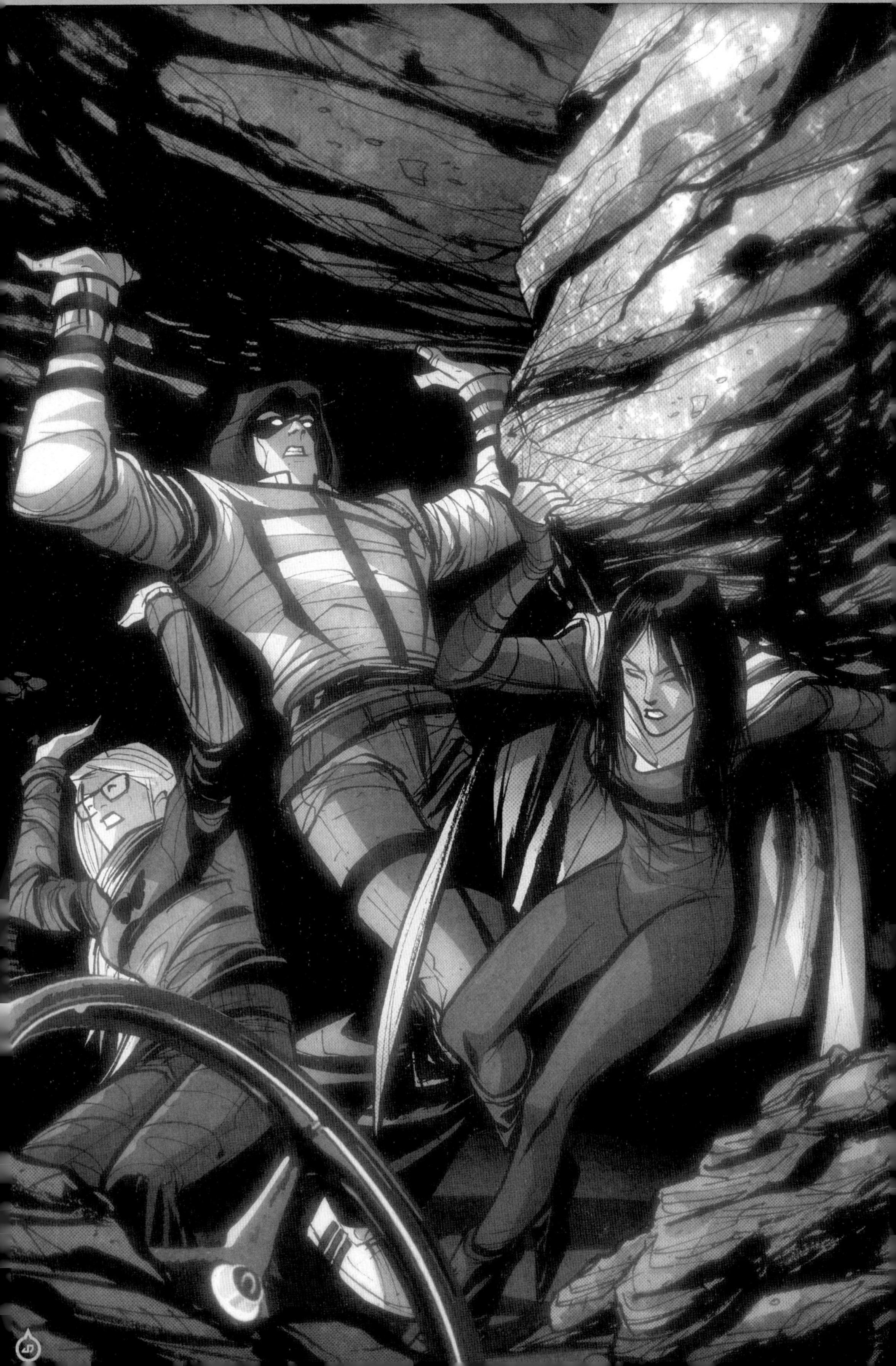

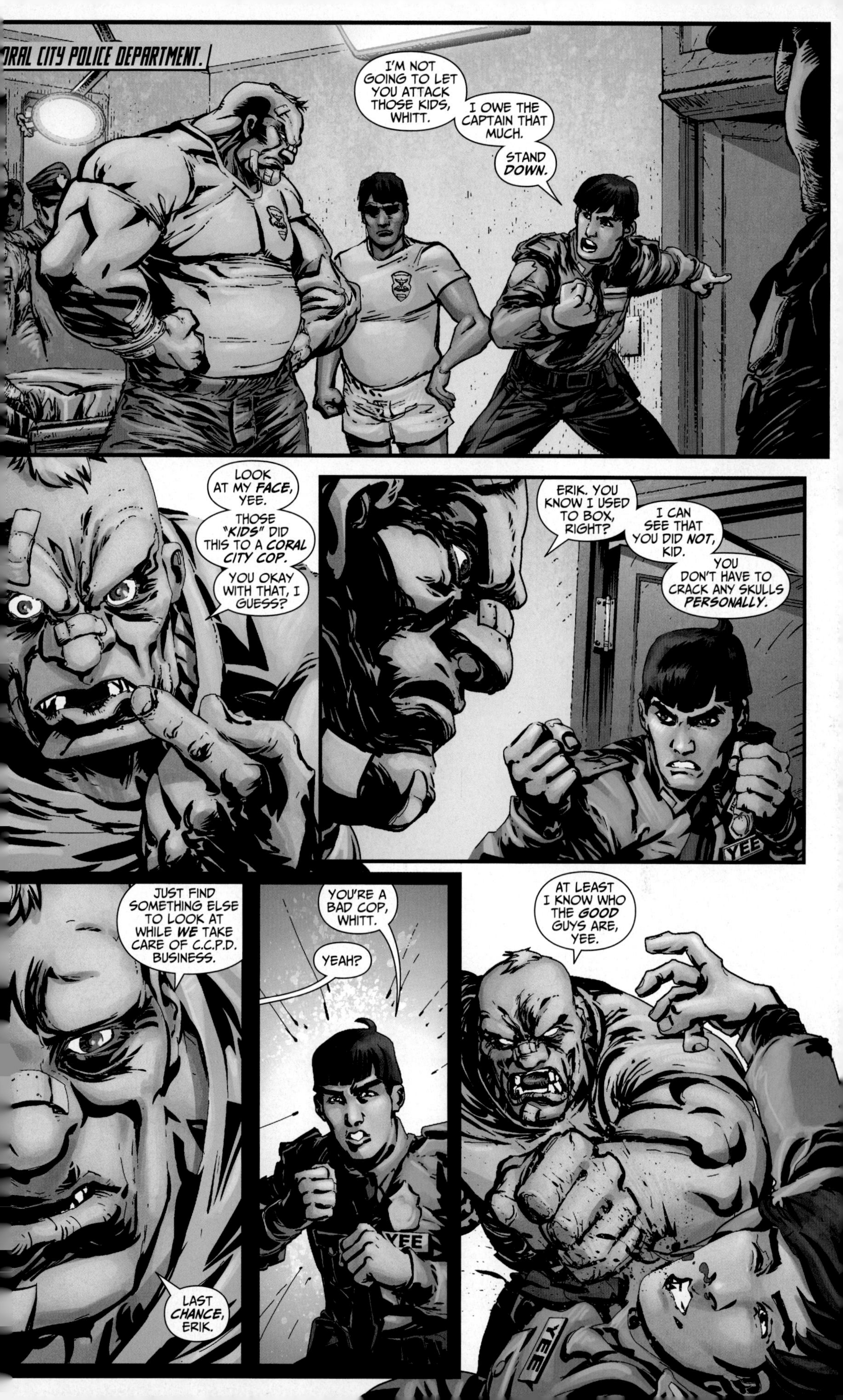
ORAL CITY POLICE DEPARTMENT.
I'M NOT GOING TO LET YOU ATTACK THOSE KIDS, WHITT.
I OWE THE CAPTAIN THAT MUCH.
STAND DOWN.
LOOK AT MY FACE, YEE.
THOSE "KIDS" DID THIS TO A CORAL CITY COP.
YOU OKAY WITH THAT, I GUESS?
ERIK. YOU KNOW I USED TO BOX, RIGHT?
I CAN SEE THAT YOU DID NOT, KID.
YOU DON'T HAVE TO CRACK ANY SKULLS PERSONALLY.
YEE
JUST FIND SOMETHING ELSE TO LOOK AT WHILE WE TAKE CARE OF C.C.P.D. BUSINESS.
LAST CHANCE, ERIK.
YOU'RE A BAD COP, WHITT.
YEAH?
YEE
AT LEAST I KNOW WHO THE GOOD GUYS ARE, YEE.
YEE

THE SWEATSHOP. UNDERGROUND HEADQUARTERS OF THE MOVEMENT.

THEY'VE COME TO DESTROY US.

NOT MOVE US.

NOT FORCE US OUT.

DESTROY US.

OKAY. I'M READY.

THE "GRAVEYARD FACTION," THEY CALL THEMSELVES.

THEY ARE, FRANKLY, A PILE OF SNARKY BUTTHOLES.

JUST A QUICK STOP TO GET SOMETHING...

SOMETHING I HAVEN'T USED IN A WHILE.

THEY'RE GOING DOWN TO GET THE CITIZENS IN THE SUB-LEVELS OF OUR H.Q.--THE SWEATSHOP. THOSE PEOPLE ARE MY RESPONSIBILITY.

MY RESPONSIBILITY. VENGEANCE MOTH.

AND THE FACTION'S GOT A JAMMER SO I CAN'T CALL FOR HELP.

FORTUNATE

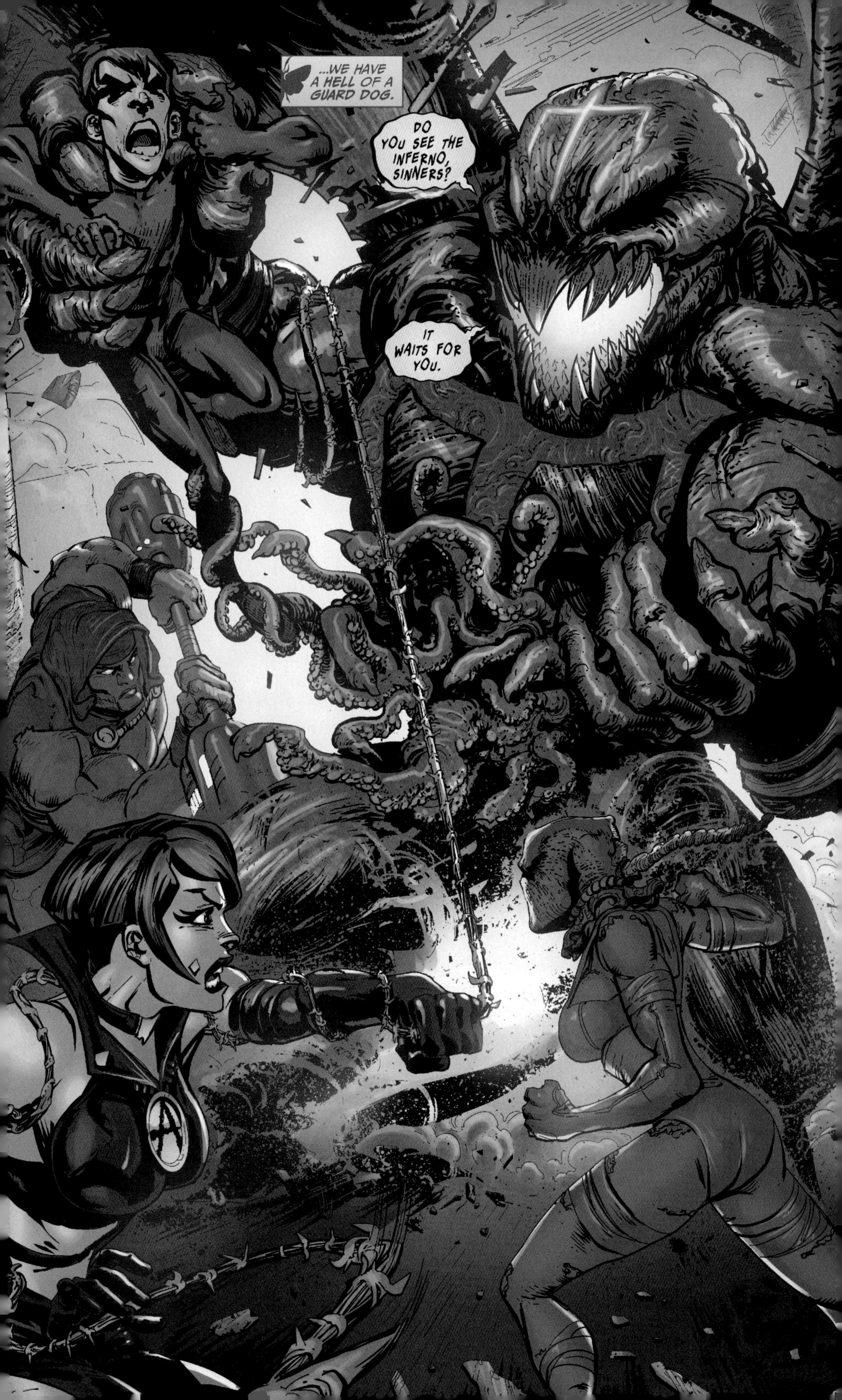

...WE HAVE A HELL OF A GUARD DOG.
DO YOU SEE THE INFERNO, SINNERS?
IT WAITS FOR YOU.

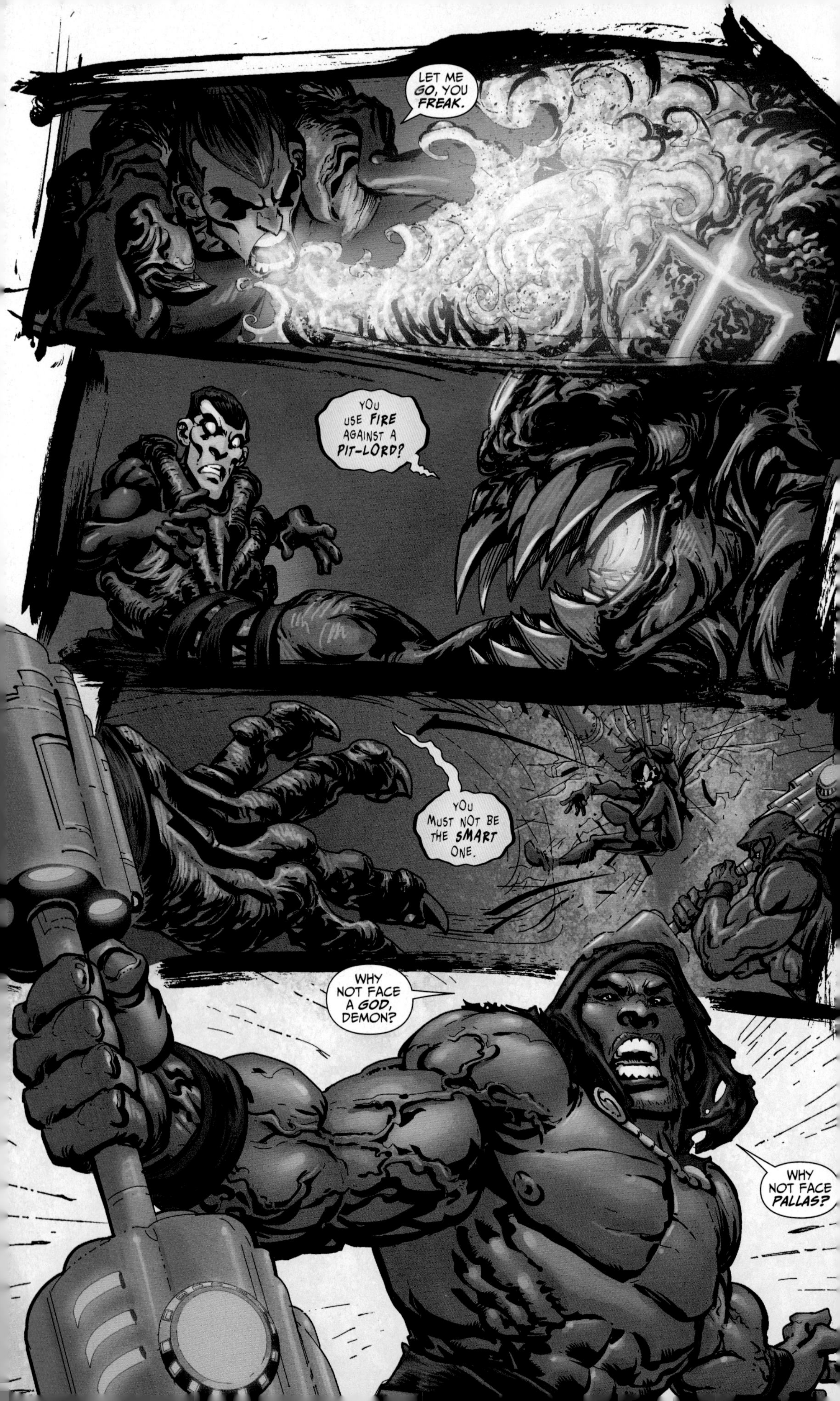
LET ME GO, YOU FREAK.
YOU USE FIRE AGAINST A PIT-LORD?
YOU MUST NOT BE THE SMART ONE.
WHY NOT FACE A GOD, DEMON?
WHY NOT FACE PALLAS?

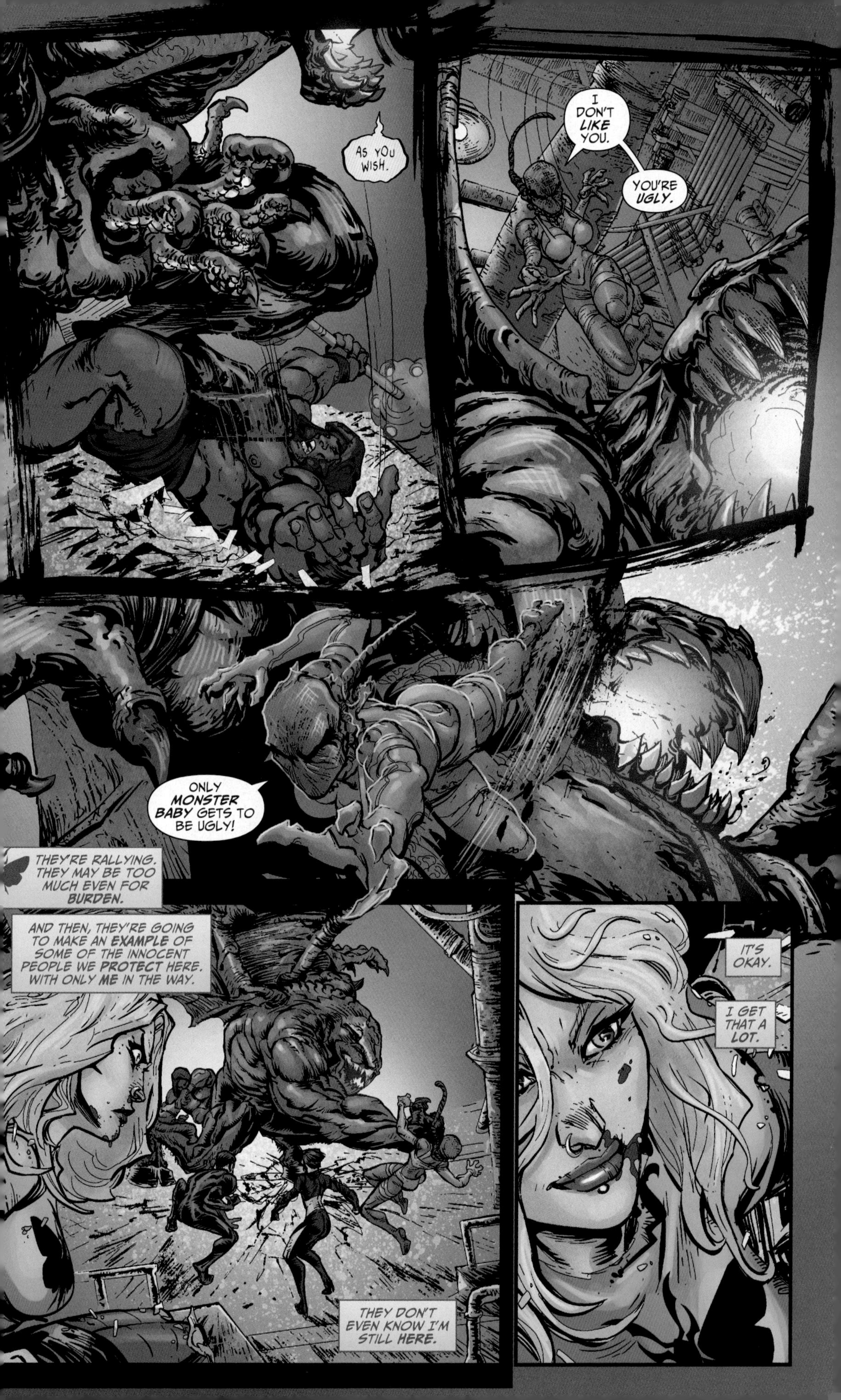

AS YOU WISH.
I DON'T LIKE YOU.
YOU'RE UGLY.
ONLY MONSTER BABY GETS TO BE UGLY!
THEY'RE RALLYING. THEY MAY BE TOO MUCH EVEN FOR BURDEN.
AND THEN, THEY'RE GOING TO MAKE AN EXAMPLE OF SOME OF THE INNOCENT PEOPLE WE PROTECT HERE. WITH ONLY ME IN THE WAY.
THEY DON'T EVEN KNOW I'M STILL HERE.
IT'S OKAY.
I GET THAT A LOT.

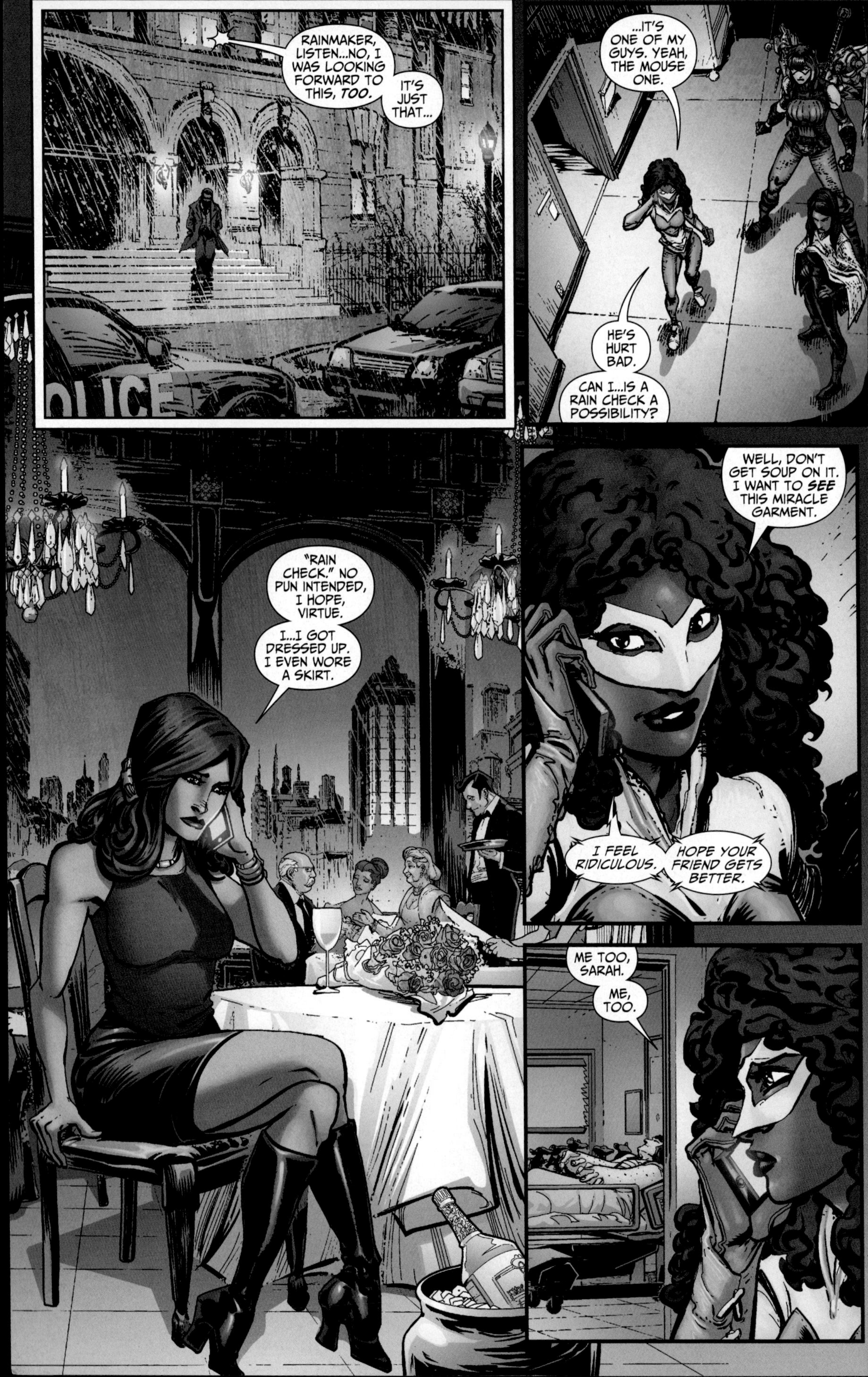
RAINMAKER, LISTEN...NO, I WAS LOOKING FORWARD TO THIS, TOO.
IT'S JUST THAT...
...IT'S ONE OF MY GUYS. YEAH, THE MOUSE ONE.
HE'S HURT BAD.
CAN I...IS A RAIN CHECK A POSSIBILITY?
"RAIN CHECK." NO PUN INTENDED, I HOPE, VIRTUE.
I...I GOT DRESSED UP. I EVEN WORE A SKIRT.
WELL, DON'T GET SOUP ON IT. I WANT TO SEE THIS MIRACLE GARMENT.
I FEEL RIDICULOUS.
HOPE YOUR FRIEND GETS BETTER.
ME TOO, SARAH.
ME, TOO.
POLICE

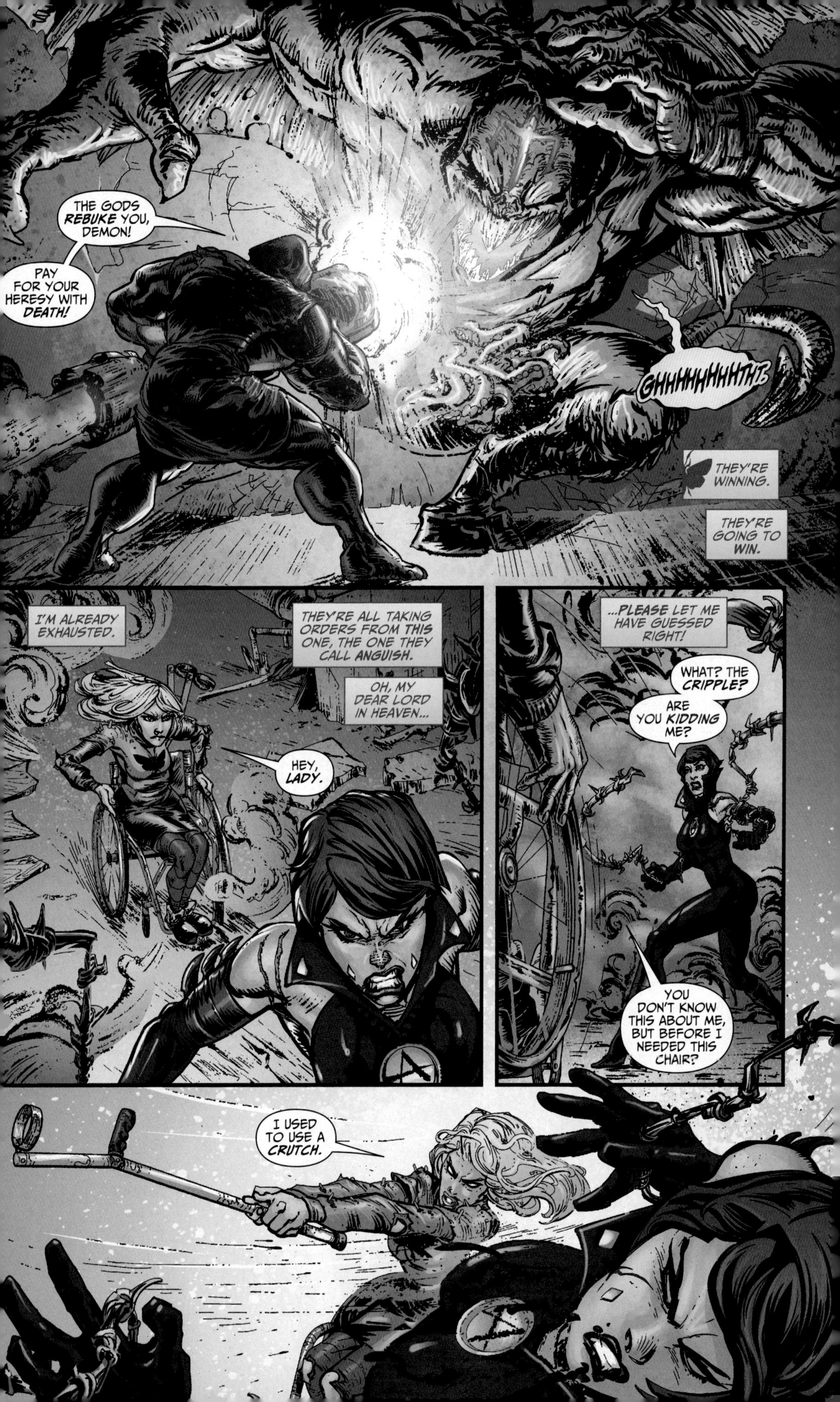

THE GODS REBUKE YOU, DEMON!
PAY FOR YOUR HERESY WITH DEATH!
GHHHHHHHHHT!
THEY'RE WINNING.
THEY'RE GOING TO WIN.
I'M ALREADY EXHAUSTED.
THEY'RE ALL TAKING ORDERS FROM THIS ONE, THE ONE THEY CALL ANGUISH.
OH, MY DEAR LORD IN HEAVEN...
HEY, LADY.
...PLEASE LET ME HAVE GUESSED RIGHT!
WHAT? THE CRIPPLE?
ARE YOU KIDDING ME?
YOU DON'T KNOW THIS ABOUT ME, BUT BEFORE I NEEDED THIS CHAIR?
I USED TO USE A CRUTCH.

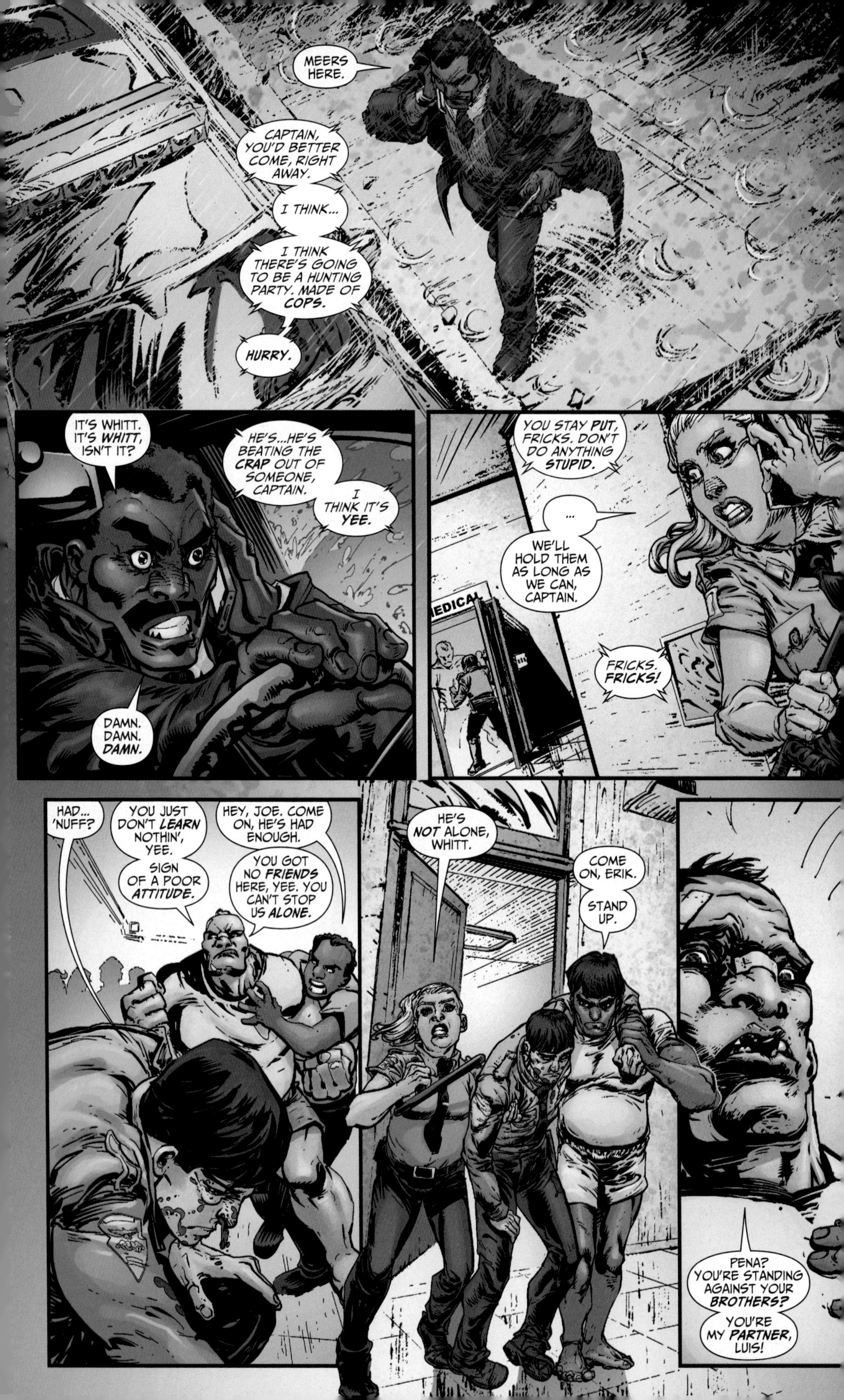
MEERS HERE.
CAPTAIN, YOU'D BETTER COME, RIGHT AWAY.
I THINK...
I THINK THERE'S GOING TO BE A HUNTING PARTY. MADE OF COPS.
HURRY.
IT'S WHITT. IT'S WHITT, ISN'T IT?
HE'S...HE'S BEATING THE CRAP OUT OF SOMEONE, CAPTAIN.
I THINK IT'S YEE.
DAMN. DAMN. DAMN.
YOU STAY PUT, FRICKS. DON'T DO ANYTHING STUPID.
...
WE'LL HOLD THEM AS LONG AS WE CAN, CAPTAIN.
MEDICAL
FRICKS. FRICKS!
HAD... 'NUFF?
YOU JUST DON'T LEARN NOTHIN', YEE.
SIGN OF A POOR ATTITUDE.
HEY, JOE. COME ON, HE'S HAD ENOUGH.
YOU GOT NO FRIENDS HERE, YEE. YOU CAN'T STOP US ALONE.
HE'S NOT ALONE, WHITT.
COME ON, ERIK.
STAND UP.
PENA? YOU'RE STANDING AGAINST YOUR BROTHERS?
YOU'RE MY PARTNER, LUIS!

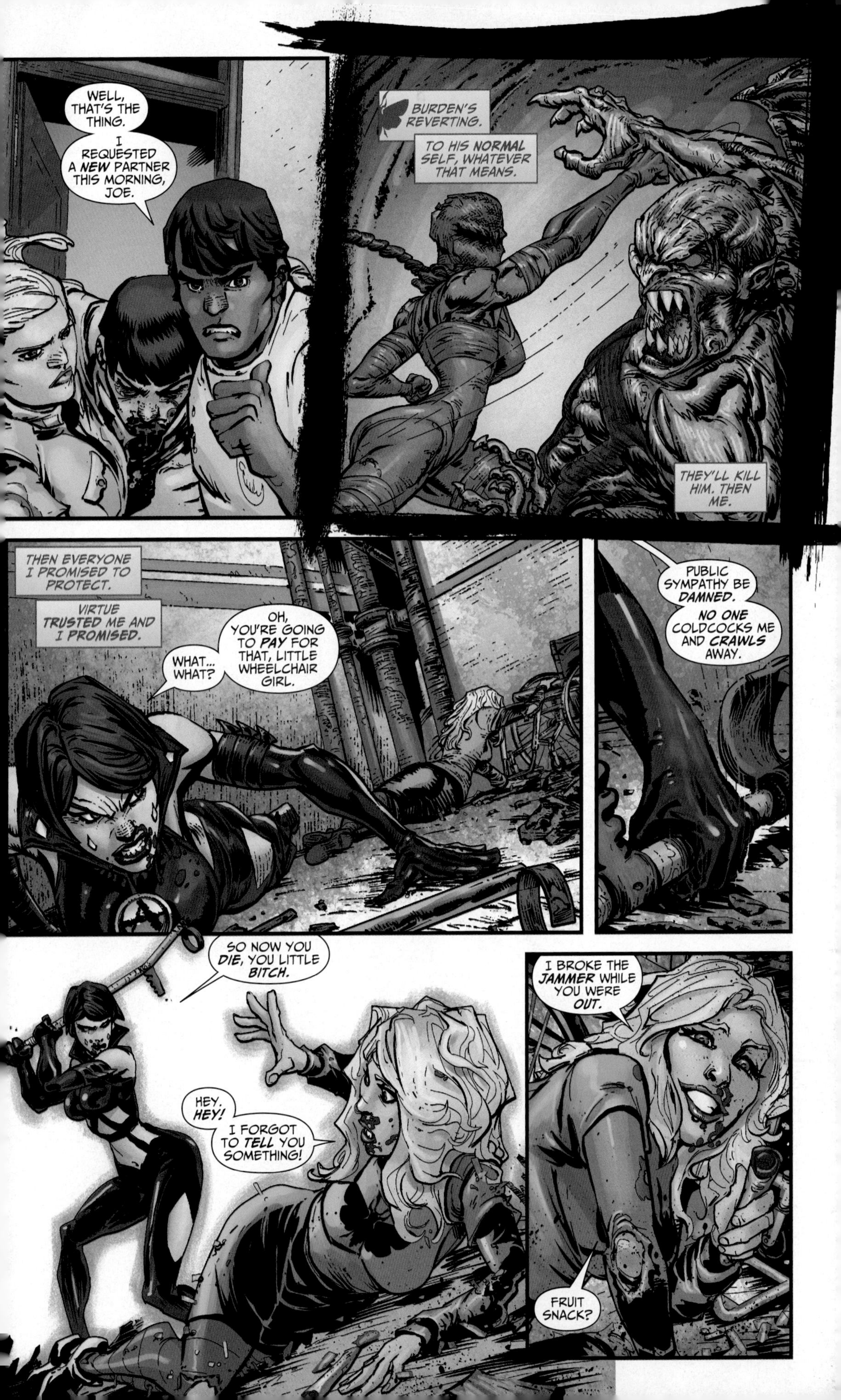
WELL, THAT'S THE THING.
I REQUESTED A NEW PARTNER THIS MORNING, JOE.
BURDEN'S REVERTING.
TO HIS NORMAL SELF, WHATEVER THAT MEANS.
THEY'LL KILL HIM. THEN ME.
THEN EVERYONE I PROMISED TO PROTECT.
VIRTUE TRUSTED ME AND I PROMISED.
WHAT... WHAT?
OH, YOU'RE GOING TO PAY FOR THAT, LITTLE WHEELCHAIR GIRL.
PUBLIC SYMPATHY BE DAMNED.
NO ONE COLDCOCKS ME AND CRAWLS AWAY.
SO NOW YOU DIE, YOU LITTLE BITCH.
HEY. HEY!
I FORGOT TO TELL YOU SOMETHING!
I BROKE THE JAMMER WHILE YOU WERE OUT.
FRUIT SNACK?

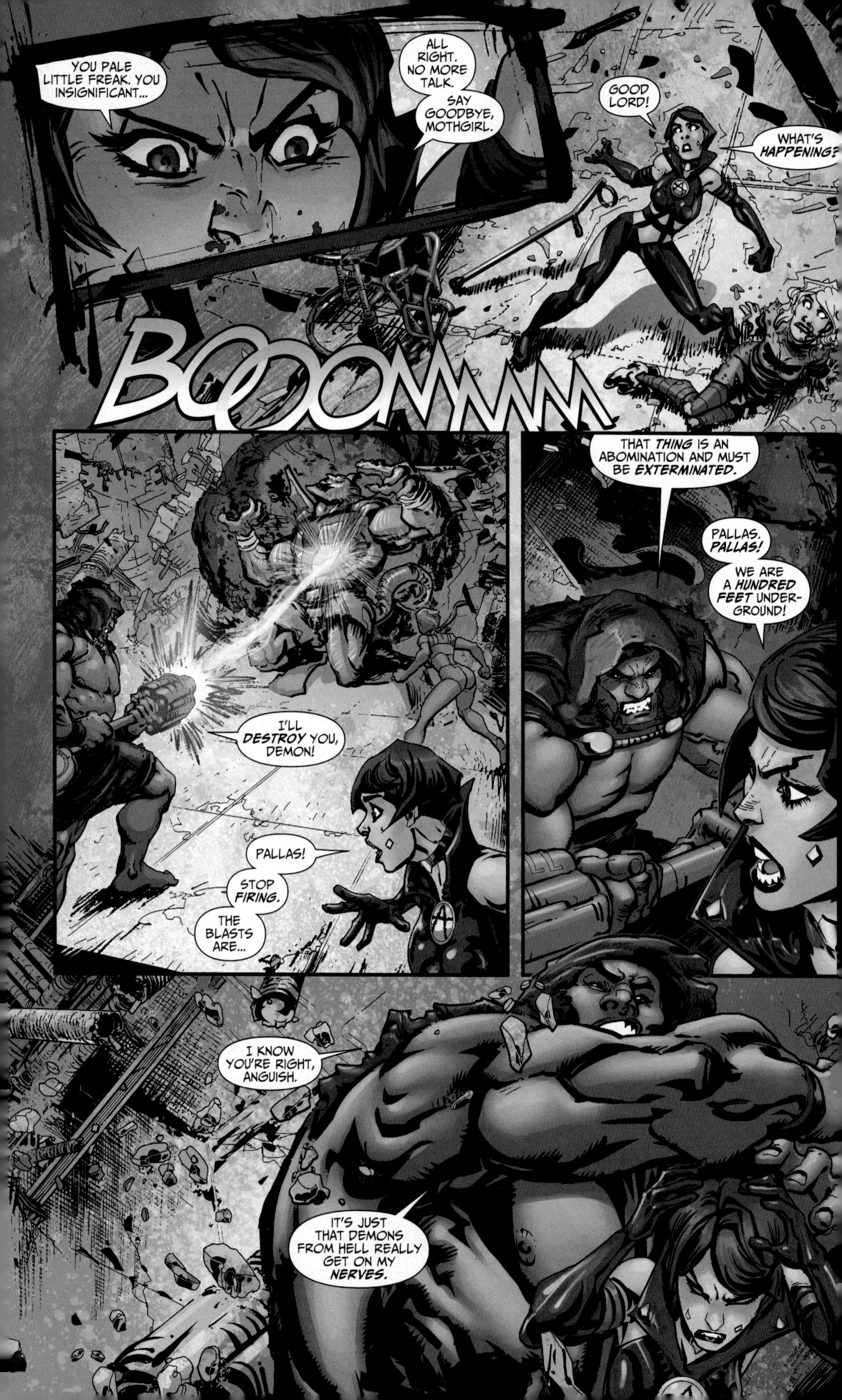
YOU PALE LITTLE FREAK. YOU INSIGNIFICANT...
ALL RIGHT. NO MORE TALK.
SAY GOODBYE, MOTHGIRL.
GOOD LORD!
WHAT'S *HAPPENING?*
BOOOMMMM
I'LL *DESTROY* YOU, DEMON!
PALLAS!
STOP *FIRING.*
THE BLASTS ARE...
THAT *THING* IS AN ABOMINATION AND MUST BE *EXTERMINATED.*
PALLAS. *PALLAS!*
WE ARE A *HUNDRED FEET* UNDER-GROUND!
I KNOW YOU'RE RIGHT, ANGUISH.
IT'S JUST THAT DEMONS FROM HELL REALLY GET ON MY *NERVES.*

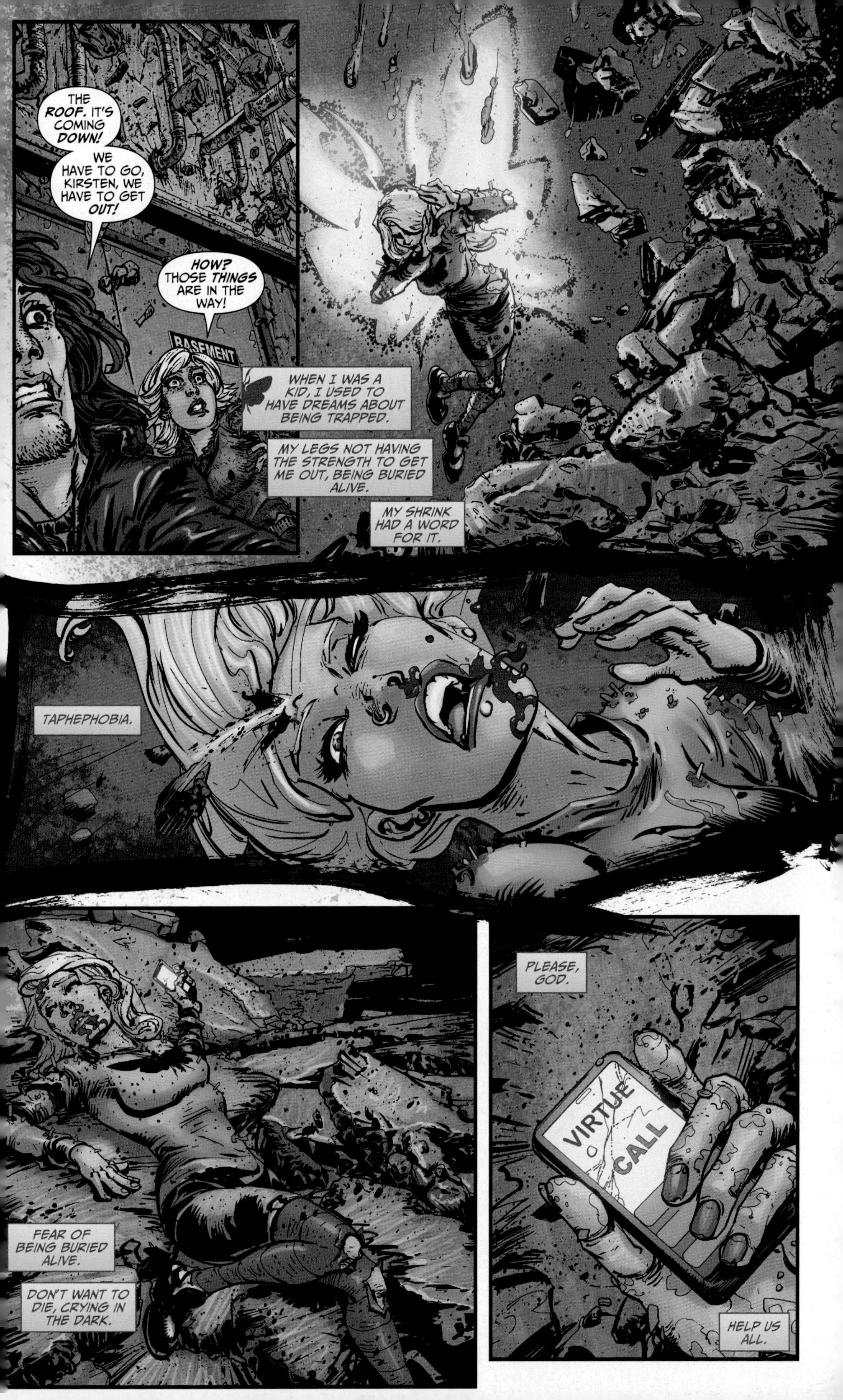
THE ROOF. IT'S COMING DOWN!
WE HAVE TO GO, KIRSTEN, WE HAVE TO GET OUT!
HOW? THOSE THINGS ARE IN THE WAY!
BASEMENT
WHEN I WAS A KID, I USED TO HAVE DREAMS ABOUT BEING TRAPPED.
MY LEGS NOT HAVING THE STRENGTH TO GET ME OUT, BEING BURIED ALIVE.
MY SHRINK HAD A WORD FOR IT.
TAPHEPHOBIA.
FEAR OF BEING BURIED ALIVE.
DON'T WANT TO DIE, CRYING IN THE DARK.
PLEASE, GOD.
VIRTUE
CALL
HELP US ALL.

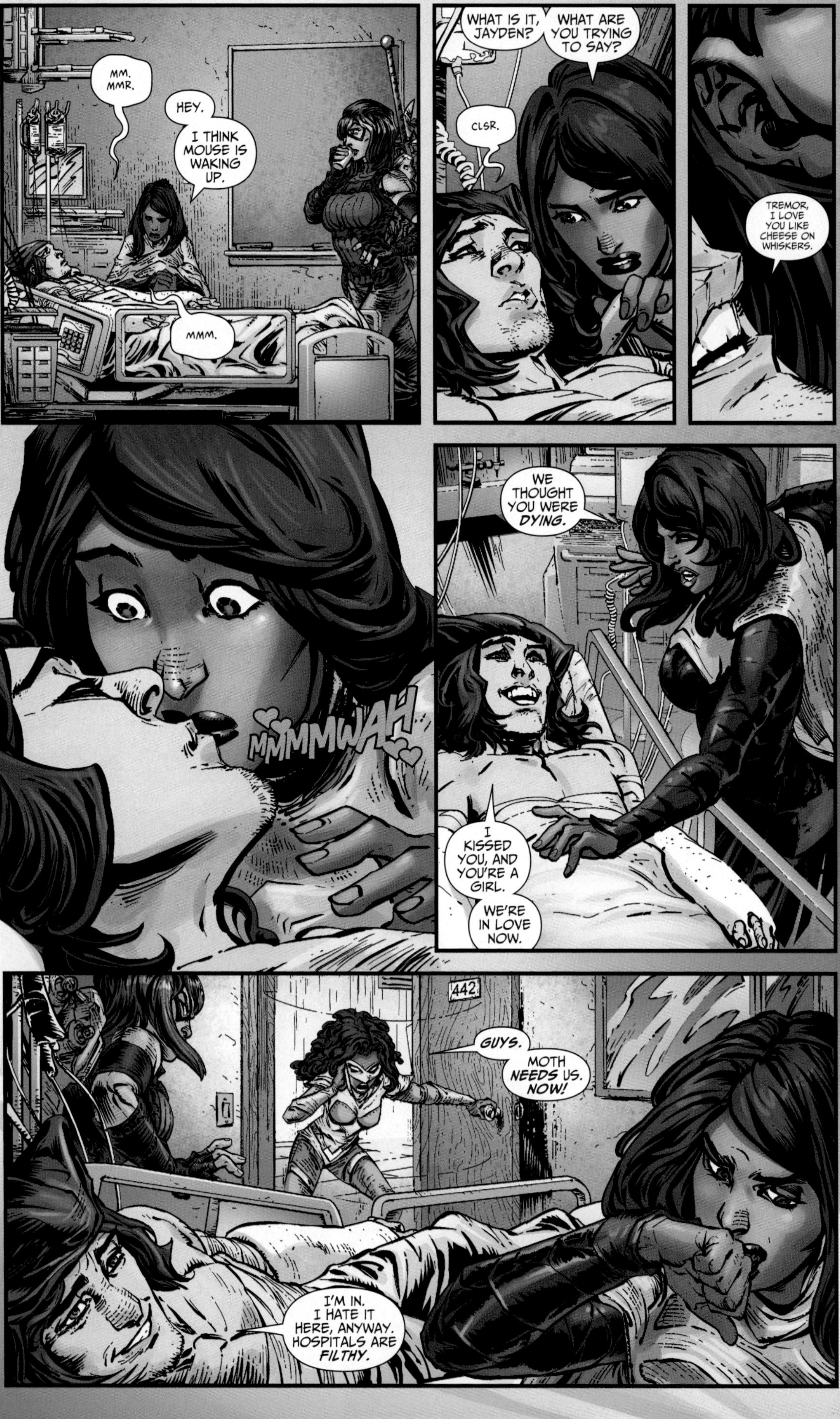
MM. MMR.
HEY.
I THINK MOUSE IS WAKING UP.
MMM.
WHAT IS IT, JAYDEN?
WHAT ARE YOU TRYING TO SAY?
CLSR.
TREMOR, I LOVE YOU LIKE CHEESE ON WHISKERS.
MMMMWAH
WE THOUGHT YOU WERE *DYING.*
I KISSED YOU, AND YOU'RE A GIRL.
WE'RE IN LOVE NOW.
442
GUYS.
MOTH *NEEDS* US. *NOW!*
I'M IN. I HATE IT HERE, ANYWAY. HOSPITALS ARE *FILTHY.*

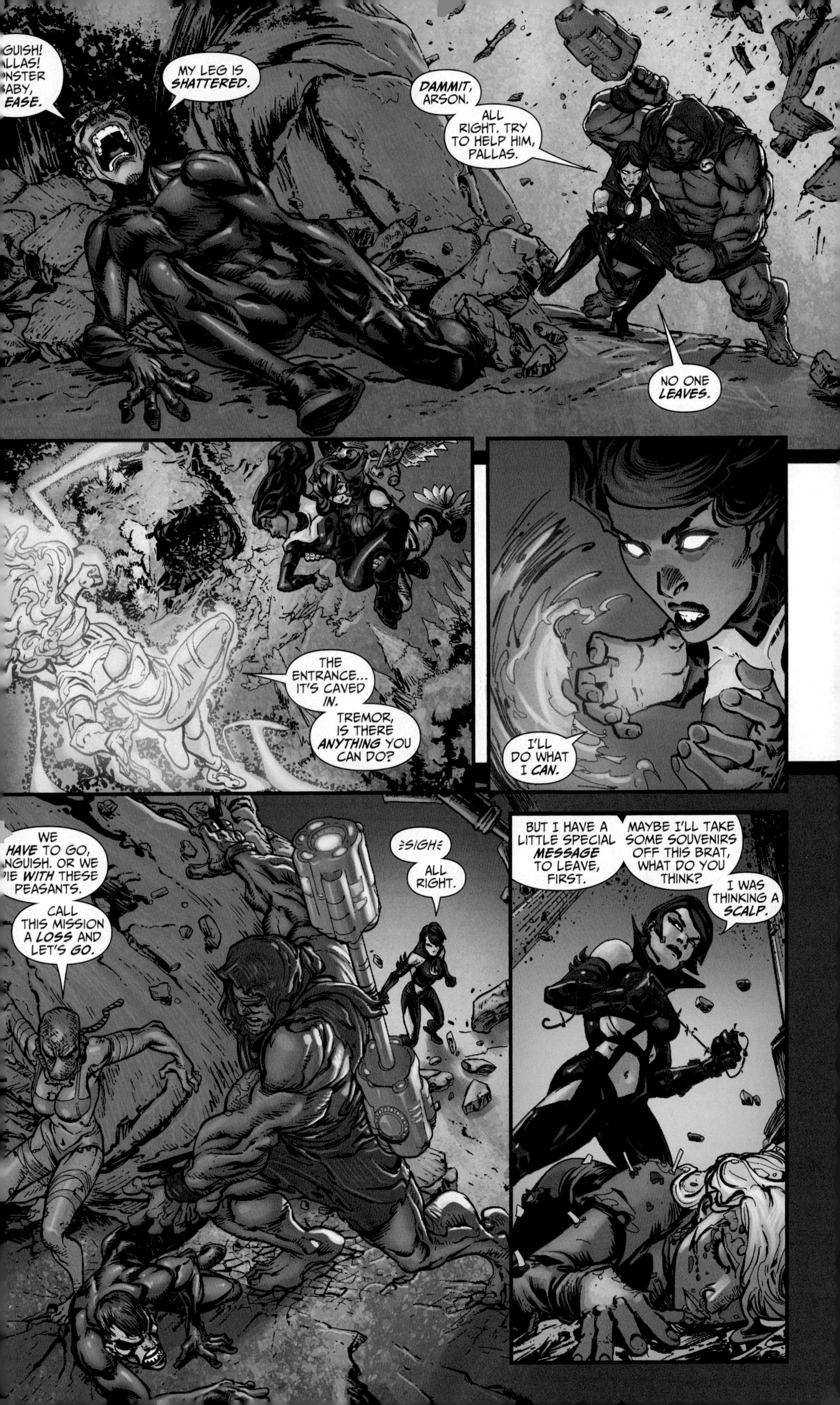

GUISH!
ALLAS!
ONSTER
BABY,
EASE.
MY LEG IS SHATTERED.
DAMMIT, ARSON.
ALL RIGHT. TRY TO HELP HIM, PALLAS.
NO ONE LEAVES.
THE ENTRANCE... IT'S CAVED IN.
TREMOR, IS THERE ANYTHING YOU CAN DO?
I'LL DO WHAT I CAN.
WE HAVE TO GO, ANGUISH. OR WE DIE WITH THESE PEASANTS.
CALL THIS MISSION A LOSS AND LET'S GO.
SIGH
ALL RIGHT.
BUT I HAVE A LITTLE SPECIAL MESSAGE TO LEAVE, FIRST.
MAYBE I'LL TAKE SOME SOUVENIRS OFF THIS BRAT, WHAT DO YOU THINK?
I WAS THINKING A SCALP.

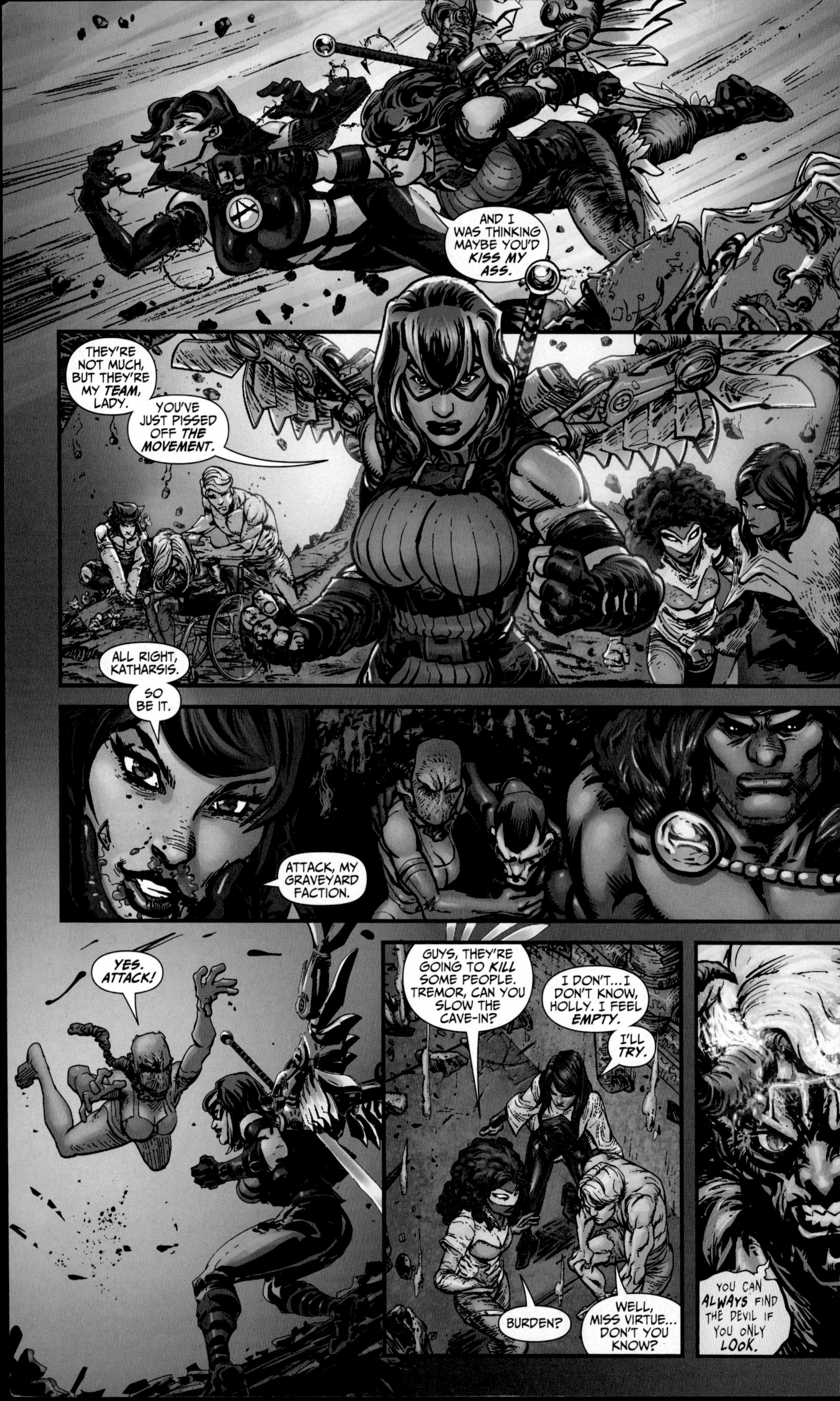
AND I WAS THINKING MAYBE YOU'D KISS MY ASS.
THEY'RE NOT MUCH, BUT THEY'RE MY TEAM, LADY.
YOU'VE JUST PISSED OFF THE MOVEMENT.
ALL RIGHT, KATHARSIS.
SO BE IT.
ATTACK, MY GRAVEYARD FACTION.
YES. ATTACK!
GUYS, THEY'RE GOING TO KILL SOME PEOPLE. TREMOR, CAN YOU SLOW THE CAVE-IN?
I DON'T... I DON'T KNOW, HOLLY. I FEEL EMPTY.
I'LL TRY.
BURDEN?
WELL, MISS VIRTUE... DON'T YOU KNOW?
YOU CAN ALWAYS FIND THE DEVIL IF YOU ONLY LOOK.

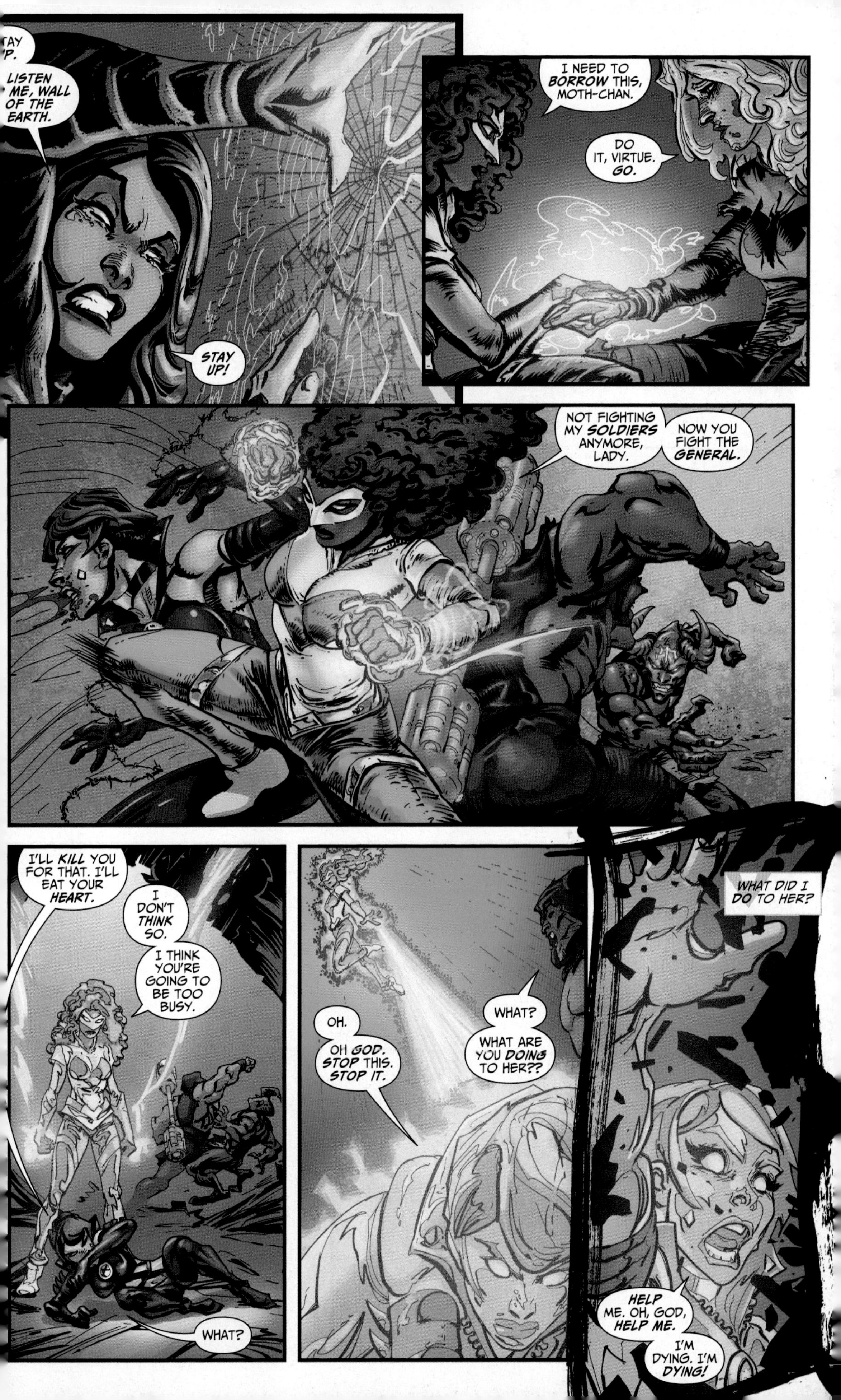

STAY UP.
LISTEN ME, WALL OF THE EARTH.
STAY UP!
I NEED TO BORROW THIS, MOTH-CHAN.
DO IT, VIRTUE. GO.
NOT FIGHTING MY SOLDIERS ANYMORE, LADY.
NOW YOU FIGHT THE GENERAL.
I'LL KILL YOU FOR THAT. I'LL EAT YOUR HEART.
I DON'T THINK SO.
I THINK YOU'RE GOING TO BE TOO BUSY.
WHAT?
OH.
OH GOD. STOP THIS. STOP IT.
WHAT?
WHAT ARE YOU DOING TO HER??
WHAT DID I DO TO HER?
HELP ME. OH, GOD, HELP ME.
I'M DYING. I'M DYING!

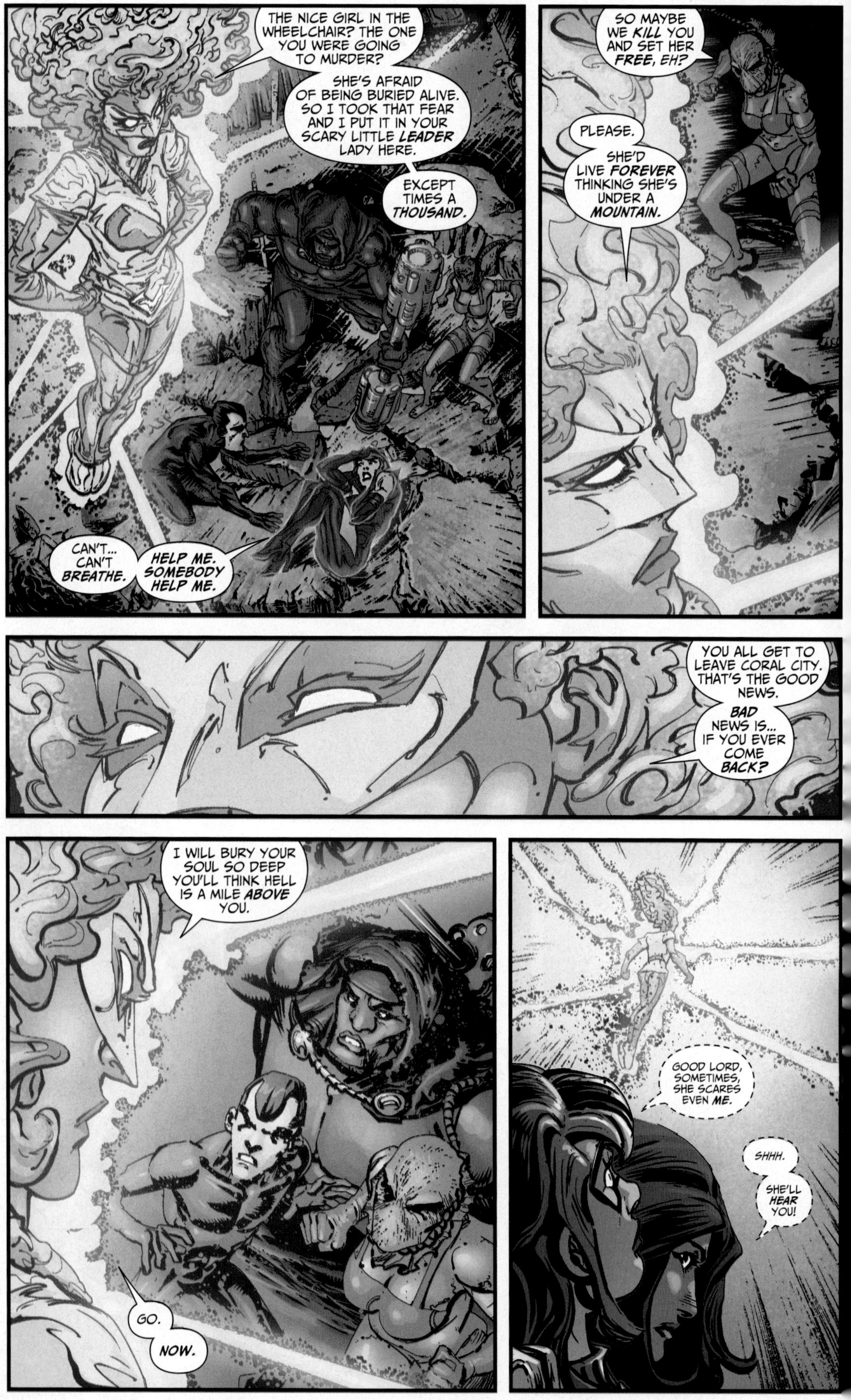
THE NICE GIRL IN THE WHEELCHAIR? THE ONE YOU WERE GOING TO MURDER?
SHE'S AFRAID OF BEING BURIED ALIVE. SO I TOOK THAT FEAR AND I PUT IT IN YOUR SCARY LITTLE LEADER LADY HERE.
EXCEPT TIMES A THOUSAND.
CAN'T... CAN'T BREATHE.
HELP ME. SOMEBODY HELP ME.
SO MAYBE WE KILL YOU AND SET HER FREE, EH?
PLEASE.
SHE'D LIVE FOREVER THINKING SHE'S UNDER A MOUNTAIN.
YOU ALL GET TO LEAVE CORAL CITY. THAT'S THE GOOD NEWS.
BAD NEWS IS... IF YOU EVER COME BACK?
I WILL BURY YOUR SOUL SO DEEP YOU'LL THINK HELL IS A MILE ABOVE YOU.
GO.
NOW.
GOOD LORD, SOMETIMES, SHE SCARES EVEN ME.
SHHH.
SHE'LL HEAR YOU!

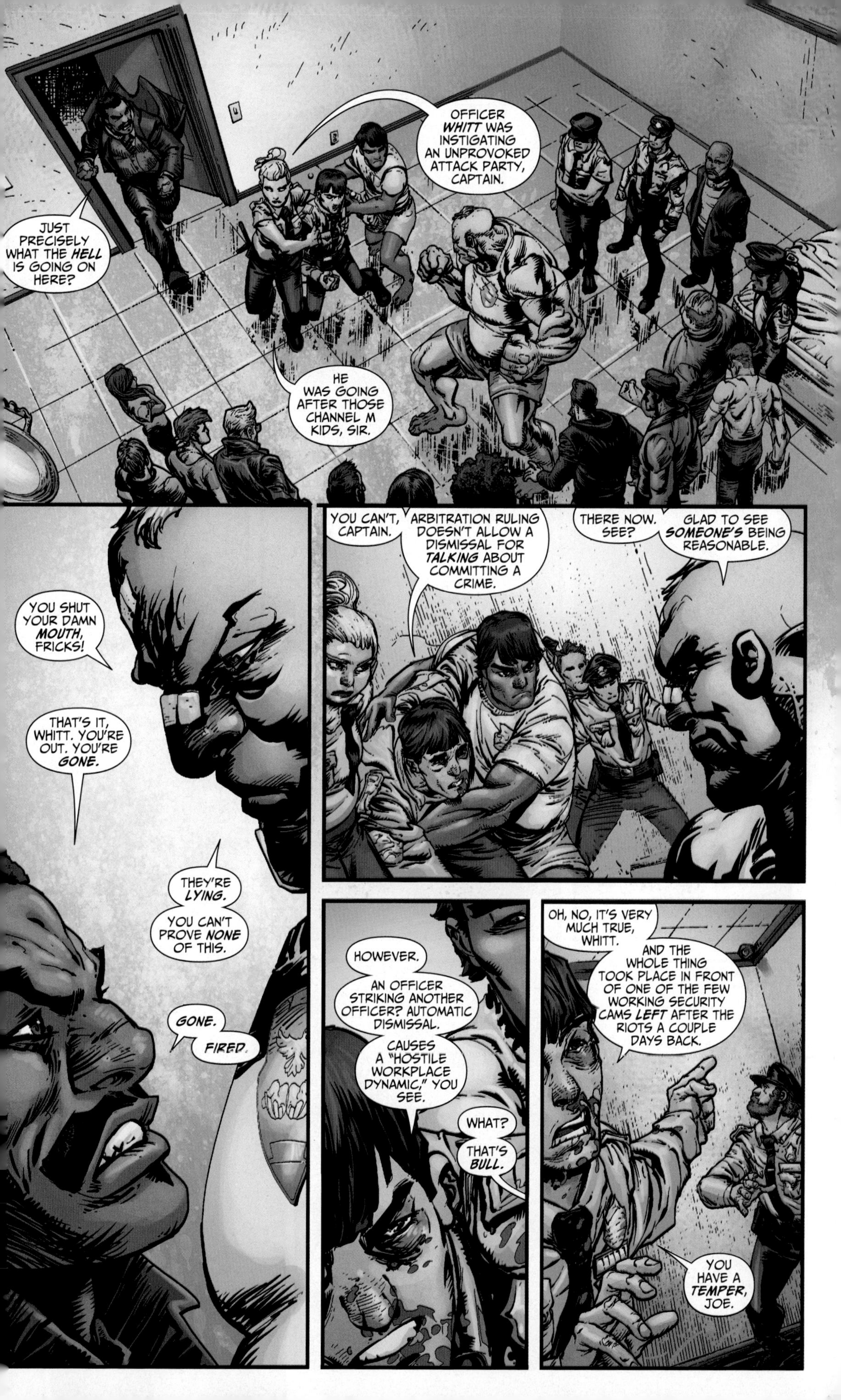

JUST PRECISELY WHAT THE HELL IS GOING ON HERE?
OFFICER WHITT WAS INSTIGATING AN UNPROVOKED ATTACK PARTY, CAPTAIN.
HE WAS GOING AFTER THOSE CHANNEL M KIDS, SIR.
YOU SHUT YOUR DAMN MOUTH, FRICKS!
THAT'S IT, WHITT. YOU'RE OUT. YOU'RE GONE.
THEY'RE LYING.
YOU CAN'T PROVE NONE OF THIS.
GONE.
FIRED.
YOU CAN'T, CAPTAIN.
ARBITRATION RULING DOESN'T ALLOW A DISMISSAL FOR TALKING ABOUT COMMITTING A CRIME.
THERE NOW. SEE?
GLAD TO SEE SOMEONE'S BEING REASONABLE.
HOWEVER.
AN OFFICER STRIKING ANOTHER OFFICER? AUTOMATIC DISMISSAL.
CAUSES A "HOSTILE WORKPLACE DYNAMIC," YOU SEE.
WHAT?
THAT'S BULL.
OH, NO, IT'S VERY MUCH TRUE, WHITT.
AND THE WHOLE THING TOOK PLACE IN FRONT OF ONE OF THE FEW WORKING SECURITY CAMS LEFT AFTER THE RIOTS A COUPLE DAYS BACK.
YOU HAVE A TEMPER, JOE.

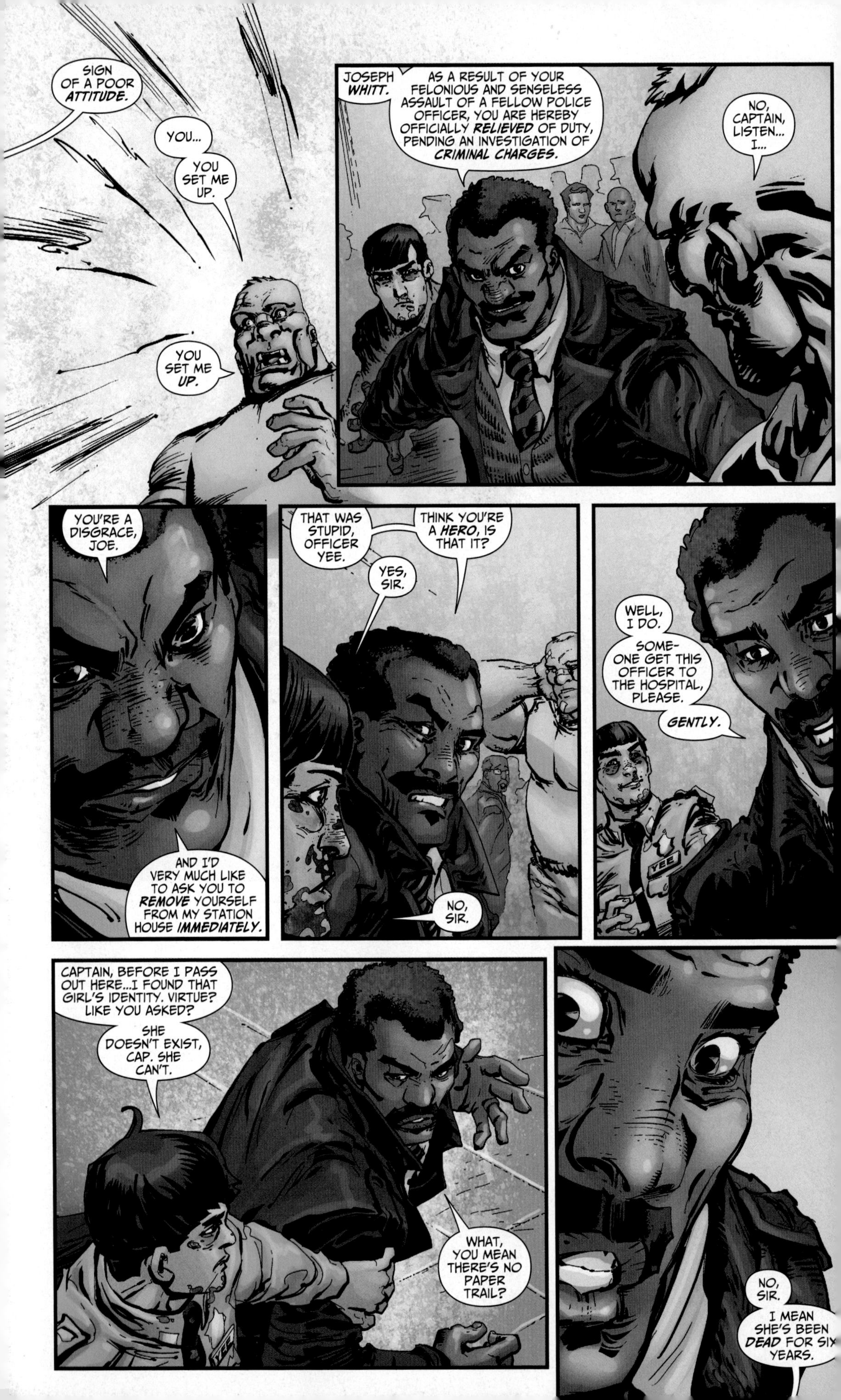
SIGN OF A POOR ATTITUDE.
YOU...
YOU SET ME UP.
YOU SET ME UP.
JOSEPH WHITT.
AS A RESULT OF YOUR FELONIOUS AND SENSELESS ASSAULT OF A FELLOW POLICE OFFICER, YOU ARE HEREBY OFFICIALLY RELIEVED OF DUTY, PENDING AN INVESTIGATION OF CRIMINAL CHARGES.
NO, CAPTAIN, LISTEN... I...
YOU'RE A DISGRACE, JOE.
AND I'D VERY MUCH LIKE TO ASK YOU TO REMOVE YOURSELF FROM MY STATION HOUSE IMMEDIATELY.
THAT WAS STUPID, OFFICER YEE.
YES, SIR.
THINK YOU'RE A HERO, IS THAT IT?
NO, SIR.
WELL, I DO.
SOME-ONE GET THIS OFFICER TO THE HOSPITAL, PLEASE.
GENTLY.
YEE
CAPTAIN, BEFORE I PASS OUT HERE...I FOUND THAT GIRL'S IDENTITY. VIRTUE? LIKE YOU ASKED?
SHE DOESN'T EXIST, CAP. SHE CAN'T.
WHAT, YOU MEAN THERE'S NO PAPER TRAIL?
NO, SIR.
I MEAN SHE'S BEEN DEAD FOR SIX YEARS.

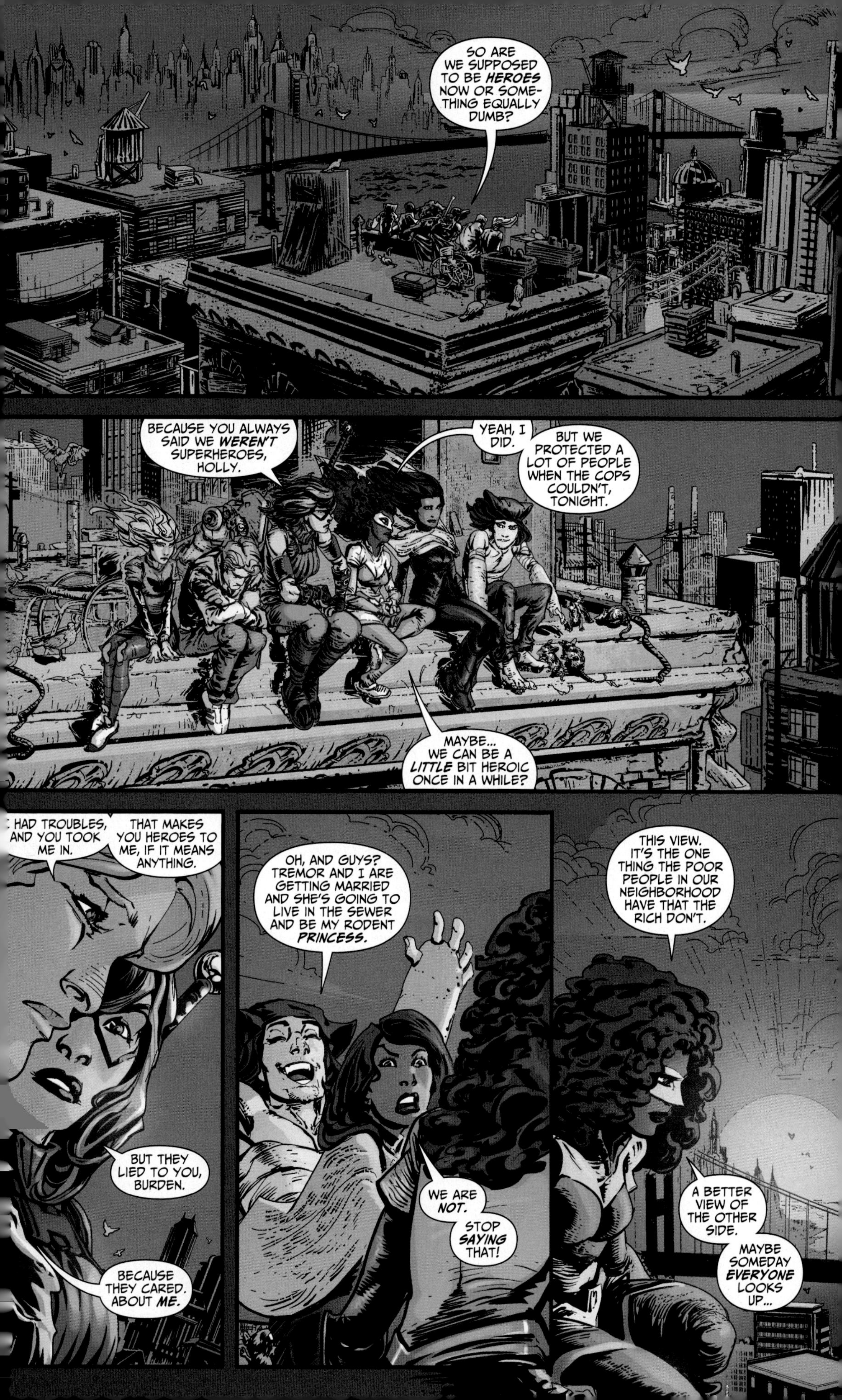

SO ARE WE SUPPOSED TO BE HEROES NOW OR SOMETHING EQUALLY DUMB?
BECAUSE YOU ALWAYS SAID WE WEREN'T SUPERHEROES, HOLLY.
YEAH, I DID.
BUT WE PROTECTED A LOT OF PEOPLE WHEN THE COPS COULDN'T, TONIGHT.
MAYBE... WE CAN BE A LITTLE BIT HEROIC ONCE IN A WHILE?
HAD TROUBLES, AND YOU TOOK ME IN.
THAT MAKES YOU HEROES TO ME, IF IT MEANS ANYTHING.
BUT THEY LIED TO YOU, BURDEN.
BECAUSE THEY CARED. ABOUT ME.
OH, AND GUYS? TREMOR AND I ARE GETTING MARRIED AND SHE'S GOING TO LIVE IN THE SEWER AND BE MY RODENT PRINCESS.
WE ARE NOT.
STOP SAYING THAT!
THIS VIEW. IT'S THE ONE THING THE POOR PEOPLE IN OUR NEIGHBORHOOD HAVE THAT THE RICH DON'T.
A BETTER VIEW OF THE OTHER SIDE.
MAYBE SOMEDAY EVERYONE LOOKS UP...

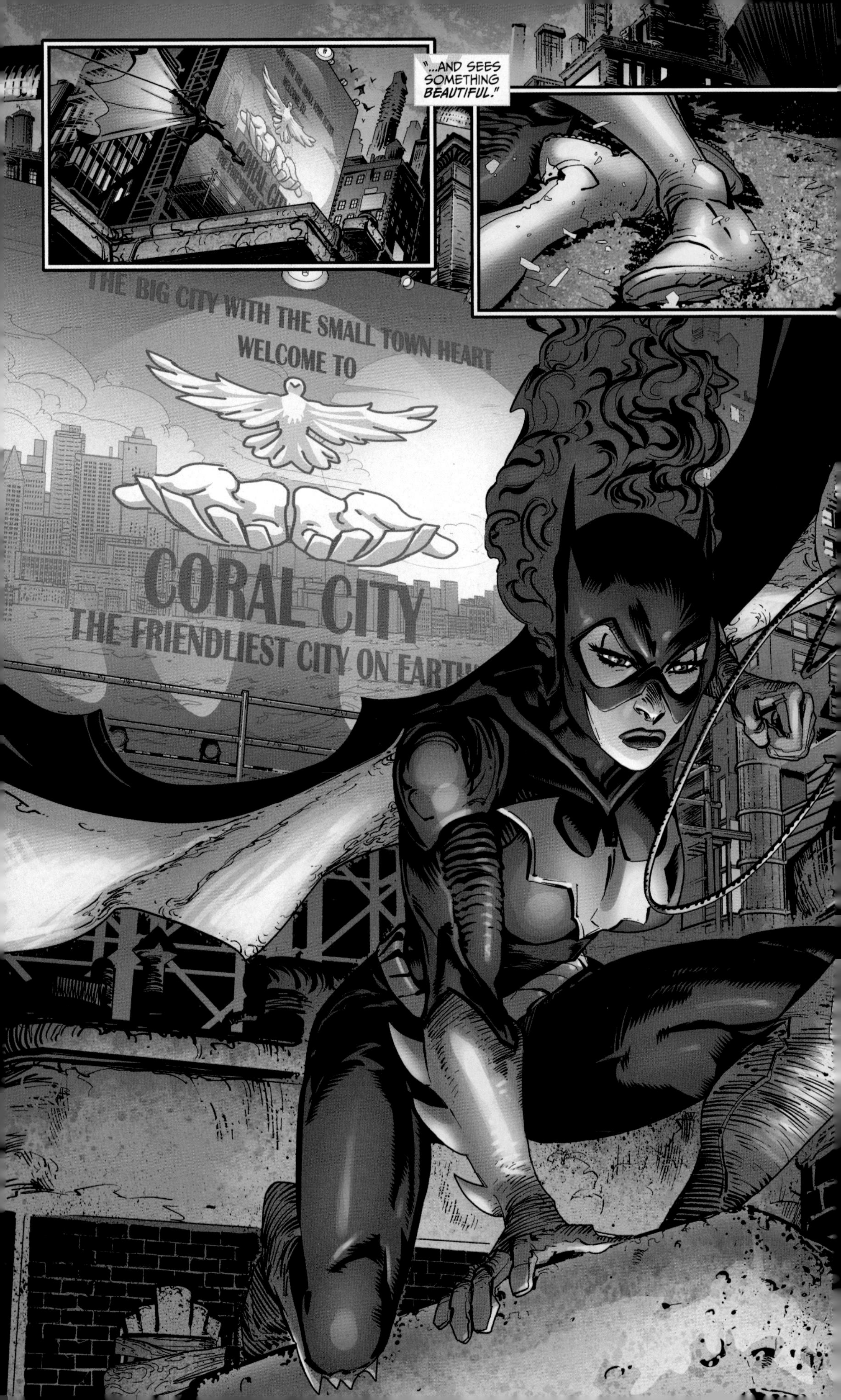
"...AND SEES SOMETHING *BEAUTIFUL*."
THE BIG CITY WITH THE SMALL TOWN HEART
WELCOME TO
CORAL CITY
THE FRIENDLIEST CITY ON EARTH

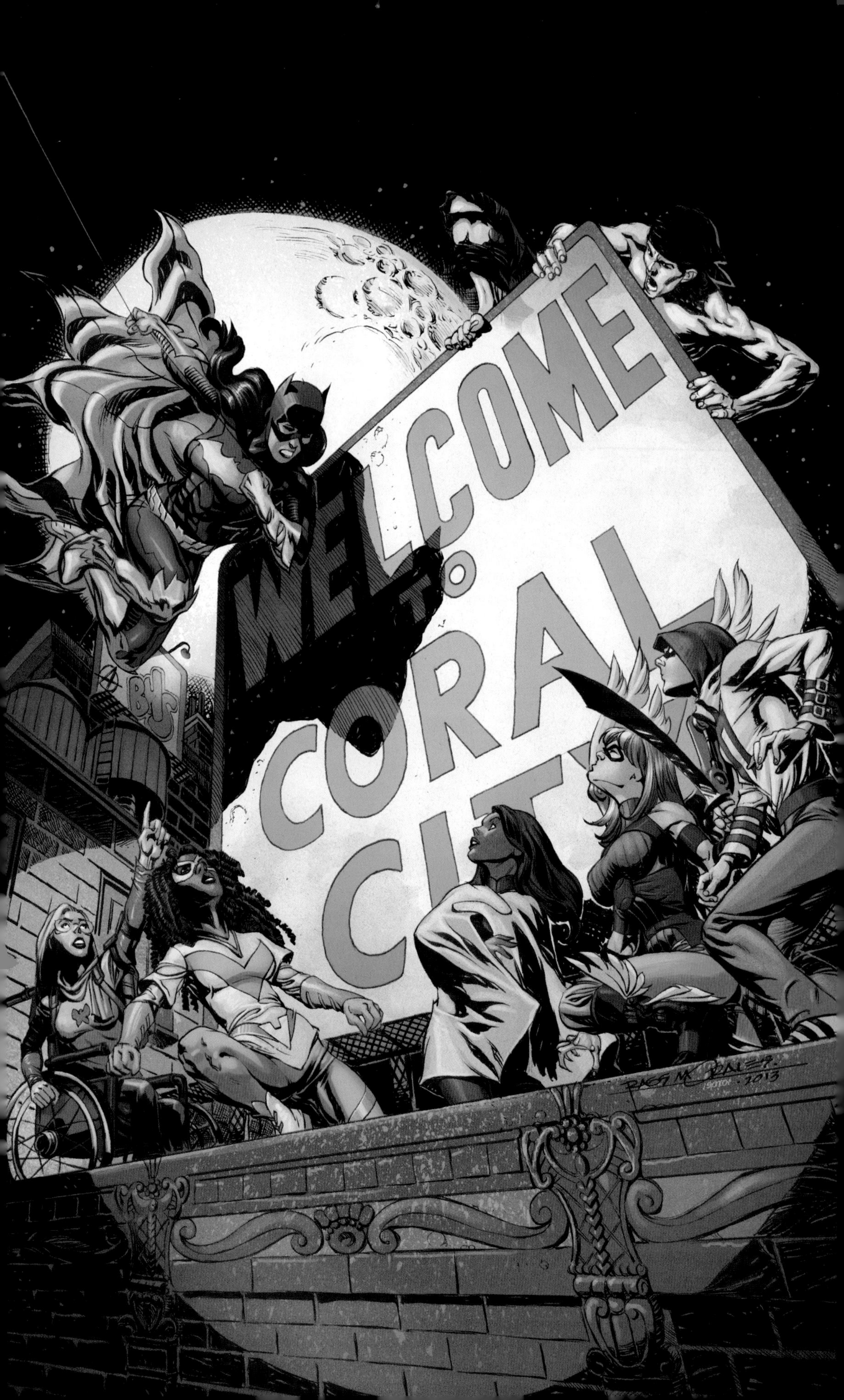
WELCOME
TO
CORAL
CIT

Cover Art by Rags Morales

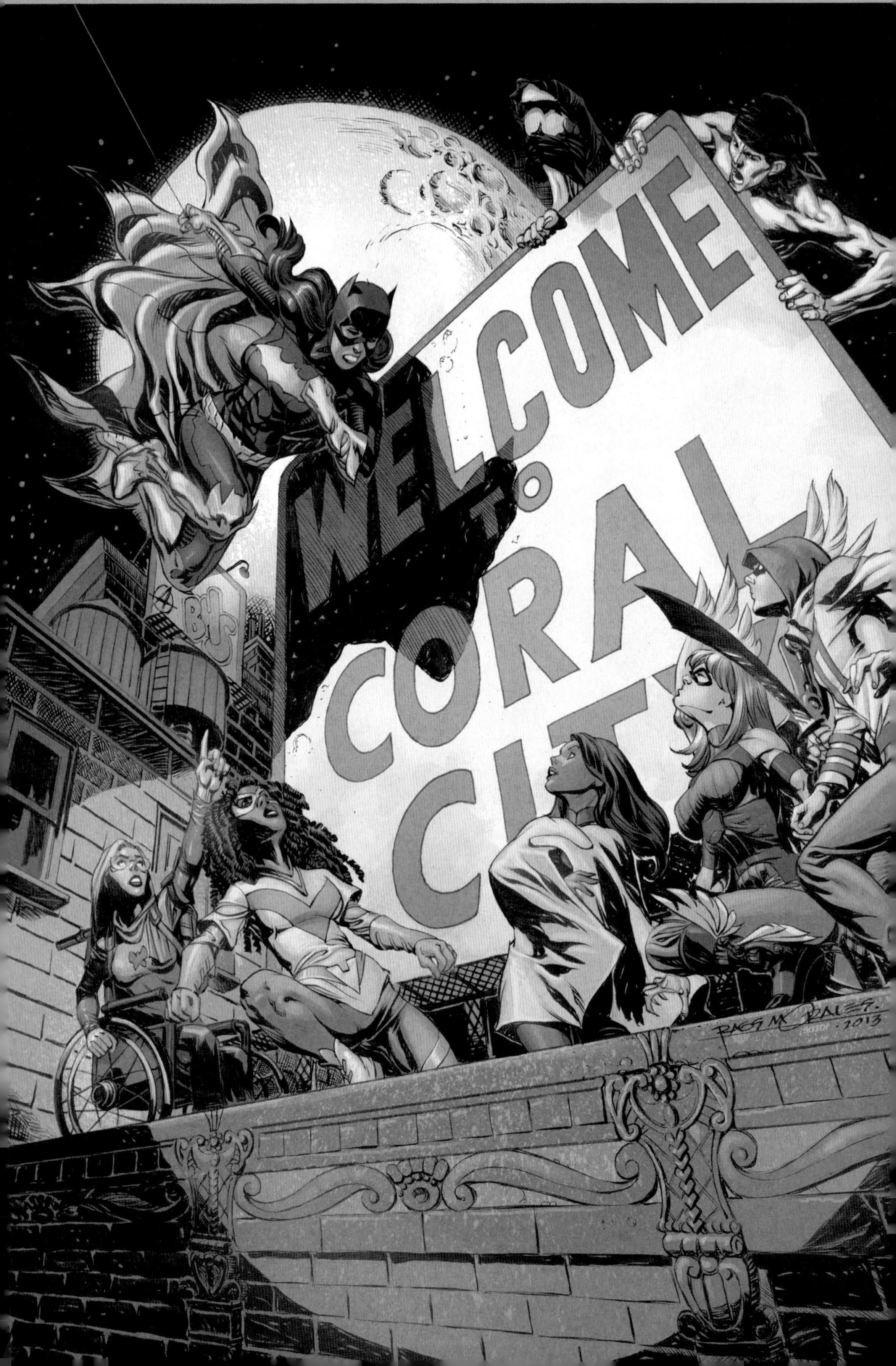
WELCOME TO CORAL CITY

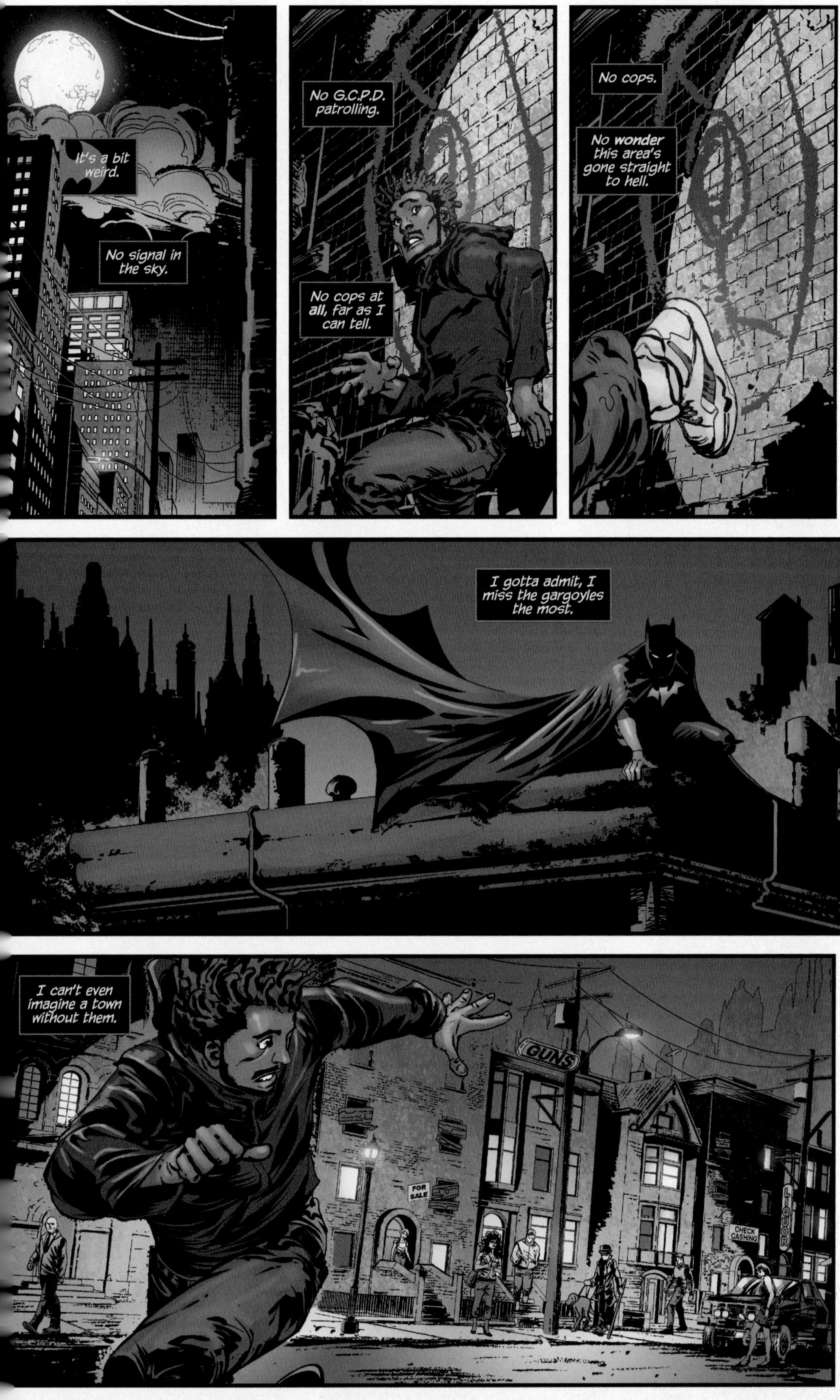
It's a bit weird.
No signal in the sky.
No G.C.P.D. patrolling.
No cops at all, far as I can tell.
No cops.
No wonder this area's gone straight to hell.
I gotta admit, I miss the gargoyles the most.
I can't even imagine a town without them.
GUNS
FOR SALE
CHECK CASHING
LIQUOR

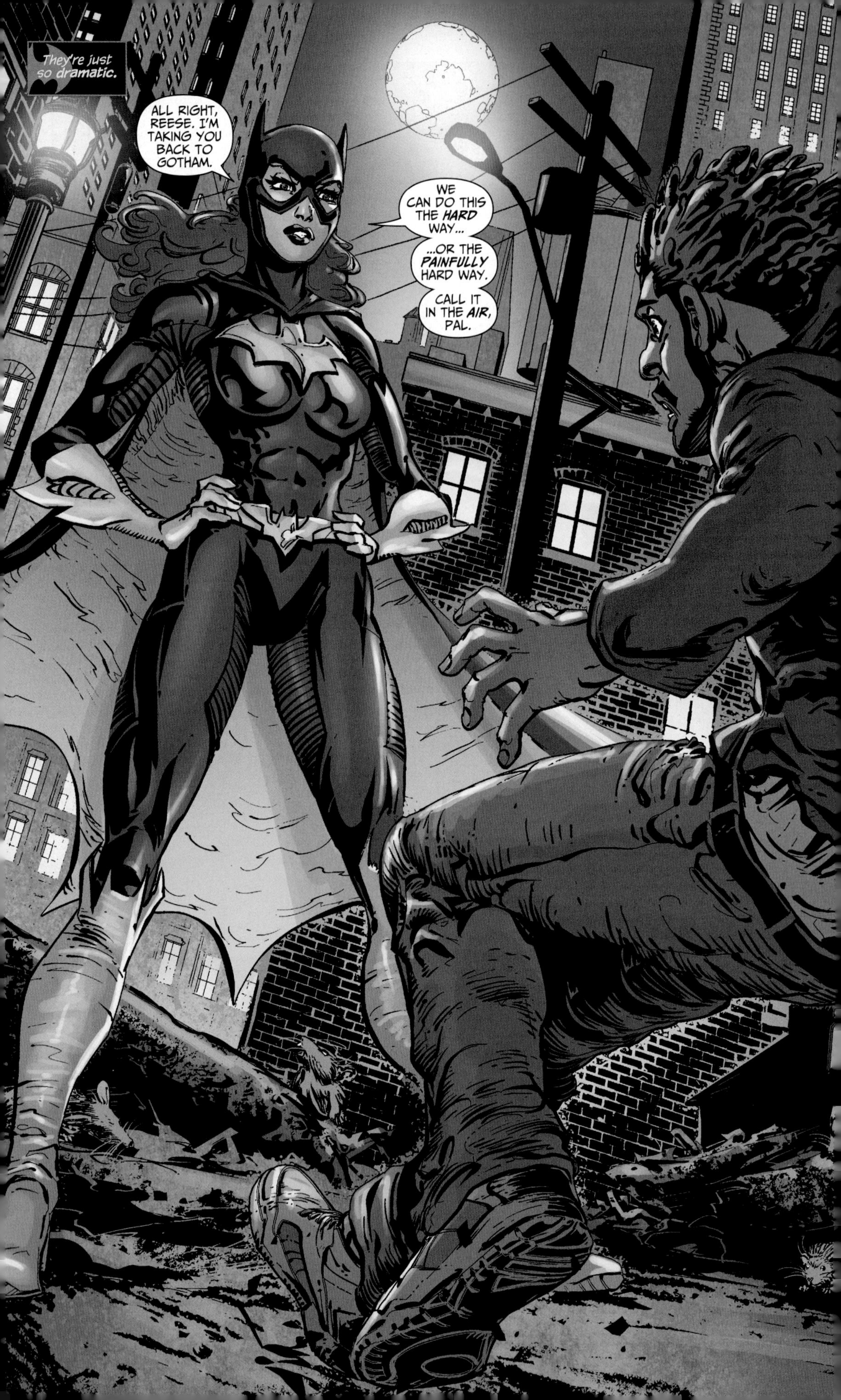
They're just so *dramatic.*
ALL RIGHT, REESE. I'M TAKING YOU BACK TO GOTHAM.
WE CAN DO THIS THE *HARD* WAY...
...OR THE *PAINFULLY* HARD WAY.
CALL IT IN THE *AIR,* PAL.

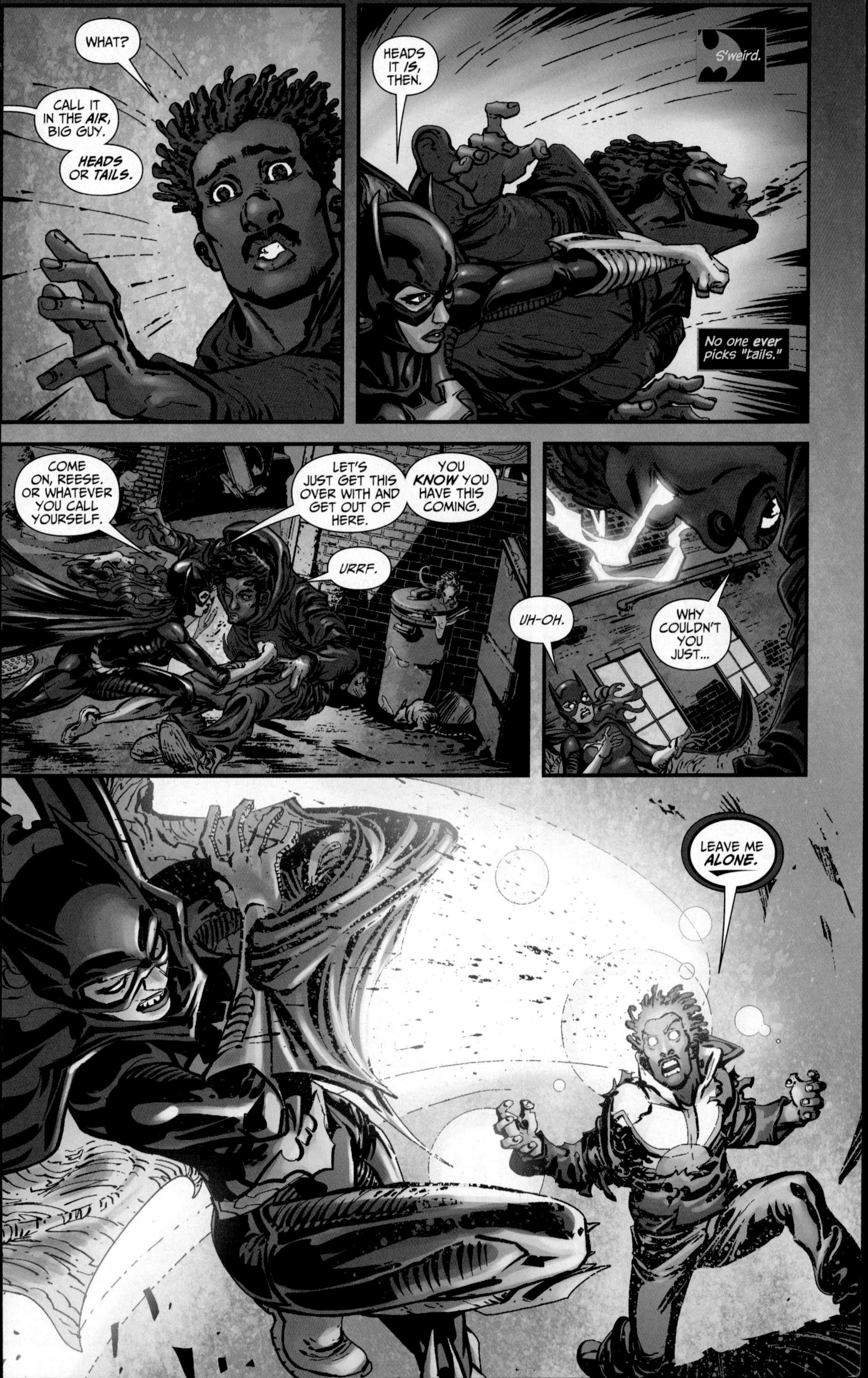

WHAT?
CALL IT IN THE AIR, BIG GUY.
HEADS OR TAILS.
HEADS IT IS, THEN.
S'weird.
No one ever picks "tails."
COME ON, REESE. OR WHATEVER YOU CALL YOURSELF.
LET'S JUST GET THIS OVER WITH AND GET OUT OF HERE.
YOU KNOW YOU HAVE THIS COMING.
URRF.
UH-OH.
WHY COULDN'T YOU JUST...
LEAVE ME ALONE.

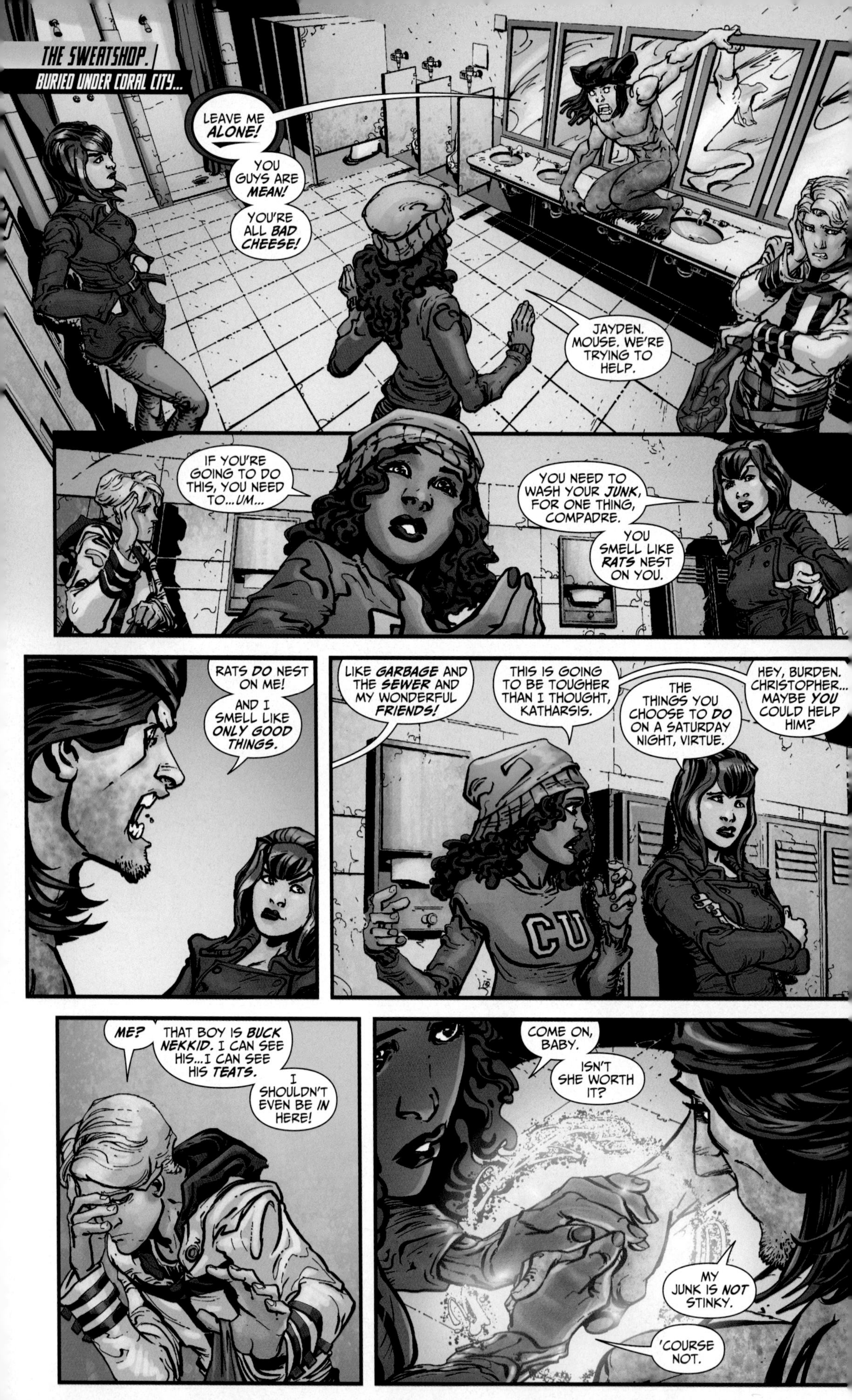
THE SWEATSHOP.
BURIED UNDER CORAL CITY...
LEAVE ME ALONE!
YOU GUYS ARE MEAN!
YOU'RE ALL BAD CHEESE!
JAYDEN. MOUSE. WE'RE TRYING TO HELP.
IF YOU'RE GOING TO DO THIS, YOU NEED TO...UM...
YOU NEED TO WASH YOUR JUNK, FOR ONE THING, COMPADRE.
YOU SMELL LIKE RATS NEST ON YOU.
RATS DO NEST ON ME!
AND I SMELL LIKE ONLY GOOD THINGS.
LIKE GARBAGE AND THE SEWER AND MY WONDERFUL FRIENDS!
THIS IS GOING TO BE TOUGHER THAN I THOUGHT, KATHARSIS.
THE THINGS YOU CHOOSE TO DO ON A SATURDAY NIGHT, VIRTUE.
HEY, BURDEN. CHRISTOPHER... MAYBE YOU COULD HELP HIM?
CU
ME?
THAT BOY IS BUCK NEKKID. I CAN SEE HIS...I CAN SEE HIS TEATS.
I SHOULDN'T EVEN BE IN HERE!
COME ON, BABY.
ISN'T SHE WORTH IT?
MY JUNK IS NOT STINKY.
'COURSE NOT.

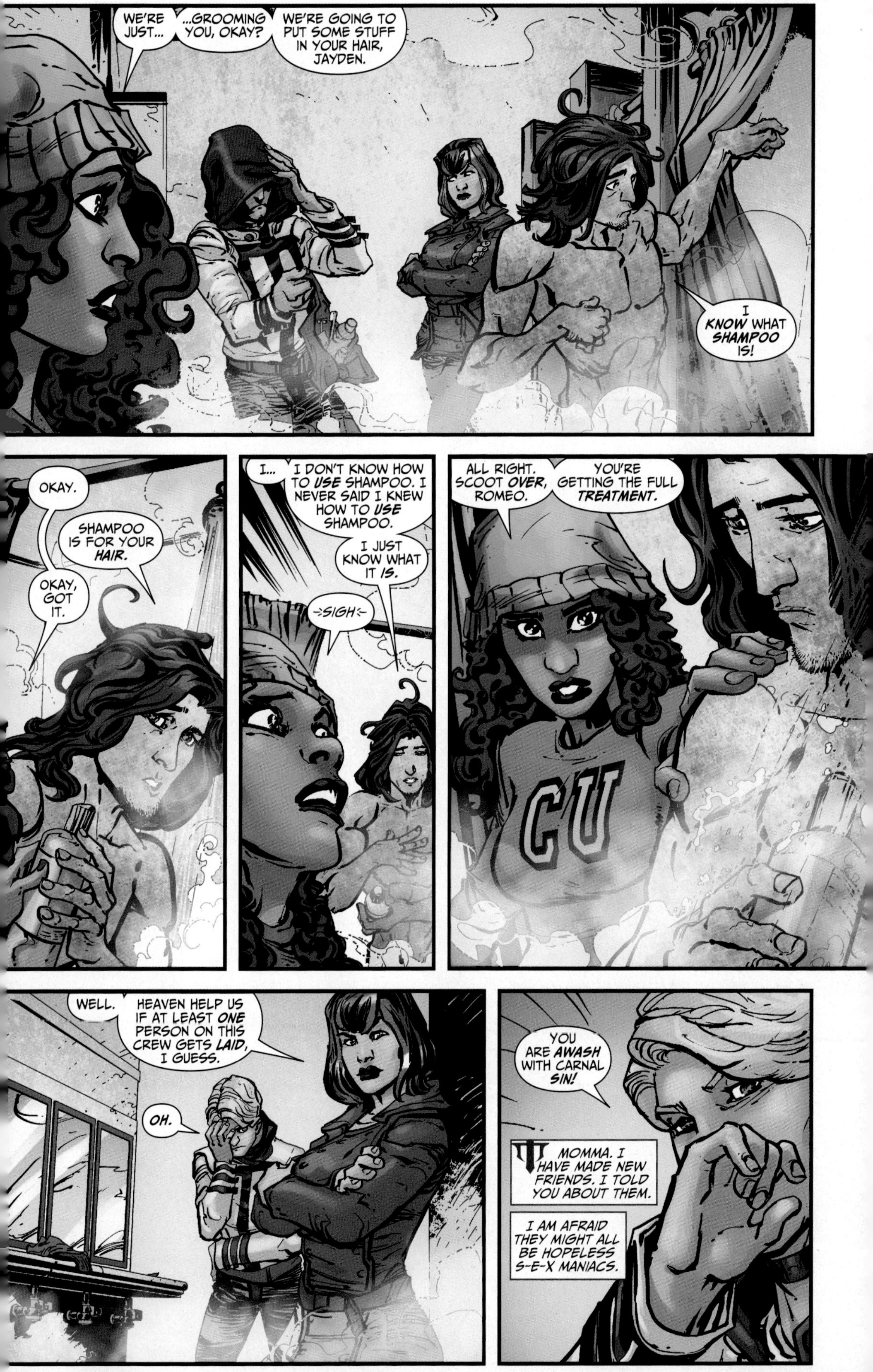
WE'RE JUST...
...GROOMING YOU, OKAY?
WE'RE GOING TO PUT SOME STUFF IN YOUR HAIR, JAYDEN.
I KNOW WHAT SHAMPOO IS!
OKAY.
SHAMPOO IS FOR YOUR HAIR.
OKAY, GOT IT.
I...
I DON'T KNOW HOW TO USE SHAMPOO. I NEVER SAID I KNEW HOW TO USE SHAMPOO.
I JUST KNOW WHAT IT IS.
SIGH
ALL RIGHT. SCOOT OVER, ROMEO.
YOU'RE GETTING THE FULL TREATMENT.
CU
WELL.
HEAVEN HELP US IF AT LEAST ONE PERSON ON THIS CREW GETS LAID, I GUESS.
OH.
YOU ARE AWASH WITH CARNAL SIN!
MOMMA. I HAVE MADE NEW FRIENDS. I TOLD YOU ABOUT THEM.
I AM AFRAID THEY MIGHT ALL BE HOPELESS S-E-X MANIACS.

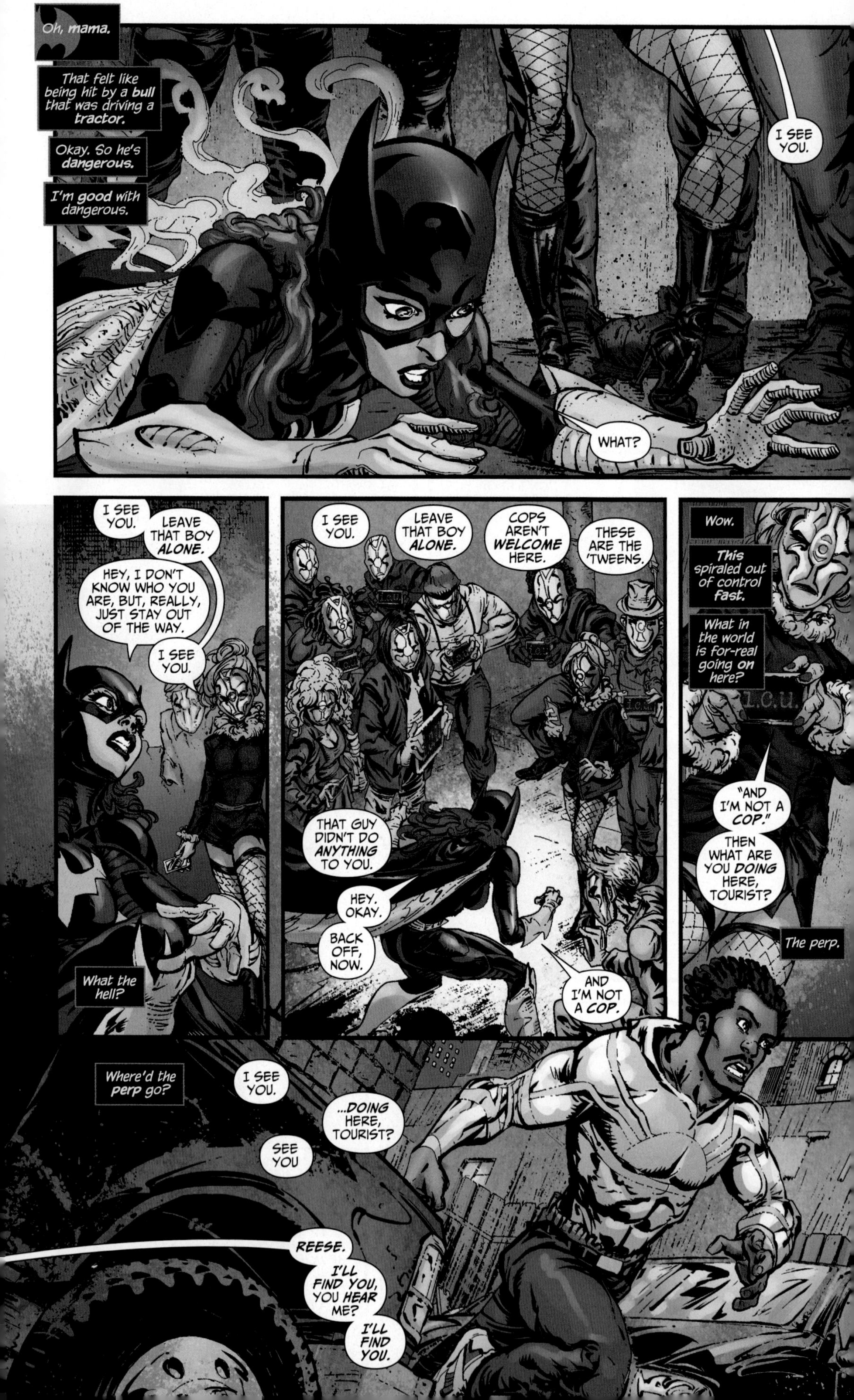

Oh, mama.
That felt like being hit by a bull that was driving a tractor.
Okay. So he's dangerous.
I'm good with dangerous.
I SEE YOU.
WHAT?
I SEE YOU.
LEAVE THAT BOY ALONE.
HEY, I DON'T KNOW WHO YOU ARE, BUT, REALLY, JUST STAY OUT OF THE WAY.
I SEE YOU.
What the hell?
I SEE YOU.
LEAVE THAT BOY ALONE.
COPS AREN'T WELCOME HERE.
THESE ARE THE 'TWEENS.
THAT GUY DIDN'T DO ANYTHING TO YOU.
HEY. OKAY.
BACK OFF, NOW.
AND I'M NOT A COP.
Wow.
This spiraled out of control fast.
What in the world is for-real going on here?
"AND I'M NOT A COP."
THEN WHAT ARE YOU DOING HERE, TOURIST?
The perp.
Where'd the perp go?
I SEE YOU.
...DOING HERE, TOURIST?
SEE YOU
REESE.
I'LL FIND YOU, YOU HEAR ME?
I'LL FIND YOU.

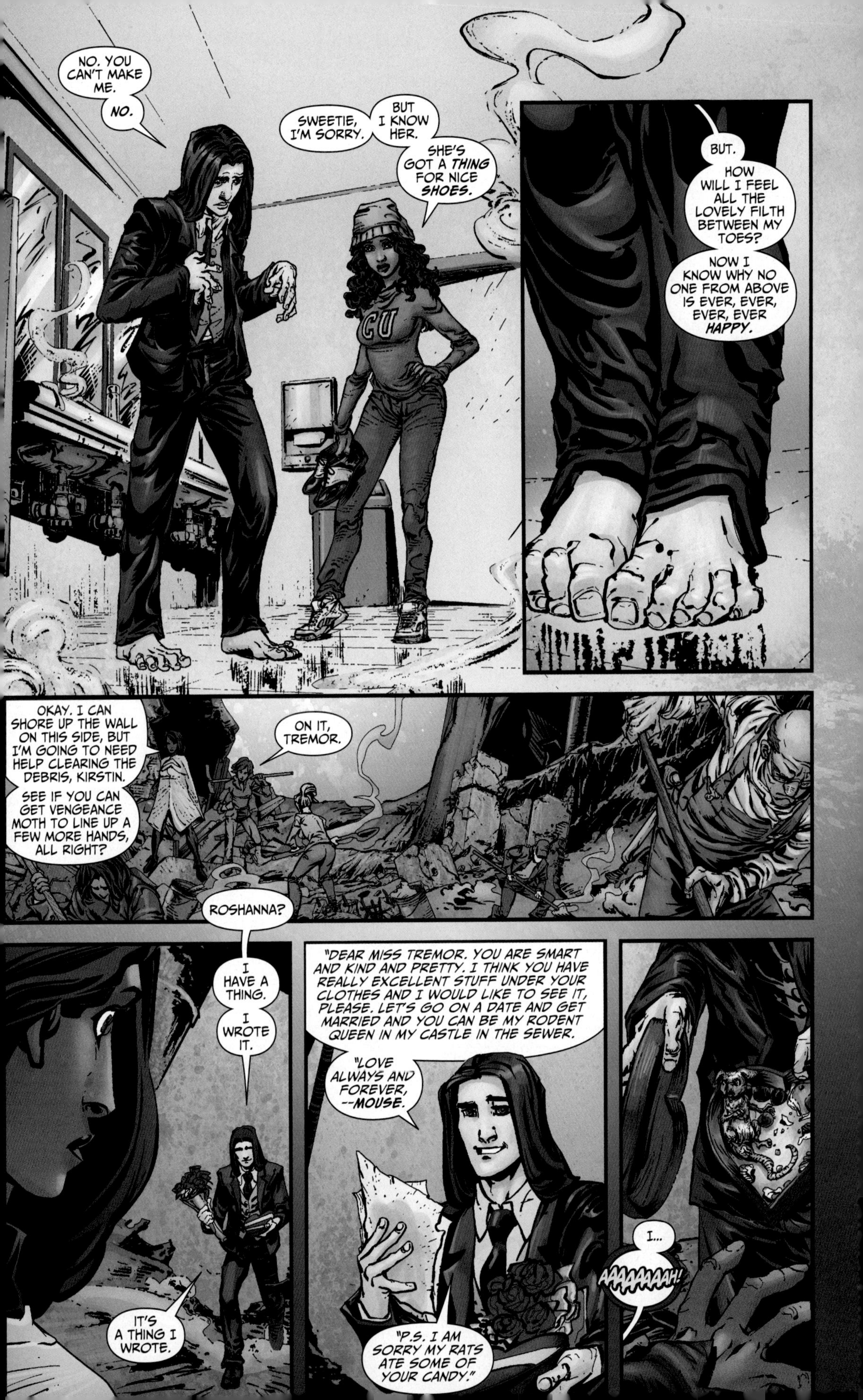
NO. YOU CAN'T MAKE ME.
NO.
SWEETIE, I'M SORRY.
BUT I KNOW HER.
SHE'S GOT A THING FOR NICE SHOES.
BUT.
HOW WILL I FEEL ALL THE LOVELY FILTH BETWEEN MY TOES?
NOW I KNOW WHY NO ONE FROM ABOVE IS EVER, EVER, EVER, EVER HAPPY.
OKAY. I CAN SHORE UP THE WALL ON THIS SIDE, BUT I'M GOING TO NEED HELP CLEARING THE DEBRIS, KIRSTIN.
SEE IF YOU CAN GET VENGEANCE MOTH TO LINE UP A FEW MORE HANDS, ALL RIGHT?
ON IT, TREMOR.
ROSHANNA?
I HAVE A THING.
I WROTE IT.
IT'S A THING I WROTE.
"DEAR MISS TREMOR. YOU ARE SMART AND KIND AND PRETTY. I THINK YOU HAVE REALLY EXCELLENT STUFF UNDER YOUR CLOTHES AND I WOULD LIKE TO SEE IT, PLEASE. LET'S GO ON A DATE AND GET MARRIED AND YOU CAN BE MY RODENT QUEEN IN MY CASTLE IN THE SEWER.
"LOVE ALWAYS AND FOREVER, --MOUSE.
"P.S. I AM SORRY MY RATS ATE SOME OF YOUR CANDY."
I...
AAAAAAAH!

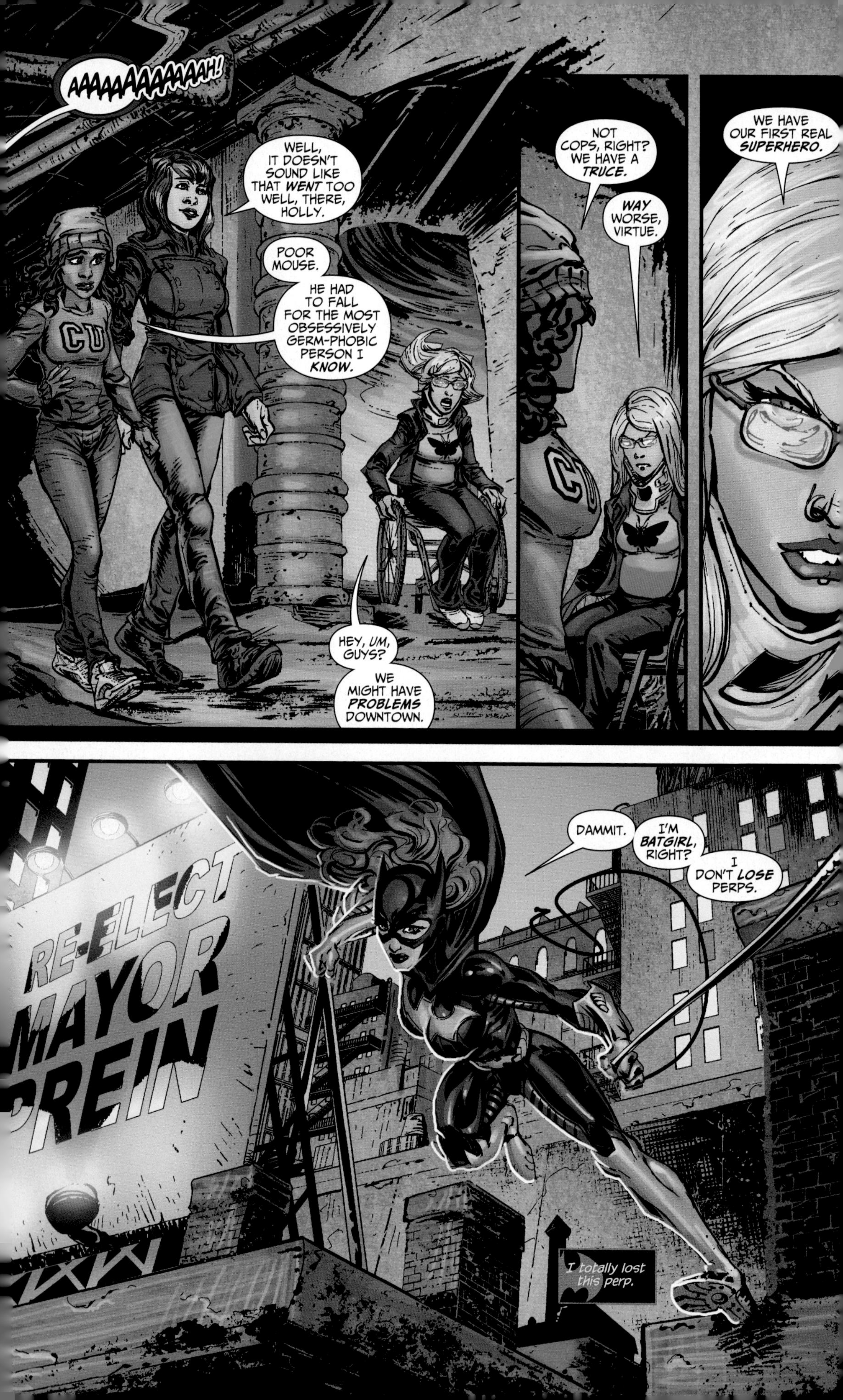
AAAAAAAAAAAAH!
WELL, IT DOESN'T SOUND LIKE THAT WENT TOO WELL, THERE, HOLLY.
POOR MOUSE.
HE HAD TO FALL FOR THE MOST OBSESSIVELY GERM-PHOBIC PERSON I KNOW.
HEY, UM, GUYS?
WE MIGHT HAVE PROBLEMS DOWNTOWN.
NOT COPS, RIGHT? WE HAVE A TRUCE.
WAY WORSE, VIRTUE.
WE HAVE OUR FIRST REAL SUPERHERO.
RE-ELECT MAYOR DREIN
DAMMIT.
I'M BATGIRL, RIGHT?
I DON'T LOSE PERPS.
I totally lost this perp.

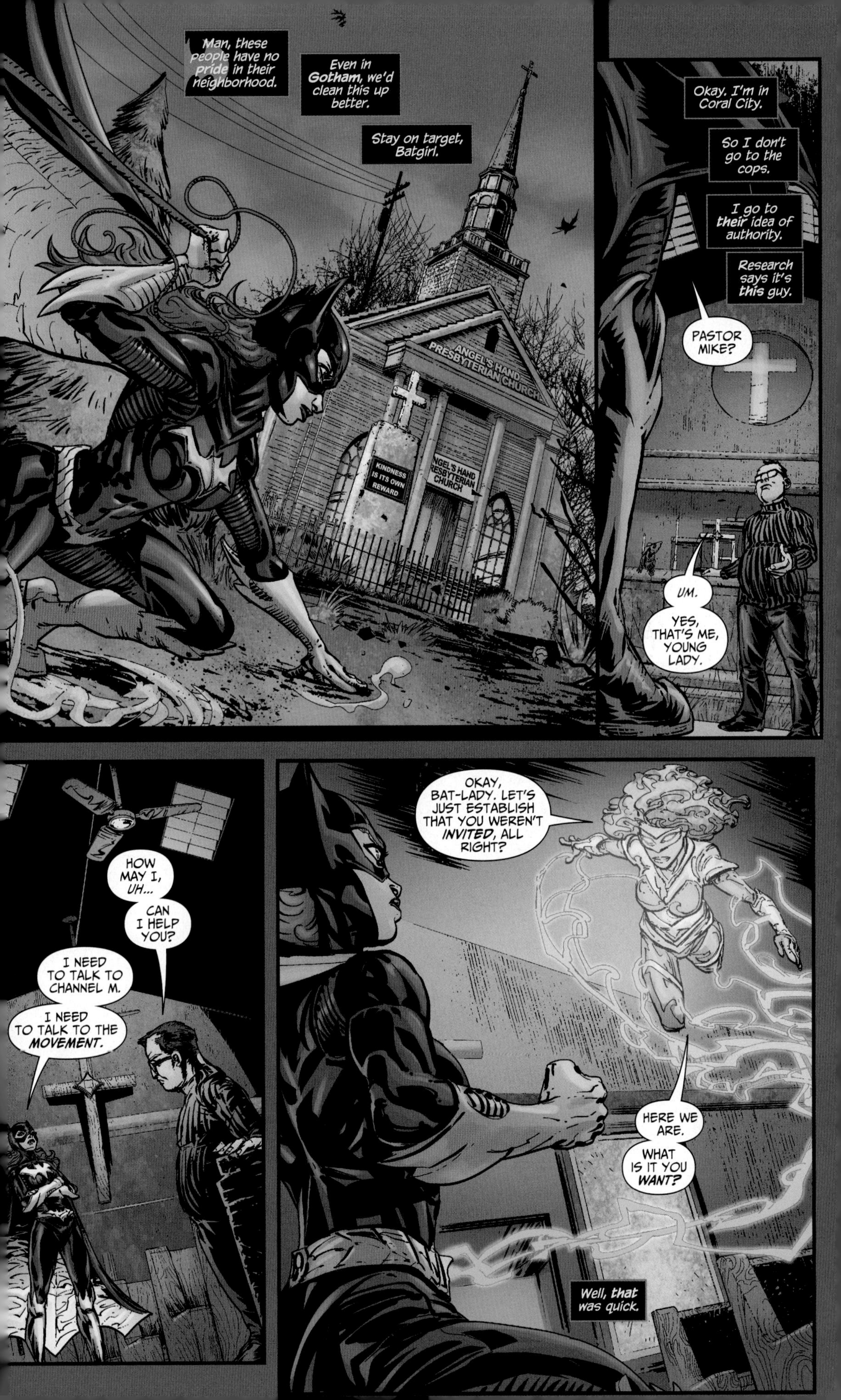

Man, these people have no pride in their neighborhood.
Even in Gotham, we'd clean this up better.
Stay on target, Batgirl.
ANGEL'S HAND PRESBYTERIAN CHURCH
KINDNESS IS ITS OWN REWARD
ANGEL'S HAND PRESBYTERIAN CHURCH
Okay. I'm in Coral City.
So I don't go to the cops.
I go to their idea of authority.
Research says it's this guy.
PASTOR MIKE?
UM.
YES, THAT'S ME, YOUNG LADY.
HOW MAY I, UH...
CAN I HELP YOU?
I NEED TO TALK TO CHANNEL M.
I NEED TO TALK TO THE MOVEMENT.
OKAY, BAT-LADY. LET'S JUST ESTABLISH THAT YOU WEREN'T INVITED, ALL RIGHT?
HERE WE ARE.
WHAT IS IT YOU WANT?
Well, that was quick.

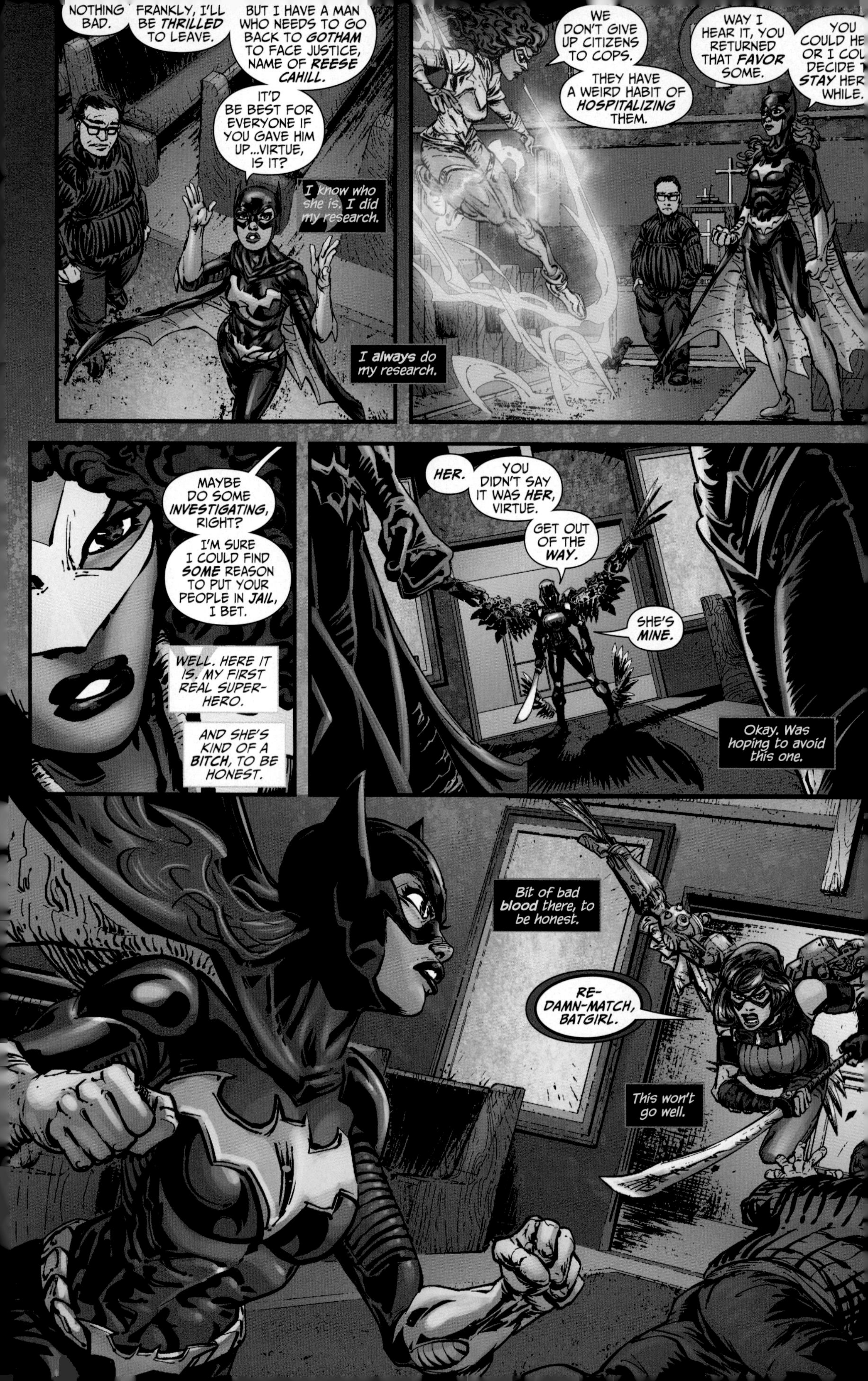

NOTHING BAD.
FRANKLY, I'LL BE THRILLED TO LEAVE.
BUT I HAVE A MAN WHO NEEDS TO GO BACK TO GOTHAM TO FACE JUSTICE, NAME OF REESE CAHILL.
IT'D BE BEST FOR EVERYONE IF YOU GAVE HIM UP...VIRTUE, IS IT?
I know who she is. I did my research.
I always do my research.
WE DON'T GIVE UP CITIZENS TO COPS.
THEY HAVE A WEIRD HABIT OF HOSPITALIZING THEM.
WAY I HEAR IT, YOU RETURNED THAT FAVOR SOME.
YOU COULD HE OR I COU DECIDE T STAY HER WHILE.
MAYBE DO SOME INVESTIGATING, RIGHT?
I'M SURE I COULD FIND SOME REASON TO PUT YOUR PEOPLE IN JAIL, I BET.
WELL. HERE IT IS. MY FIRST REAL SUPER-HERO.
AND SHE'S KIND OF A BITCH, TO BE HONEST.
HER.
YOU DIDN'T SAY IT WAS HER, VIRTUE.
GET OUT OF THE WAY.
SHE'S MINE.
Okay. Was hoping to avoid this one.
Bit of bad blood there, to be honest.
RE-DAMN-MATCH, BATGIRL.
This won't go well.

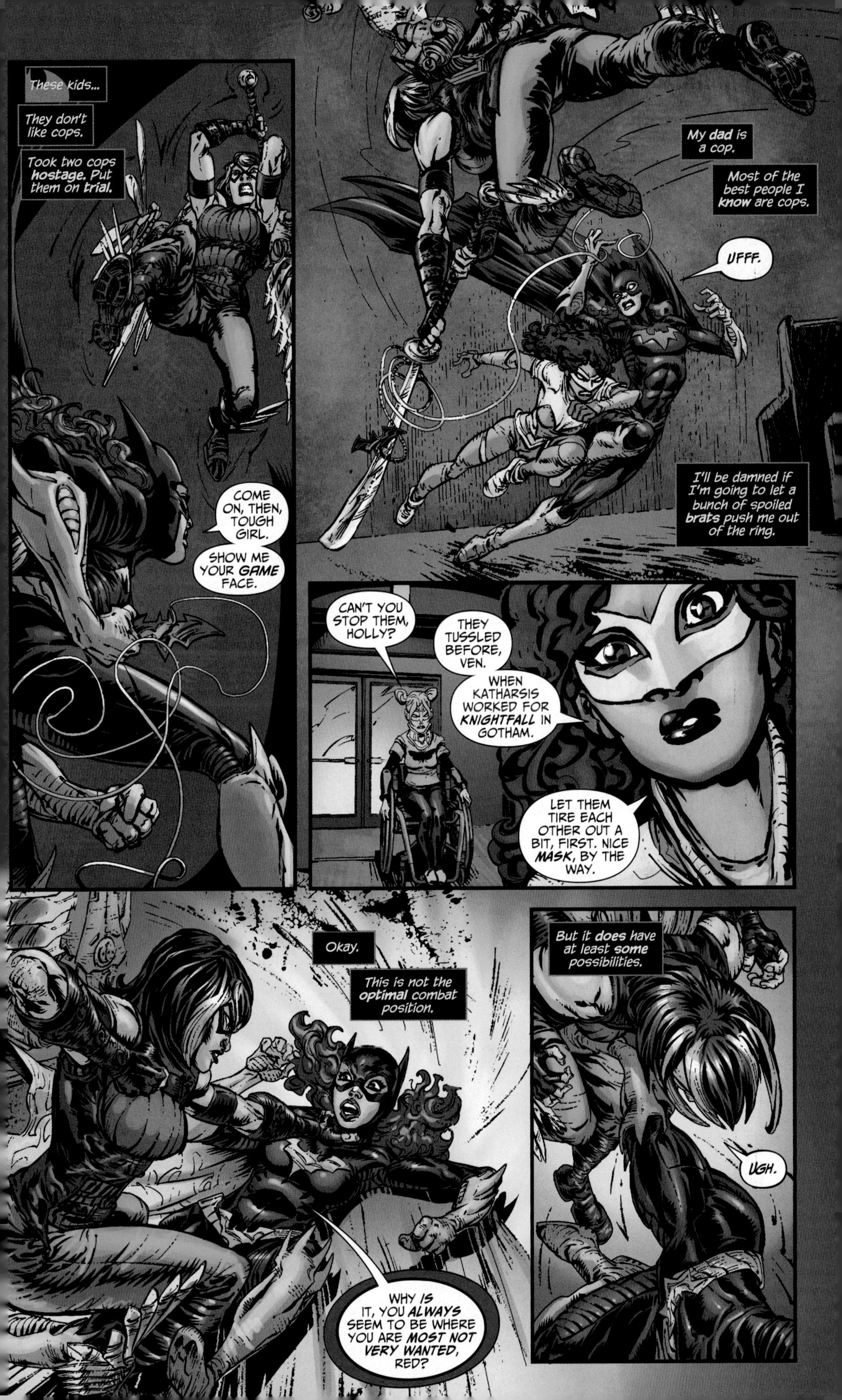

These kids...
They don't like cops.
Took two cops hostage. Put them on trial.
My dad is a cop.
Most of the best people I know are cops.
UFFF.
COME ON, THEN, TOUGH GIRL.
SHOW ME YOUR GAME FACE.
I'll be damned if I'm going to let a bunch of spoiled brats push me out of the ring.
CAN'T YOU STOP THEM, HOLLY?
THEY TUSSLED BEFORE, VEN.
WHEN KATHARSIS WORKED FOR KNIGHTFALL IN GOTHAM.
LET THEM TIRE EACH OTHER OUT A BIT, FIRST. NICE MASK, BY THE WAY.
Okay.
This is not the optimal combat position.
WHY IS IT, YOU ALWAYS SEEM TO BE WHERE YOU ARE MOST NOT VERY WANTED, RED?
But it does have at least some possibilities.
UGH.

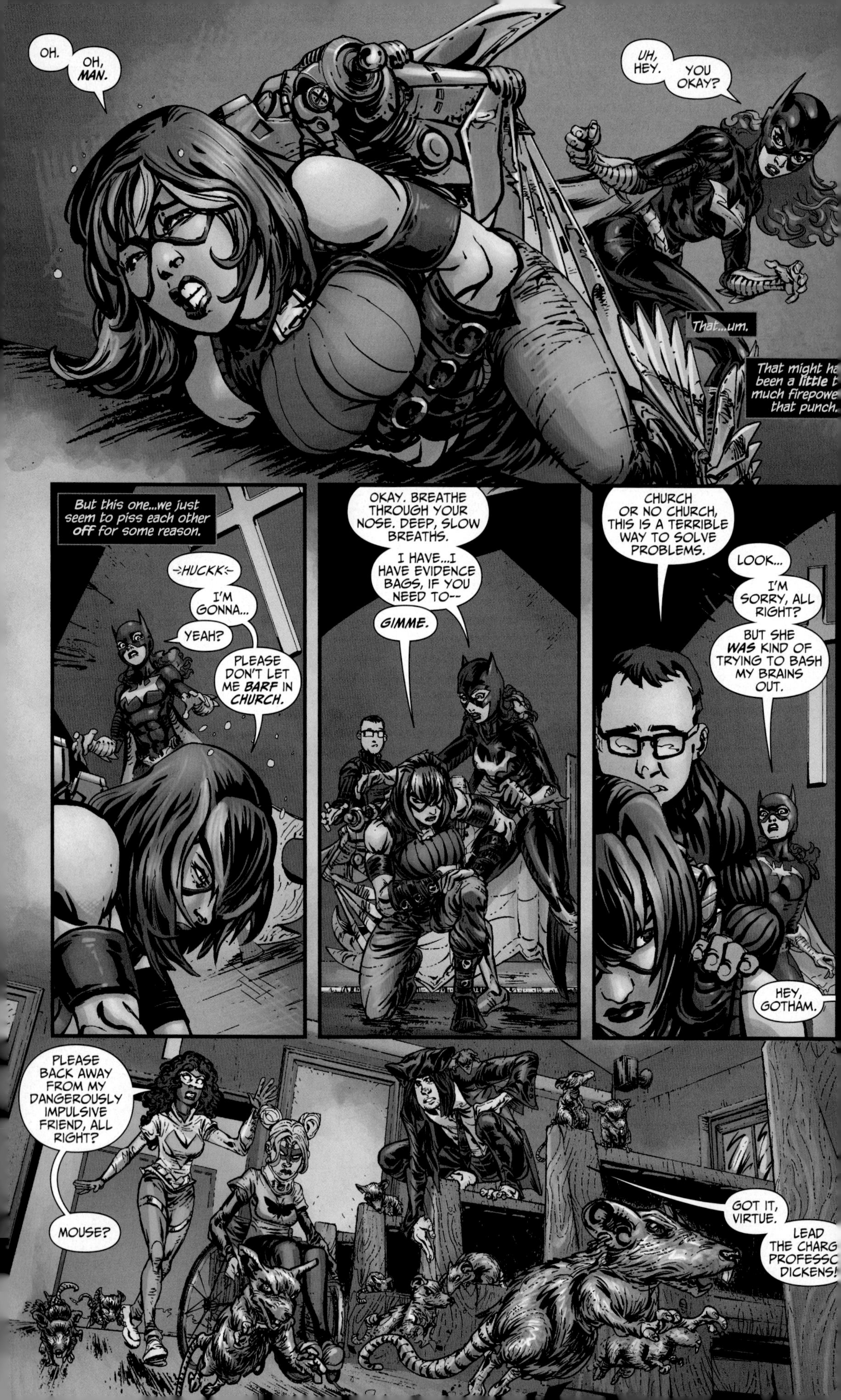

OH.
OH, MAN.
UH, HEY.
YOU OKAY?
That...um.
That might ha been a little t much firepowe that punch.
But this one...we just seem to piss each other off for some reason.
HUCKK
I'M GONNA...
YEAH?
PLEASE DON'T LET ME BARF IN CHURCH.
OKAY. BREATHE THROUGH YOUR NOSE. DEEP, SLOW BREATHS.
I HAVE...I HAVE EVIDENCE BAGS, IF YOU NEED TO--
GIMME.
CHURCH OR NO CHURCH, THIS IS A TERRIBLE WAY TO SOLVE PROBLEMS.
LOOK...
I'M SORRY, ALL RIGHT?
BUT SHE WAS KIND OF TRYING TO BASH MY BRAINS OUT.
HEY, GOTHAM.
PLEASE BACK AWAY FROM MY DANGEROUSLY IMPULSIVE FRIEND, ALL RIGHT?
MOUSE?
GOT IT, VIRTUE.
LEAD THE CHARG PROFESSO DICKENS!

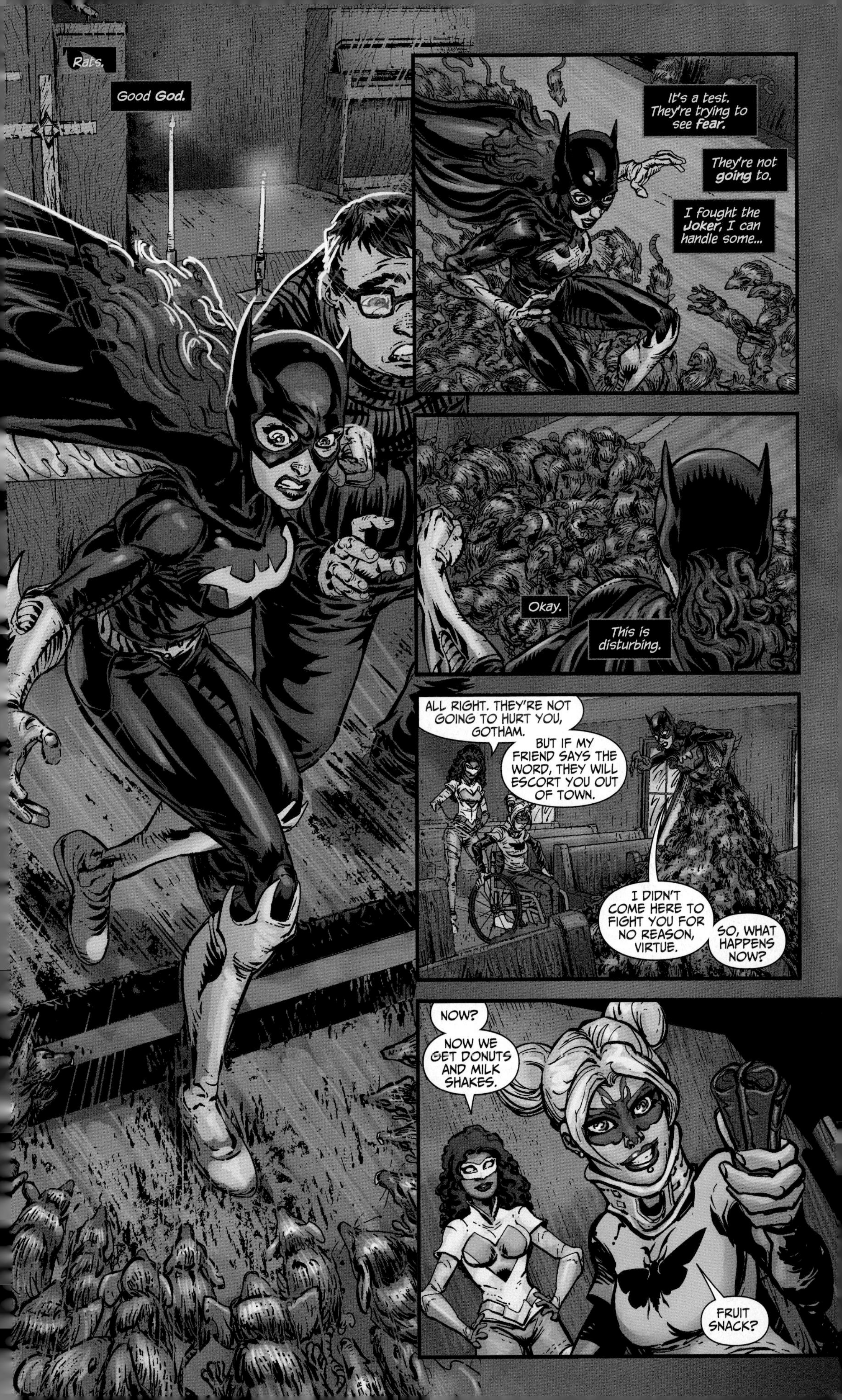
Rats.
Good God.
It's a test. They're trying to see fear.
They're not going to.
I fought the Joker, I can handle some...
Okay.
This is disturbing.
ALL RIGHT. THEY'RE NOT GOING TO HURT YOU, GOTHAM.
BUT IF MY FRIEND SAYS THE WORD, THEY WILL ESCORT YOU OUT OF TOWN.
I DIDN'T COME HERE TO FIGHT YOU FOR NO REASON, VIRTUE.
SO, WHAT HAPPENS NOW?
NOW?
NOW WE GET DONUTS AND MILK SHAKES.
FRUIT SNACK?

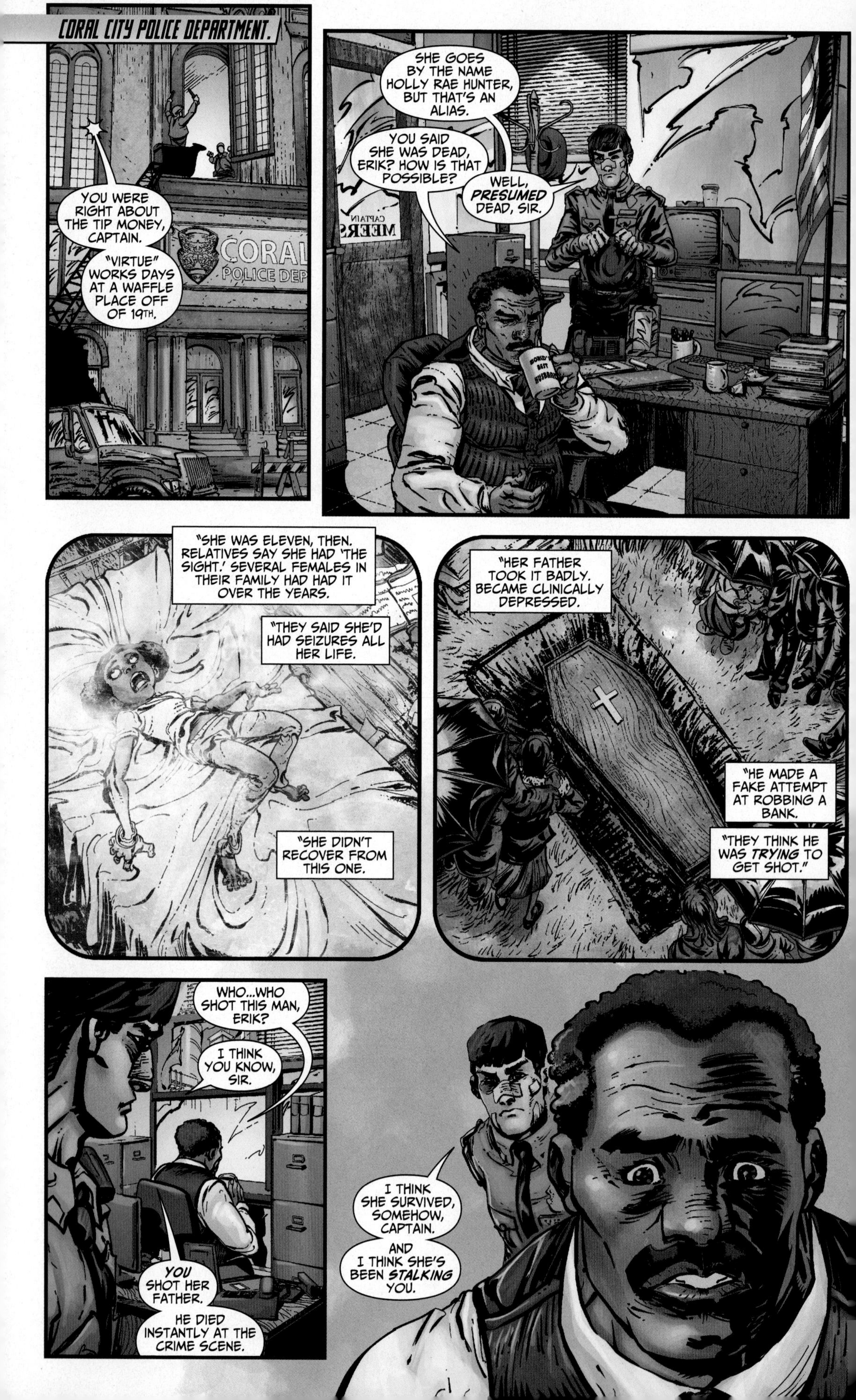

CORAL CITY POLICE DEPARTMENT.
YOU WERE RIGHT ABOUT THE TIP MONEY, CAPTAIN.
"VIRTUE" WORKS DAYS AT A WAFFLE PLACE OFF OF 19TH.
CORAL POLICE DEP
SHE GOES BY THE NAME HOLLY RAE HUNTER, BUT THAT'S AN ALIAS.
YOU SAID SHE WAS DEAD, ERIK? HOW IS THAT POSSIBLE?
WELL, PRESUMED DEAD, SIR.
CAPTAIN MEERS
"SHE WAS ELEVEN, THEN. RELATIVES SAY SHE HAD 'THE SIGHT.' SEVERAL FEMALES IN THEIR FAMILY HAD HAD IT OVER THE YEARS.
"THEY SAID SHE'D HAD SEIZURES ALL HER LIFE.
"SHE DIDN'T RECOVER FROM THIS ONE.
"HER FATHER TOOK IT BADLY. BECAME CLINICALLY DEPRESSED.
"HE MADE A FAKE ATTEMPT AT ROBBING A BANK.
"THEY THINK HE WAS TRYING TO GET SHOT."
WHO...WHO SHOT THIS MAN, ERIK?
I THINK YOU KNOW, SIR.
YOU SHOT HER FATHER.
HE DIED INSTANTLY AT THE CRIME SCENE.
I THINK SHE SURVIVED, SOMEHOW, CAPTAIN.
AND I THINK SHE'S BEEN STALKING YOU.

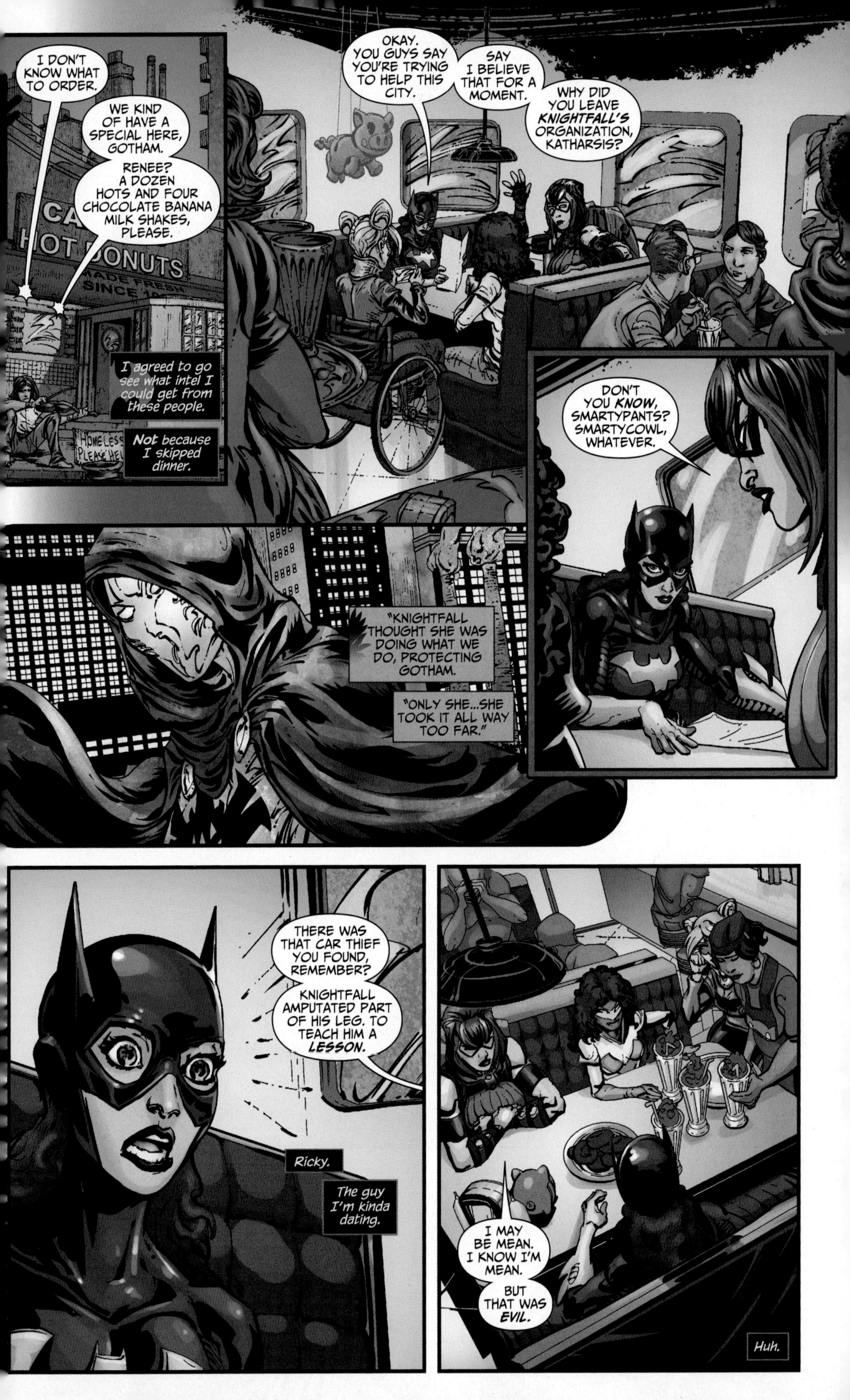

I DON'T KNOW WHAT TO ORDER.
WE KIND OF HAVE A SPECIAL HERE, GOTHAM.
RENEE? A DOZEN HOTS AND FOUR CHOCOLATE BANANA MILK SHAKES, PLEASE.
HOT DONUTS
MADE FRESH
I agreed to go see what intel I could get from these people.
Not because I skipped dinner.
OKAY. YOU GUYS SAY YOU'RE TRYING TO HELP THIS CITY.
SAY I BELIEVE THAT FOR A MOMENT.
WHY DID YOU LEAVE KNIGHTFALL'S ORGANIZATION, KATHARSIS?
DON'T YOU KNOW, SMARTYPANTS? SMARTYCOWL, WHATEVER.
"KNIGHTFALL THOUGHT SHE WAS DOING WHAT WE DO, PROTECTING GOTHAM.
"ONLY SHE...SHE TOOK IT ALL WAY TOO FAR."
THERE WAS THAT CAR THIEF YOU FOUND, REMEMBER?
KNIGHTFALL AMPUTATED PART OF HIS LEG. TO TEACH HIM A LESSON.
Ricky.
The guy I'm kinda dating.
I MAY BE MEAN. I KNOW I'M MEAN.
BUT THAT WAS EVIL.
Huh.

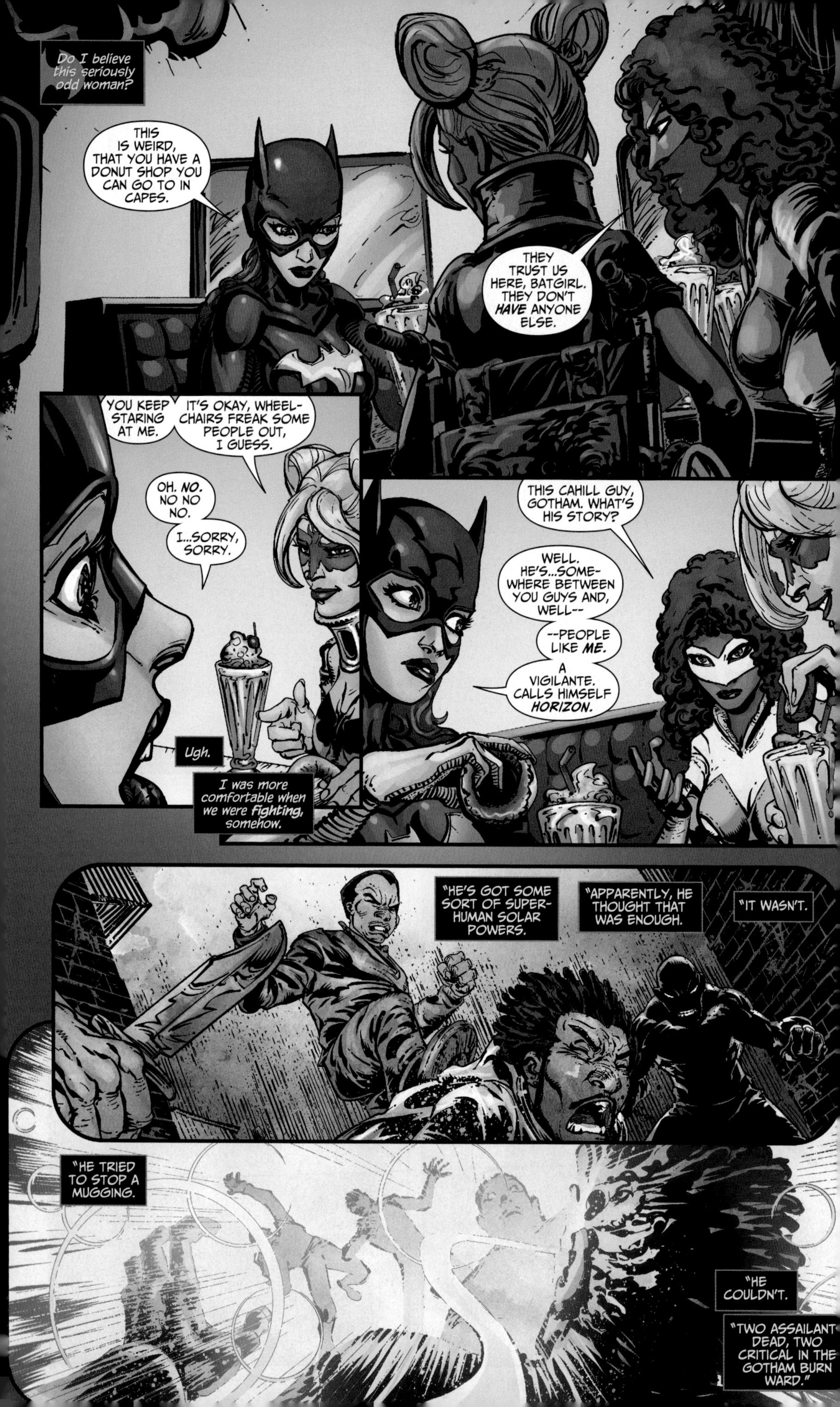

Do I believe this seriously odd woman?
THIS IS WEIRD, THAT YOU HAVE A DONUT SHOP YOU CAN GO TO IN CAPES.
THEY TRUST US HERE, BATGIRL. THEY DON'T HAVE ANYONE ELSE.
YOU KEEP STARING AT ME.
IT'S OKAY, WHEEL-CHAIRS FREAK SOME PEOPLE OUT, I GUESS.
OH. NO. NO NO NO.
I...SORRY, SORRY.
Ugh.
I was more comfortable when we were fighting, somehow.
THIS CAHILL GUY, GOTHAM. WHAT'S HIS STORY?
WELL. HE'S...SOME-WHERE BETWEEN YOU GUYS AND, WELL--
--PEOPLE LIKE ME.
A VIGILANTE. CALLS HIMSELF HORIZON.
"HE'S GOT SOME SORT OF SUPER-HUMAN SOLAR POWERS.
"APPARENTLY, HE THOUGHT THAT WAS ENOUGH.
"IT WASN'T.
"HE TRIED TO STOP A MUGGING.
"HE COULDN'T.
"TWO ASSAILANT DEAD, TWO CRITICAL IN THE GOTHAM BURN WARD."

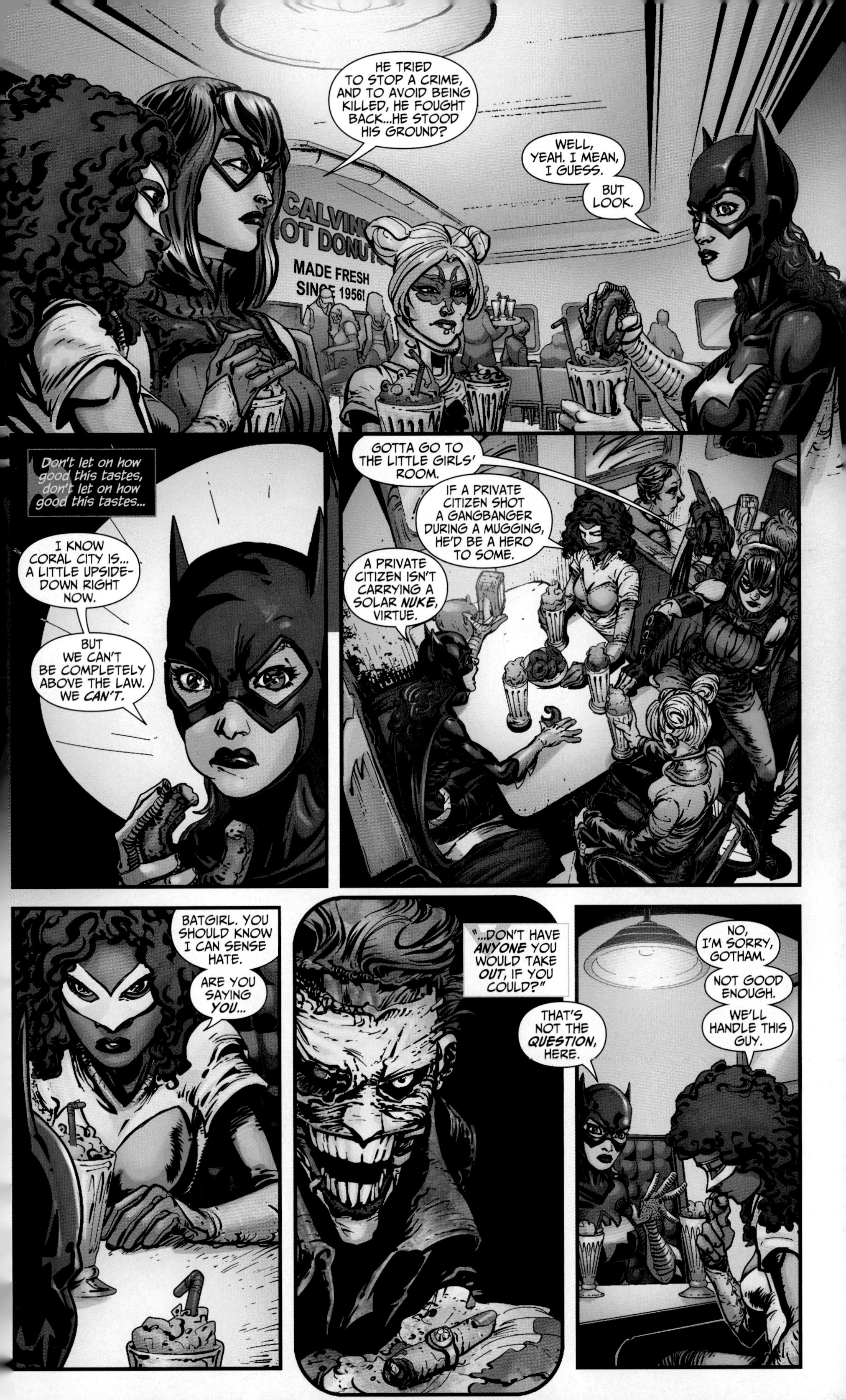
HE TRIED TO STOP A CRIME, AND TO AVOID BEING KILLED, HE FOUGHT BACK...HE STOOD HIS GROUND?
WELL, YEAH. I MEAN, I GUESS.
BUT LOOK.
CALVIN'S HOT DONUTS
MADE FRESH SINCE 1956!
Don't let on how good this tastes, don't let on how good this tastes...
I KNOW CORAL CITY IS... A LITTLE UPSIDE-DOWN RIGHT NOW.
BUT WE CAN'T BE COMPLETELY ABOVE THE LAW. WE *CAN'T.*
GOTTA GO TO THE LITTLE GIRLS' ROOM.
IF A PRIVATE CITIZEN SHOT A GANGBANGER DURING A MUGGING, HE'D BE A HERO TO SOME.
A PRIVATE CITIZEN ISN'T CARRYING A SOLAR *NUKE,* VIRTUE.
BATGIRL. YOU SHOULD KNOW I CAN SENSE HATE.
ARE YOU SAYING *YOU*...
"...DON'T HAVE *ANYONE* YOU WOULD TAKE *OUT*, IF YOU COULD?"
THAT'S NOT THE *QUESTION,* HERE.
NO, I'M SORRY, GOTHAM.
NOT GOOD ENOUGH.
WE'LL HANDLE THIS GUY.

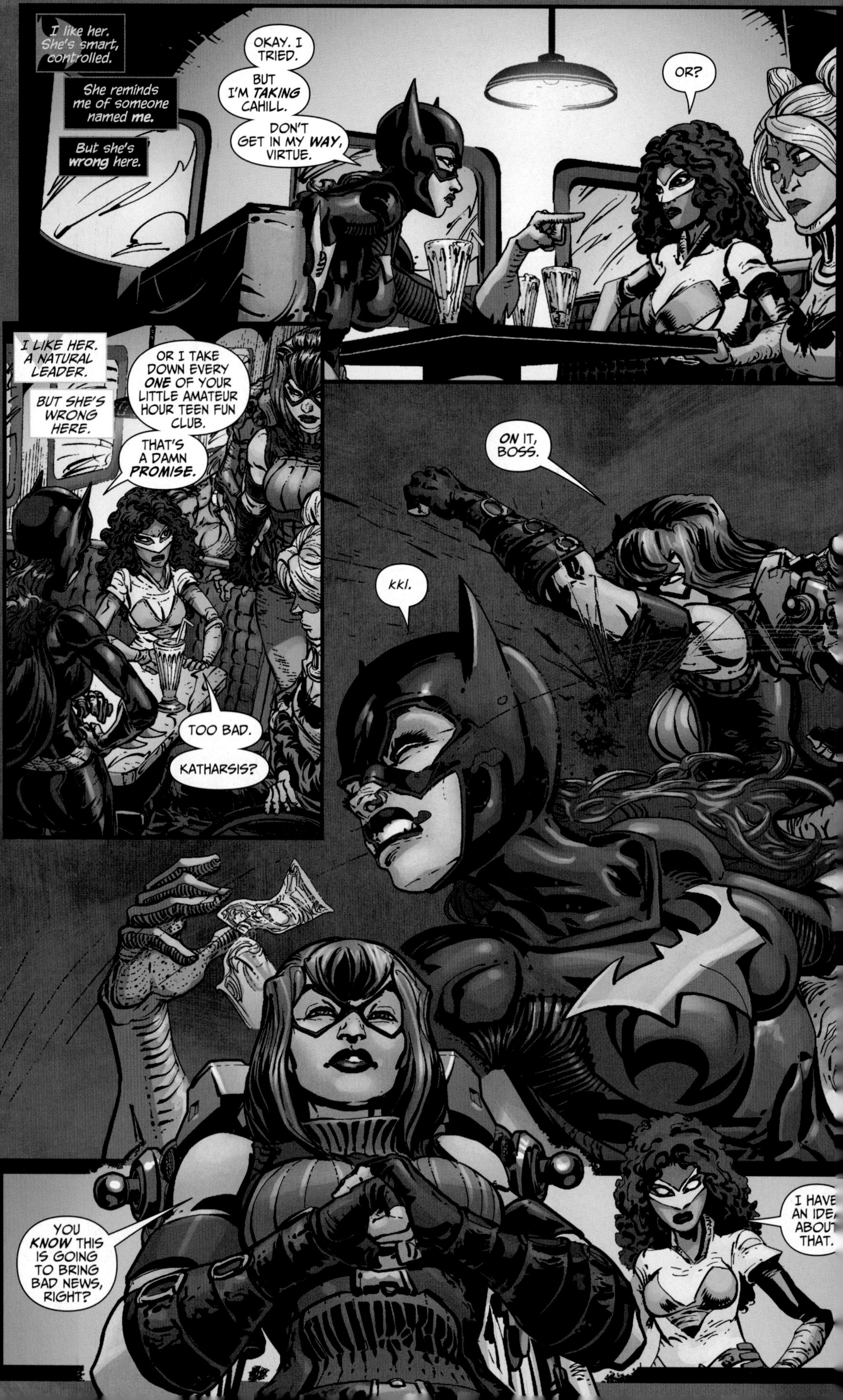

I like her. She's smart, controlled.
She reminds me of someone named me.
But she's wrong here.
OKAY. I TRIED.
BUT I'M TAKING CAHILL.
DON'T GET IN MY WAY, VIRTUE.
OR?
I LIKE HER. A NATURAL LEADER.
BUT SHE'S WRONG HERE.
OR I TAKE DOWN EVERY ONE OF YOUR LITTLE AMATEUR HOUR TEEN FUN CLUB.
THAT'S A DAMN PROMISE.
TOO BAD.
KATHARSIS?
ON IT, BOSS.
KKL.
YOU KNOW THIS IS GOING TO BRING BAD NEWS, RIGHT?
I HAVE AN IDE ABOUT THAT.

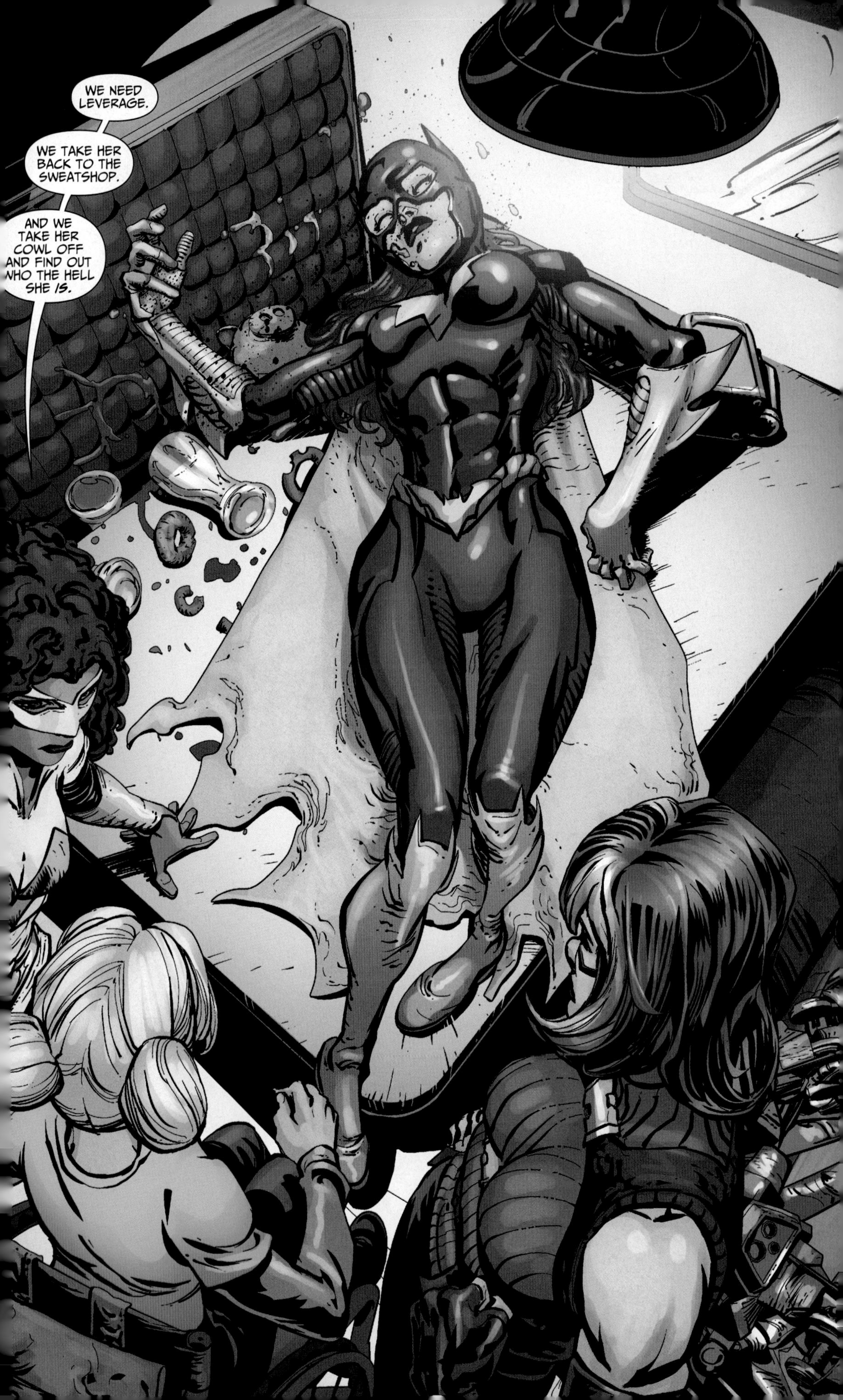
WE NEED LEVERAGE.
WE TAKE HER BACK TO THE SWEATSHOP.
AND WE TAKE HER COWL OFF AND FIND OUT WHO THE HELL SHE IS.

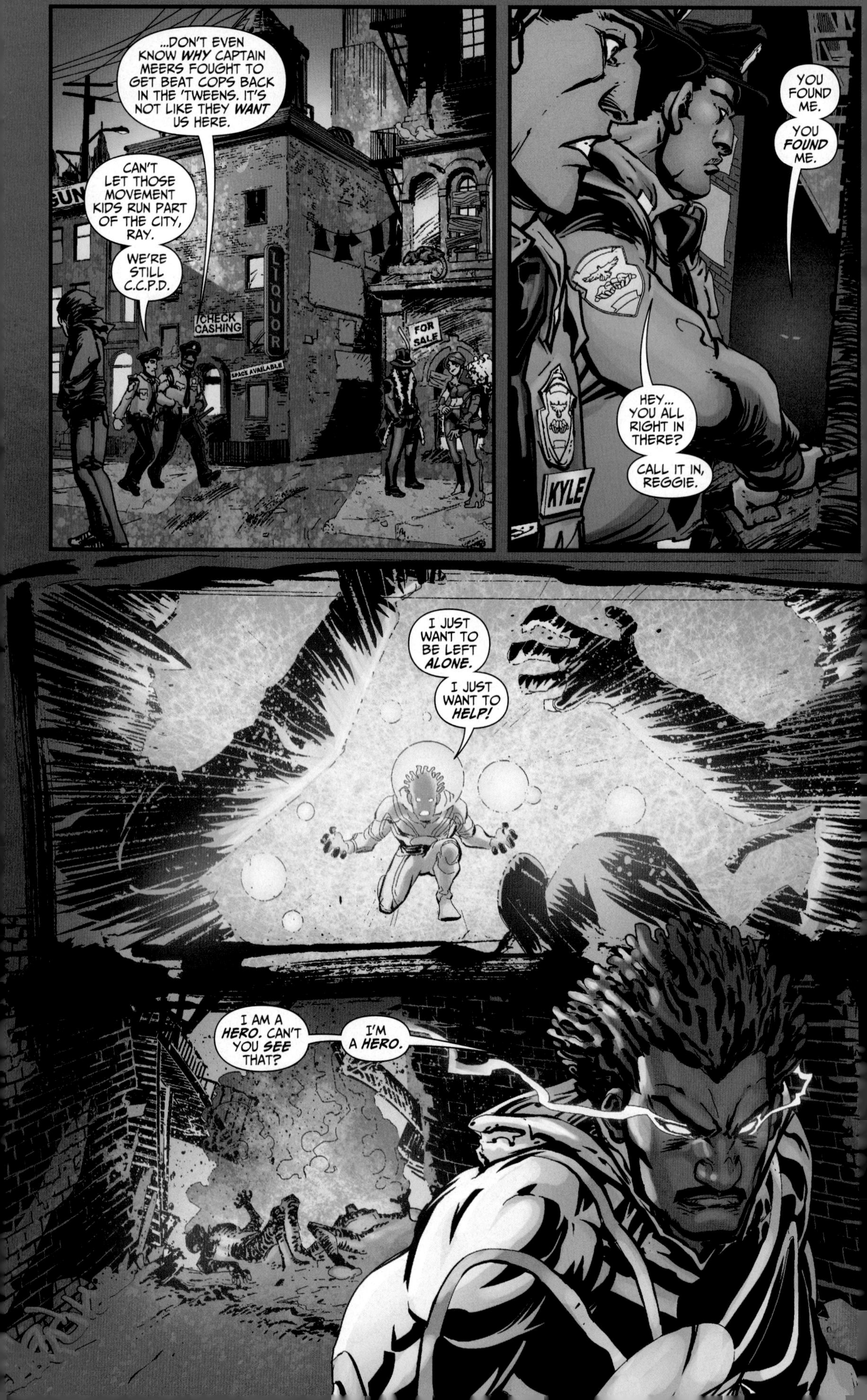

...DON'T EVEN KNOW *WHY* CAPTAIN MEERS FOUGHT TO GET BEAT COPS BACK IN THE 'TWEENS. IT'S NOT LIKE THEY *WANT* US HERE.
CAN'T LET THOSE MOVEMENT KIDS RUN PART OF THE CITY, RAY.
WE'RE STILL C.C.P.D.
CHECK CASHING
LIQUOR
SPACE AVAILABLE
FOR SALE
YOU FOUND ME.
YOU *FOUND* ME.
HEY... YOU ALL RIGHT IN THERE?
CALL IT IN, REGGIE.
KYLE
I JUST WANT TO BE LEFT *ALONE*.
I JUST WANT TO *HELP!*
I AM A *HERO*. CAN'T YOU *SEE* THAT?
I'M A *HERO*.

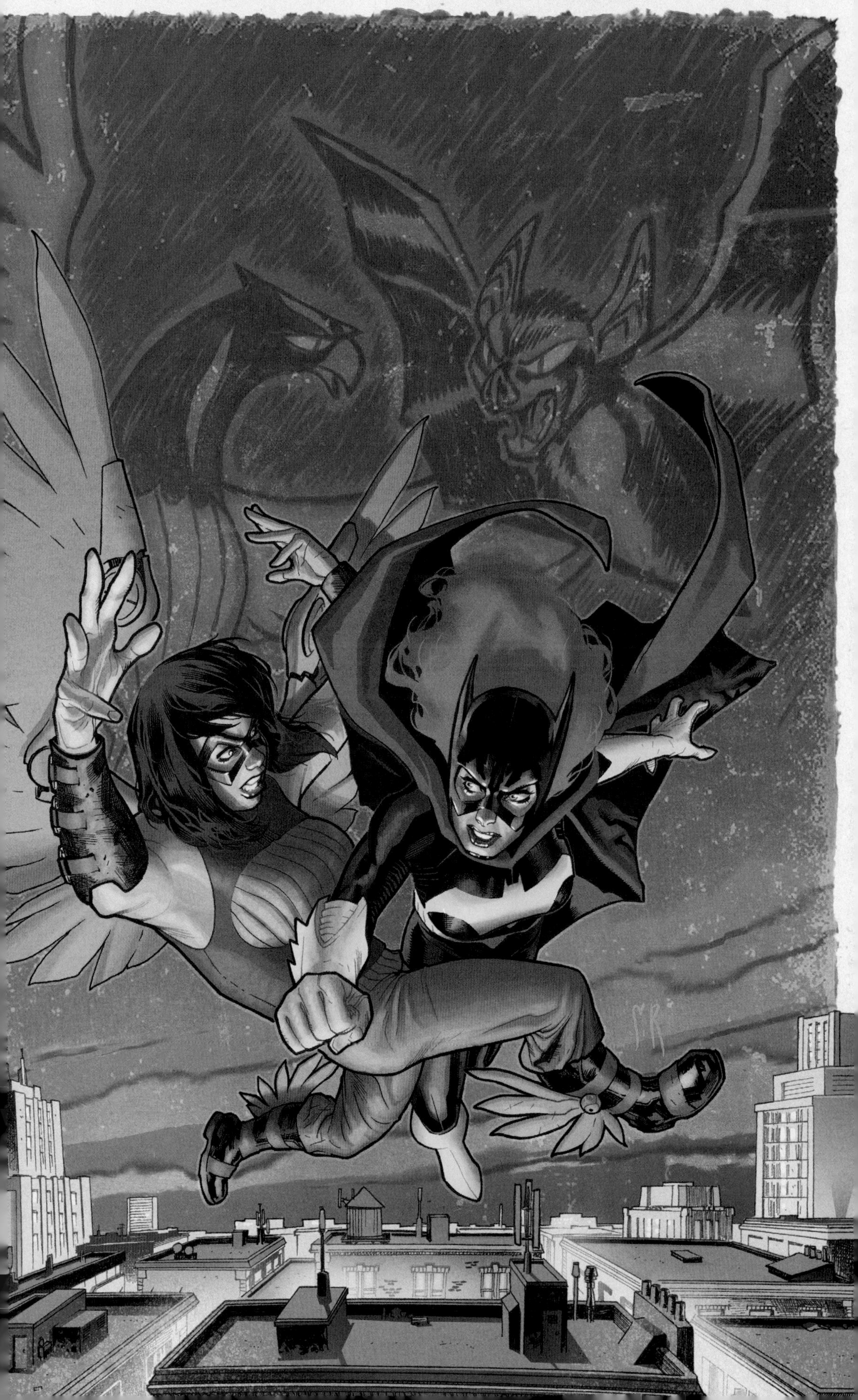

Cover Art by Stephane Roux

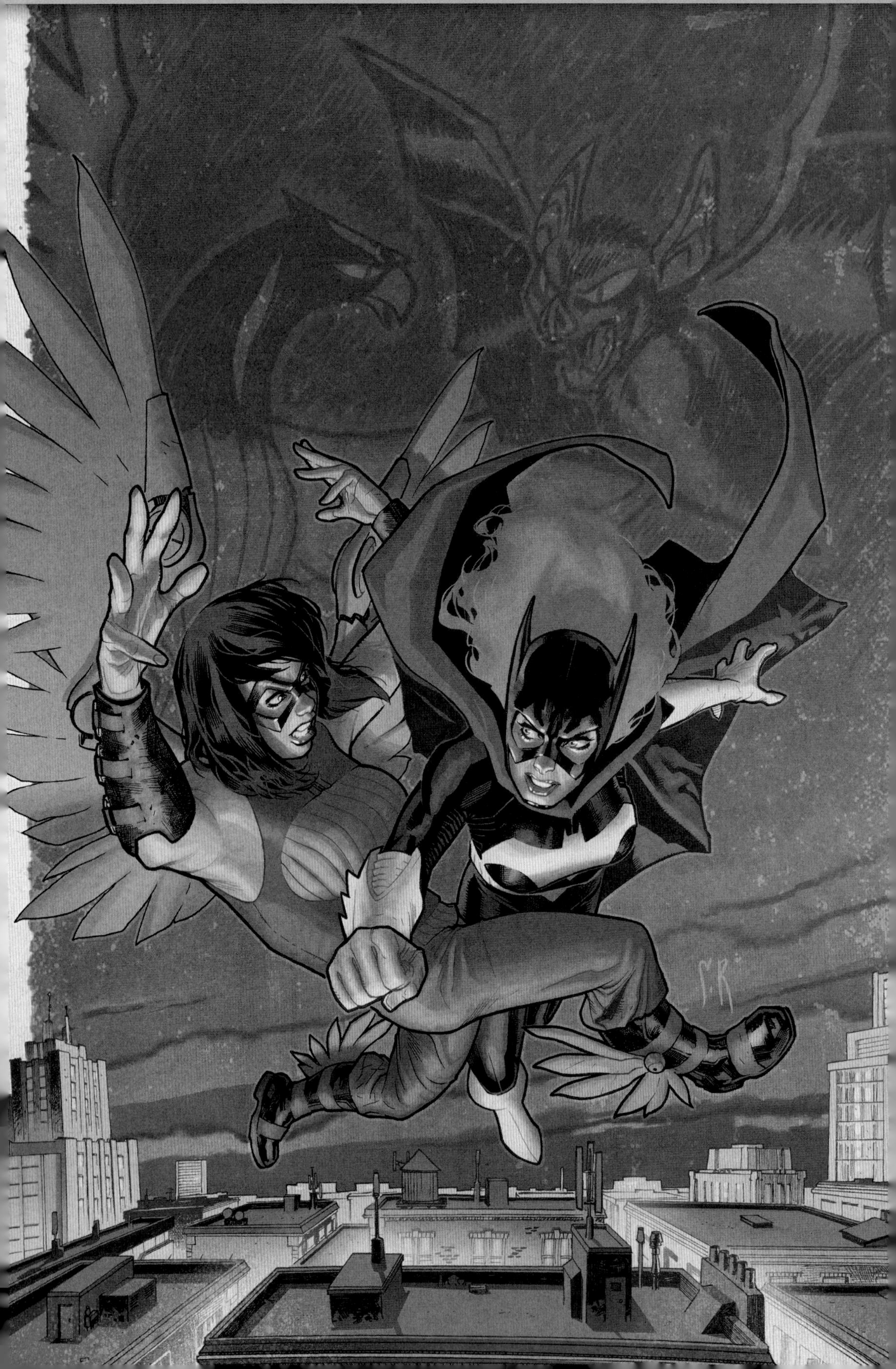

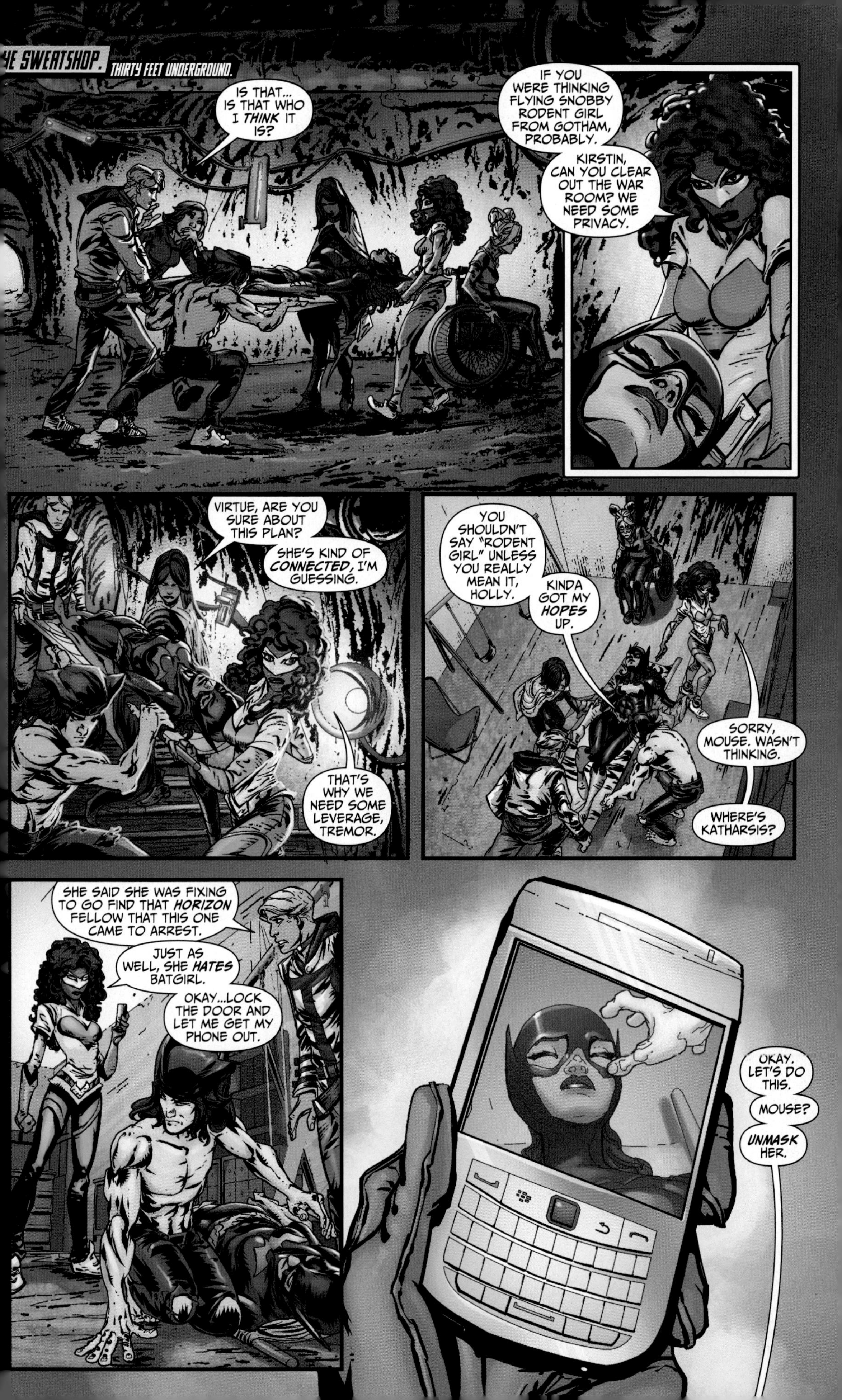
HE SWEATSHOP. THIRTY FEET UNDERGROUND.
IS THAT... IS THAT WHO I *THINK* IT IS?
IF YOU WERE THINKING FLYING SNOBBY RODENT GIRL FROM GOTHAM, PROBABLY.
KIRSTIN, CAN YOU CLEAR OUT THE WAR ROOM? WE NEED SOME PRIVACY.
VIRTUE, ARE YOU SURE ABOUT THIS PLAN?
SHE'S KIND OF *CONNECTED,* I'M GUESSING.
THAT'S WHY WE NEED SOME LEVERAGE, TREMOR.
YOU SHOULDN'T SAY "RODENT GIRL" UNLESS YOU REALLY MEAN IT, HOLLY.
KINDA GOT MY *HOPES* UP.
SORRY, MOUSE. WASN'T THINKING.
WHERE'S KATHARSIS?
SHE SAID SHE WAS FIXING TO GO FIND THAT *HORIZON* FELLOW THAT THIS ONE CAME TO ARREST.
JUST AS WELL, SHE *HATES* BATGIRL.
OKAY...LOCK THE DOOR AND LET ME GET MY PHONE OUT.
OKAY. LET'S DO THIS.
MOUSE?
UNMASK HER.

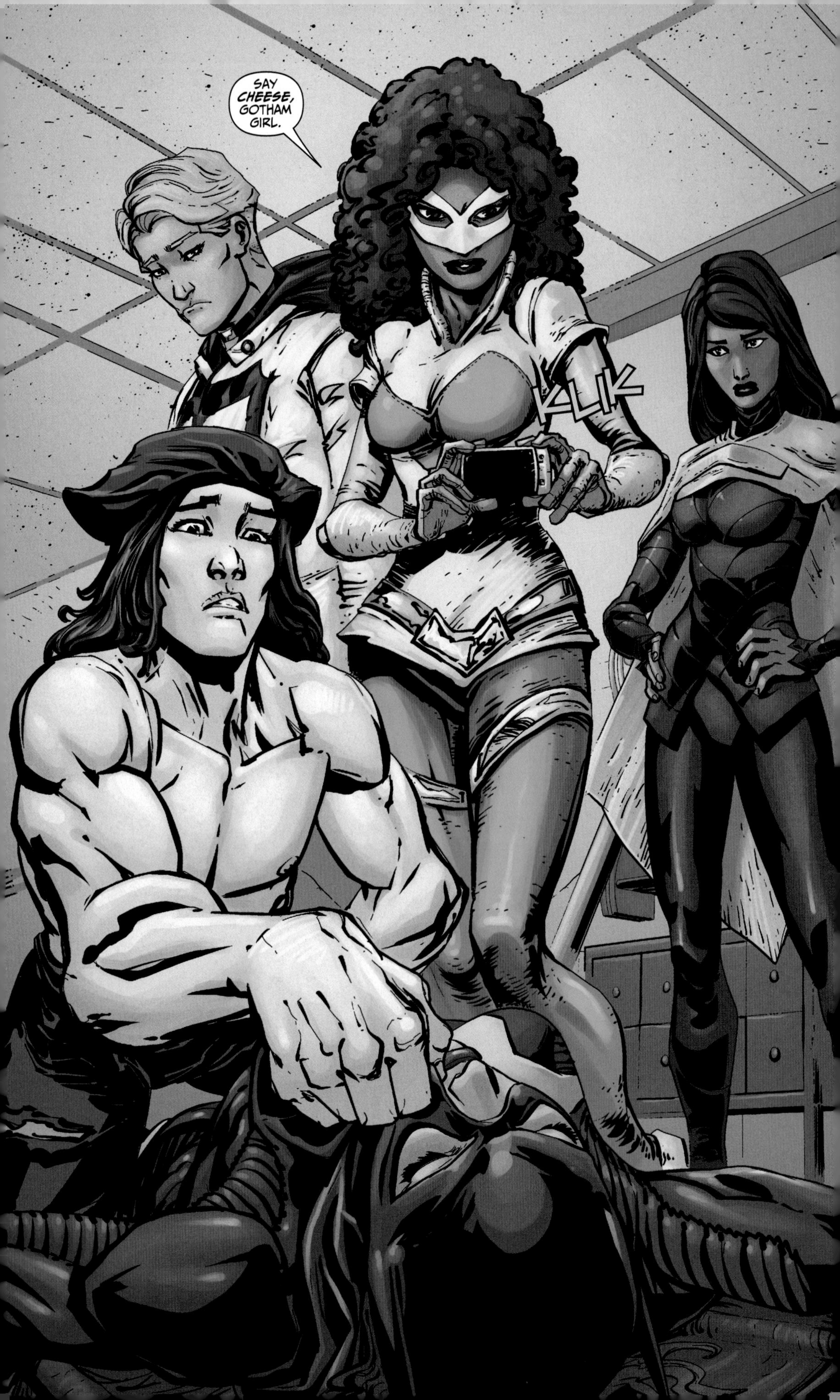
SAY CHEESE, GOTHAM GIRL.
KLIK

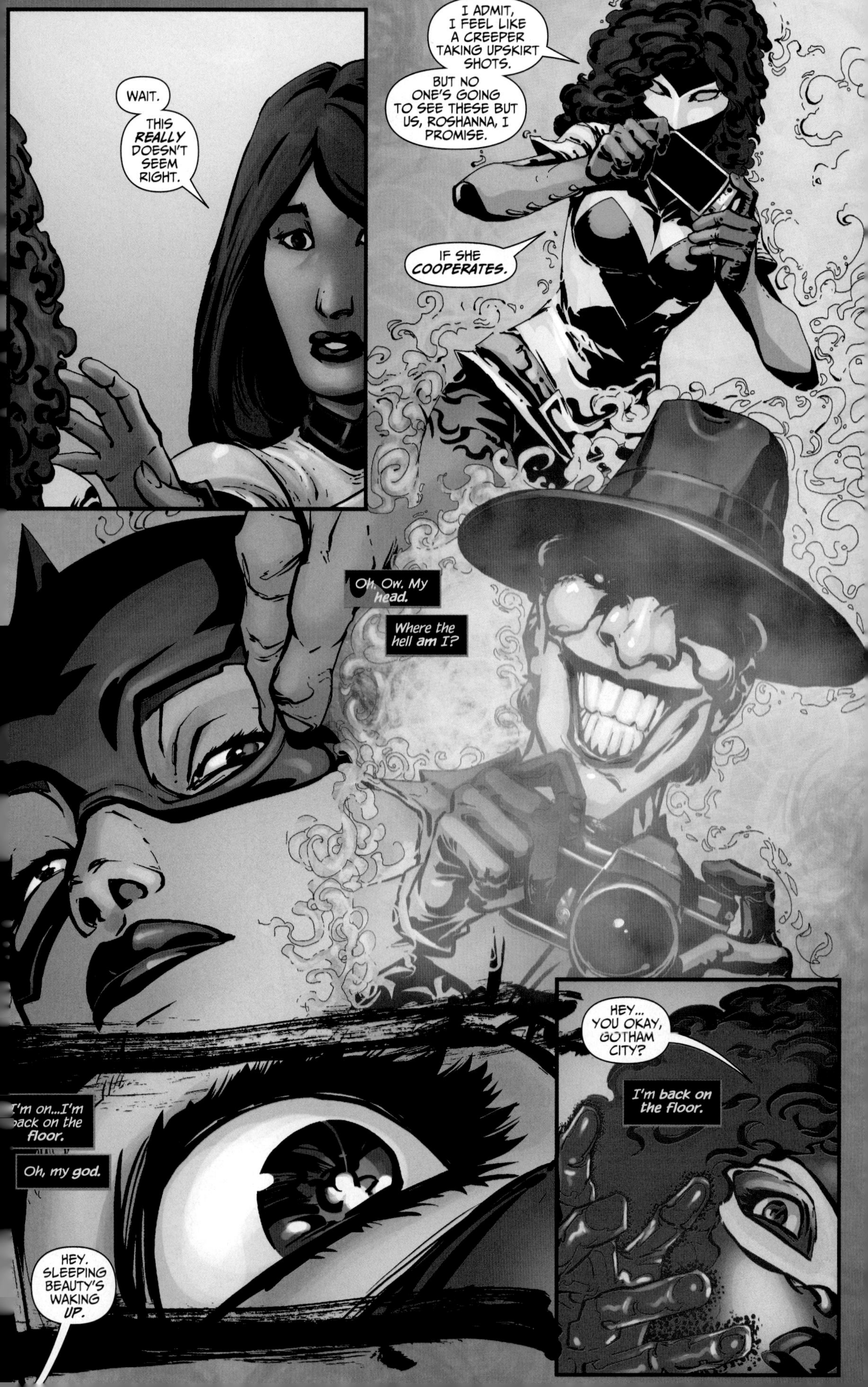
WAIT.
THIS *REALLY* DOESN'T SEEM RIGHT.
I ADMIT, I FEEL LIKE A CREEPER TAKING UPSKIRT SHOTS.
BUT NO ONE'S GOING TO SEE THESE BUT US, ROSHANNA, I PROMISE.
IF SHE *COOPERATES.*
Oh. Ow. My head.
Where the hell am I?
I'm on...I'm back on the floor.
Oh, my god.
HEY. SLEEPING BEAUTY'S WAKING *UP*.
HEY... YOU OKAY, GOTHAM CITY?
I'm back on the floor.

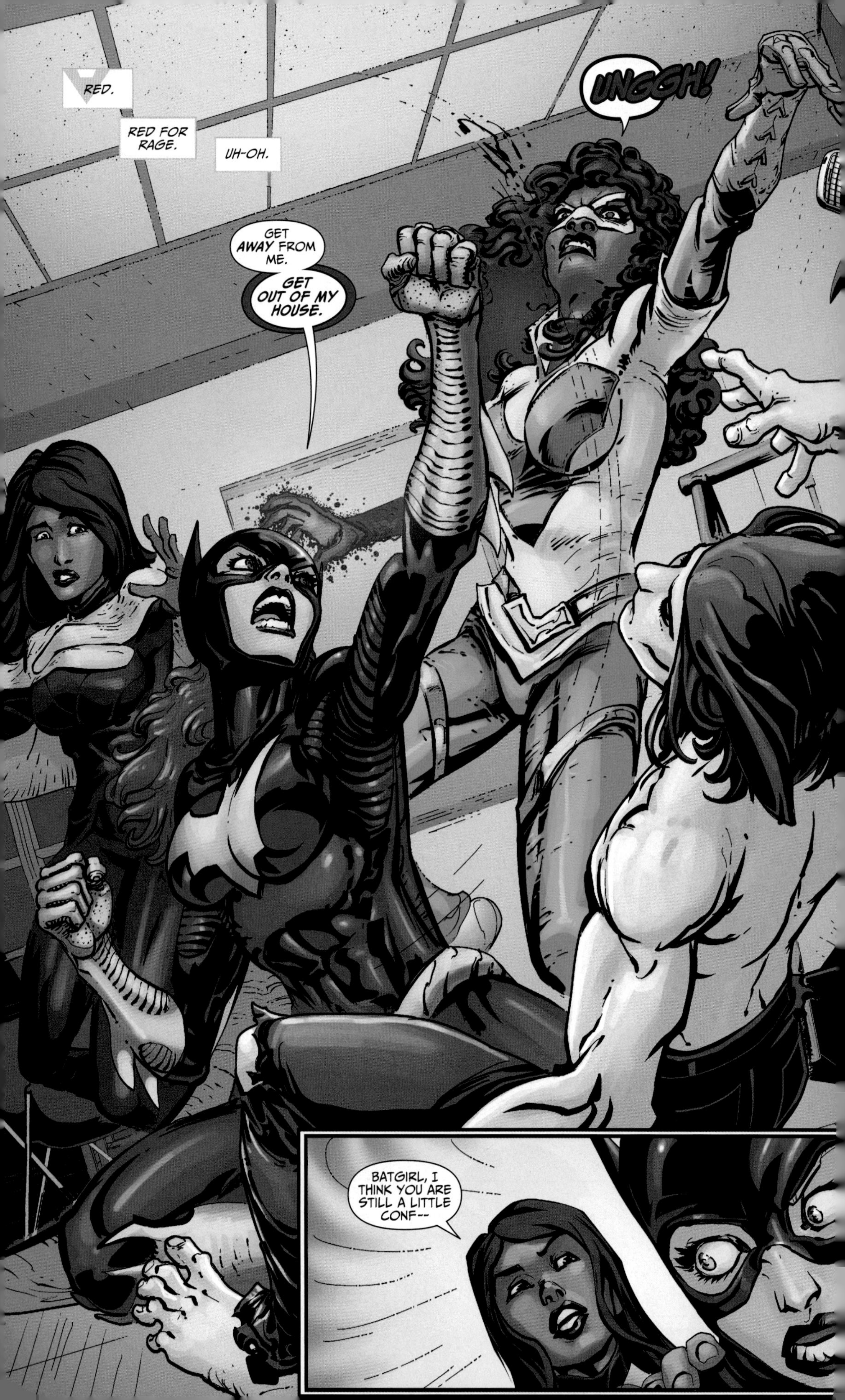
RED.
RED FOR RAGE.
UH-OH.
UNGGH!
GET AWAY FROM ME.
GET OUT OF MY HOUSE.
BATGIRL, I THINK YOU ARE STILL A LITTLE CONF--

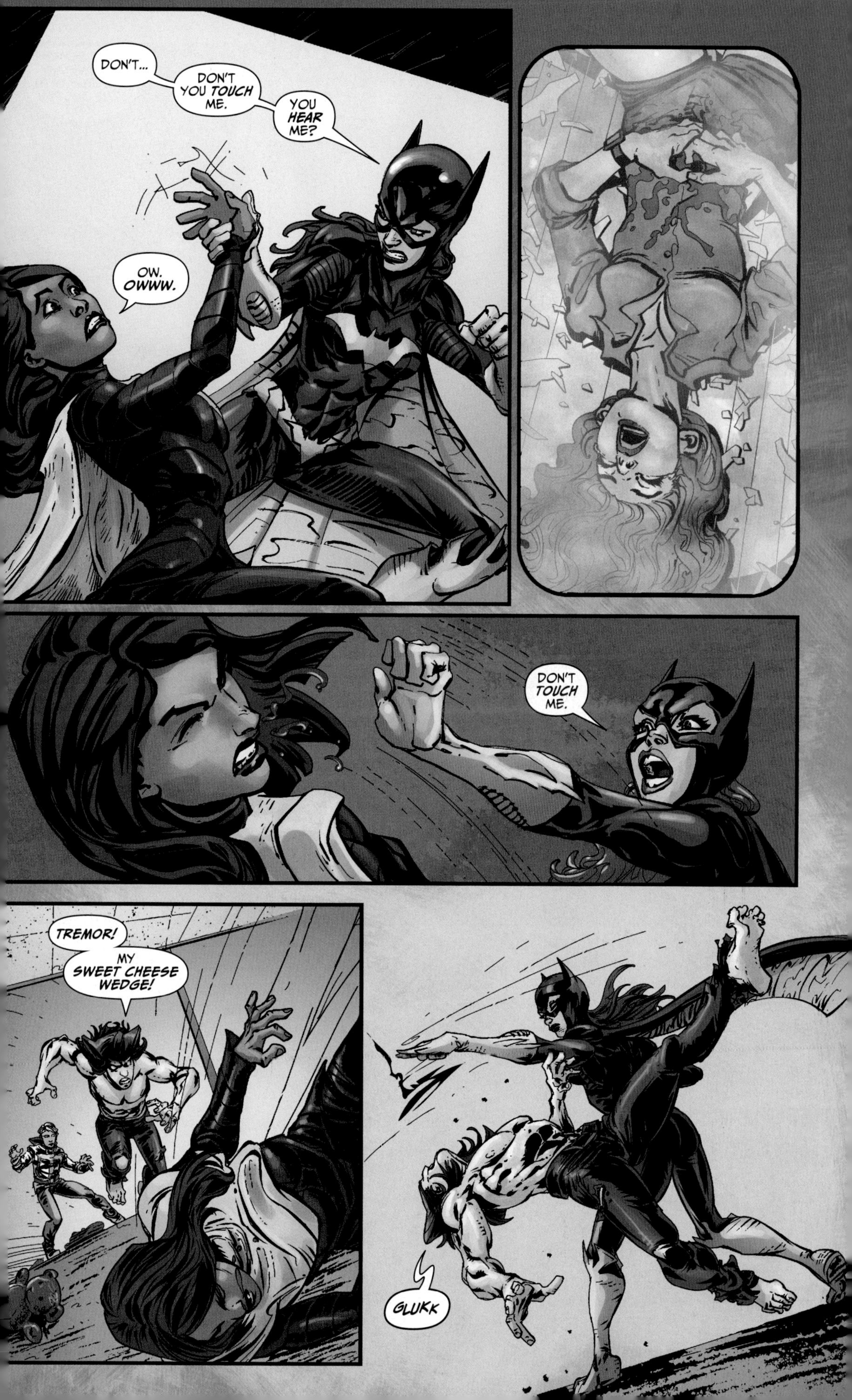
DON'T...
DON'T YOU TOUCH ME.
YOU HEAR ME?
OW. OWWW.
DON'T TOUCH ME.
TREMOR!
MY SWEET CHEESE WEDGE!
GLUKK

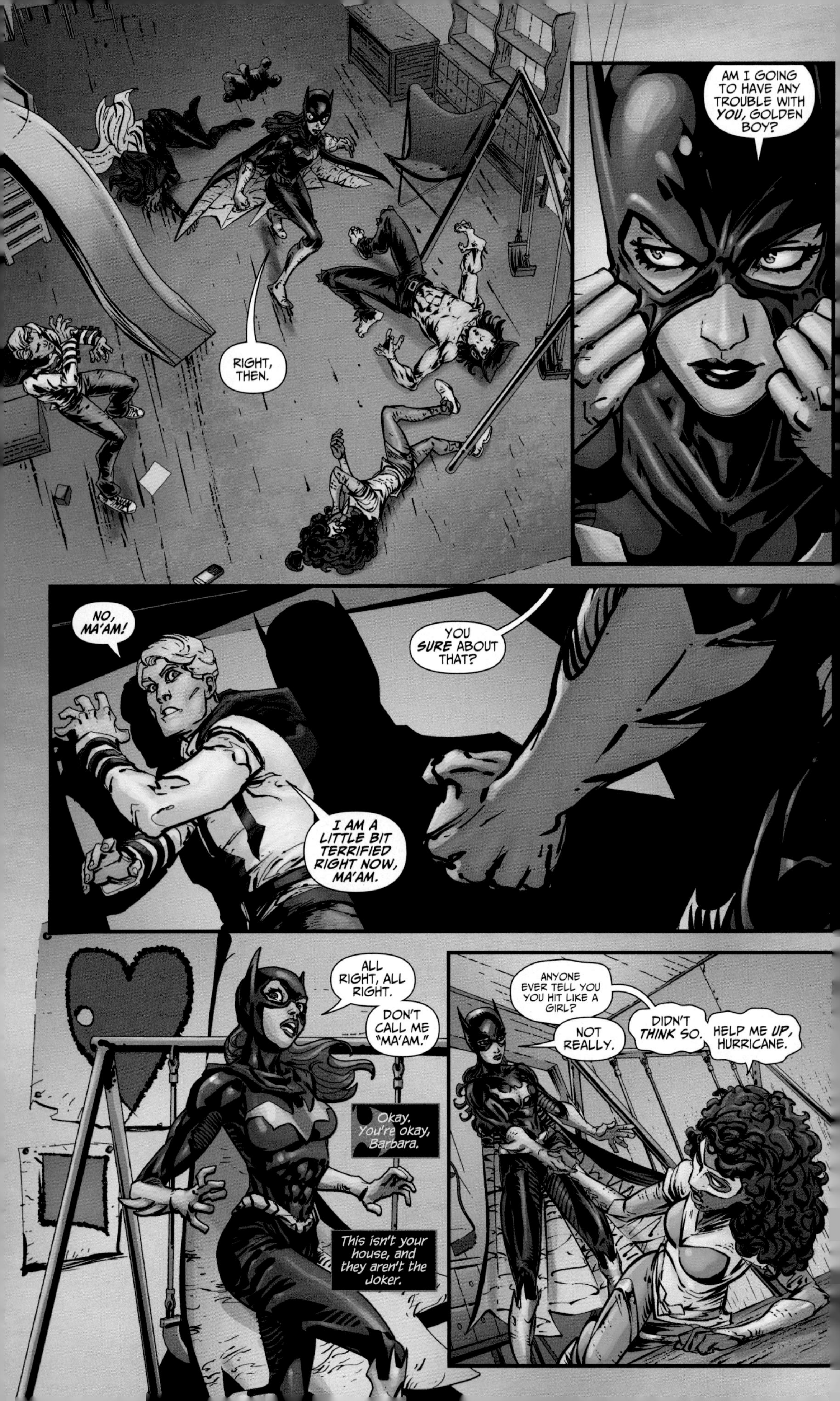
RIGHT, THEN.
AM I GOING TO HAVE ANY TROUBLE WITH YOU, GOLDEN BOY?
NO, MA'AM!
YOU SURE ABOUT THAT?
I AM A LITTLE BIT TERRIFIED RIGHT NOW, MA'AM.
ALL RIGHT, ALL RIGHT.
DON'T CALL ME "MA'AM."
Okay. You're okay, Barbara.
This isn't your house, and they aren't the Joker.
ANYONE EVER TELL YOU YOU HIT LIKE A GIRL?
NOT REALLY.
DIDN'T THINK SO.
HELP ME UP, HURRICANE.

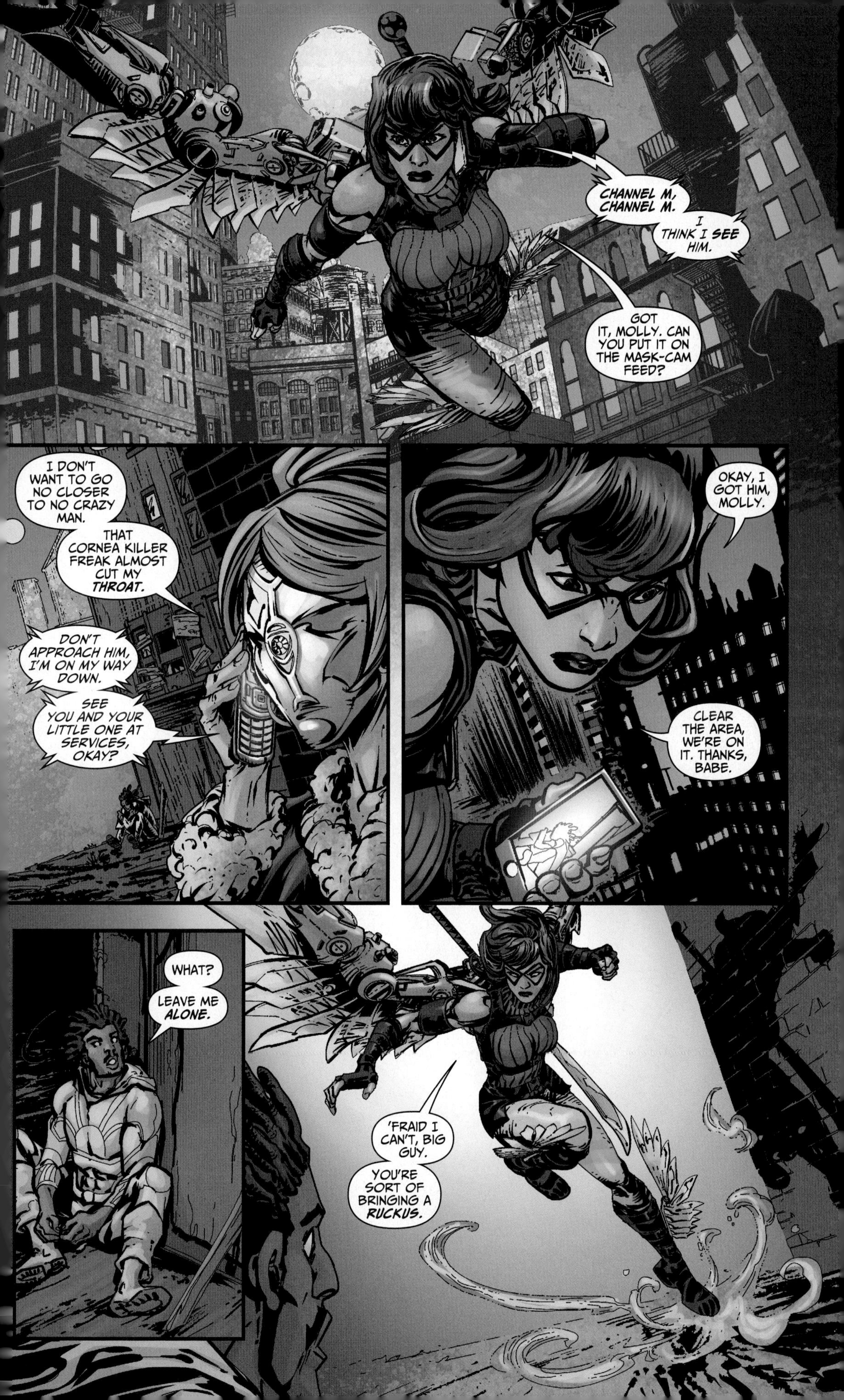
CHANNEL M, CHANNEL M.
I THINK I SEE HIM.
GOT IT, MOLLY. CAN YOU PUT IT ON THE MASK-CAM FEED?
I DON'T WANT TO GO NO CLOSER TO NO CRAZY MAN.
THAT CORNEA KILLER FREAK ALMOST CUT MY THROAT.
DON'T APPROACH HIM, I'M ON MY WAY DOWN.
SEE YOU AND YOUR LITTLE ONE AT SERVICES, OKAY?
OKAY, I GOT HIM, MOLLY.
CLEAR THE AREA, WE'RE ON IT. THANKS, BABE.
WHAT?
LEAVE ME ALONE.
'FRAID I CAN'T, BIG GUY.
YOU'RE SORT OF BRINGING A RUCKUS.

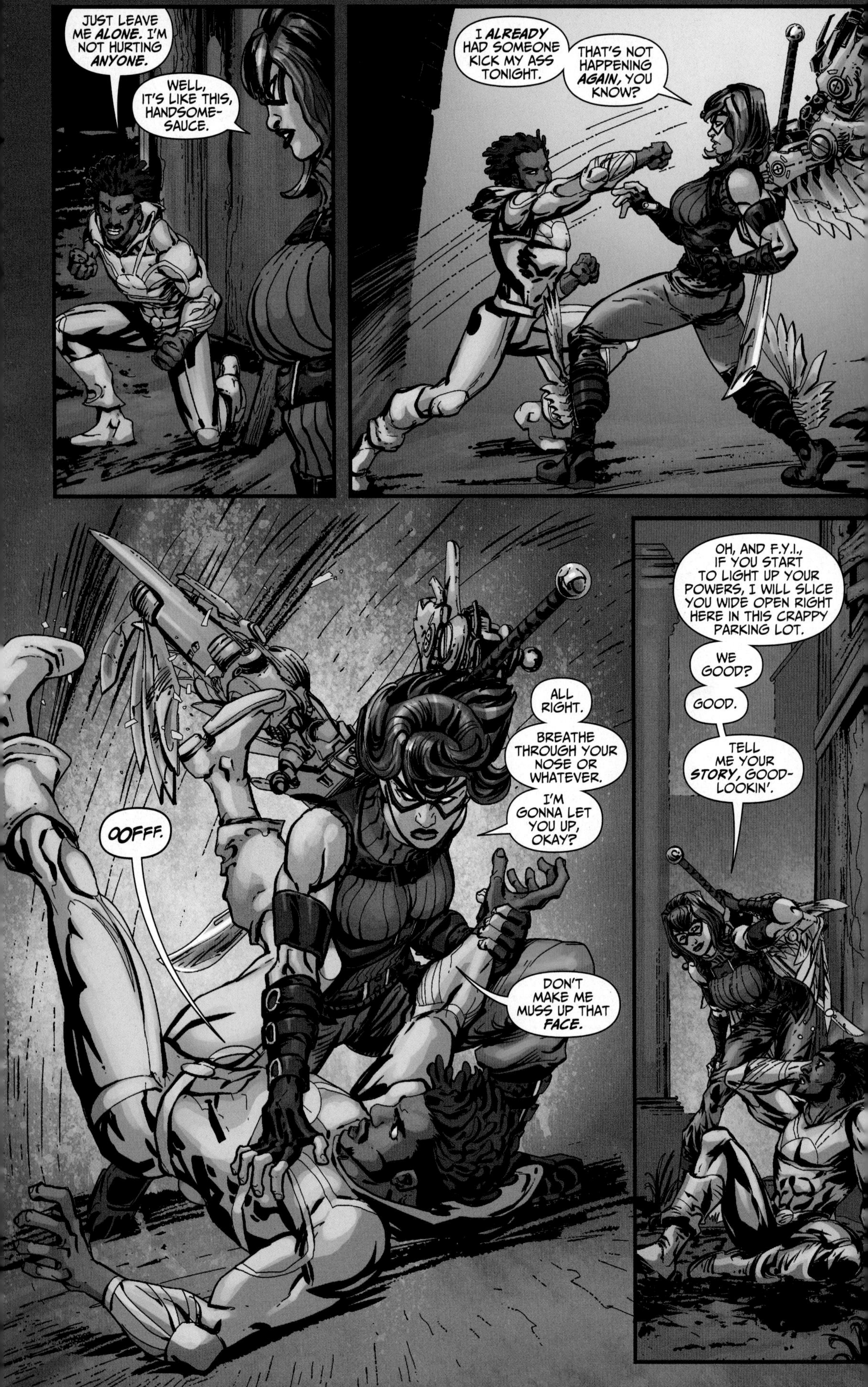

JUST LEAVE ME ALONE. I'M NOT HURTING ANYONE.
WELL, IT'S LIKE THIS, HANDSOME-SAUCE.
I ALREADY HAD SOMEONE KICK MY ASS TONIGHT.
THAT'S NOT HAPPENING AGAIN, YOU KNOW?
OOFFF.
ALL RIGHT.
BREATHE THROUGH YOUR NOSE OR WHATEVER.
I'M GONNA LET YOU UP, OKAY?
DON'T MAKE ME MUSS UP THAT FACE.
OH, AND F.Y.I., IF YOU START TO LIGHT UP YOUR POWERS, I WILL SLICE YOU WIDE OPEN RIGHT HERE IN THIS CRAPPY PARKING LOT.
WE GOOD?
GOOD.
TELL ME YOUR STORY, GOOD-LOOKIN'.

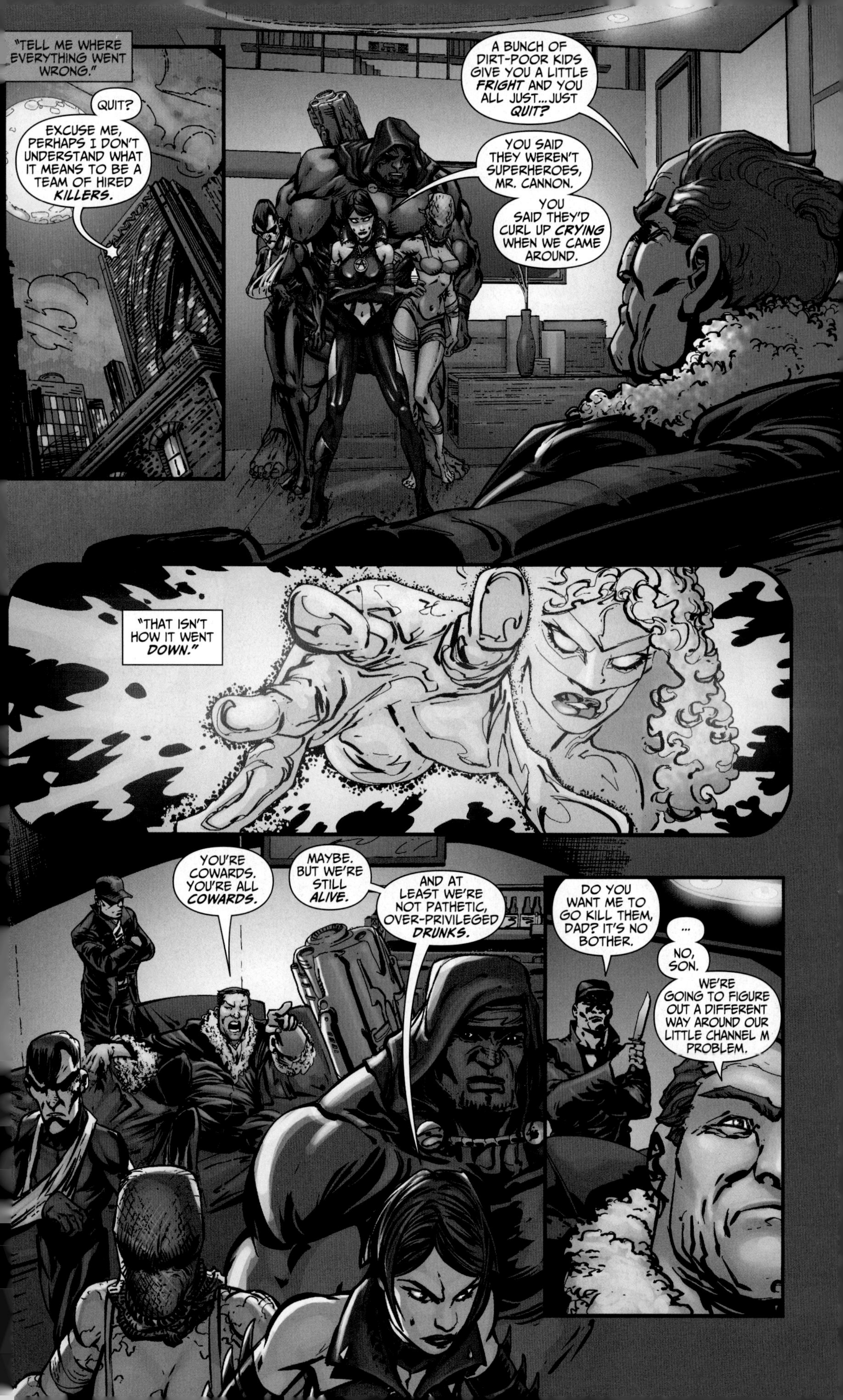
"TELL ME WHERE EVERYTHING WENT WRONG."
QUIT?
EXCUSE ME, PERHAPS I DON'T UNDERSTAND WHAT IT MEANS TO BE A TEAM OF HIRED KILLERS.
A BUNCH OF DIRT-POOR KIDS GIVE YOU A LITTLE FRIGHT AND YOU ALL JUST...JUST QUIT?
YOU SAID THEY WEREN'T SUPERHEROES, MR. CANNON.
YOU SAID THEY'D CURL UP CRYING WHEN WE CAME AROUND.
"THAT ISN'T HOW IT WENT DOWN."
YOU'RE COWARDS. YOU'RE ALL COWARDS.
MAYBE. BUT WE'RE STILL ALIVE.
AND AT LEAST WE'RE NOT PATHETIC, OVER-PRIVILEGED DRUNKS.
DO YOU WANT ME TO GO KILL THEM, DAD? IT'S NO BOTHER.
...
NO, SON.
WE'RE GOING TO FIGURE OUT A DIFFERENT WAY AROUND OUR LITTLE CHANNEL M PROBLEM.

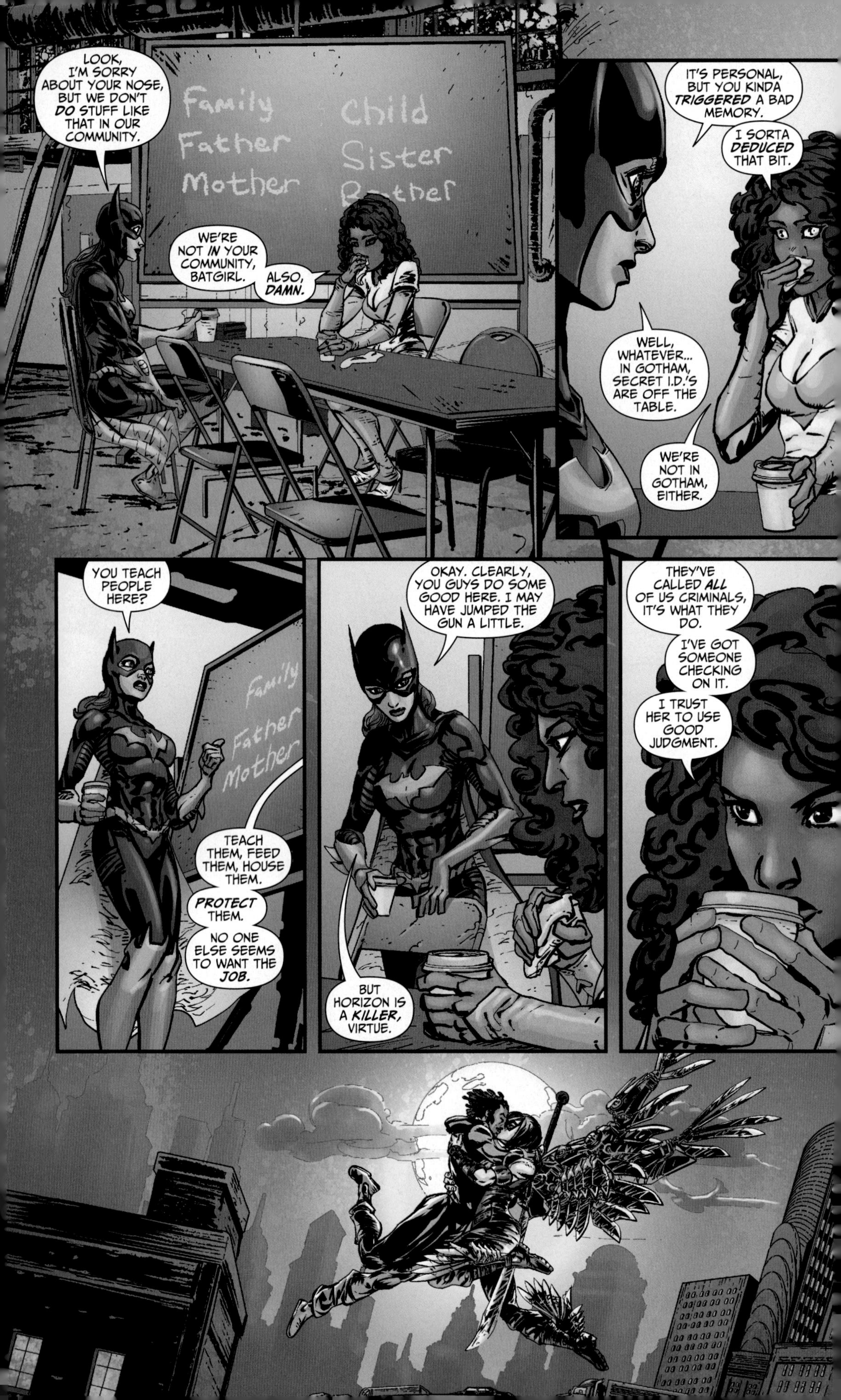

LOOK, I'M SORRY ABOUT YOUR NOSE, BUT WE DON'T DO STUFF LIKE THAT IN OUR COMMUNITY.
Family
Father
Mother
Child
Sister
Brother
WE'RE NOT IN YOUR COMMUNITY, BATGIRL.
ALSO, DAMN.
IT'S PERSONAL, BUT YOU KINDA TRIGGERED A BAD MEMORY.
I SORTA DEDUCED THAT BIT.
WELL, WHATEVER... IN GOTHAM, SECRET I.D.'S ARE OFF THE TABLE.
WE'RE NOT IN GOTHAM, EITHER.
YOU TEACH PEOPLE HERE?
TEACH THEM, FEED THEM, HOUSE THEM.
PROTECT THEM.
NO ONE ELSE SEEMS TO WANT THE JOB.
OKAY. CLEARLY, YOU GUYS DO SOME GOOD HERE. I MAY HAVE JUMPED THE GUN A LITTLE.
BUT HORIZON IS A KILLER, VIRTUE.
THEY'VE CALLED ALL OF US CRIMINALS, IT'S WHAT THEY DO.
I'VE GOT SOMEONE CHECKING ON IT.
I TRUST HER TO USE GOOD JUDGMENT.

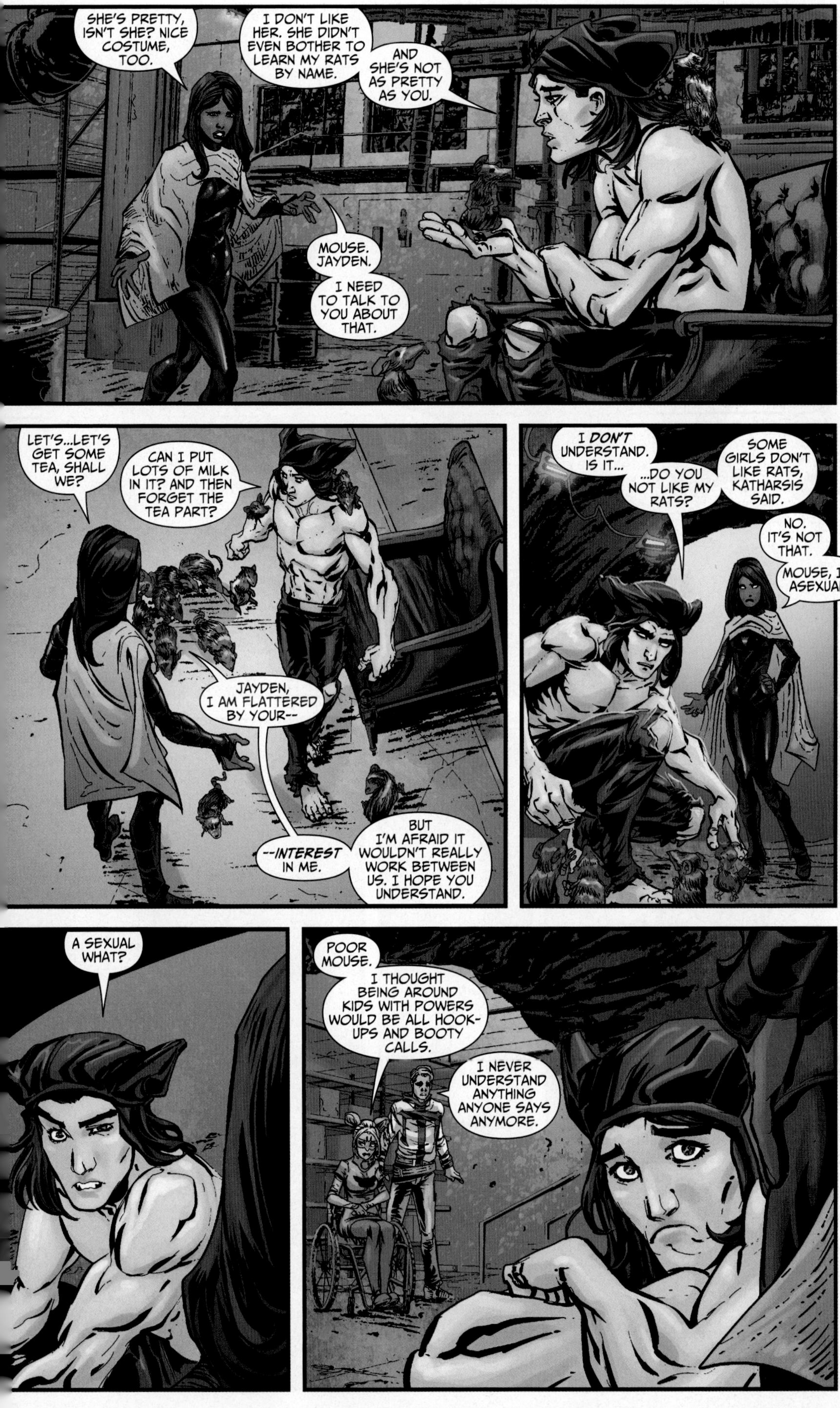

SHE'S PRETTY, ISN'T SHE? NICE COSTUME, TOO.
I DON'T LIKE HER. SHE DIDN'T EVEN BOTHER TO LEARN MY RATS BY NAME.
AND SHE'S NOT AS PRETTY AS YOU.
MOUSE. JAYDEN.
I NEED TO TALK TO YOU ABOUT THAT.
LET'S...LET'S GET SOME TEA, SHALL WE?
CAN I PUT LOTS OF MILK IN IT? AND THEN FORGET THE TEA PART?
JAYDEN, I AM FLATTERED BY YOUR--
--INTEREST IN ME.
BUT I'M AFRAID IT WOULDN'T REALLY WORK BETWEEN US. I HOPE YOU UNDERSTAND.
I DON'T UNDERSTAND. IS IT...
...DO YOU NOT LIKE MY RATS?
SOME GIRLS DON'T LIKE RATS, KATHARSIS SAID.
NO. IT'S NOT THAT.
MOUSE, I'M ASEXUAL.
A SEXUAL WHAT?
POOR MOUSE.
I THOUGHT BEING AROUND KIDS WITH POWERS WOULD BE ALL HOOK-UPS AND BOOTY CALLS.
I NEVER UNDERSTAND ANYTHING ANYONE SAYS ANYMORE.

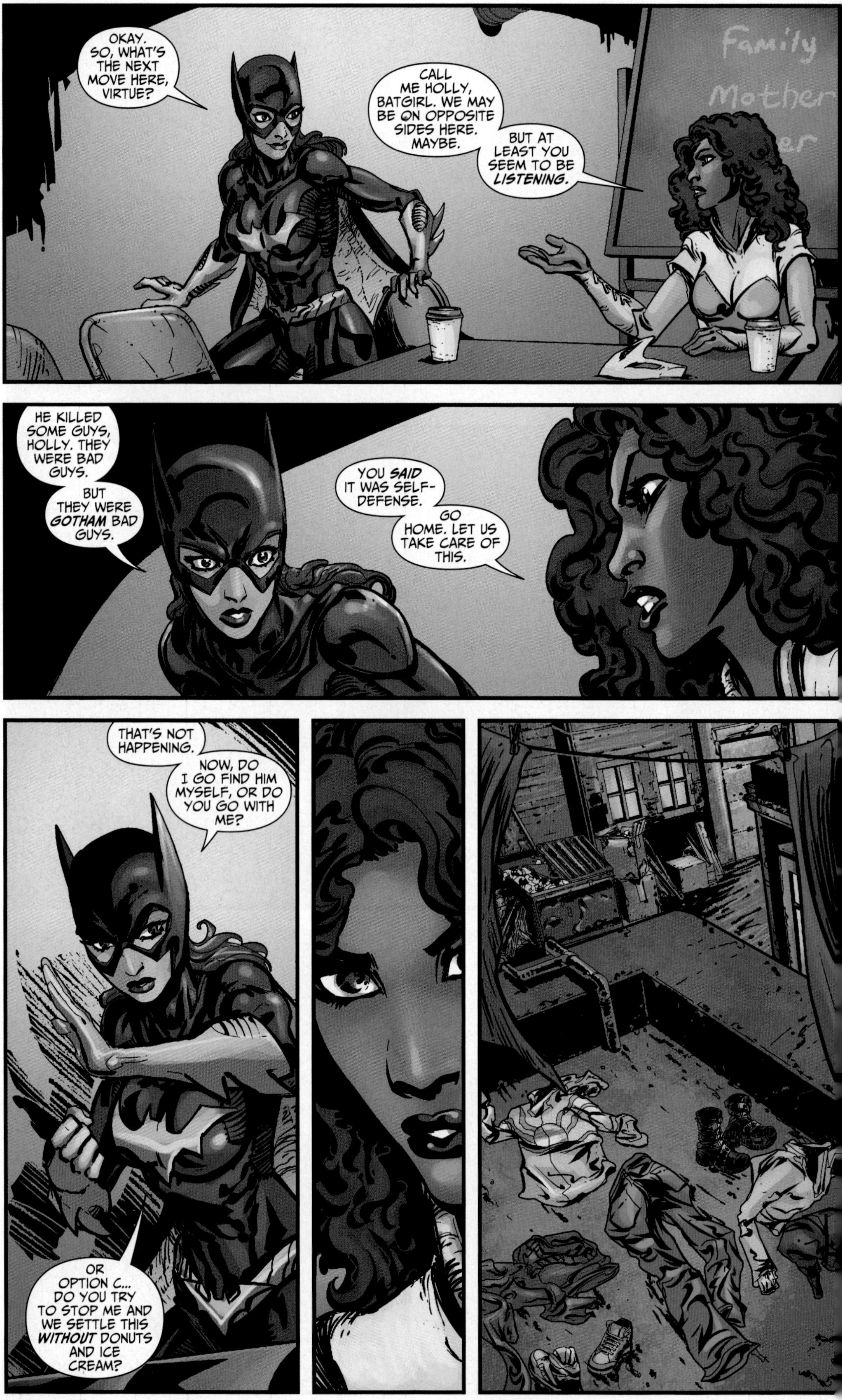

Family
Mother
OKAY. SO, WHAT'S THE NEXT MOVE HERE, VIRTUE?
CALL ME HOLLY, BATGIRL. WE MAY BE ON OPPOSITE SIDES HERE. MAYBE.
BUT AT LEAST YOU SEEM TO BE LISTENING.
HE KILLED SOME GUYS, HOLLY. THEY WERE BAD GUYS.
BUT THEY WERE GOTHAM BAD GUYS.
YOU SAID IT WAS SELF-DEFENSE.
GO HOME. LET US TAKE CARE OF THIS.
THAT'S NOT HAPPENING.
NOW, DO I GO FIND HIM MYSELF, OR DO YOU GO WITH ME?
OR OPTION C... DO YOU TRY TO STOP ME AND WE SETTLE THIS WITHOUT DONUTS AND ICE CREAM?

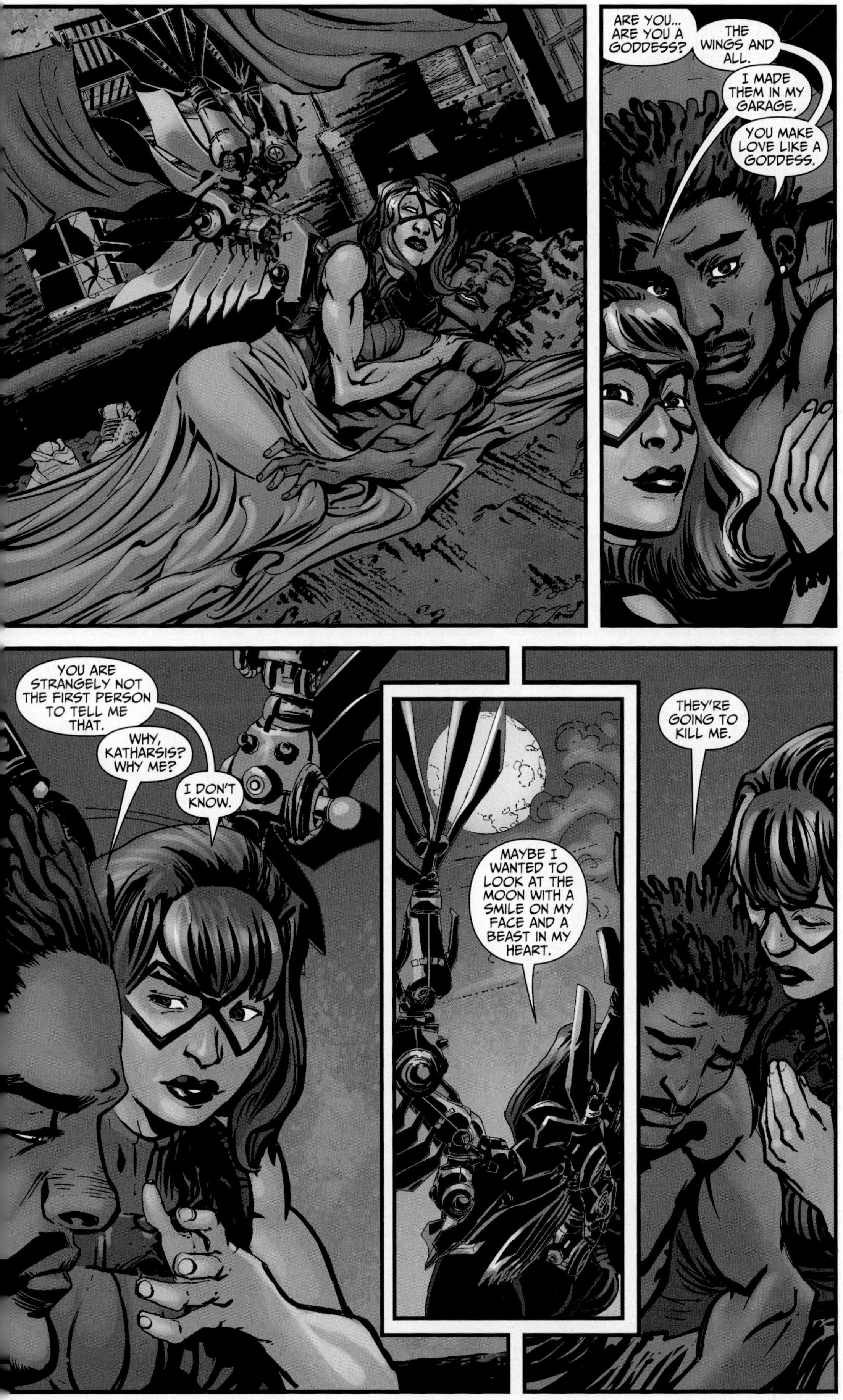
ARE YOU... ARE YOU A GODDESS?
THE WINGS AND ALL.
I MADE THEM IN MY GARAGE.
YOU MAKE LOVE LIKE A GODDESS.
YOU ARE STRANGELY NOT THE FIRST PERSON TO TELL ME THAT.
WHY, KATHARSIS? WHY ME?
I DON'T KNOW.
MAYBE I WANTED TO LOOK AT THE MOON WITH A SMILE ON MY FACE AND A BEAST IN MY HEART.
THEY'RE GOING TO KILL ME.

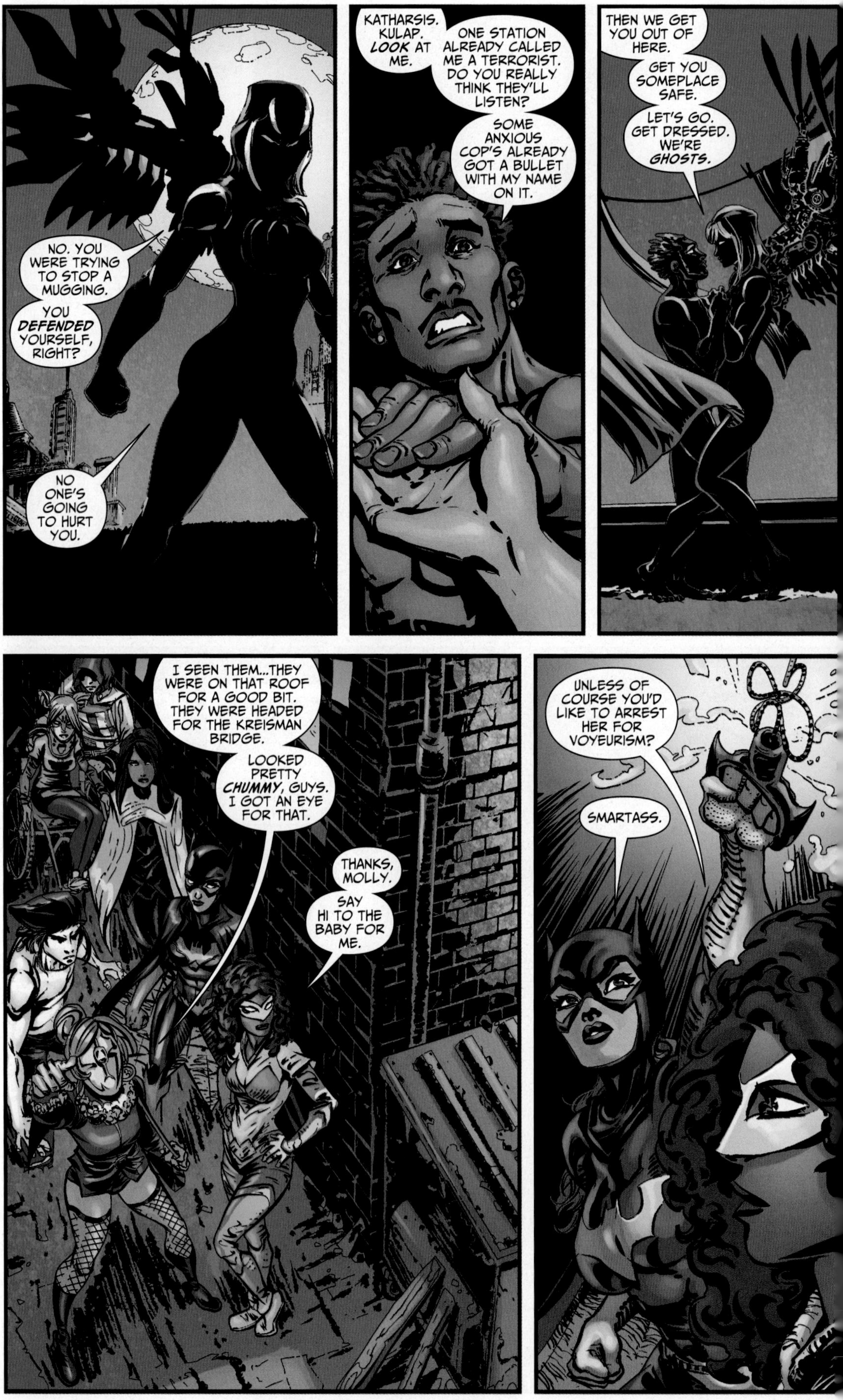
NO. YOU WERE TRYING TO STOP A MUGGING.
YOU *DEFENDED* YOURSELF, RIGHT?
NO ONE'S GOING TO HURT YOU.
KATHARSIS. KULAP. *LOOK* AT ME.
ONE STATION ALREADY CALLED ME A TERRORIST. DO YOU REALLY THINK THEY'LL LISTEN?
SOME ANXIOUS COP'S ALREADY GOT A BULLET WITH MY NAME ON IT.
THEN WE GET YOU OUT OF HERE.
GET YOU SOMEPLACE SAFE.
LET'S GO. GET DRESSED. WE'RE *GHOSTS.*
I SEEN THEM...THEY WERE ON THAT ROOF FOR A GOOD BIT. THEY WERE HEADED FOR THE KREISMAN BRIDGE.
LOOKED PRETTY *CHUMMY,* GUYS. I GOT AN EYE FOR THAT.
THANKS, MOLLY.
SAY HI TO THE BABY FOR ME.
UNLESS OF COURSE YOU'D LIKE TO ARREST HER FOR VOYEURISM?
SMARTASS.

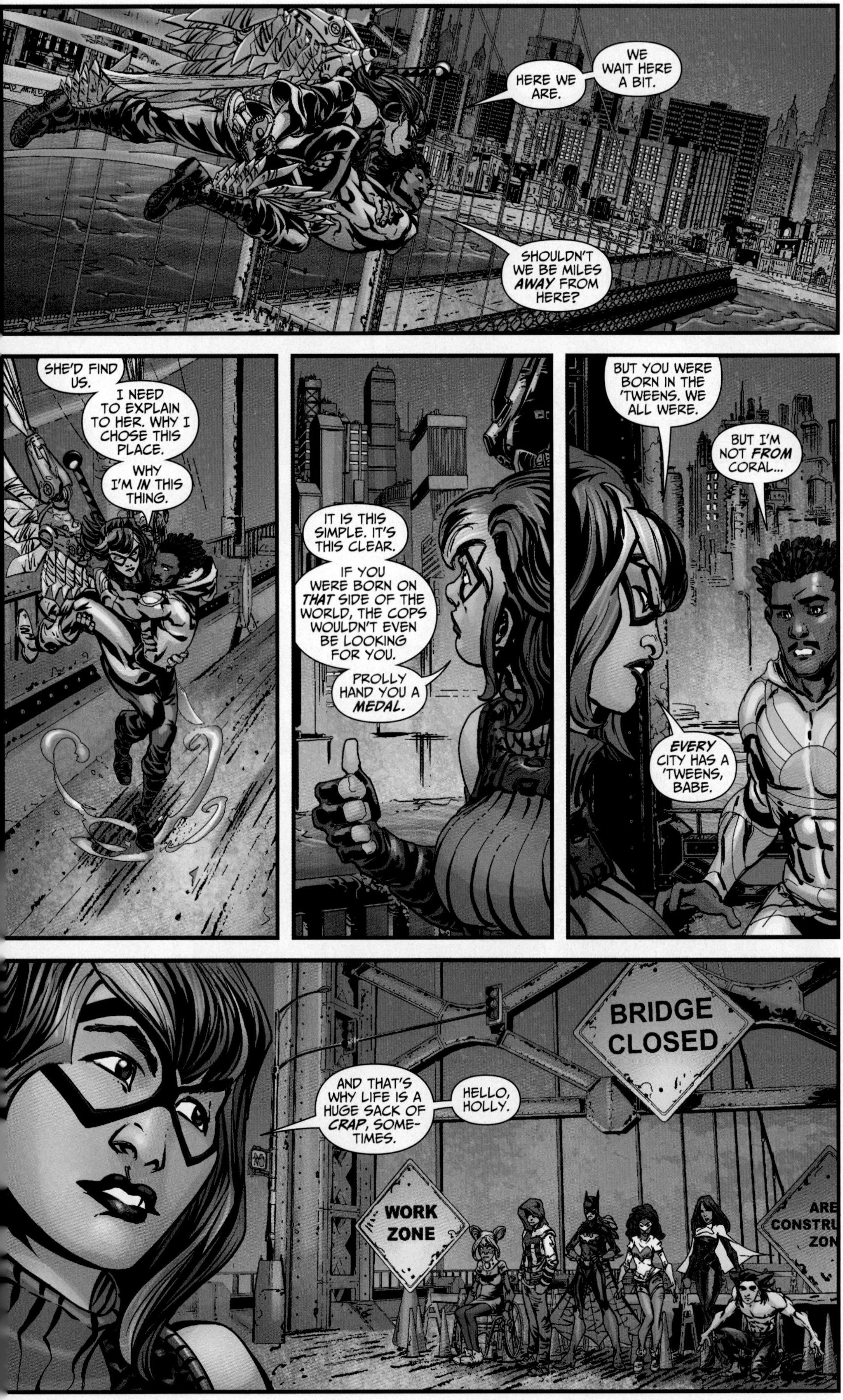
HERE WE ARE.
WE WAIT HERE A BIT.
SHOULDN'T WE BE MILES AWAY FROM HERE?
SHE'D FIND US.
I NEED TO EXPLAIN TO HER. WHY I CHOSE THIS PLACE.
WHY I'M IN THIS THING.
IT IS THIS SIMPLE. IT'S THIS CLEAR.
IF YOU WERE BORN ON THAT SIDE OF THE WORLD, THE COPS WOULDN'T EVEN BE LOOKING FOR YOU.
PROLLY HAND YOU A MEDAL.
BUT YOU WERE BORN IN THE 'TWEENS. WE ALL WERE.
BUT I'M NOT FROM CORAL...
EVERY CITY HAS A 'TWEENS, BABE.
BRIDGE CLOSED
AND THAT'S WHY LIFE IS A HUGE SACK OF CRAP, SOMETIMES.
HELLO, HOLLY.
WORK ZONE

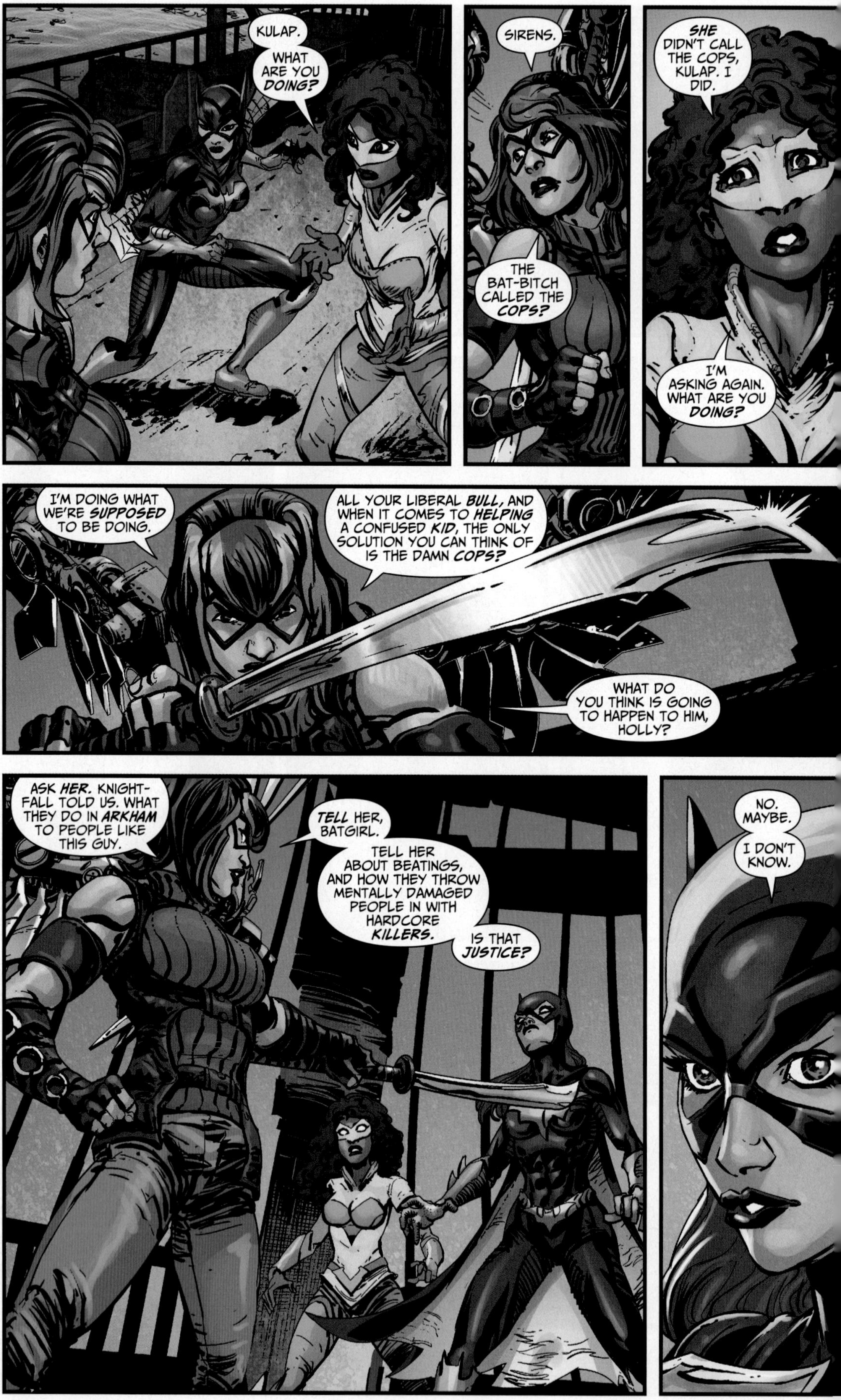
KULAP.
WHAT ARE YOU DOING?
SIRENS.
THE BAT-BITCH CALLED THE COPS?
SHE DIDN'T CALL THE COPS, KULAP. I DID.
I'M ASKING AGAIN. WHAT ARE YOU DOING?
I'M DOING WHAT WE'RE SUPPOSED TO BE DOING.
ALL YOUR LIBERAL BULL, AND WHEN IT COMES TO HELPING A CONFUSED KID, THE ONLY SOLUTION YOU CAN THINK OF IS THE DAMN COPS?
WHAT DO YOU THINK IS GOING TO HAPPEN TO HIM, HOLLY?
ASK HER. KNIGHT-FALL TOLD US. WHAT THEY DO IN ARKHAM TO PEOPLE LIKE THIS GUY.
TELL HER, BATGIRL.
TELL HER ABOUT BEATINGS, AND HOW THEY THROW MENTALLY DAMAGED PEOPLE IN WITH HARDCORE KILLERS.
IS THAT JUSTICE?
NO. MAYBE.
I DON'T KNOW.

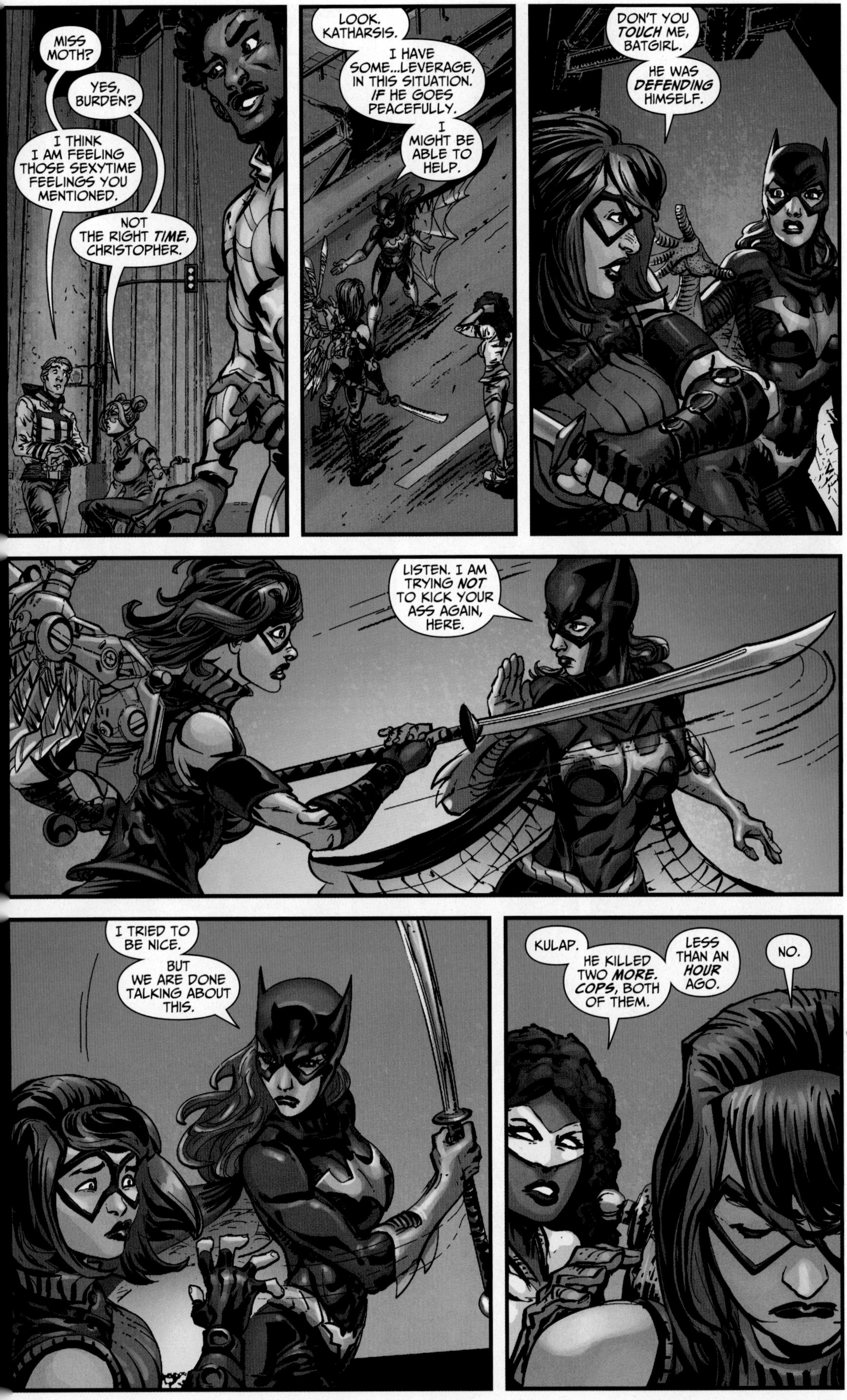
MISS MOTH?
YES, BURDEN?
I THINK I AM FEELING THOSE SEXYTIME FEELINGS YOU MENTIONED.
NOT THE RIGHT *TIME*, CHRISTOPHER.
LOOK. KATHARSIS.
I HAVE SOME...LEVERAGE, IN THIS SITUATION. *IF* HE GOES PEACEFULLY.
I MIGHT BE ABLE TO HELP.
DON'T YOU *TOUCH* ME, BATGIRL.
HE WAS *DEFENDING* HIMSELF.
LISTEN. I AM TRYING *NOT* TO KICK YOUR ASS AGAIN, HERE.
I TRIED TO BE NICE.
BUT WE ARE DONE TALKING ABOUT THIS.
KULAP.
HE KILLED TWO *MORE. COPS,* BOTH OF THEM.
LESS THAN AN *HOUR* AGO.
NO.

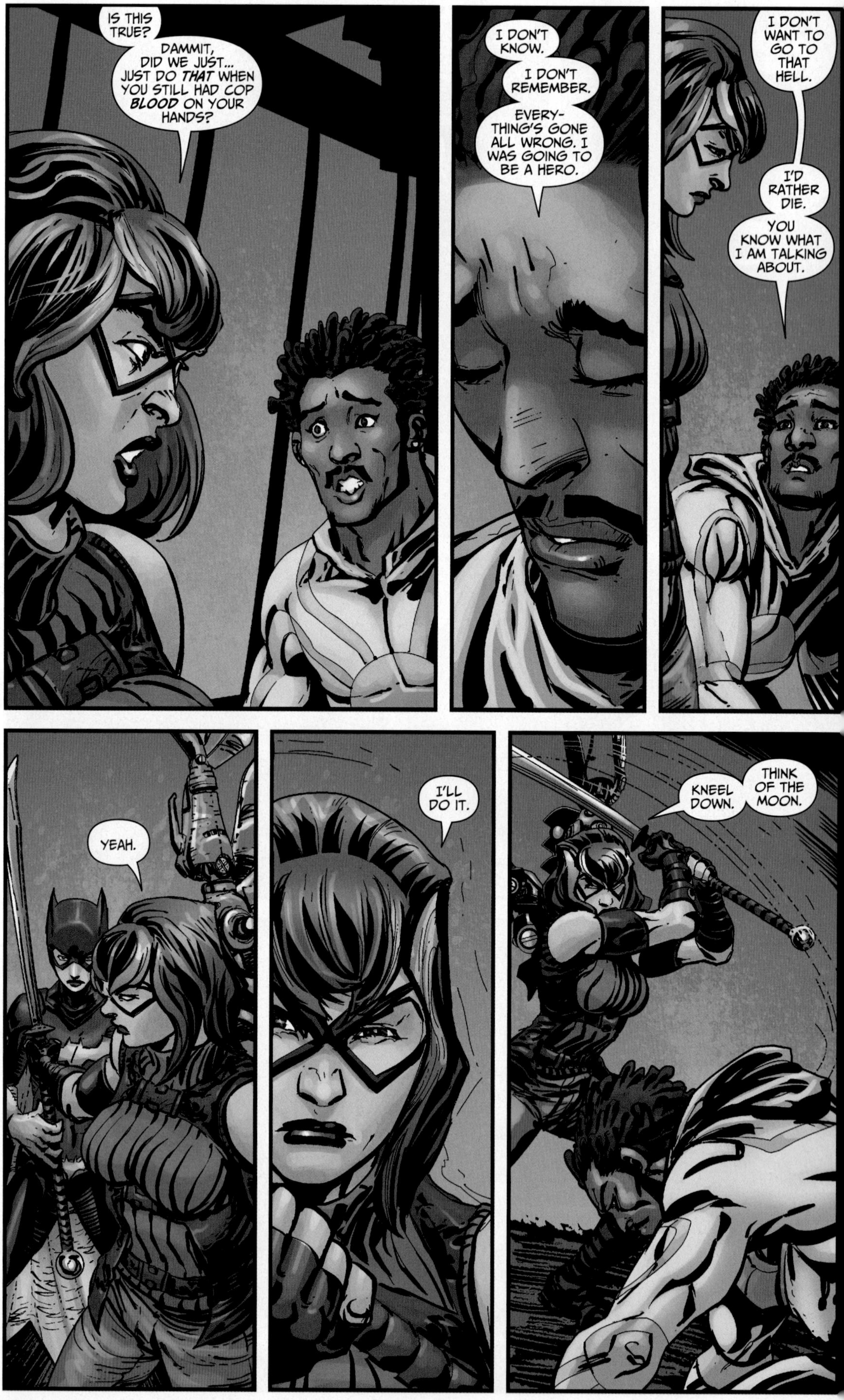
IS THIS TRUE?
DAMMIT, DID WE JUST... JUST DO *THAT* WHEN YOU STILL HAD COP *BLOOD* ON YOUR HANDS?
I DON'T KNOW.
I DON'T REMEMBER.
EVERY-THING'S GONE ALL WRONG. I WAS GOING TO BE A HERO.
I DON'T WANT TO GO TO THAT HELL.
I'D RATHER DIE.
YOU KNOW WHAT I AM TALKING ABOUT.
YEAH.
I'LL DO IT.
KNEEL DOWN.
THINK OF THE MOON.

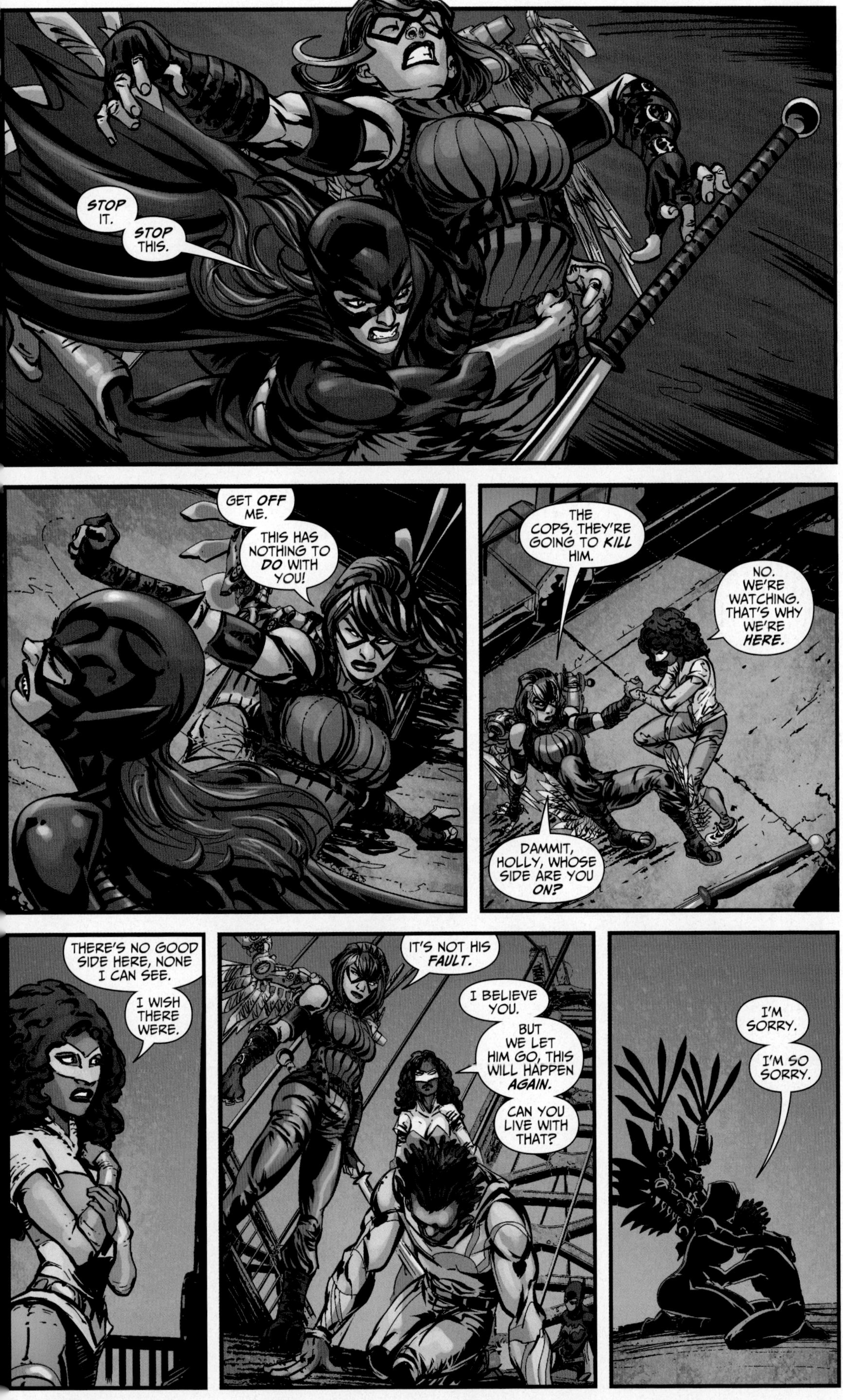
STOP IT.
STOP THIS.
GET OFF ME.
THIS HAS NOTHING TO DO WITH YOU!
THE COPS, THEY'RE GOING TO KILL HIM.
NO. WE'RE WATCHING. THAT'S WHY WE'RE HERE.
DAMMIT, HOLLY, WHOSE SIDE ARE YOU ON?
THERE'S NO GOOD SIDE HERE, NONE I CAN SEE.
I WISH THERE WERE.
IT'S NOT HIS FAULT.
I BELIEVE YOU.
BUT WE LET HIM GO, THIS WILL HAPPEN AGAIN.
CAN YOU LIVE WITH THAT?
I'M SORRY.
I'M SO SORRY.

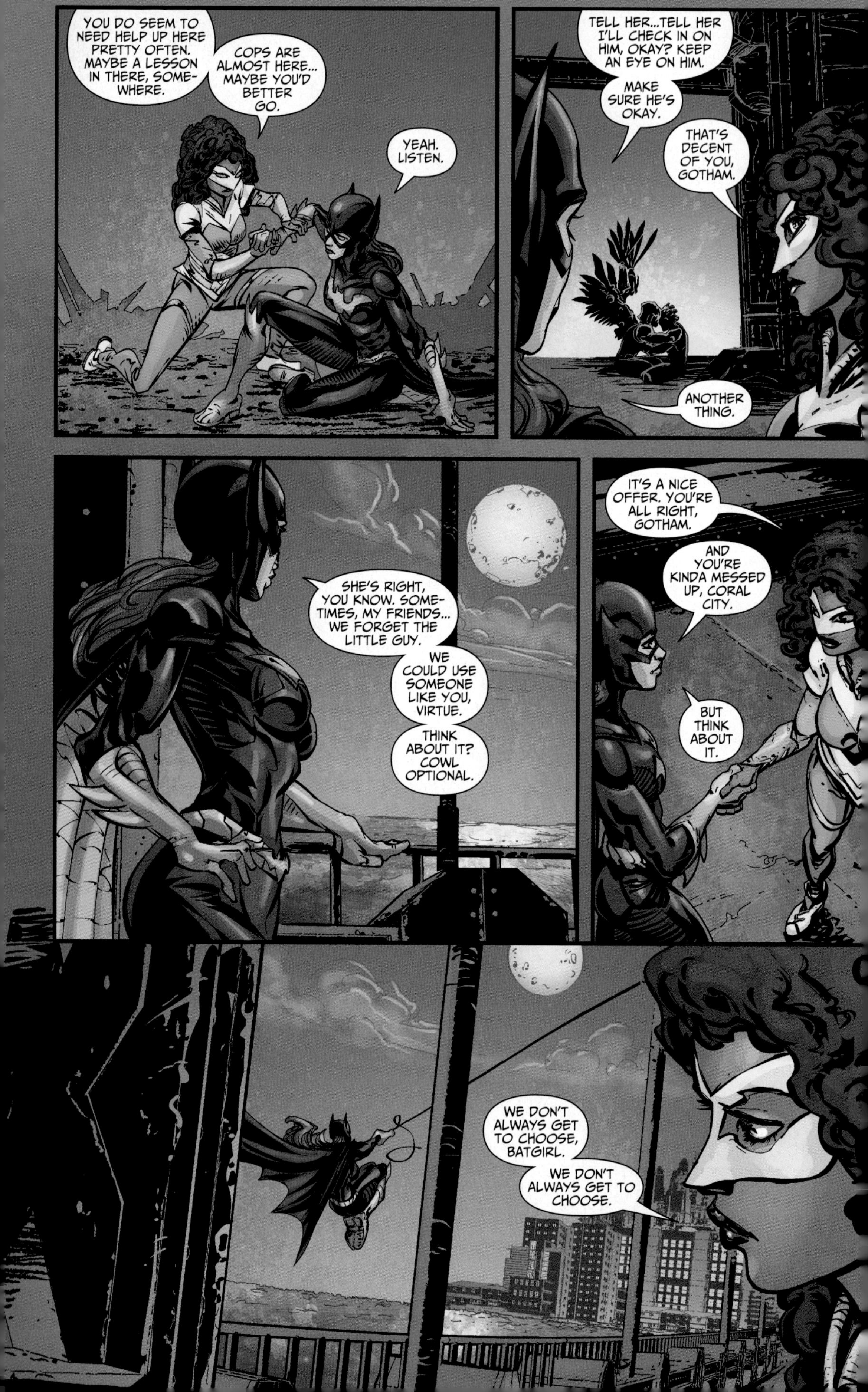

YOU DO SEEM TO NEED HELP UP HERE PRETTY OFTEN. MAYBE A LESSON IN THERE, SOME-WHERE.
COPS ARE ALMOST HERE... MAYBE YOU'D BETTER GO.
YEAH. LISTEN.
TELL HER...TELL HER I'LL CHECK IN ON HIM, OKAY? KEEP AN EYE ON HIM.
MAKE SURE HE'S OKAY.
THAT'S DECENT OF YOU, GOTHAM.
ANOTHER THING.
SHE'S RIGHT, YOU KNOW. SOME-TIMES, MY FRIENDS... WE FORGET THE LITTLE GUY.
WE COULD USE SOMEONE LIKE YOU, VIRTUE.
THINK ABOUT IT? COWL OPTIONAL.
IT'S A NICE OFFER. YOU'RE ALL RIGHT, GOTHAM.
AND YOU'RE KINDA MESSED UP, CORAL CITY.
BUT THINK ABOUT IT.
WE DON'T ALWAYS GET TO CHOOSE, BATGIRL.
WE DON'T ALWAYS GET TO CHOOSE.

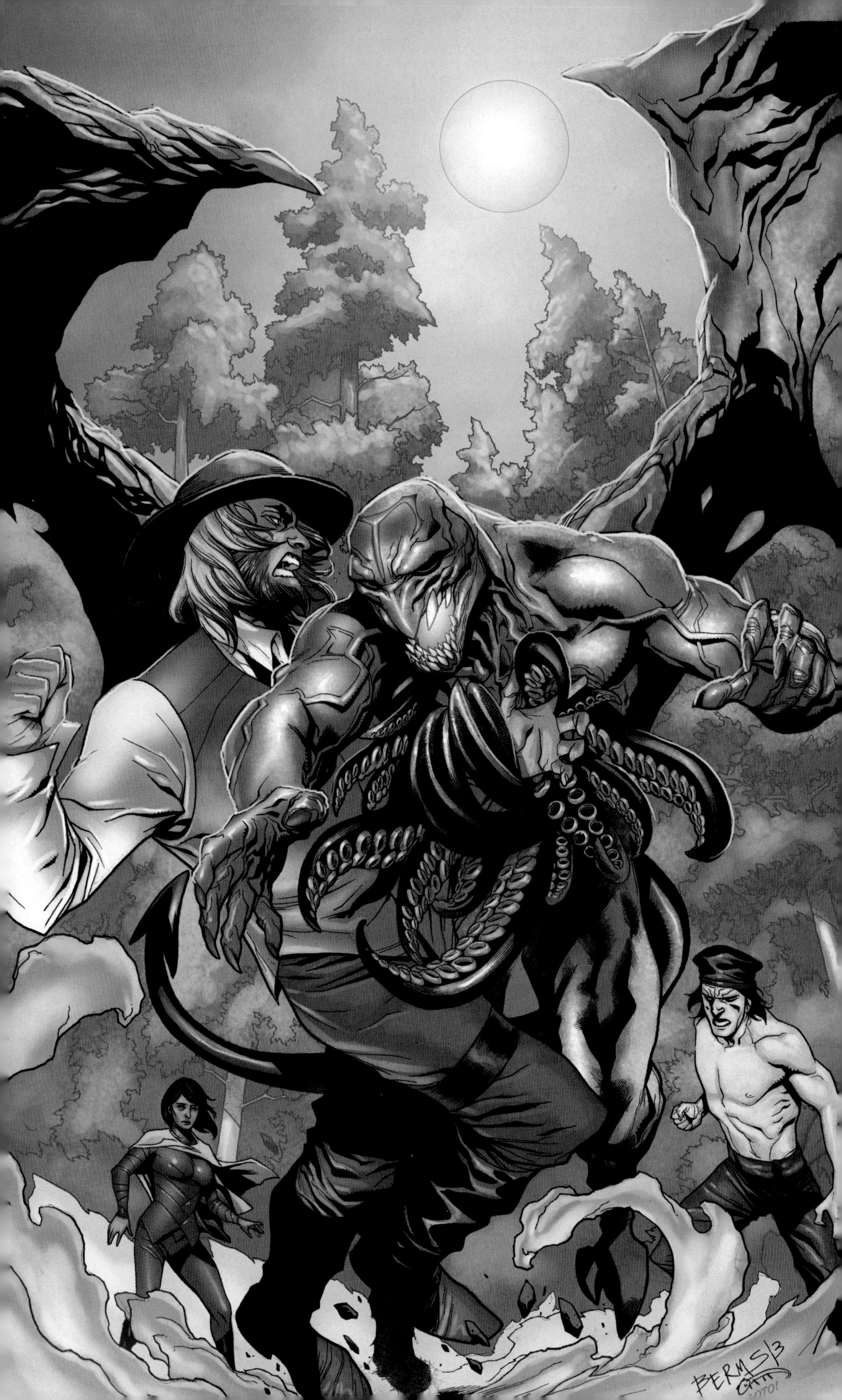

Cover Art by Raymund Bermudez

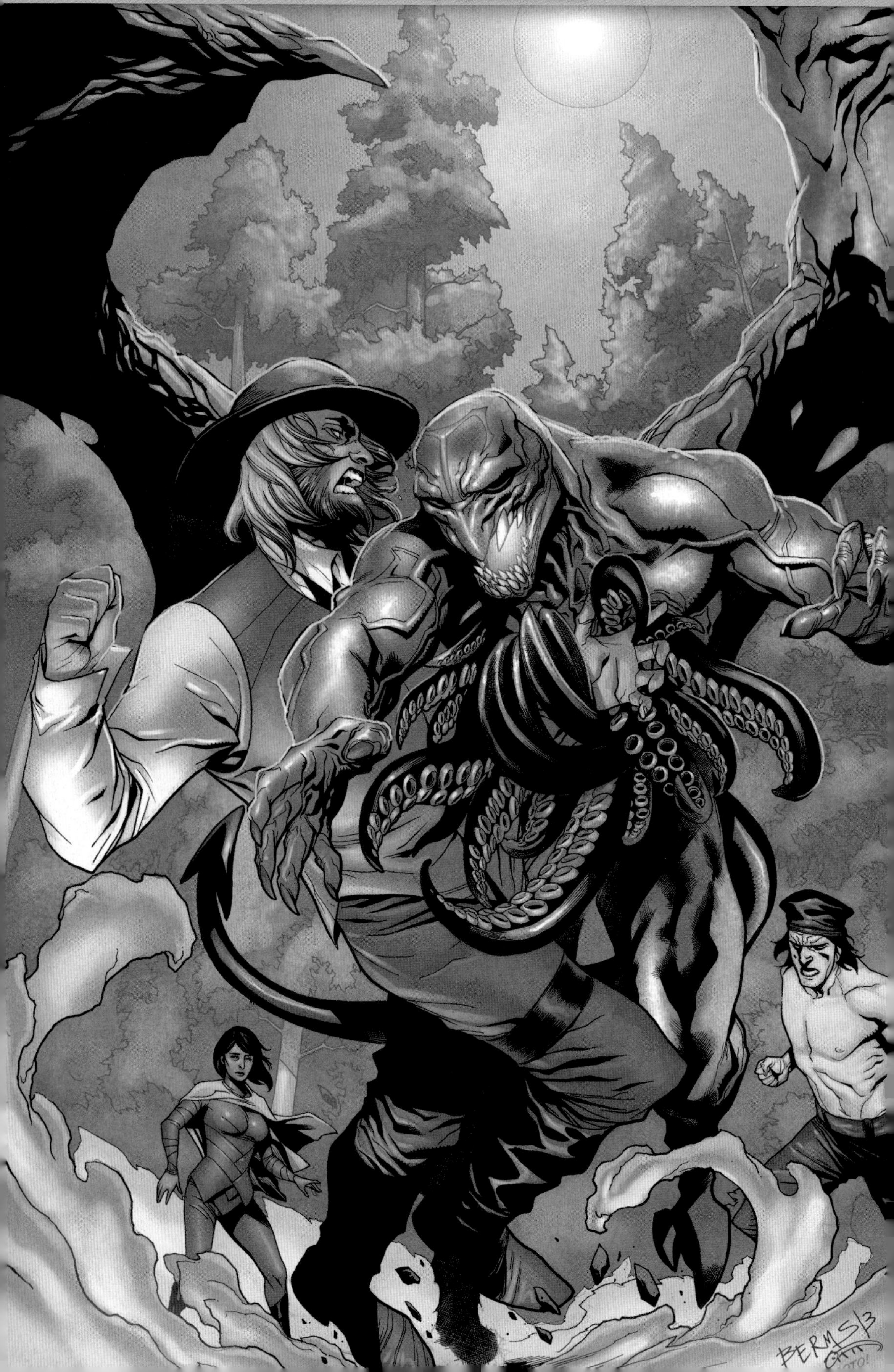

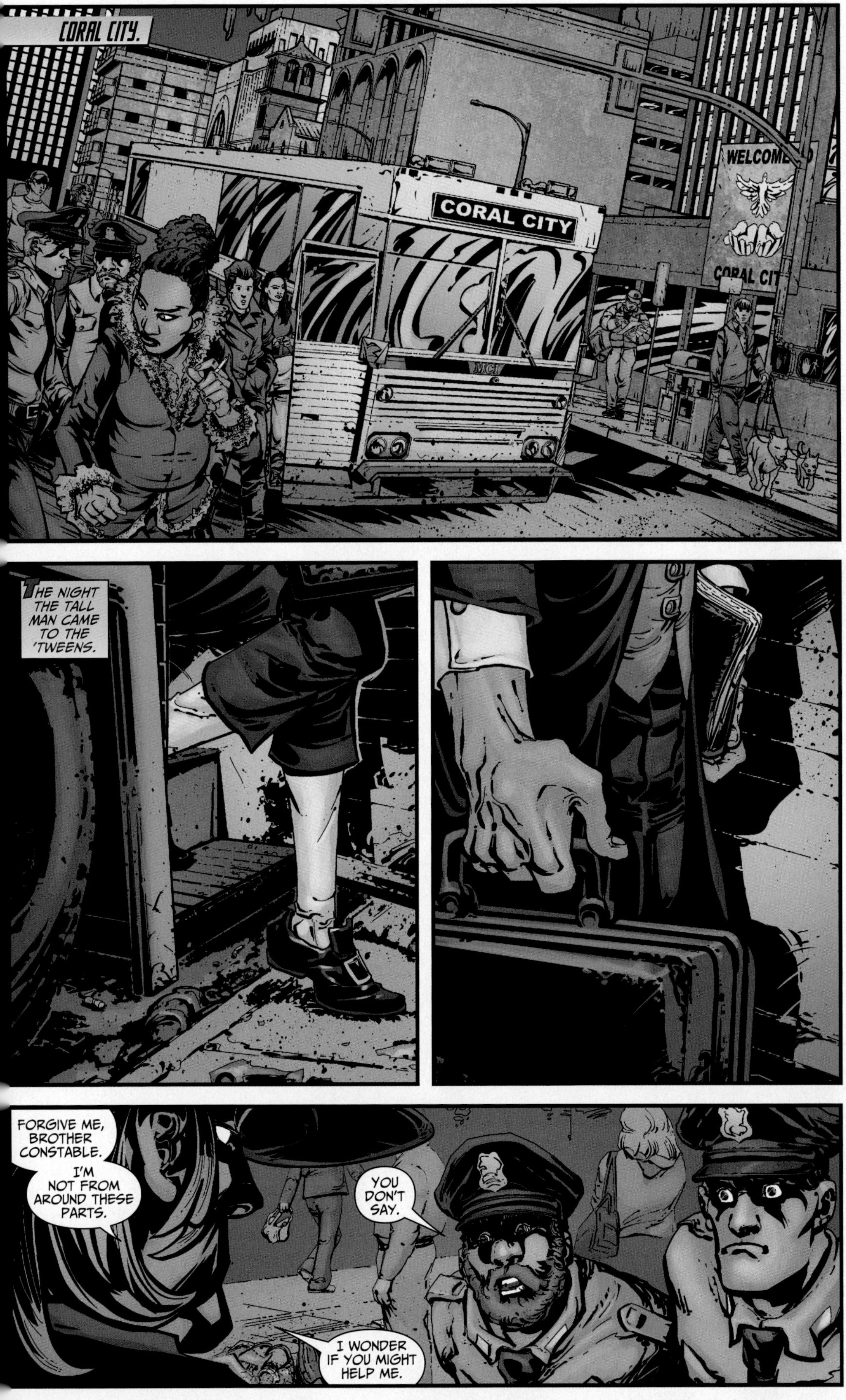
CORAL CITY.
CORAL CITY
WELCOME
THE NIGHT THE TALL MAN CAME TO THE 'TWEENS.
FORGIVE ME, BROTHER CONSTABLE.
I'M NOT FROM AROUND THESE PARTS.
YOU DON'T SAY.
I WONDER IF YOU MIGHT HELP ME.

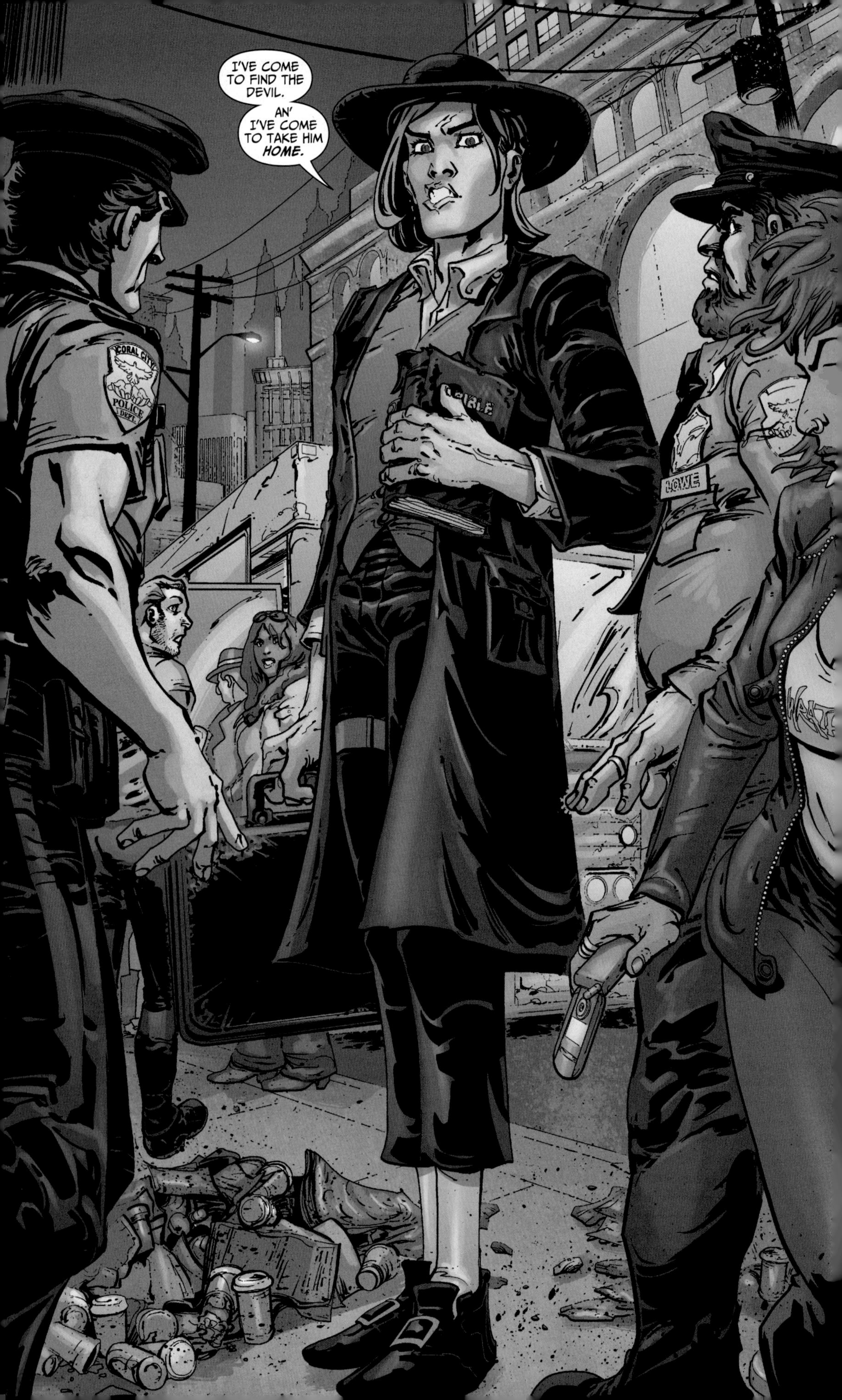
I'VE COME TO FIND THE DEVIL.
AN' I'VE COME TO TAKE HIM *HOME.*
CORAL CITY POLICE DEPT.
BIBLE
LOWE

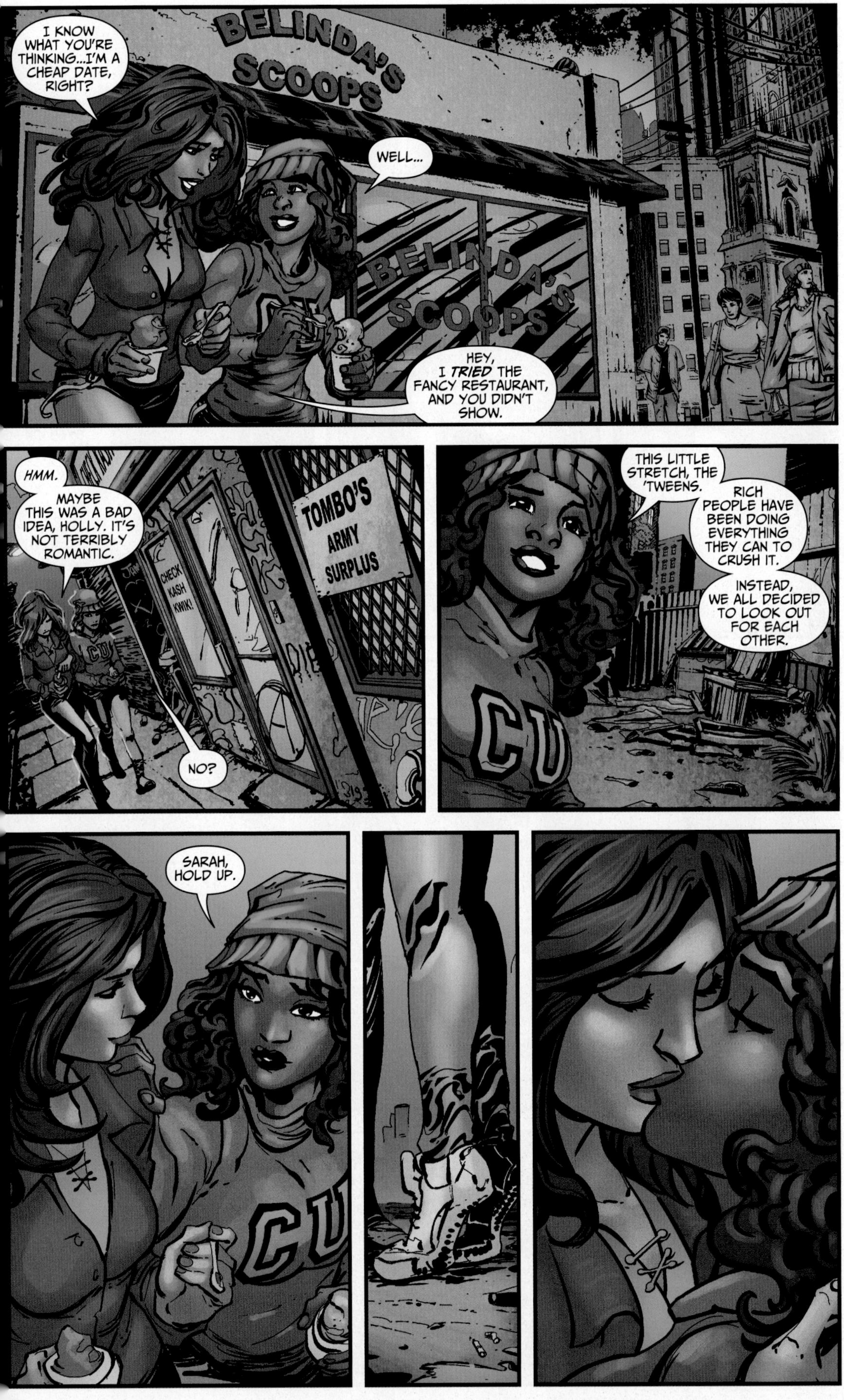

BELINDA'S SCOOPS
I KNOW WHAT YOU'RE THINKING...I'M A CHEAP DATE, RIGHT?
WELL...
HEY, I TRIED THE FANCY RESTAURANT, AND YOU DIDN'T SHOW.
HMM.
MAYBE THIS WAS A BAD IDEA, HOLLY. IT'S NOT TERRIBLY ROMANTIC.
TOMBO'S ARMY SURPLUS
CHECK KASH KWIK!
NO?
THIS LITTLE STRETCH, THE 'TWEENS.
RICH PEOPLE HAVE BEEN DOING EVERYTHING THEY CAN TO CRUSH IT.
INSTEAD, WE ALL DECIDED TO LOOK OUT FOR EACH OTHER.
SARAH, HOLD UP.

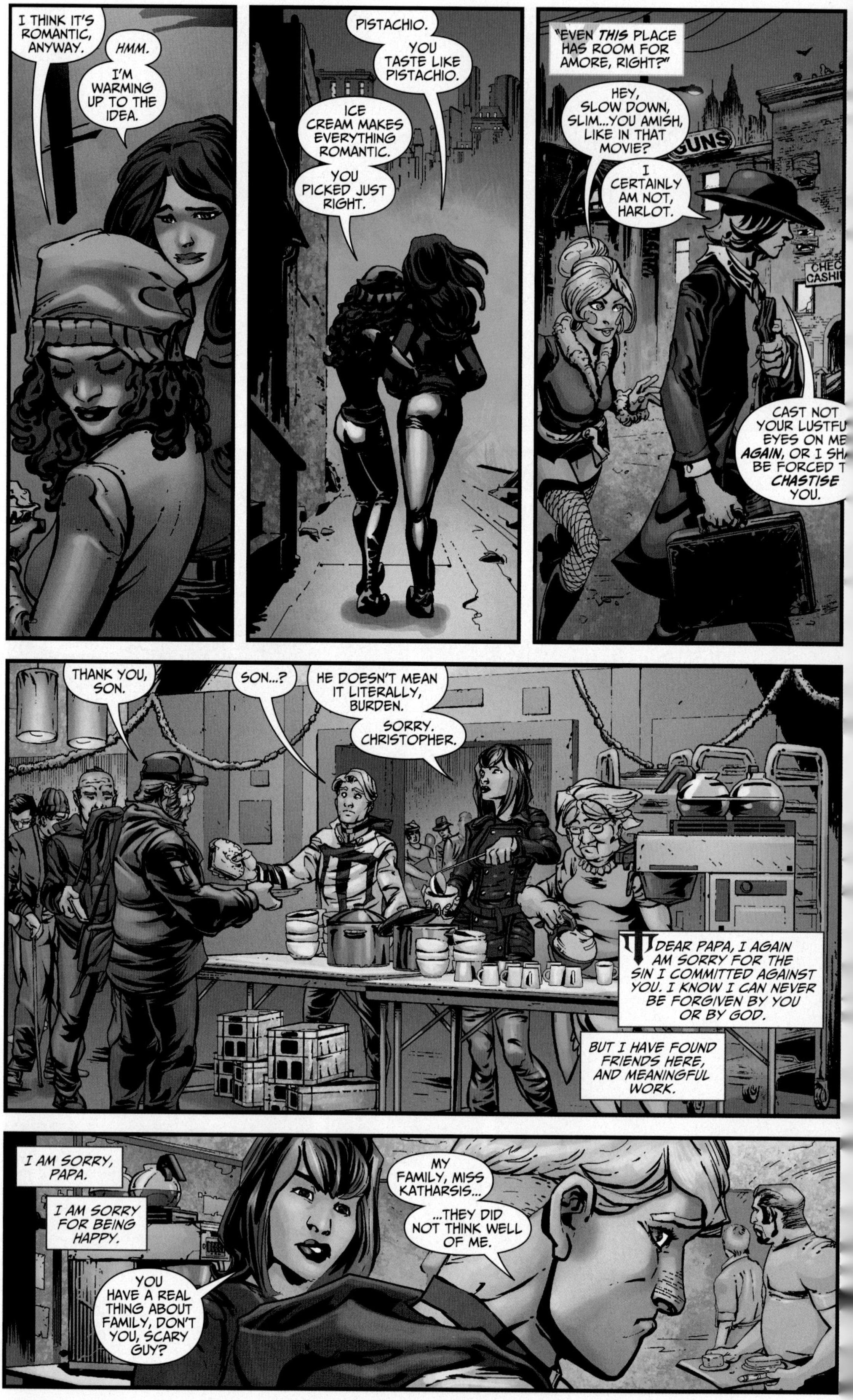
I THINK IT'S ROMANTIC, ANYWAY.
HMM.
I'M WARMING UP TO THE IDEA.
PISTACHIO.
YOU TASTE LIKE PISTACHIO.
ICE CREAM MAKES EVERYTHING ROMANTIC.
YOU PICKED JUST RIGHT.
"EVEN THIS PLACE HAS ROOM FOR AMORE, RIGHT?"
HEY, SLOW DOWN, SLIM...YOU AMISH, LIKE IN THAT MOVIE?
GUNS
I CERTAINLY AM NOT, HARLOT.
CAST NOT YOUR LUSTFU EYES ON ME AGAIN, OR I SHA BE FORCED T CHASTISE YOU.
THANK YOU, SON.
SON...?
HE DOESN'T MEAN IT LITERALLY, BURDEN.
SORRY. CHRISTOPHER.
DEAR PAPA, I AGAIN AM SORRY FOR THE SIN I COMMITTED AGAINST YOU. I KNOW I CAN NEVER BE FORGIVEN BY YOU OR BY GOD.
BUT I HAVE FOUND FRIENDS HERE, AND MEANINGFUL WORK.
I AM SORRY, PAPA.
I AM SORRY FOR BEING HAPPY.
MY FAMILY, MISS KATHARSIS...
...THEY DID NOT THINK WELL OF ME.
YOU HAVE A REAL THING ABOUT FAMILY, DON'T YOU, SCARY GUY?

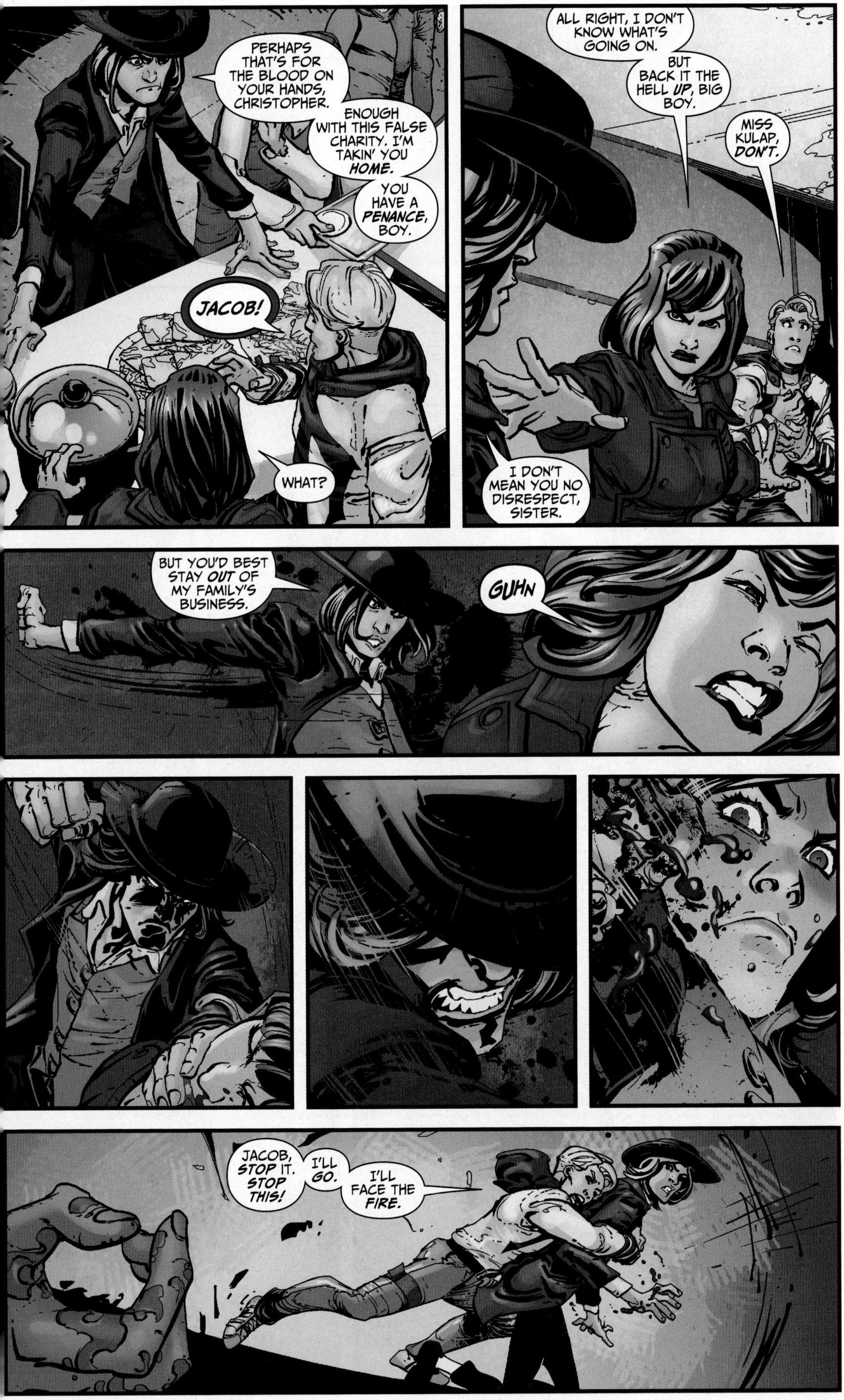
PERHAPS THAT'S FOR THE BLOOD ON YOUR HANDS, CHRISTOPHER.
ENOUGH WITH THIS FALSE CHARITY. I'M TAKIN' YOU HOME.
YOU HAVE A PENANCE, BOY.
JACOB!
WHAT?
ALL RIGHT, I DON'T KNOW WHAT'S GOING ON.
BUT BACK IT THE HELL UP, BIG BOY.
MISS KULAP, DON'T.
I DON'T MEAN YOU NO DISRESPECT, SISTER.
BUT YOU'D BEST STAY OUT OF MY FAMILY'S BUSINESS.
GUHN
JACOB, STOP IT. STOP THIS!
I'LL GO.
I'LL FACE THE FIRE.

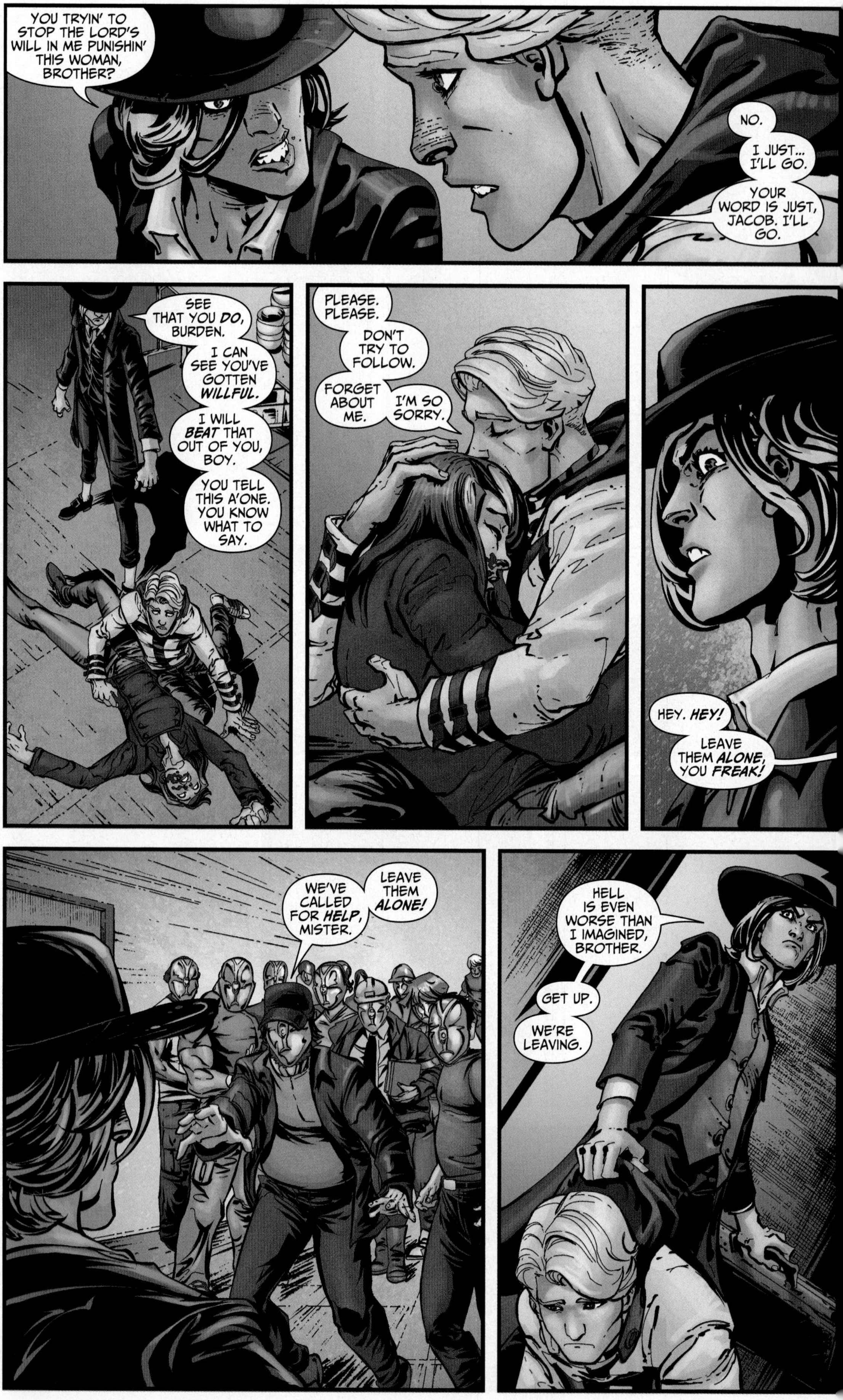
YOU TRYIN' TO STOP THE LORD'S WILL IN ME PUNISHIN' THIS WOMAN, BROTHER?
NO.
I JUST... I'LL GO.
YOUR WORD IS JUST, JACOB. I'LL GO.
SEE THAT YOU ***DO***, BURDEN.
I CAN SEE YOU'VE GOTTEN ***WILLFUL.***
I WILL ***BEAT*** THAT OUT OF YOU, BOY.
YOU TELL THIS A'ONE. YOU KNOW WHAT TO SAY.
PLEASE. PLEASE.
DON'T TRY TO FOLLOW.
FORGET ABOUT ME.
I'M SO SORRY.
HEY. ***HEY!***
LEAVE THEM ***ALONE***, YOU ***FREAK!***
WE'VE CALLED FOR ***HELP***, MISTER.
LEAVE THEM ***ALONE!***
HELL IS EVEN WORSE THAN I IMAGINED, BROTHER.
GET UP.
WE'RE LEAVING.

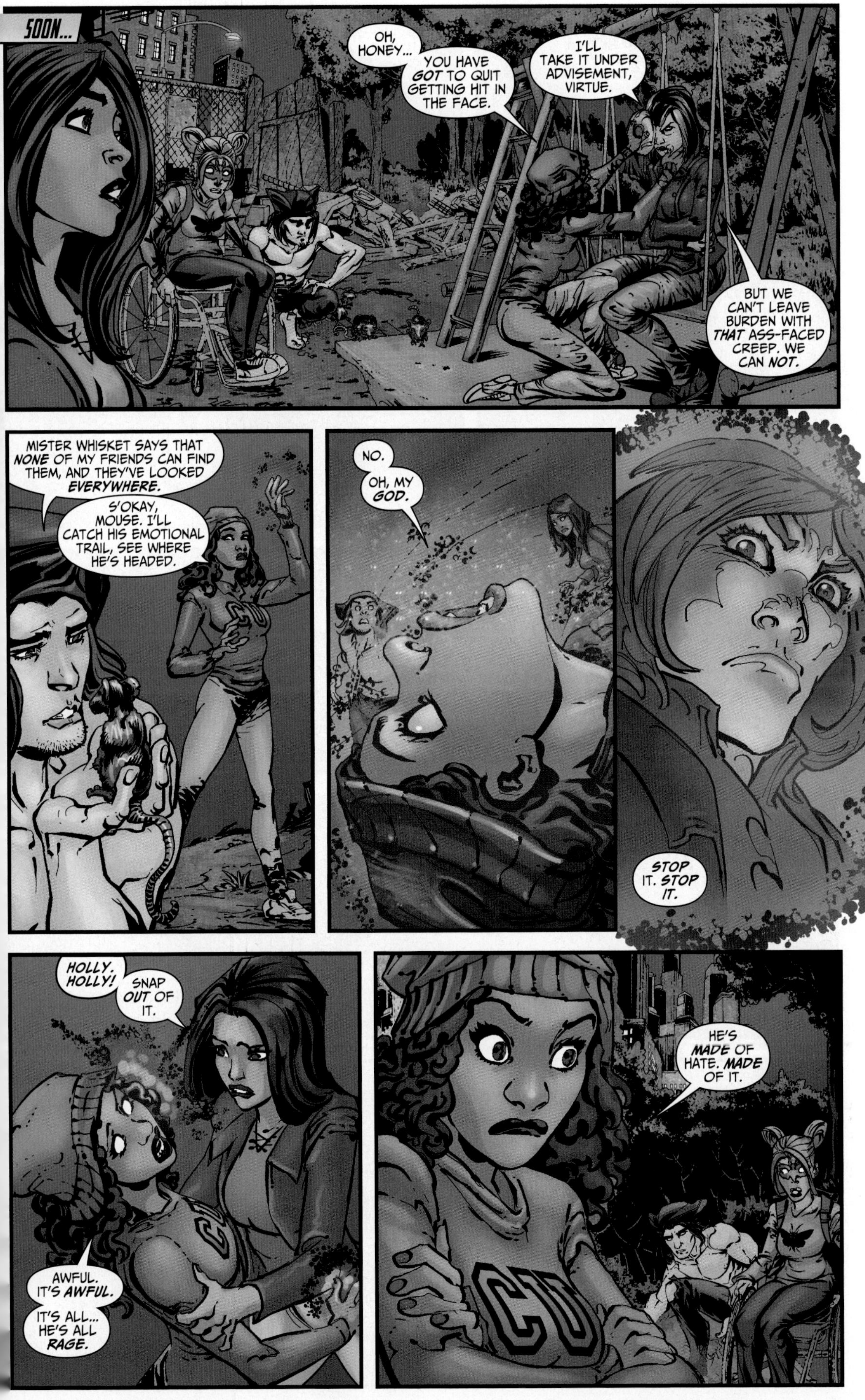
SOON...
OH, HONEY...
YOU HAVE GOT TO QUIT GETTING HIT IN THE FACE.
I'LL TAKE IT UNDER ADVISEMENT, VIRTUE.
BUT WE CAN'T LEAVE BURDEN WITH THAT ASS-FACED CREEP. WE CAN NOT.
MISTER WHISKET SAYS THAT NONE OF MY FRIENDS CAN FIND THEM, AND THEY'VE LOOKED EVERYWHERE.
S'OKAY, MOUSE. I'LL CATCH HIS EMOTIONAL TRAIL, SEE WHERE HE'S HEADED.
NO.
OH, MY GOD.
STOP IT. STOP IT.
HOLLY. HOLLY!
SNAP OUT OF IT.
AWFUL. IT'S AWFUL.
IT'S ALL... HE'S ALL RAGE.
HE'S MADE OF HATE. MADE OF IT.

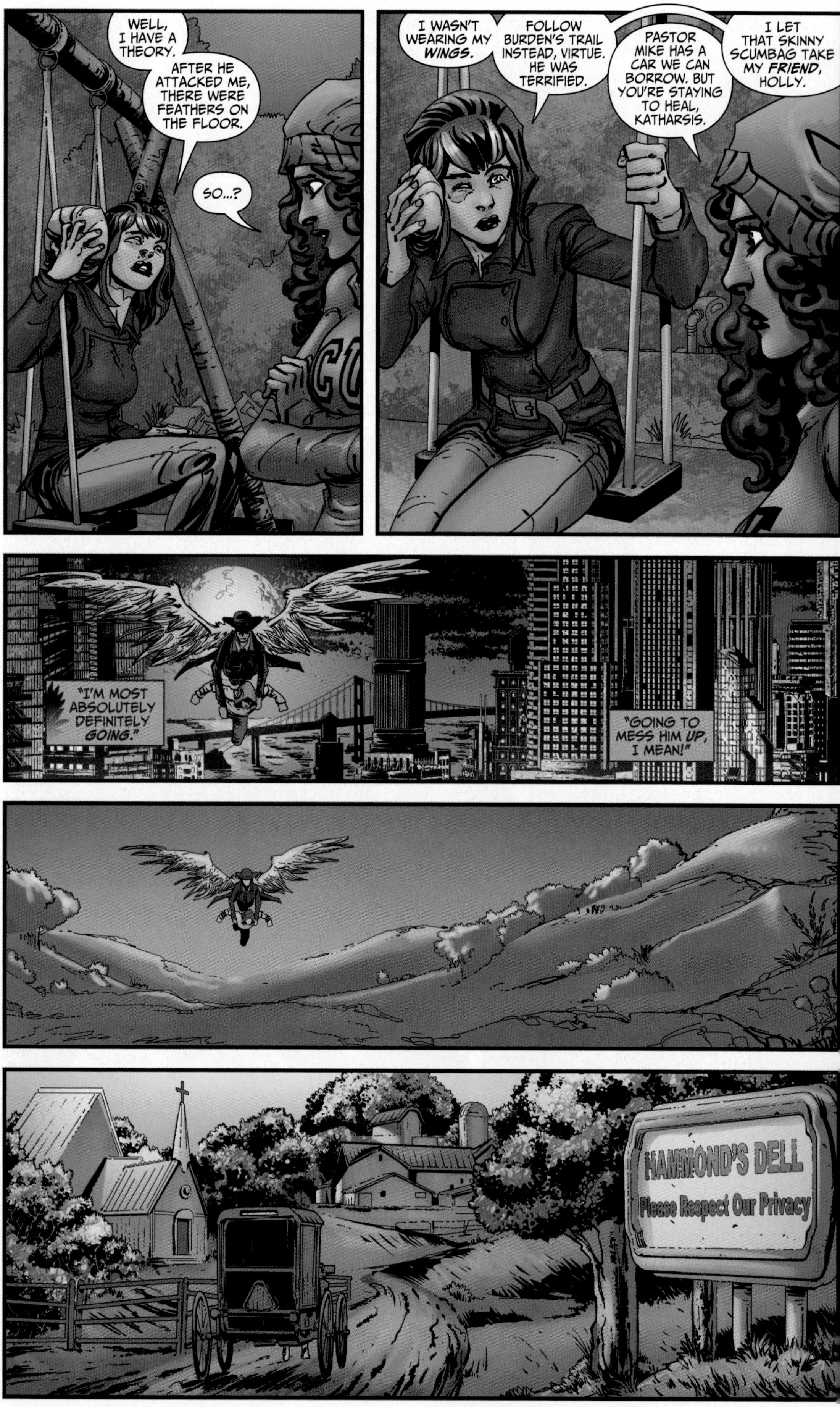
WELL, I HAVE A THEORY.
AFTER HE ATTACKED ME, THERE WERE FEATHERS ON THE FLOOR.
SO...?
I WASN'T WEARING MY *WINGS.*
FOLLOW BURDEN'S TRAIL INSTEAD, VIRTUE. HE WAS TERRIFIED.
PASTOR MIKE HAS A CAR WE CAN BORROW. BUT YOU'RE STAYING TO HEAL, KATHARSIS.
I LET THAT SKINNY SCUMBAG TAKE MY *FRIEND,* HOLLY.
"I'M MOST ABSOLUTELY DEFINITELY *GOING.*"
"GOING TO MESS HIM *UP,* I MEAN!"
HAMMOND'S DELL
Please Respect Our Privacy

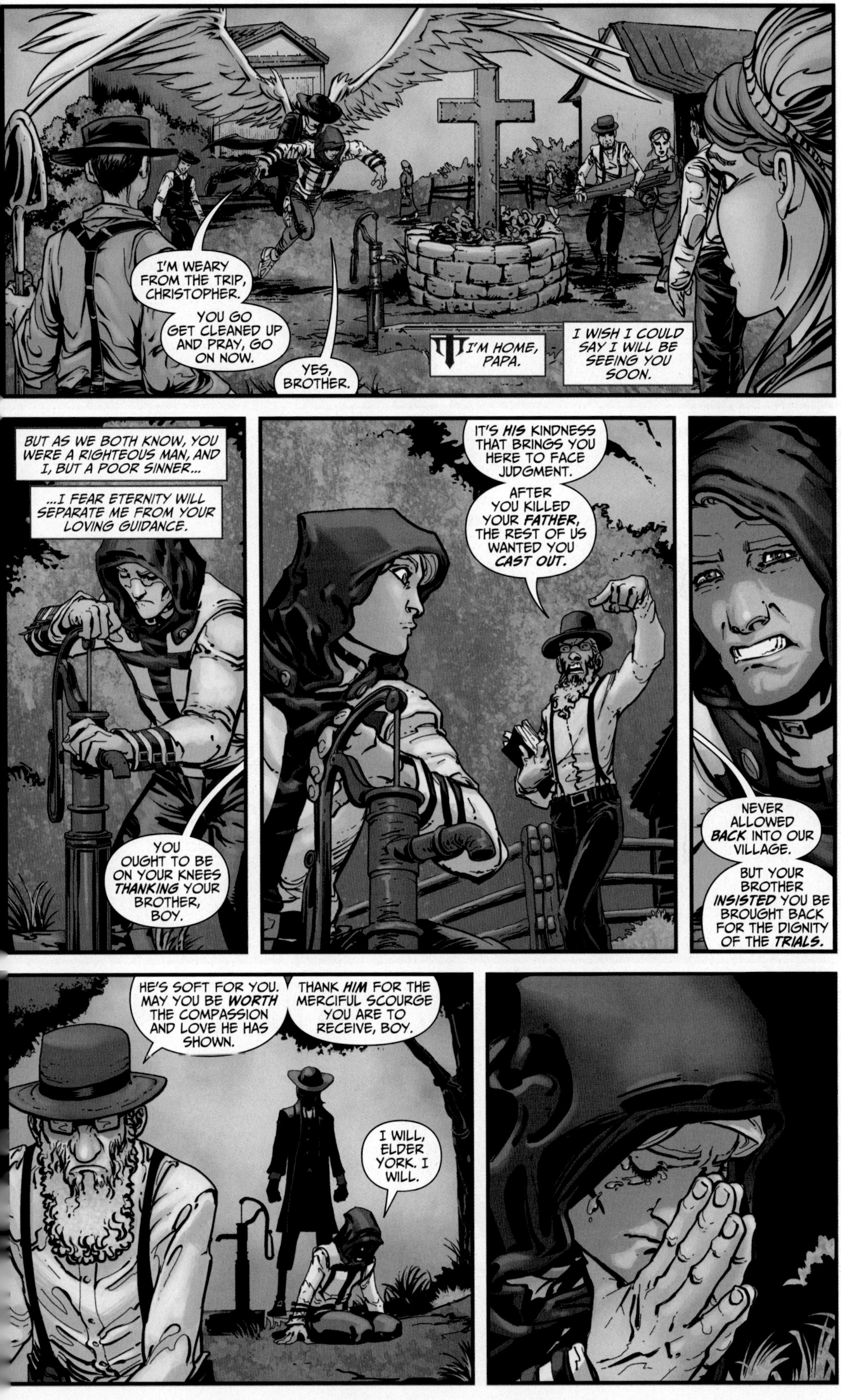
I'M WEARY FROM THE TRIP, CHRISTOPHER.
YOU GO GET CLEANED UP AND PRAY, GO ON NOW.
YES, BROTHER.
I'M HOME, PAPA.
I WISH I COULD SAY I WILL BE SEEING YOU SOON.
BUT AS WE BOTH KNOW, YOU WERE A RIGHTEOUS MAN, AND I, BUT A POOR SINNER...
...I FEAR ETERNITY WILL SEPARATE ME FROM YOUR LOVING GUIDANCE.
YOU OUGHT TO BE ON YOUR KNEES THANKING YOUR BROTHER, BOY.
IT'S HIS KINDNESS THAT BRINGS YOU HERE TO FACE JUDGMENT.
AFTER YOU KILLED YOUR FATHER, THE REST OF US WANTED YOU CAST OUT.
NEVER ALLOWED BACK INTO OUR VILLAGE.
BUT YOUR BROTHER INSISTED YOU BE BROUGHT BACK FOR THE DIGNITY OF THE TRIALS.
HE'S SOFT FOR YOU. MAY YOU BE WORTH THE COMPASSION AND LOVE HE HAS SHOWN.
THANK HIM FOR THE MERCIFUL SCOURGE YOU ARE TO RECEIVE, BOY.
I WILL, ELDER YORK. I WILL.

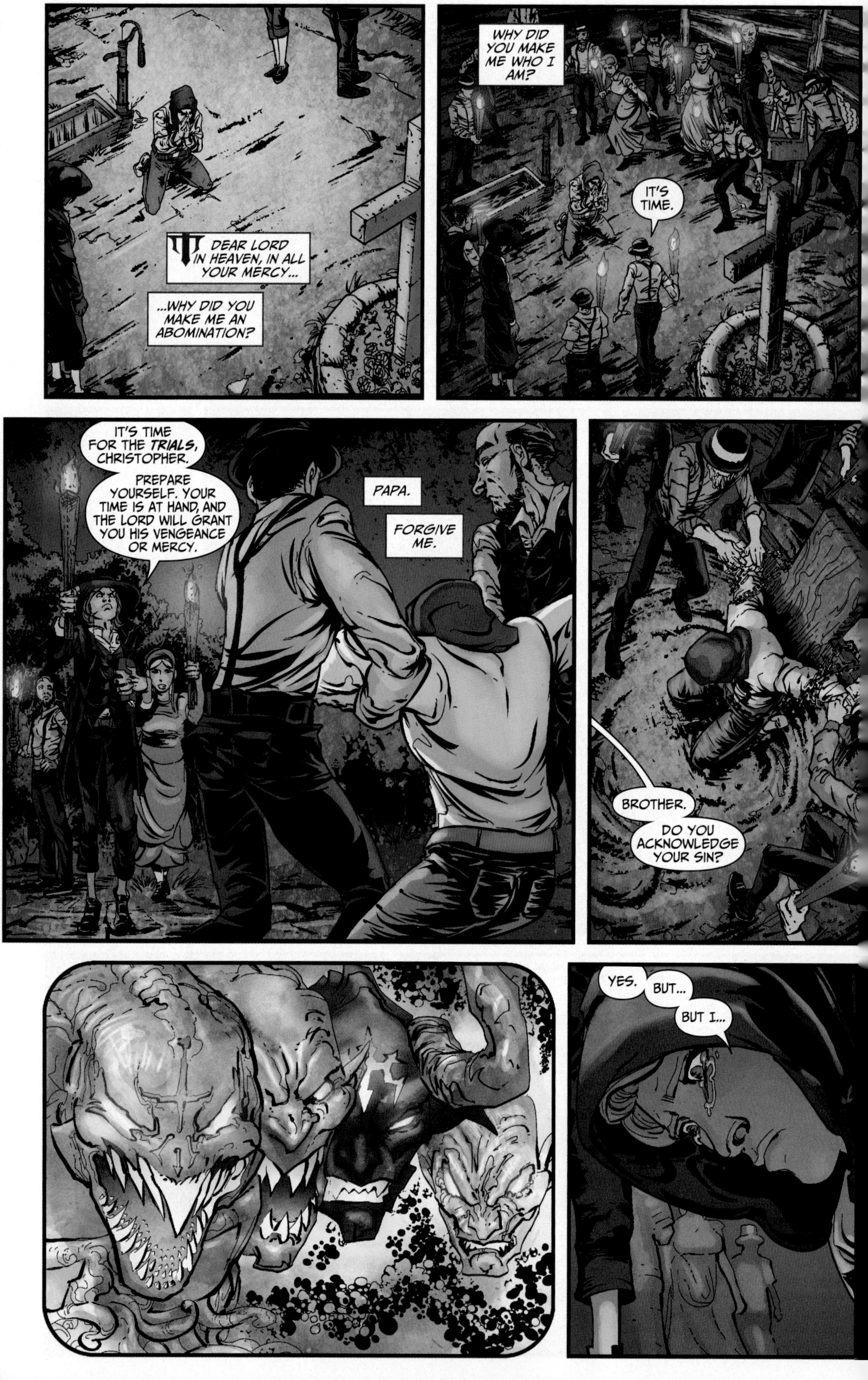
DEAR LORD IN HEAVEN, IN ALL YOUR MERCY...
...WHY DID YOU MAKE ME AN ABOMINATION?
WHY DID YOU MAKE ME WHO I AM?
IT'S TIME.
IT'S TIME FOR THE TRIALS, CHRISTOPHER.
PREPARE YOURSELF. YOUR TIME IS AT HAND, AND THE LORD WILL GRANT YOU HIS VENGEANCE OR MERCY.
PAPA.
FORGIVE ME.
BROTHER.
DO YOU ACKNOWLEDGE YOUR SIN?
YES.
BUT...
BUT I...

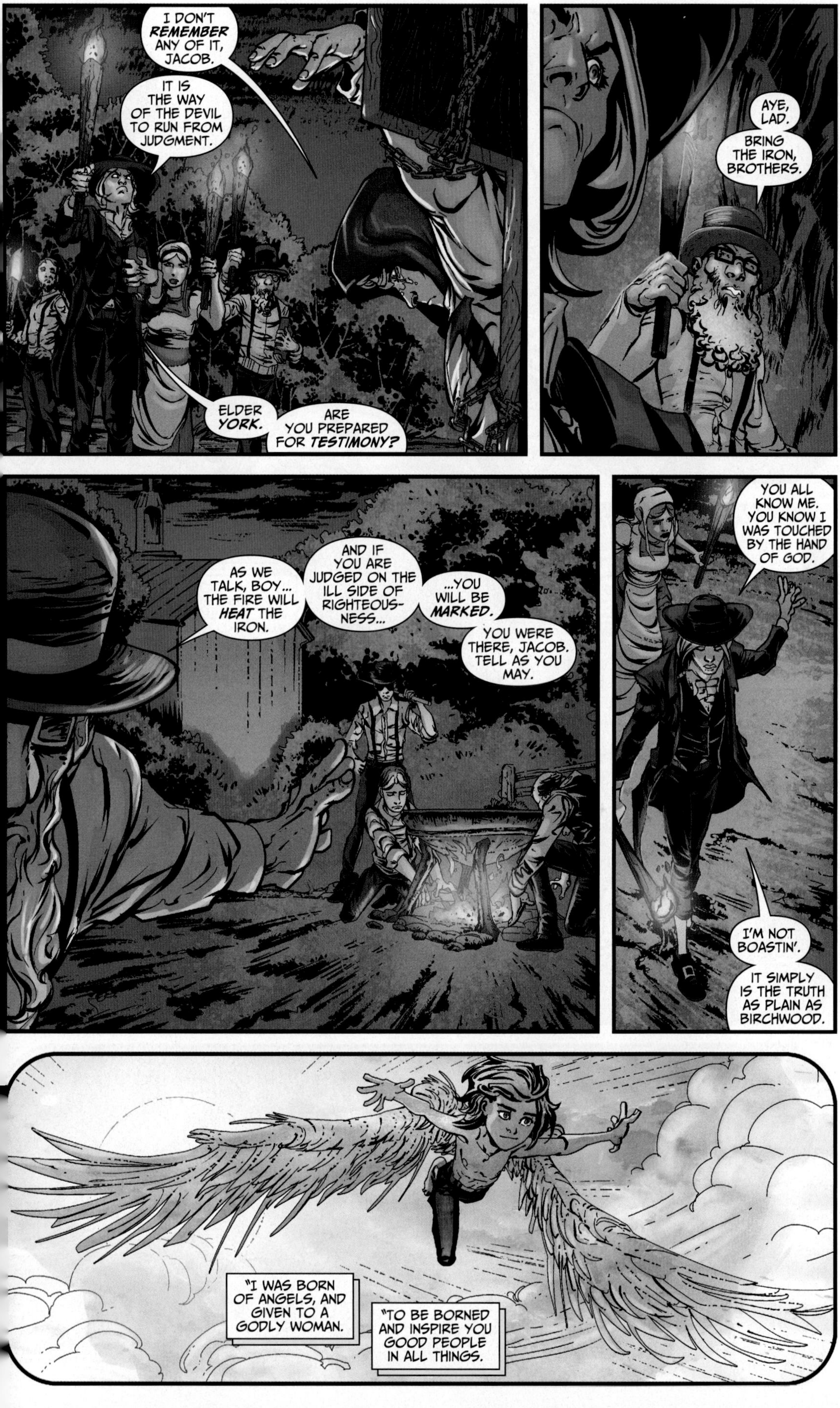

I DON'T REMEMBER ANY OF IT, JACOB.
IT IS THE WAY OF THE DEVIL TO RUN FROM JUDGMENT.
ELDER YORK.
ARE YOU PREPARED FOR TESTIMONY?
AYE, LAD.
BRING THE IRON, BROTHERS.
AS WE TALK, BOY... THE FIRE WILL HEAT THE IRON.
AND IF YOU ARE JUDGED ON THE ILL SIDE OF RIGHTEOUS-NESS...
...YOU WILL BE MARKED.
YOU WERE THERE, JACOB. TELL AS YOU MAY.
YOU ALL KNOW ME. YOU KNOW I WAS TOUCHED BY THE HAND OF GOD.
I'M NOT BOASTIN'.
IT SIMPLY IS THE TRUTH AS PLAIN AS BIRCHWOOD.
"I WAS BORN OF ANGELS, AND GIVEN TO A GODLY WOMAN.
"TO BE BORNED AND INSPIRE YOU GOOD PEOPLE IN ALL THINGS.

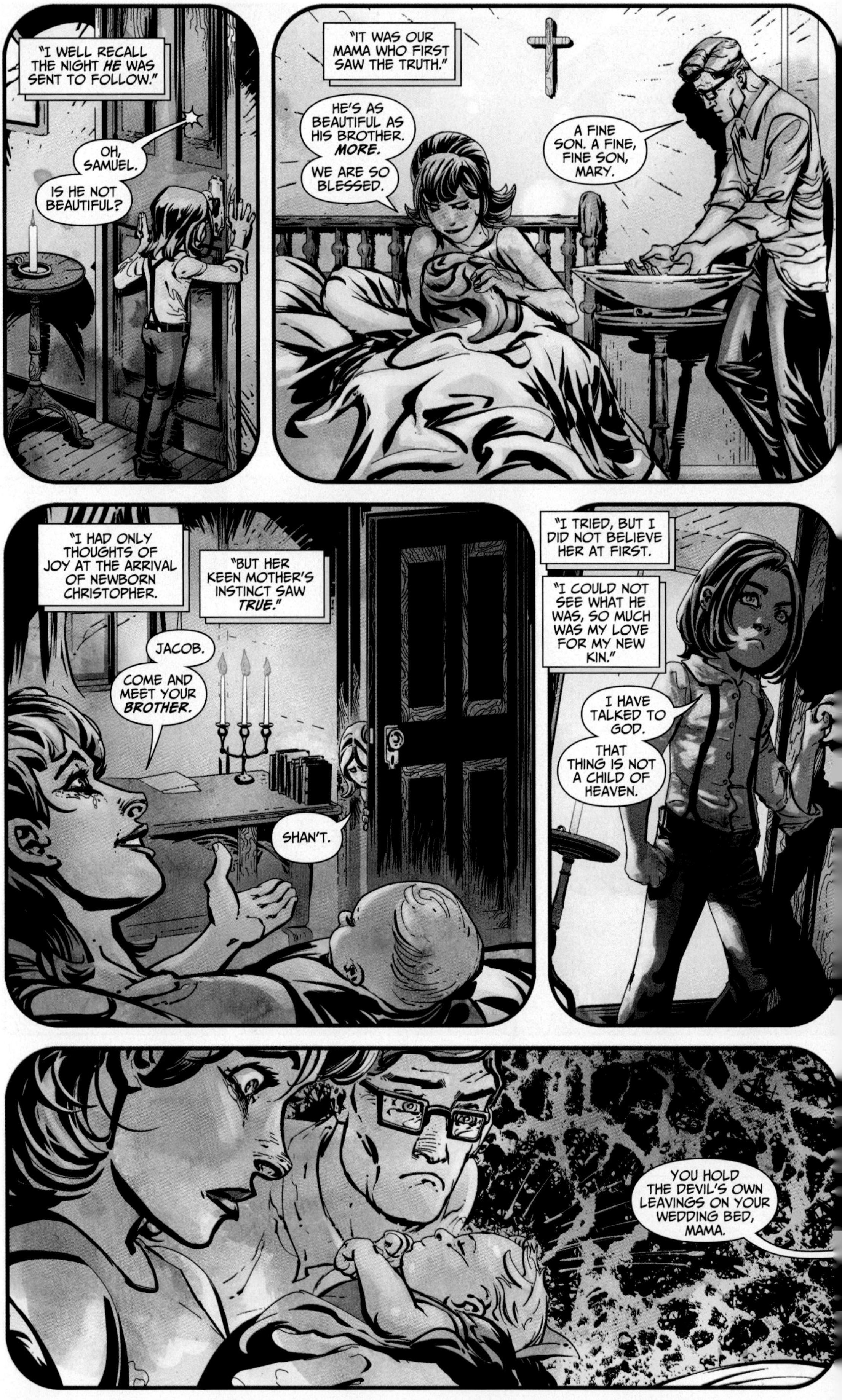
"I WELL RECALL THE NIGHT HE WAS SENT TO FOLLOW."
OH, SAMUEL.
IS HE NOT BEAUTIFUL?
"IT WAS OUR MAMA WHO FIRST SAW THE TRUTH."
HE'S AS BEAUTIFUL AS HIS BROTHER. MORE.
WE ARE SO BLESSED.
A FINE SON. A FINE, FINE SON, MARY.
"I HAD ONLY THOUGHTS OF JOY AT THE ARRIVAL OF NEWBORN CHRISTOPHER.
"BUT HER KEEN MOTHER'S INSTINCT SAW TRUE."
JACOB.
COME AND MEET YOUR BROTHER.
SHAN'T.
"I TRIED, BUT I DID NOT BELIEVE HER AT FIRST.
"I COULD NOT SEE WHAT HE WAS, SO MUCH WAS MY LOVE FOR MY NEW KIN."
I HAVE TALKED TO GOD.
THAT THING IS NOT A CHILD OF HEAVEN.
YOU HOLD THE DEVIL'S OWN LEAVINGS ON YOUR WEDDING BED, MAMA.

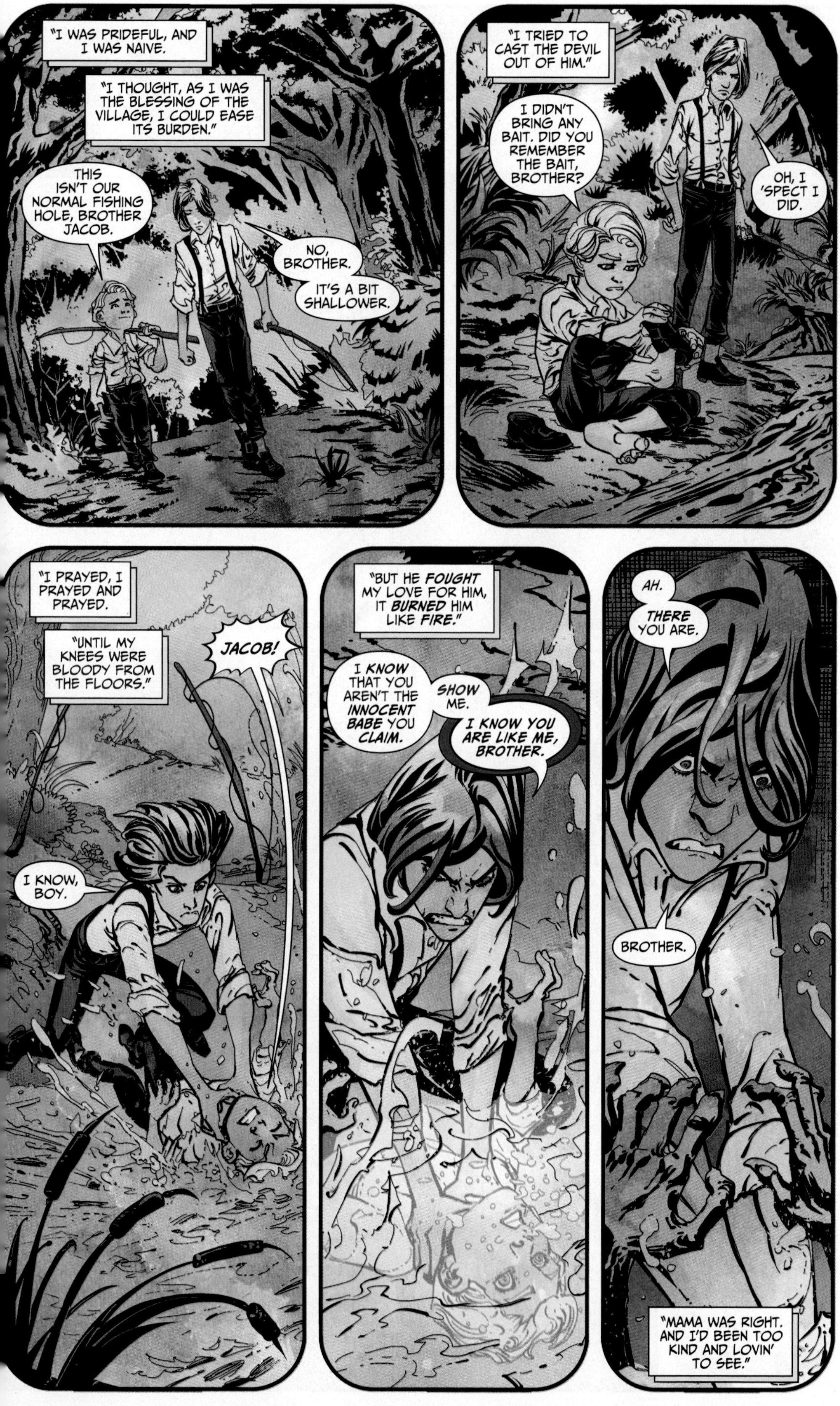
"I WAS PRIDEFUL, AND I WAS NAIVE.
"I THOUGHT, AS I WAS THE BLESSING OF THE VILLAGE, I COULD EASE ITS BURDEN."
THIS ISN'T OUR NORMAL FISHING HOLE, BROTHER JACOB.
NO, BROTHER.
IT'S A BIT SHALLOWER.
"I TRIED TO CAST THE DEVIL OUT OF HIM."
I DIDN'T BRING ANY BAIT. DID YOU REMEMBER THE BAIT, BROTHER?
OH, I 'SPECT I DID.
"I PRAYED, I PRAYED AND PRAYED.
"UNTIL MY KNEES WERE BLOODY FROM THE FLOORS."
JACOB!
I KNOW, BOY.
"BUT HE FOUGHT MY LOVE FOR HIM, IT BURNED HIM LIKE FIRE."
I KNOW THAT YOU AREN'T THE INNOCENT BABE YOU CLAIM.
SHOW ME.
I KNOW YOU ARE LIKE ME, BROTHER.
AH.
THERE YOU ARE.
BROTHER.
"MAMA WAS RIGHT. AND I'D BEEN TOO KIND AND LOVIN' TO SEE."

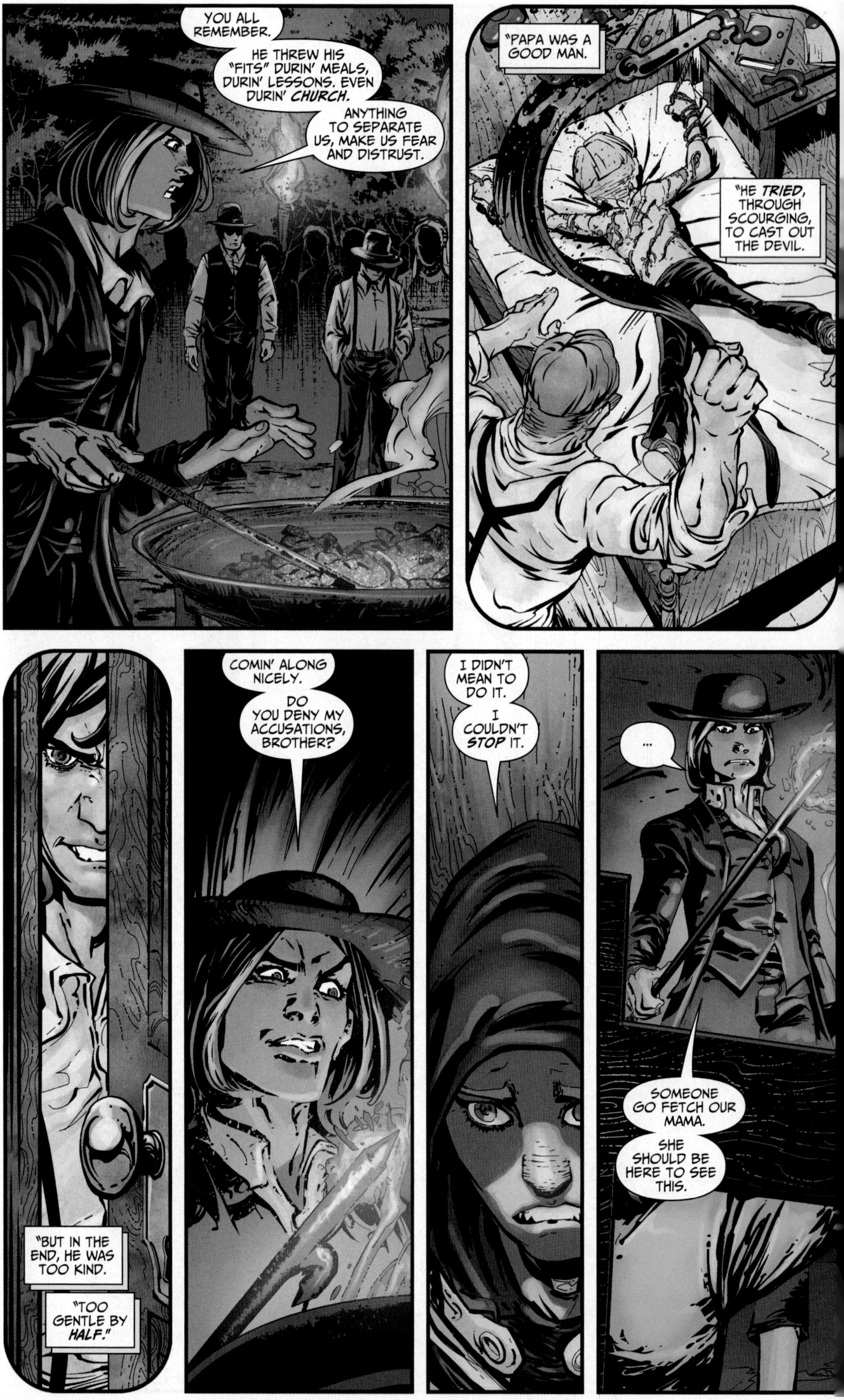

YOU ALL REMEMBER.
HE THREW HIS "FITS" DURIN' MEALS, DURIN' LESSONS. EVEN DURIN' *CHURCH.*
ANYTHING TO SEPARATE US, MAKE US FEAR AND DISTRUST.
"PAPA WAS A GOOD MAN.
"HE *TRIED,* THROUGH SCOURGING, TO CAST OUT THE DEVIL.
"BUT IN THE END, HE WAS TOO KIND.
"TOO GENTLE BY *HALF.*"
COMIN' ALONG NICELY.
DO YOU DENY MY ACCUSATIONS, BROTHER?
I DIDN'T MEAN TO DO IT.
I COULDN'T *STOP* IT.
...
SOMEONE GO FETCH OUR MAMA.
SHE SHOULD BE HERE TO SEE THIS.

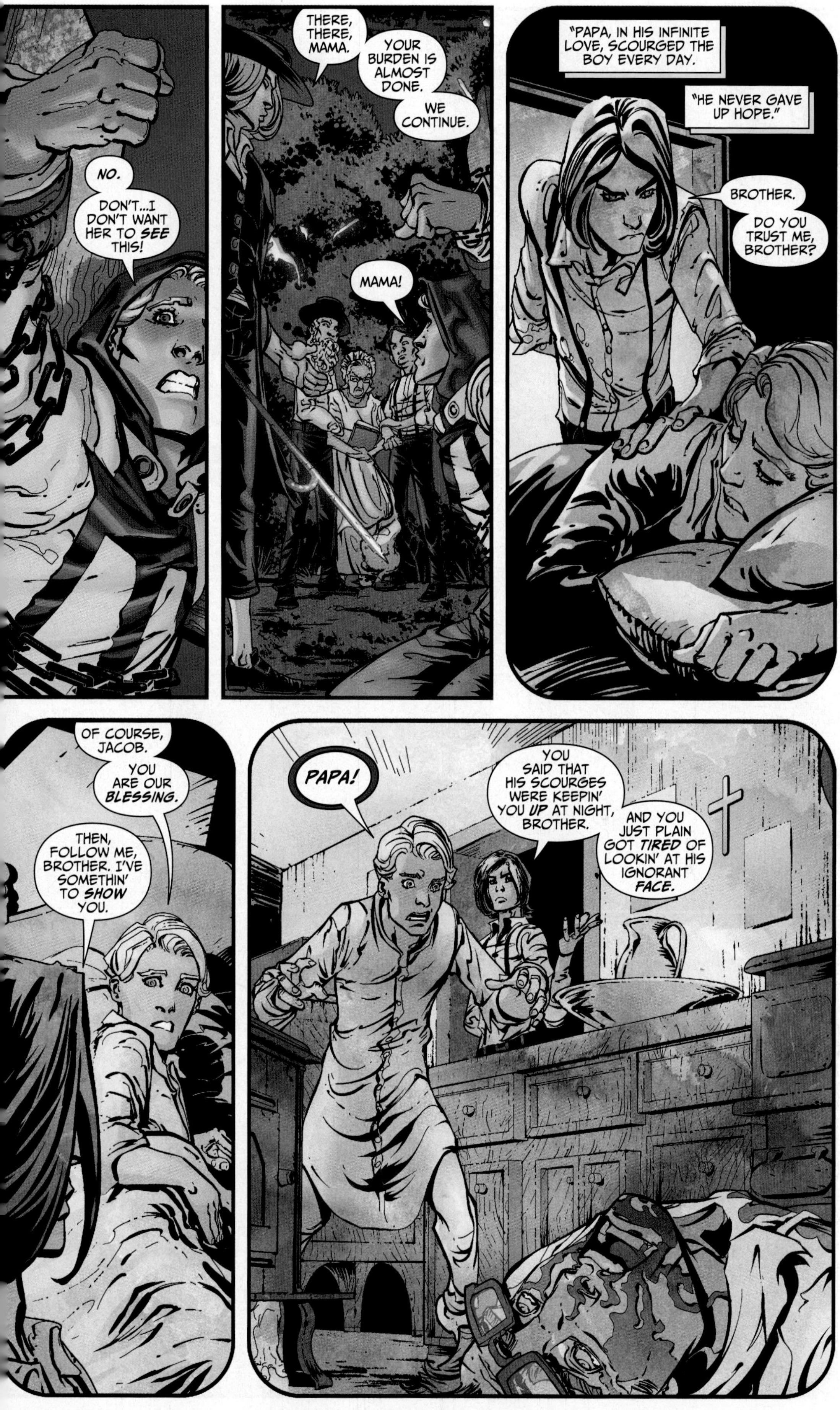

NO.
DON'T...I DON'T WANT HER TO SEE THIS!
THERE, THERE, MAMA.
YOUR BURDEN IS ALMOST DONE.
WE CONTINUE.
MAMA!
"PAPA, IN HIS INFINITE LOVE, SCOURGED THE BOY EVERY DAY.
"HE NEVER GAVE UP HOPE."
BROTHER.
DO YOU TRUST ME, BROTHER?
OF COURSE, JACOB.
YOU ARE OUR BLESSING.
THEN, FOLLOW ME, BROTHER. I'VE SOMETHIN' TO SHOW YOU.
PAPA!
YOU SAID THAT HIS SCOURGES WERE KEEPIN' YOU UP AT NIGHT, BROTHER.
AND YOU JUST PLAIN GOT TIRED OF LOOKIN' AT HIS IGNORANT FACE.

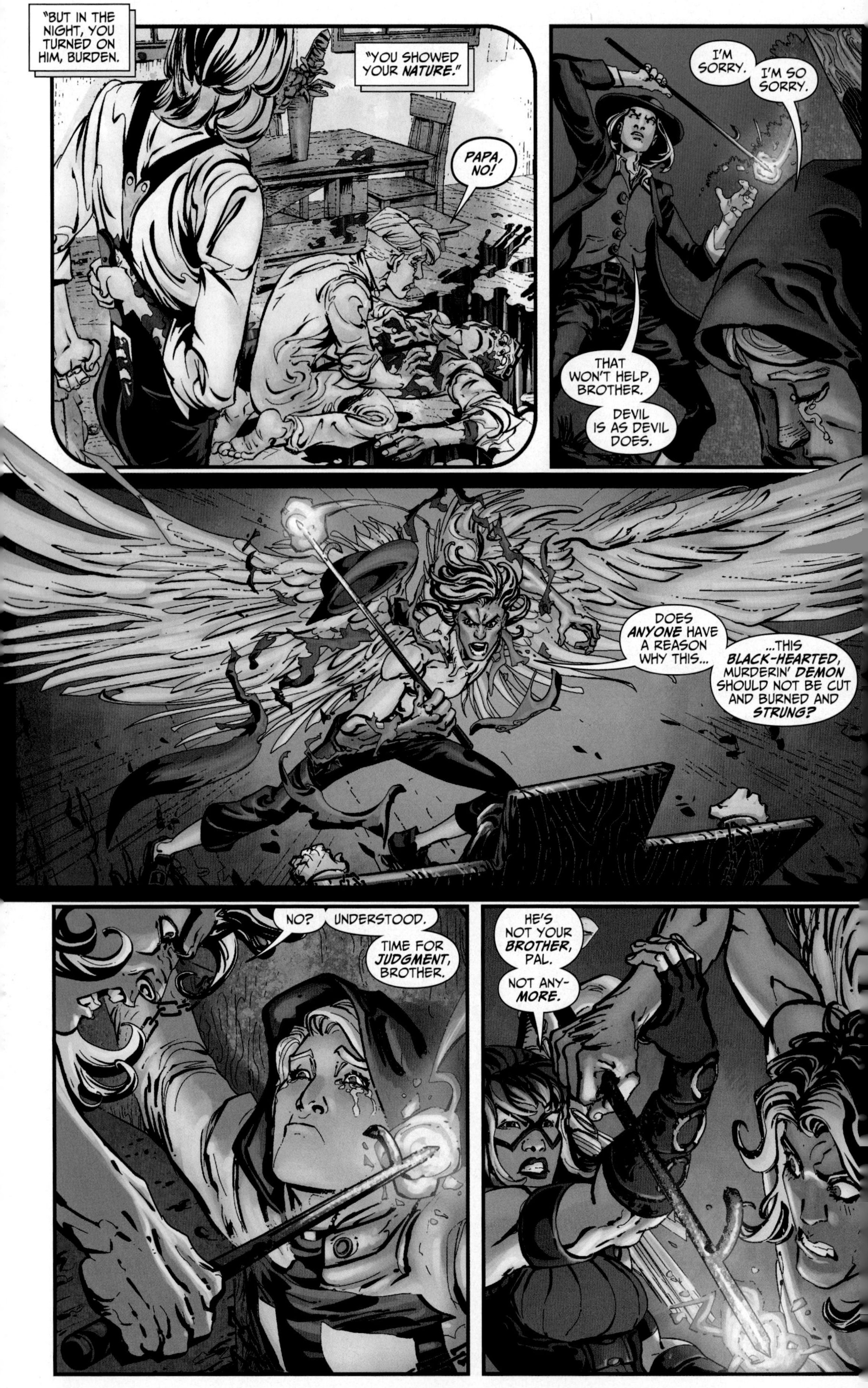
"BUT IN THE NIGHT, YOU TURNED ON HIM, BURDEN.
"YOU SHOWED YOUR NATURE."
PAPA, NO!
I'M SORRY.
I'M SO SORRY.
THAT WON'T HELP, BROTHER.
DEVIL IS AS DEVIL DOES.
DOES ANYONE HAVE A REASON WHY THIS...
...THIS BLACK-HEARTED, MURDERIN' DEMON SHOULD NOT BE CUT AND BURNED AND STRUNG?
NO?
UNDERSTOOD.
TIME FOR JUDGMENT, BROTHER.
HE'S NOT YOUR BROTHER, PAL.
NOT ANY-MORE.

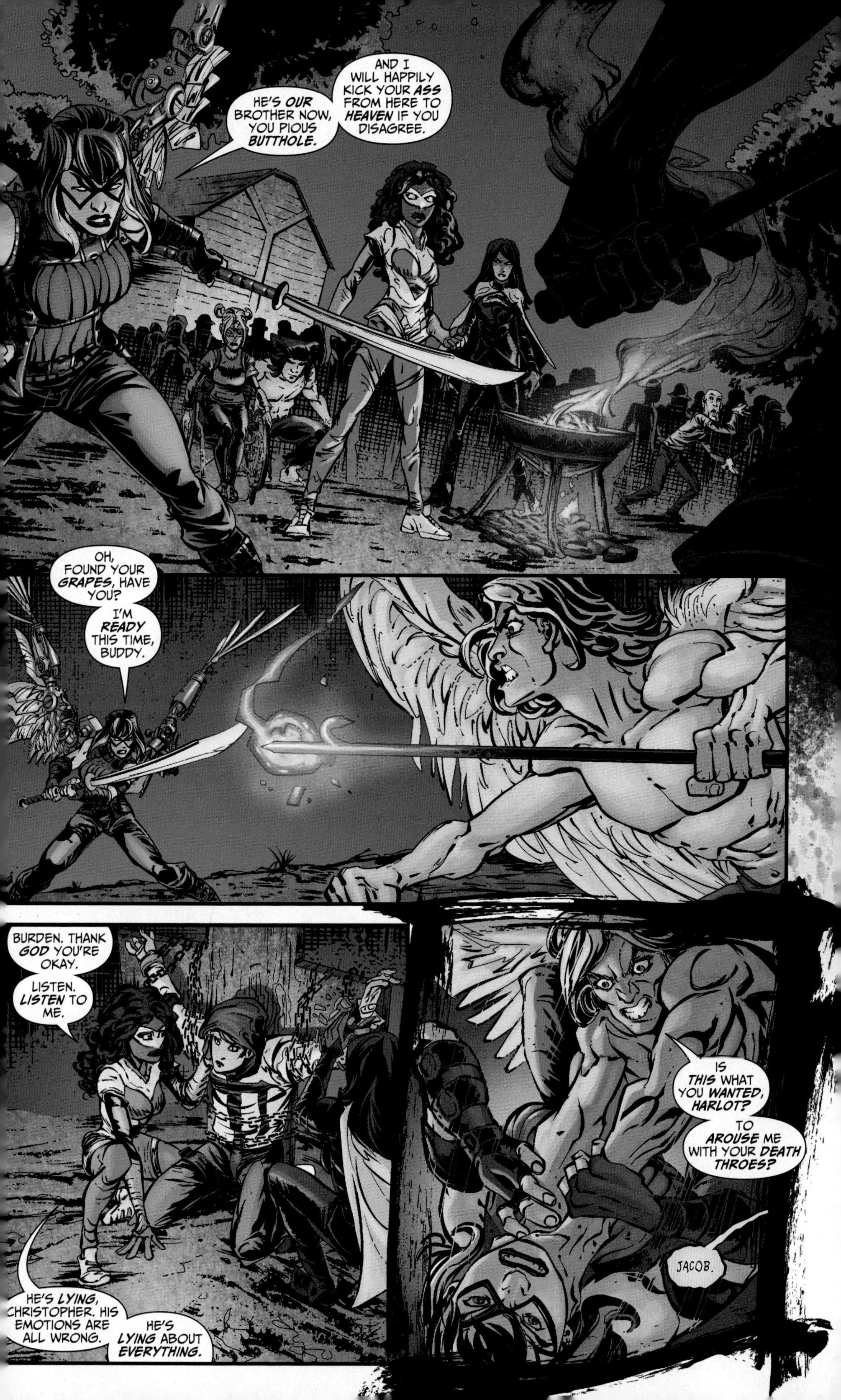
HE'S OUR BROTHER NOW, YOU PIOUS BUTTHOLE.
AND I WILL HAPPILY KICK YOUR ASS FROM HERE TO HEAVEN IF YOU DISAGREE.
OH, FOUND YOUR GRAPES, HAVE YOU?
I'M READY THIS TIME, BUDDY.
BURDEN. THANK GOD YOU'RE OKAY.
LISTEN. LISTEN TO ME.
HE'S LYING, CHRISTOPHER. HIS EMOTIONS ARE ALL WRONG.
HE'S LYING ABOUT EVERYTHING.
IS THIS WHAT YOU WANTED, HARLOT?
TO AROUSE ME WITH YOUR DEATH THROES?
JACOB.

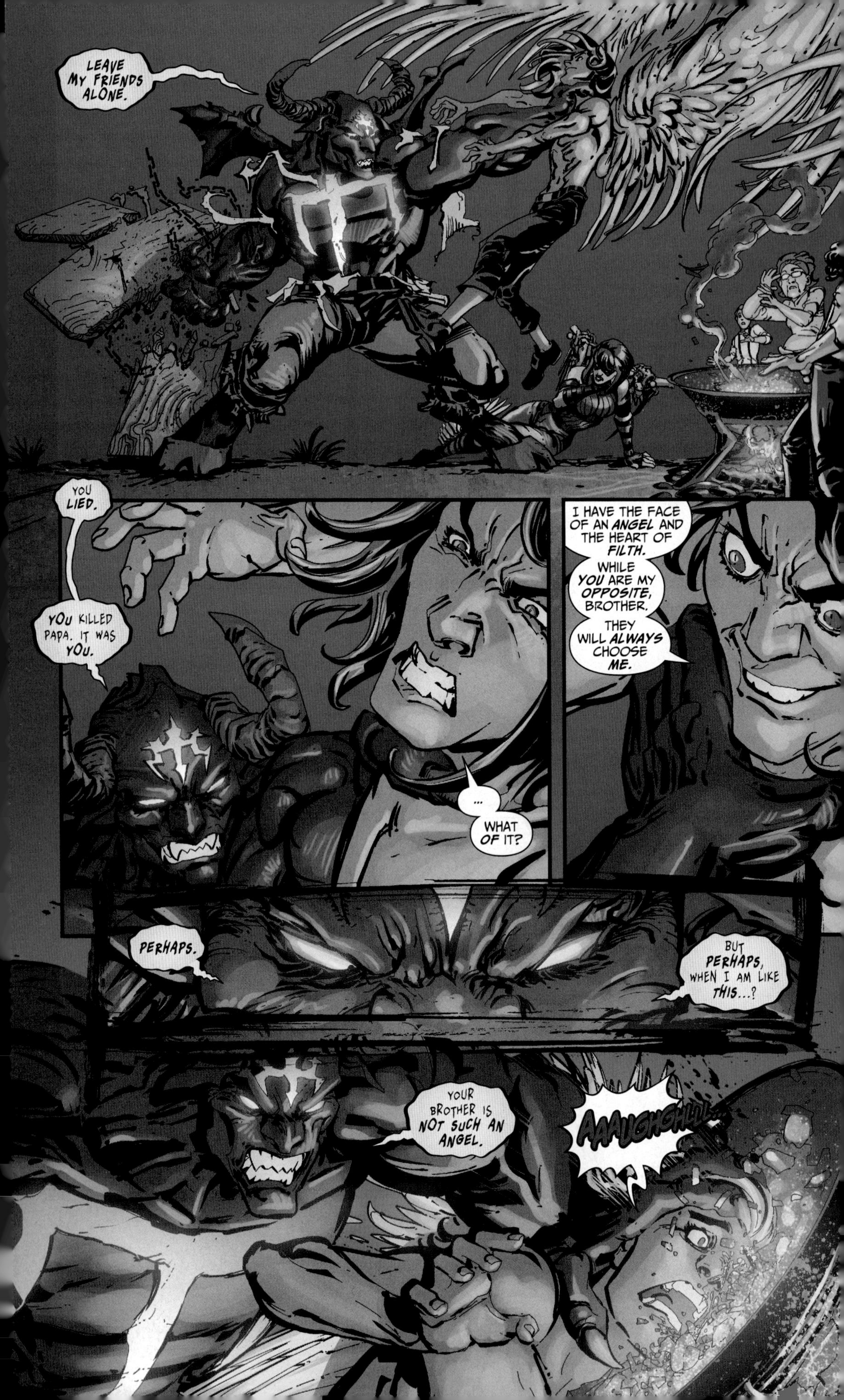
LEAVE MY FRIENDS ALONE.
YOU LIED.
YOU KILLED PAPA. IT WAS YOU.
... WHAT OF IT?
I HAVE THE FACE OF AN ANGEL AND THE HEART OF FILTH.
WHILE YOU ARE MY OPPOSITE, BROTHER.
THEY WILL ALWAYS CHOOSE ME.
PERHAPS.
BUT PERHAPS, WHEN I AM LIKE THIS...?
YOUR BROTHER IS NOT SUCH AN ANGEL.
AAAUGHGHLLL

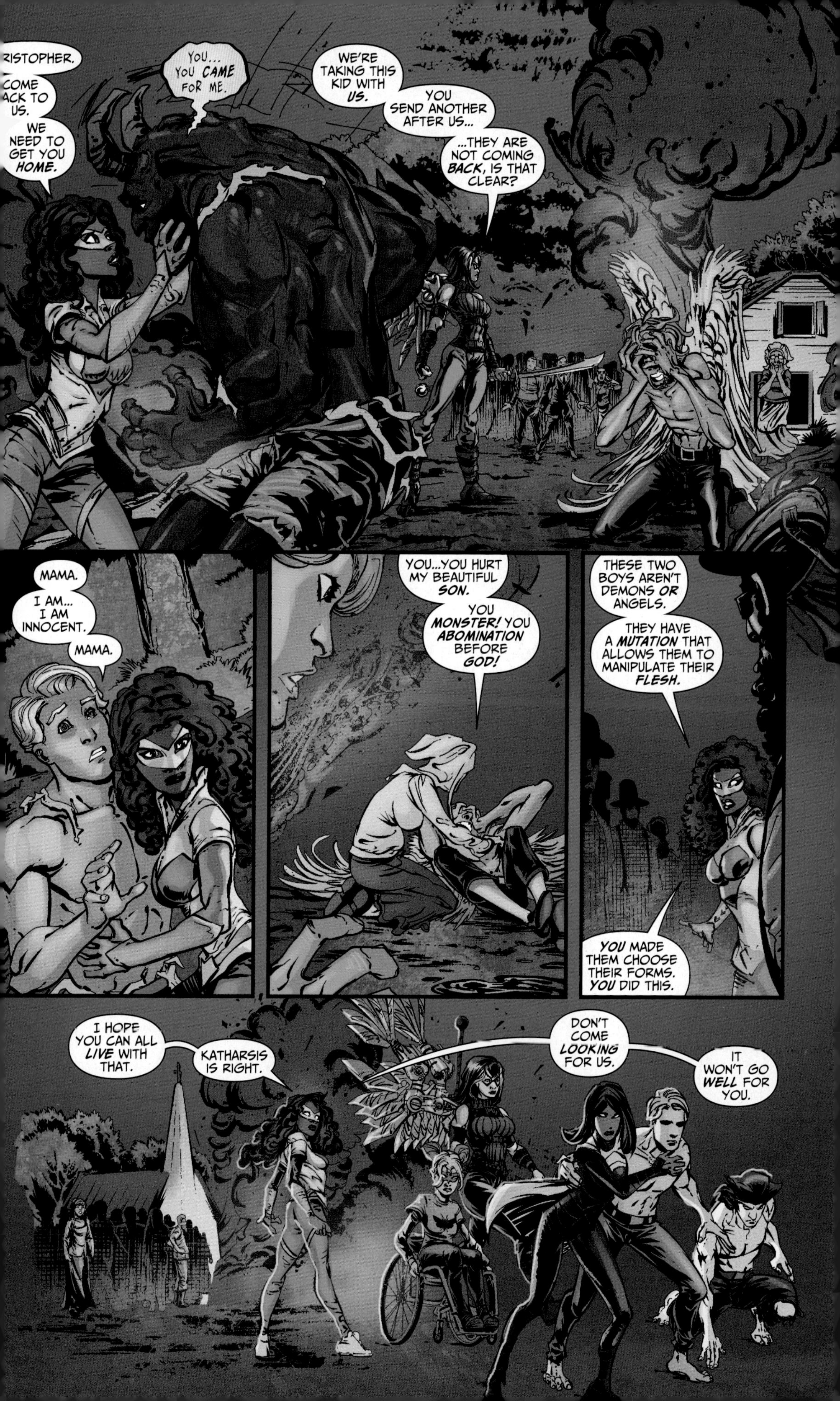
RISTOPHER.
COME
ACK TO
US.
WE
NEED TO
GET YOU
HOME.
YOU...
YOU CAME
FOR ME.
WE'RE
TAKING THIS
KID WITH
US.
YOU
SEND ANOTHER
AFTER US...
...THEY ARE
NOT COMING
BACK, IS THAT
CLEAR?
MAMA.
I AM...
I AM
INNOCENT.
MAMA.
YOU...YOU HURT
MY BEAUTIFUL
SON.
YOU
MONSTER! YOU
ABOMINATION
BEFORE
GOD!
THESE TWO
BOYS AREN'T
DEMONS OR
ANGELS.
THEY HAVE
A MUTATION THAT
ALLOWS THEM TO
MANIPULATE THEIR
FLESH.
YOU MADE
THEM CHOOSE
THEIR FORMS.
YOU DID THIS.
I HOPE
YOU CAN ALL
LIVE WITH
THAT.
KATHARSIS
IS RIGHT.
DON'T
COME
LOOKING
FOR US.
IT
WON'T GO
WELL FOR
YOU.

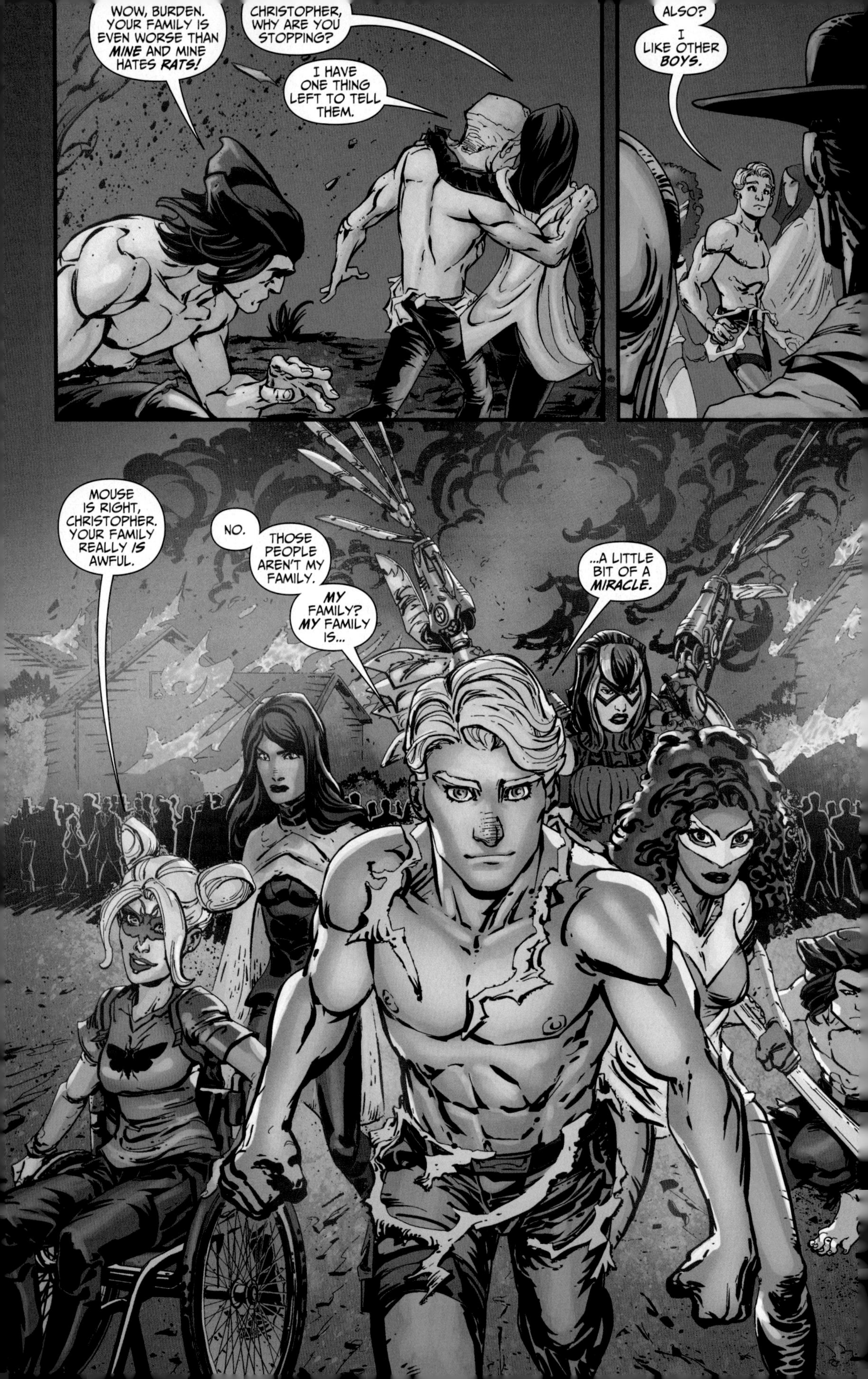
WOW, BURDEN. YOUR FAMILY IS EVEN WORSE THAN *MINE* AND MINE HATES *RATS!*
CHRISTOPHER, WHY ARE YOU STOPPING?
I HAVE ONE THING LEFT TO TELL THEM.
ALSO?
I LIKE OTHER *BOYS.*
MOUSE IS RIGHT, CHRISTOPHER. YOUR FAMILY REALLY *IS* AWFUL.
NO.
THOSE PEOPLE AREN'T MY FAMILY.
MY FAMILY? *MY* FAMILY IS...
...A LITTLE BIT OF A *MIRACLE.*

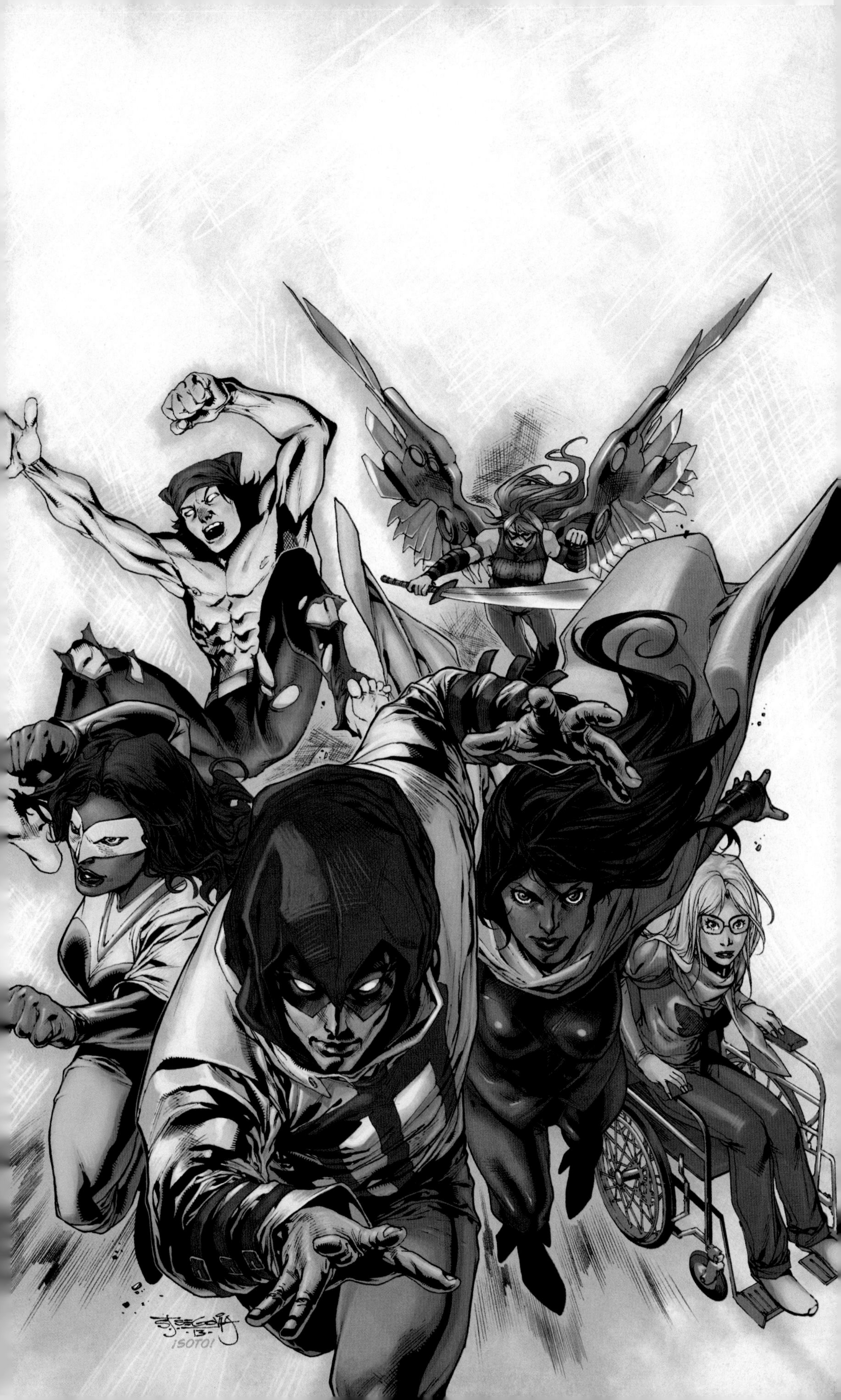

Cover Art by Stephen Segovia

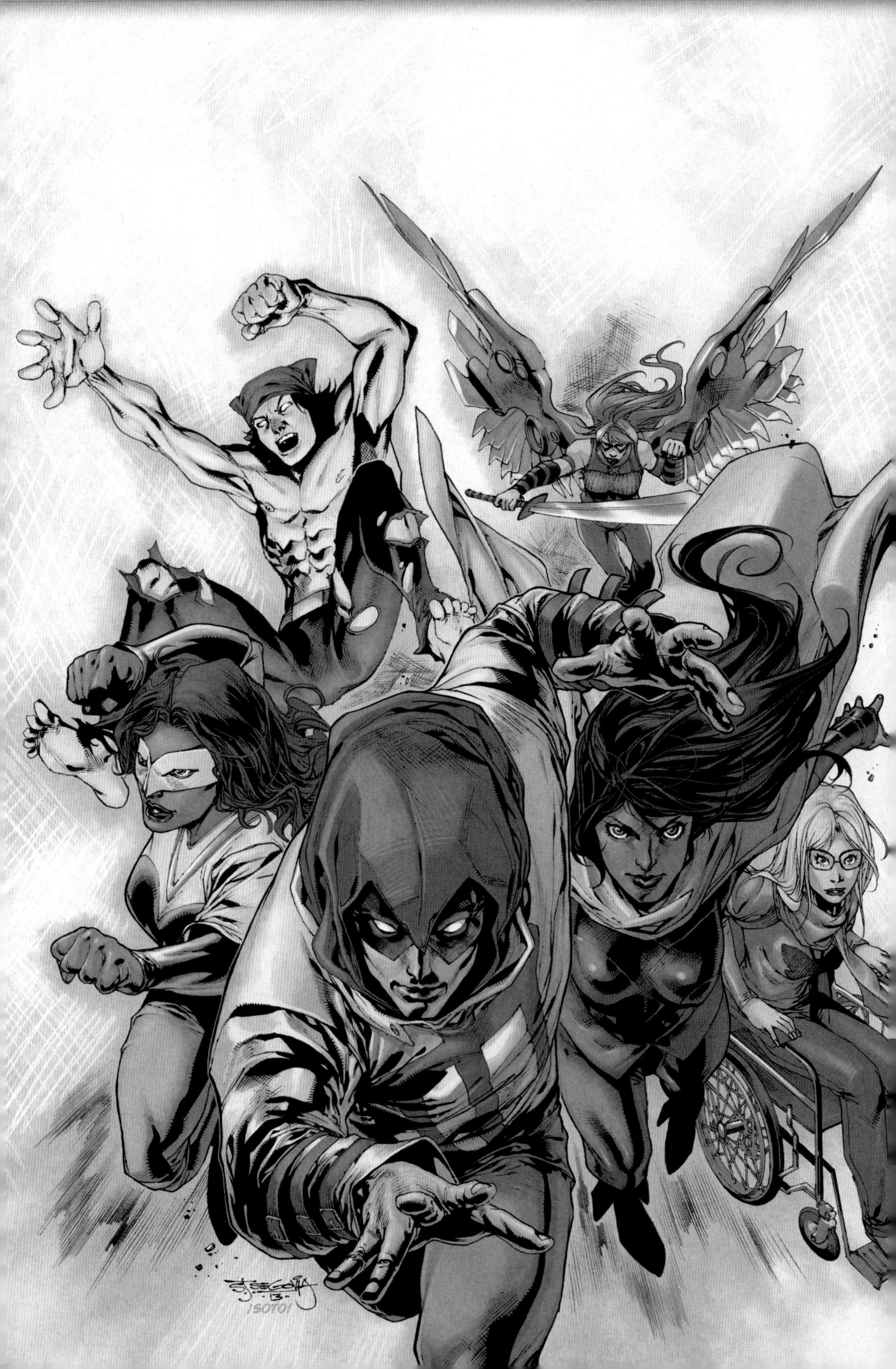
SEGOVIA
13
¡SOTO!

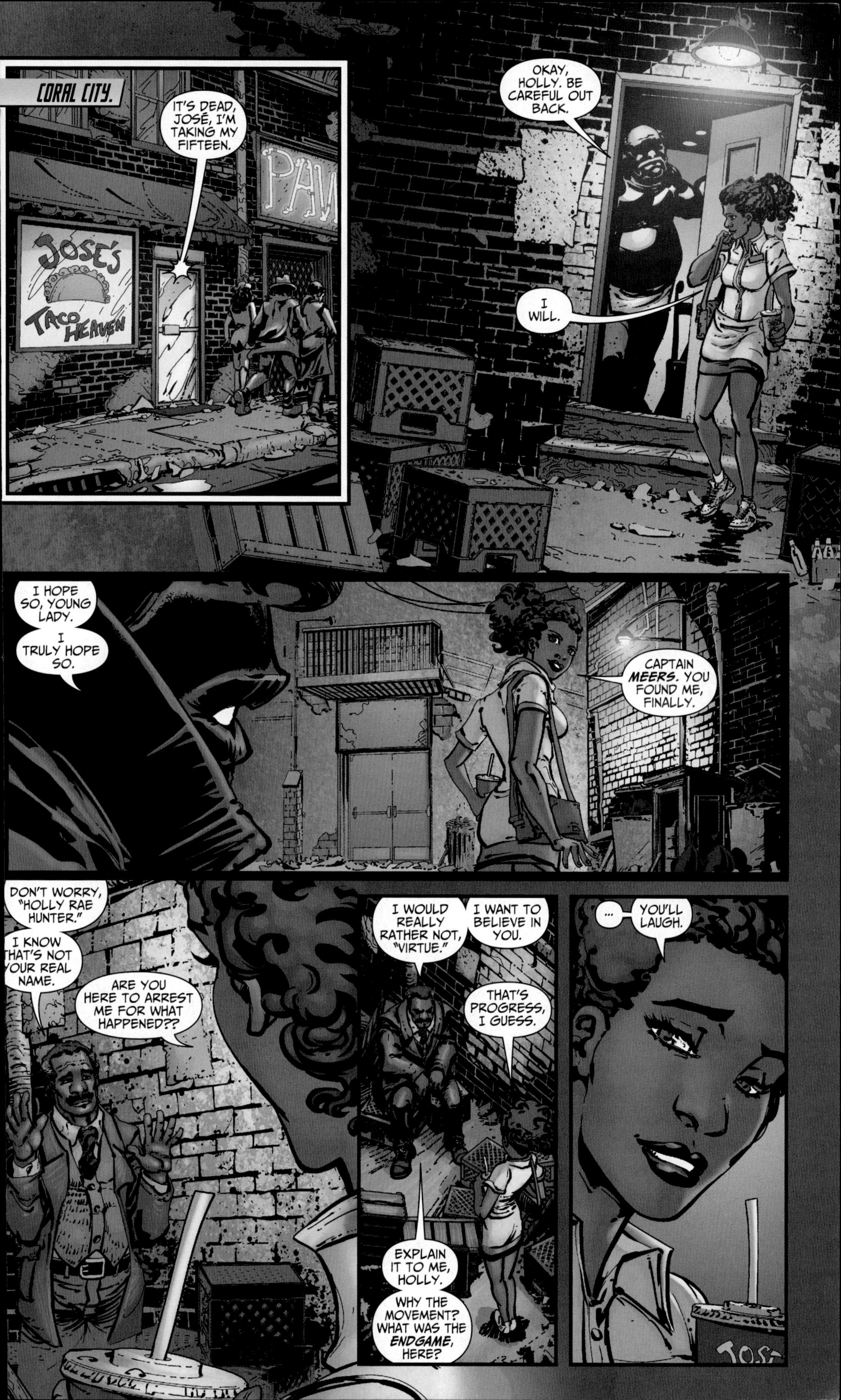

CORAL CITY.
IT'S DEAD, JOSÉ, I'M TAKING MY FIFTEEN.
JOSÉ'S TACO HEAVEN
PAW
OKAY, HOLLY. BE CAREFUL OUT BACK.
I WILL.
I HOPE SO, YOUNG LADY.
I TRULY HOPE SO.
CAPTAIN MEERS. YOU FOUND ME, FINALLY.
DON'T WORRY, "HOLLY RAE HUNTER."
I KNOW THAT'S NOT YOUR REAL NAME.
ARE YOU HERE TO ARREST ME FOR WHAT HAPPENED??
I WOULD REALLY RATHER NOT, "VIRTUE."
I WANT TO BELIEVE IN YOU.
THAT'S PROGRESS, I GUESS.
EXPLAIN IT TO ME, HOLLY.
WHY THE MOVEMENT? WHAT WAS THE ENDGAME, HERE?
...
YOU'LL LAUGH.

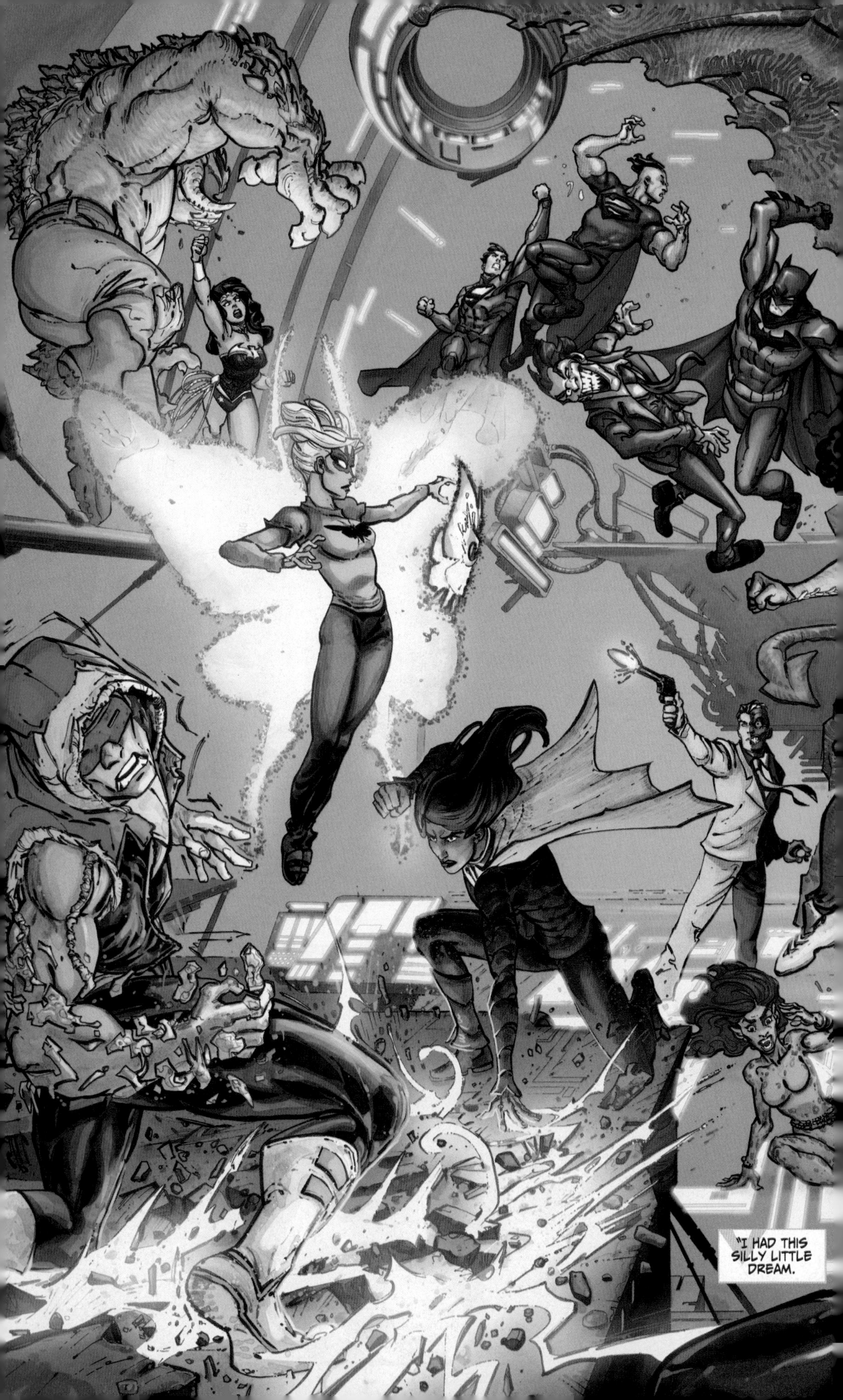
"I HAD THIS SILLY LITTLE DREAM.

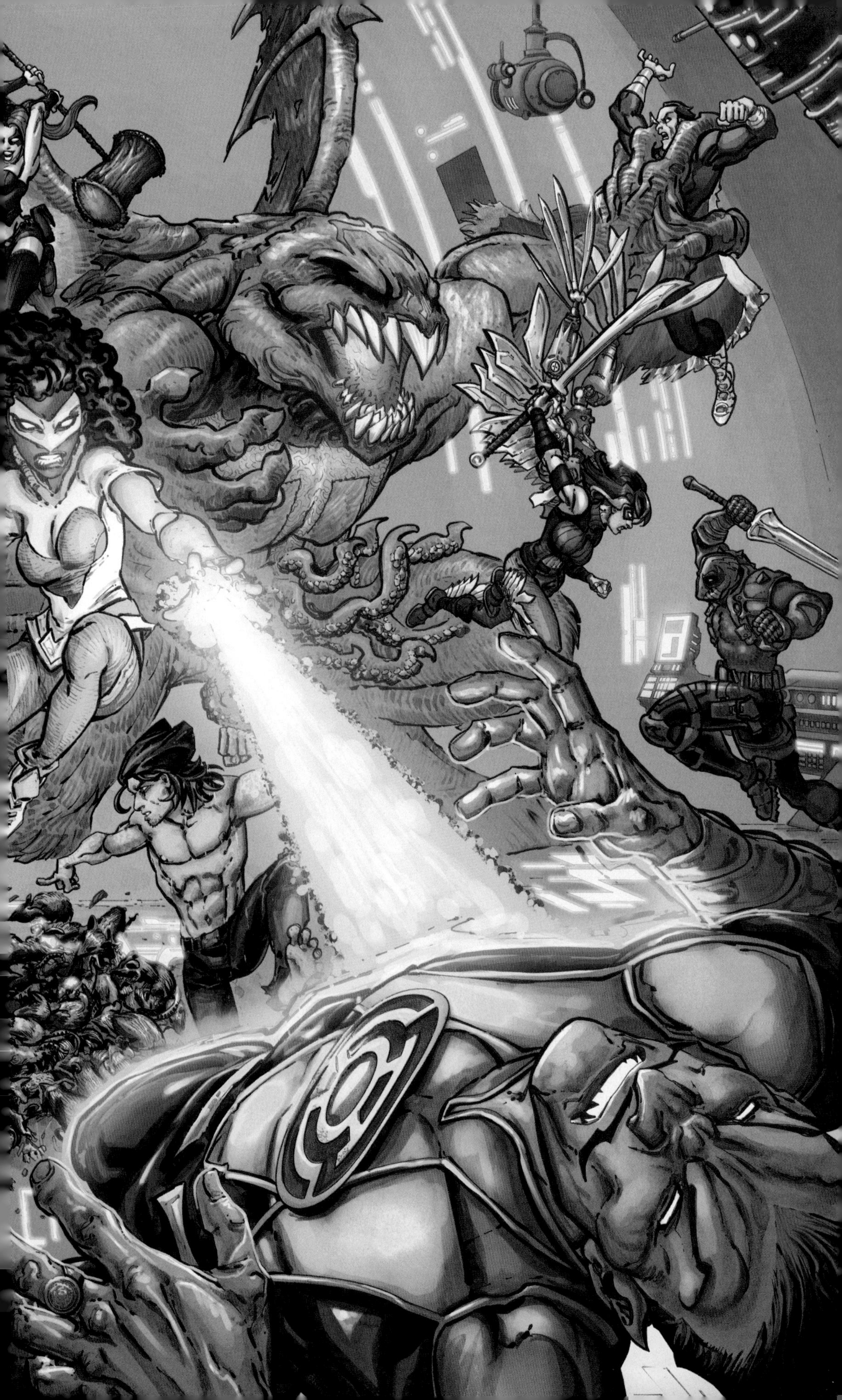

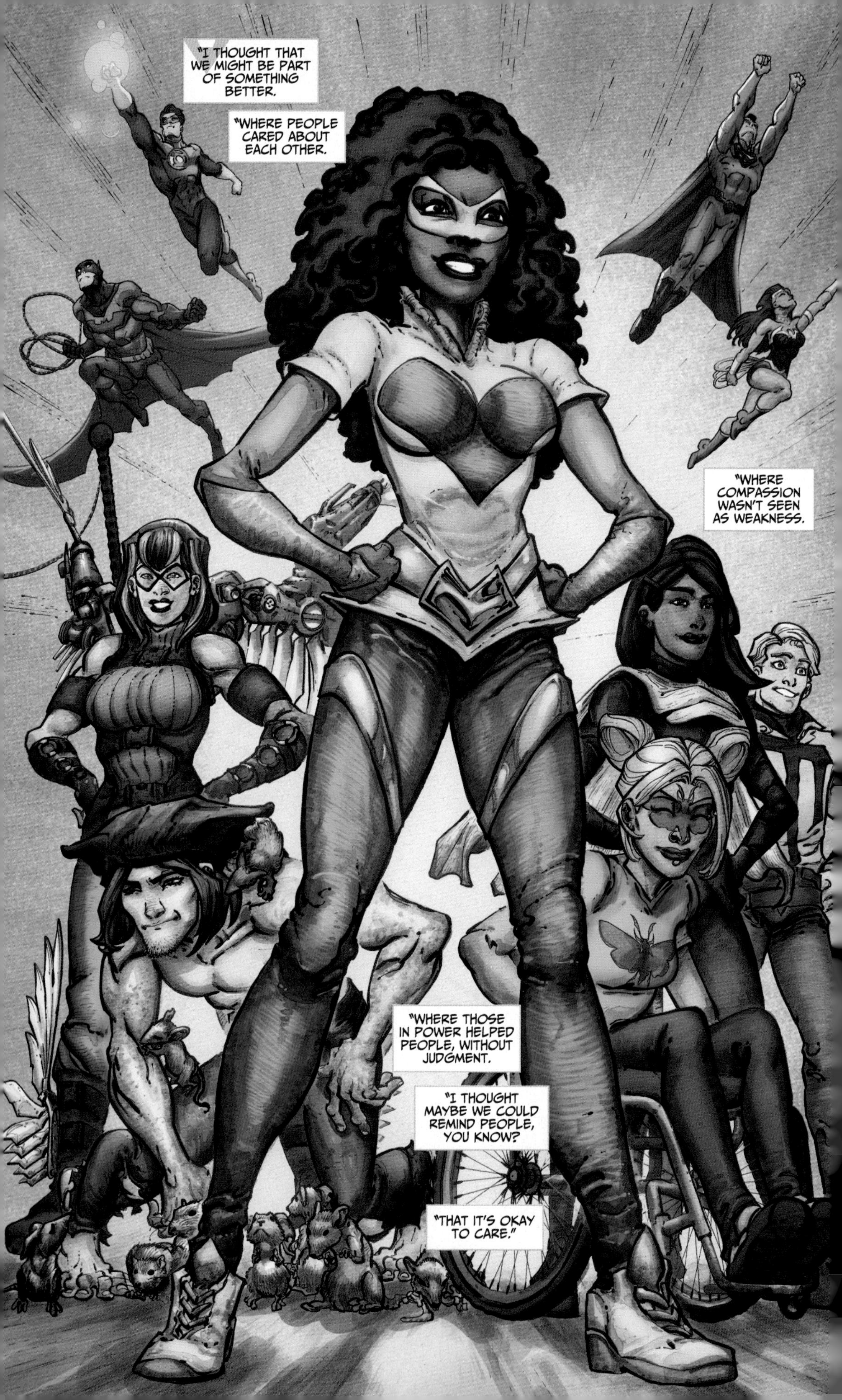

"I THOUGHT THAT WE MIGHT BE PART OF SOMETHING BETTER.
"WHERE PEOPLE CARED ABOUT EACH OTHER.
"WHERE COMPASSION WASN'T SEEN AS WEAKNESS.
"WHERE THOSE IN POWER HELPED PEOPLE, WITHOUT JUDGMENT.
"I THOUGHT MAYBE WE COULD REMIND PEOPLE, YOU KNOW?
"THAT IT'S OKAY TO CARE."

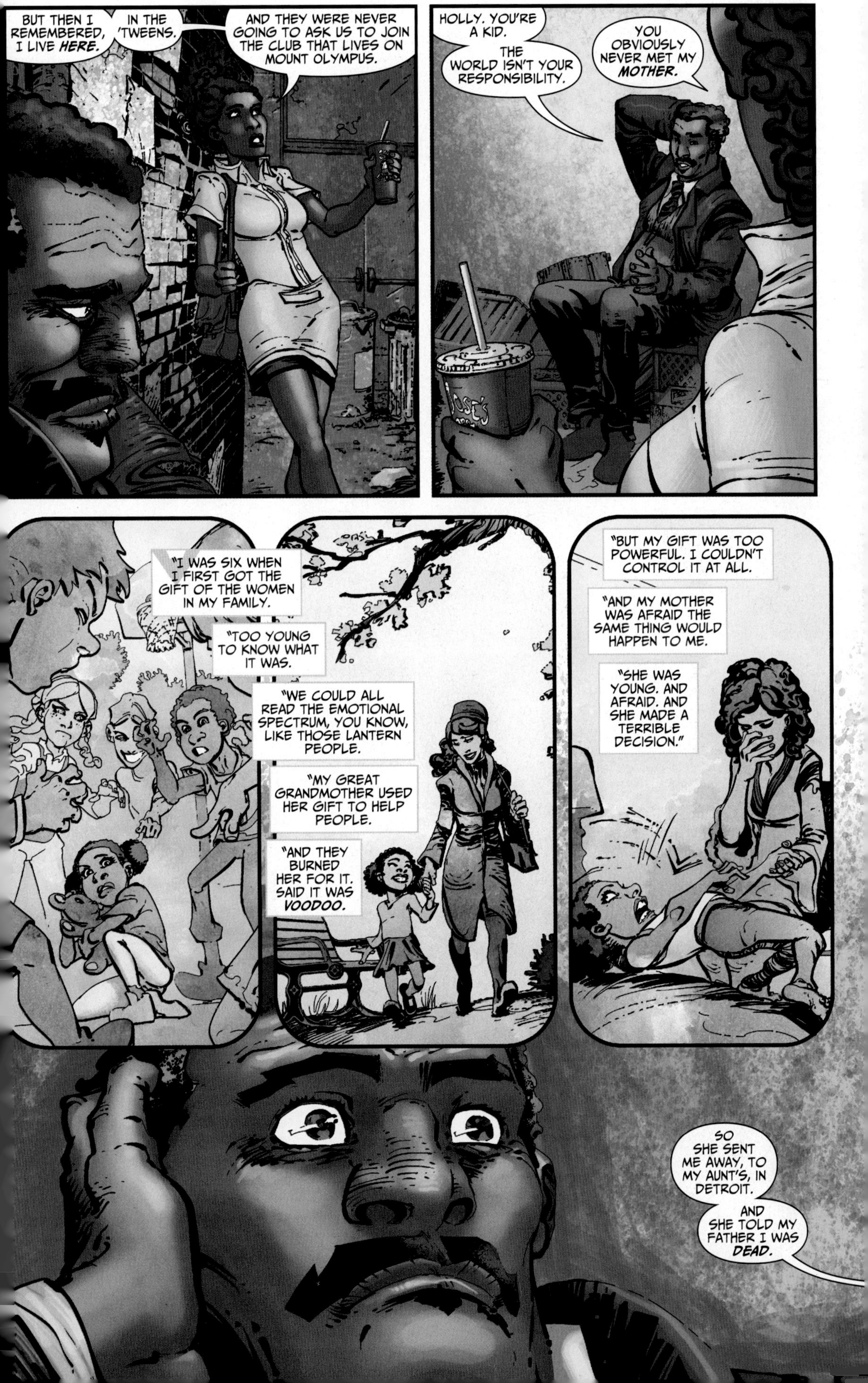

BUT THEN I REMEMBERED, I LIVE *HERE.*
IN THE 'TWEENS.
AND THEY WERE NEVER GOING TO ASK US TO JOIN THE CLUB THAT LIVES ON MOUNT OLYMPUS.
HOLLY. YOU'RE A KID.
THE WORLD ISN'T YOUR RESPONSIBILITY.
YOU OBVIOUSLY NEVER MET MY *MOTHER.*
"I WAS SIX WHEN I FIRST GOT THE GIFT OF THE WOMEN IN MY FAMILY.
"TOO YOUNG TO KNOW WHAT IT WAS.
"WE COULD ALL READ THE EMOTIONAL SPECTRUM, YOU KNOW, LIKE THOSE LANTERN PEOPLE.
"MY GREAT GRANDMOTHER USED HER GIFT TO HELP PEOPLE.
"AND THEY BURNED HER FOR IT. SAID IT WAS *VOODOO.*
"BUT MY GIFT WAS TOO POWERFUL. I COULDN'T CONTROL IT AT ALL.
"AND MY MOTHER WAS AFRAID THE SAME THING WOULD HAPPEN TO ME.
"SHE WAS YOUNG. AND AFRAID. AND SHE MADE A TERRIBLE DECISION."
SO SHE SENT ME AWAY, TO MY AUNT'S, IN DETROIT.
AND SHE TOLD MY FATHER I WAS *DEAD.*

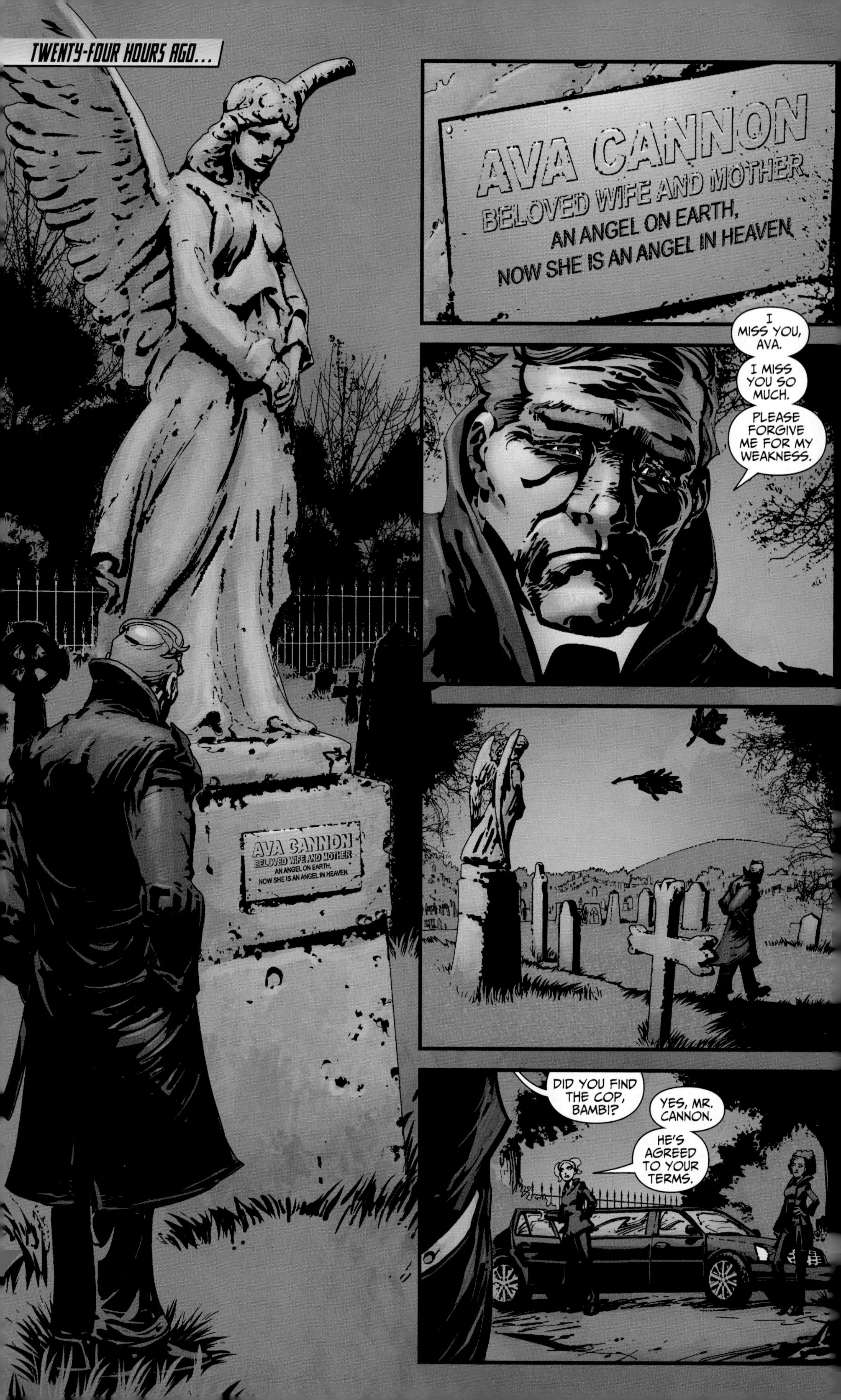

TWENTY-FOUR HOURS AGO...
AVA CANNON
BELOVED WIFE AND MOTHER
AN ANGEL ON EARTH,
NOW SHE IS AN ANGEL IN HEAVEN
AVA CANNON
BELOVED WIFE AND MOTHER
AN ANGEL ON EARTH,
NOW SHE IS AN ANGEL IN HEAVEN
I MISS YOU, AVA.
I MISS YOU SO MUCH.
PLEASE FORGIVE ME FOR MY WEAKNESS.
DID YOU FIND THE COP, BAMBI?
YES, MR. CANNON.
HE'S AGREED TO YOUR TERMS.

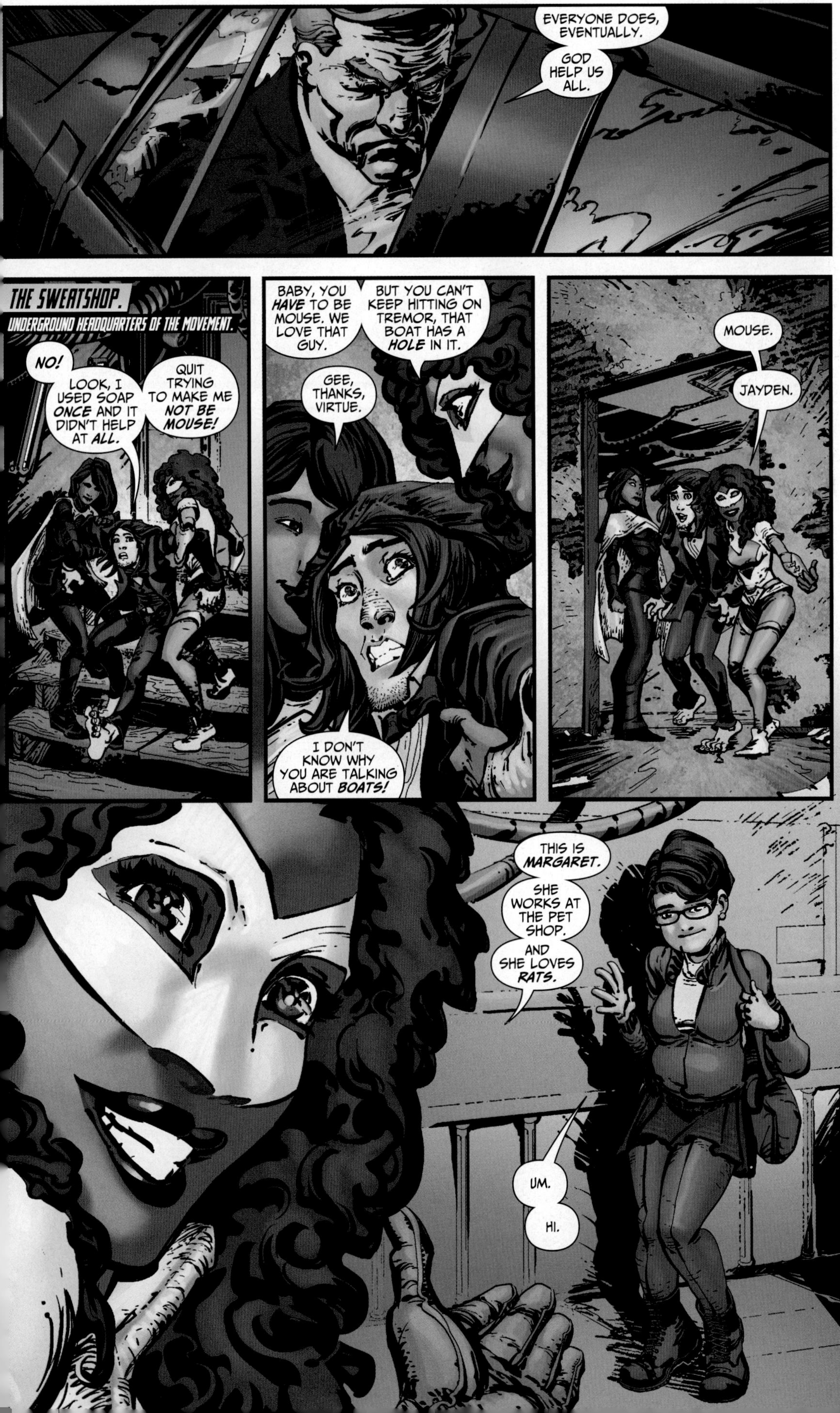

EVERYONE DOES, EVENTUALLY.
GOD HELP US ALL.
THE SWEATSHOP.
UNDERGROUND HEADQUARTERS OF THE MOVEMENT.
NO!
LOOK, I USED SOAP ONCE AND IT DIDN'T HELP AT ALL.
QUIT TRYING TO MAKE ME NOT BE MOUSE!
BABY, YOU HAVE TO BE MOUSE. WE LOVE THAT GUY.
BUT YOU CAN'T KEEP HITTING ON TREMOR, THAT BOAT HAS A HOLE IN IT.
GEE, THANKS, VIRTUE.
I DON'T KNOW WHY YOU ARE TALKING ABOUT BOATS!
MOUSE.
JAYDEN.
THIS IS MARGARET.
SHE WORKS AT THE PET SHOP.
AND SHE LOVES RATS.
UM.
HI.

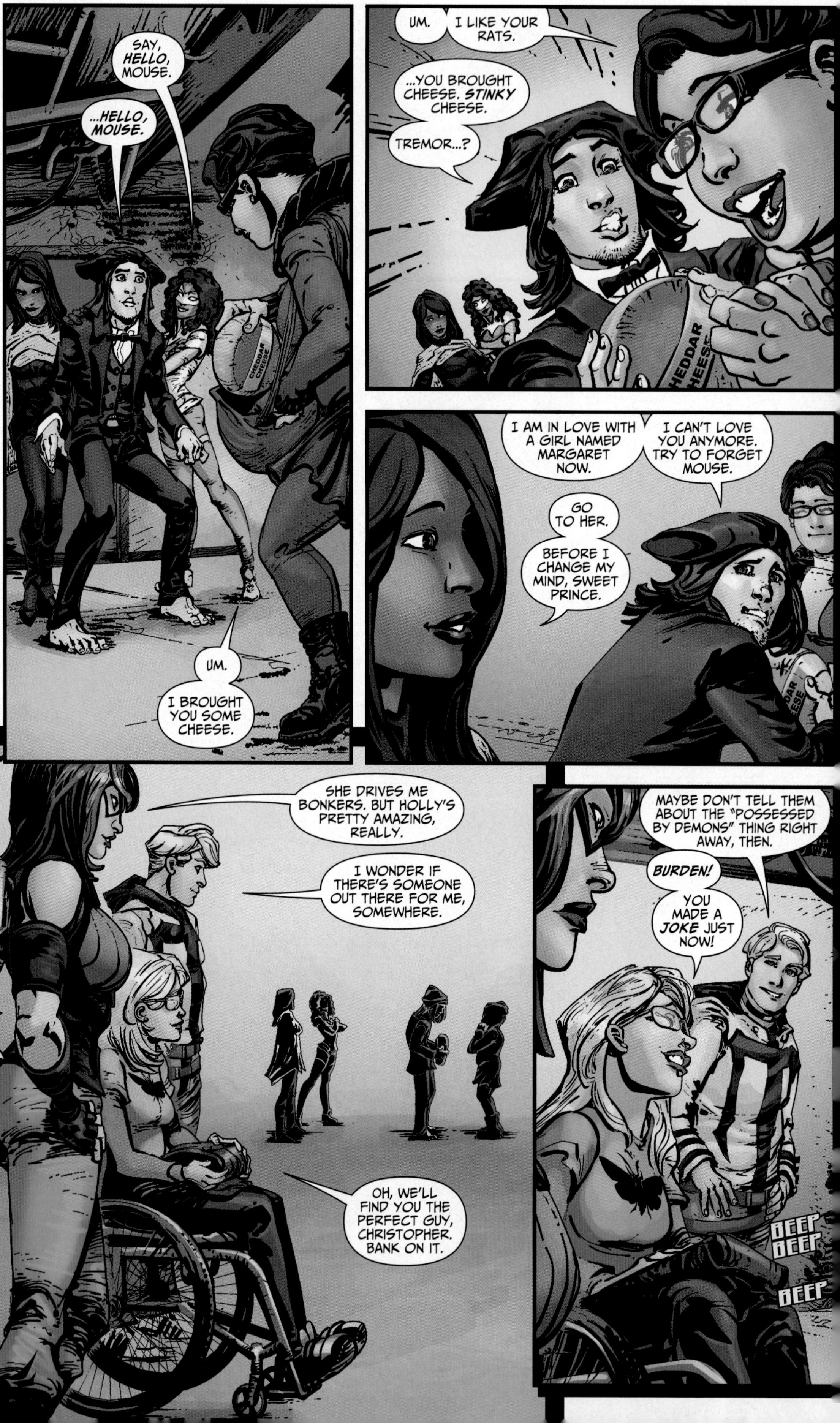
SAY, HELLO, MOUSE.
...HELLO, MOUSE.
CHEDDAR CHEESE
UM.
I BROUGHT YOU SOME CHEESE.
UM.
I LIKE YOUR RATS.
...YOU BROUGHT CHEESE. STINKY CHEESE.
TREMOR...?
CHEDDAR CHEESE
I AM IN LOVE WITH A GIRL NAMED MARGARET NOW.
I CAN'T LOVE YOU ANYMORE. TRY TO FORGET MOUSE.
GO TO HER.
BEFORE I CHANGE MY MIND, SWEET PRINCE.
SHE DRIVES ME BONKERS. BUT HOLLY'S PRETTY AMAZING, REALLY.
I WONDER IF THERE'S SOMEONE OUT THERE FOR ME, SOMEWHERE.
OH, WE'LL FIND YOU THE PERFECT GUY, CHRISTOPHER. BANK ON IT.
MAYBE DON'T TELL THEM ABOUT THE "POSSESSED BY DEMONS" THING RIGHT AWAY, THEN.
BURDEN!
YOU MADE A JOKE JUST NOW!
BEEP BEEP
BEEP

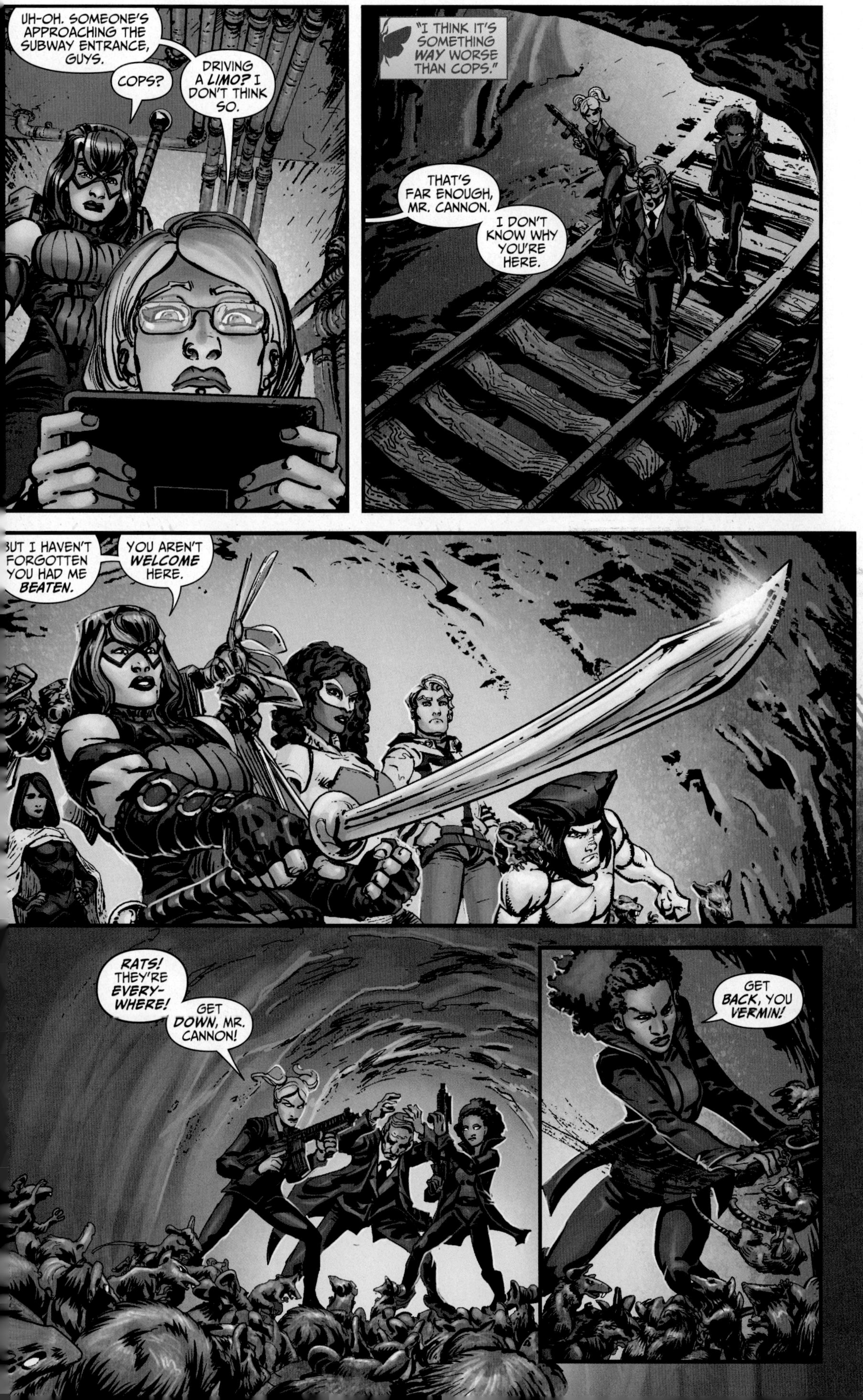
UH-OH. SOMEONE'S APPROACHING THE SUBWAY ENTRANCE, GUYS.
COPS?
DRIVING A LIMO? I DON'T THINK SO.
"I THINK IT'S SOMETHING WAY WORSE THAN COPS."
THAT'S FAR ENOUGH, MR. CANNON.
I DON'T KNOW WHY YOU'RE HERE.
BUT I HAVEN'T FORGOTTEN YOU HAD ME BEATEN.
YOU AREN'T WELCOME HERE.
RATS! THEY'RE EVERY-WHERE!
GET DOWN, MR. CANNON!
GET BACK, YOU VERMIN!

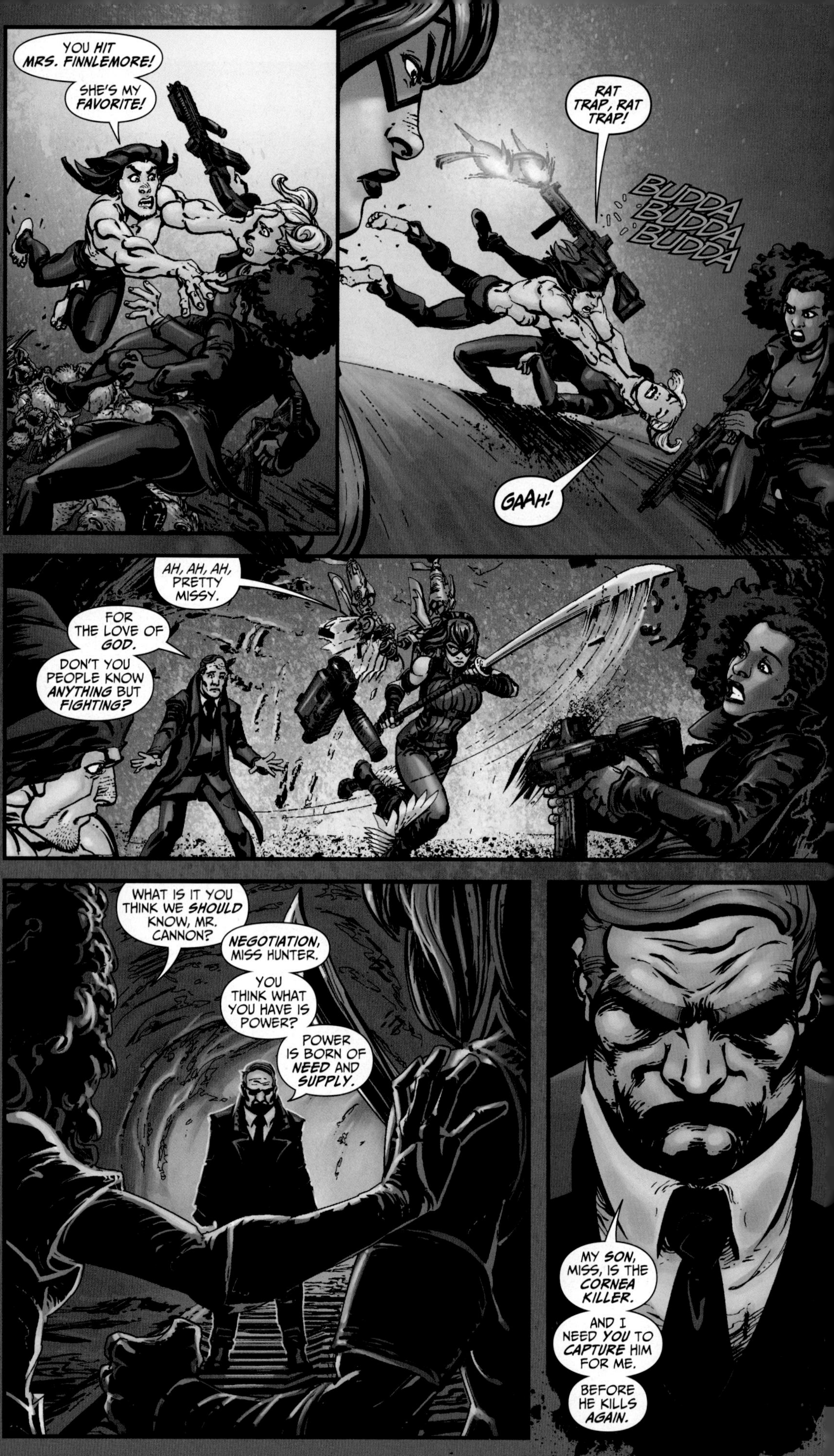

YOU HIT MRS. FINNLEMORE!
SHE'S MY FAVORITE!
RAT TRAP, RAT TRAP!
BUDDA BUDDA BUDDA
GAAH!
AH, AH, AH, PRETTY MISSY.
FOR THE LOVE OF GOD.
DON'T YOU PEOPLE KNOW ANYTHING BUT FIGHTING?
WHAT IS IT YOU THINK WE SHOULD KNOW, MR. CANNON?
NEGOTIATION, MISS HUNTER.
YOU THINK WHAT YOU HAVE IS POWER?
POWER IS BORN OF NEED AND SUPPLY.
MY SON, MISS, IS THE CORNEA KILLER.
AND I NEED YOU TO CAPTURE HIM FOR ME.
BEFORE HE KILLS AGAIN.

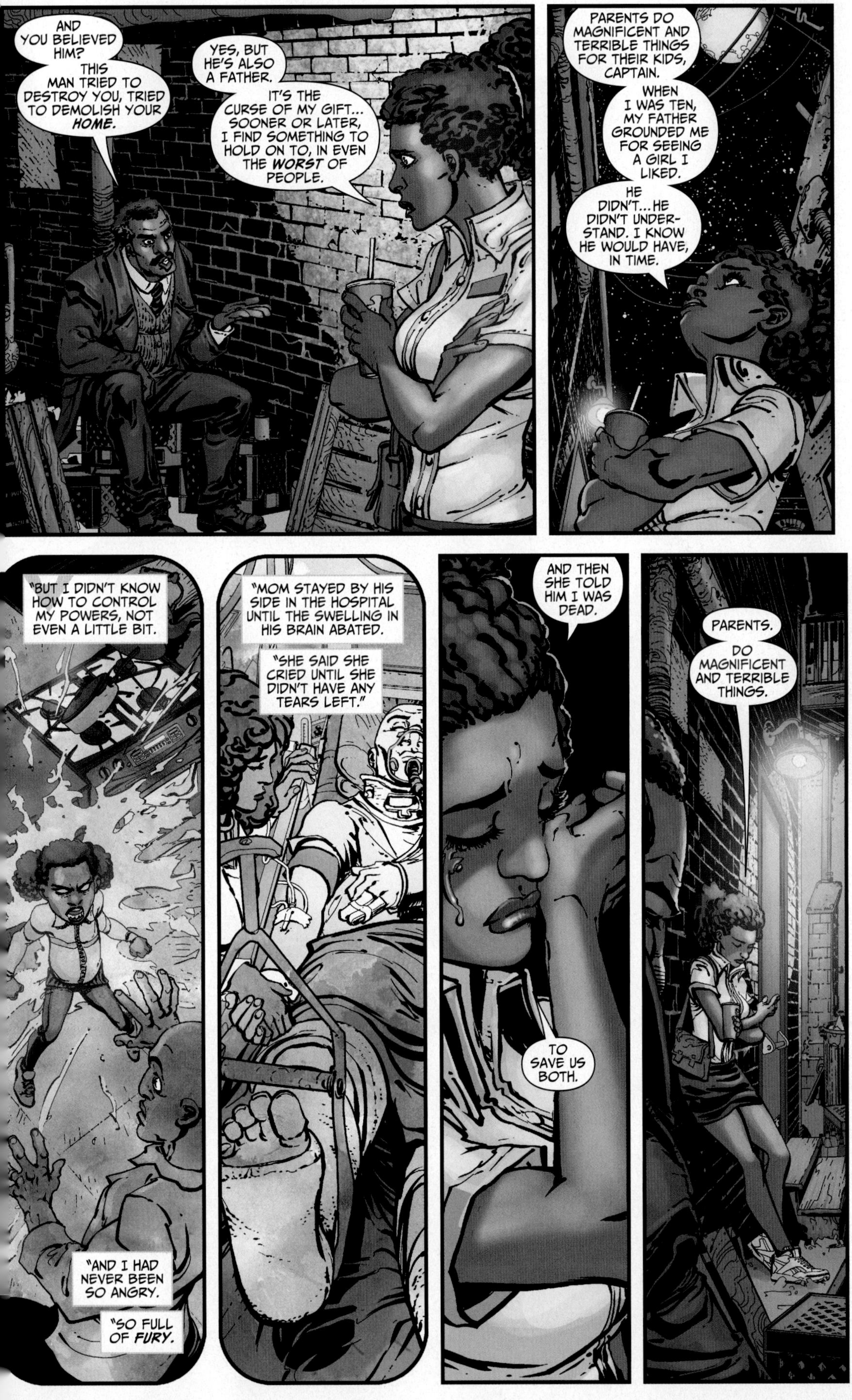
AND YOU BELIEVED HIM?
THIS MAN TRIED TO DESTROY YOU, TRIED TO DEMOLISH YOUR HOME.
YES, BUT HE'S ALSO A FATHER.
IT'S THE CURSE OF MY GIFT... SOONER OR LATER, I FIND SOMETHING TO HOLD ON TO, IN EVEN THE WORST OF PEOPLE.
PARENTS DO MAGNIFICENT AND TERRIBLE THINGS FOR THEIR KIDS, CAPTAIN.
WHEN I WAS TEN, MY FATHER GROUNDED ME FOR SEEING A GIRL I LIKED.
HE DIDN'T... HE DIDN'T UNDER-STAND. I KNOW HE WOULD HAVE, IN TIME.
"BUT I DIDN'T KNOW HOW TO CONTROL MY POWERS, NOT EVEN A LITTLE BIT.
"AND I HAD NEVER BEEN SO ANGRY.
"SO FULL OF FURY.
"MOM STAYED BY HIS SIDE IN THE HOSPITAL UNTIL THE SWELLING IN HIS BRAIN ABATED.
"SHE SAID SHE CRIED UNTIL SHE DIDN'T HAVE ANY TEARS LEFT."
AND THEN SHE TOLD HIM I WAS DEAD.
TO SAVE US BOTH.
PARENTS.
DO MAGNIFICENT AND TERRIBLE THINGS.

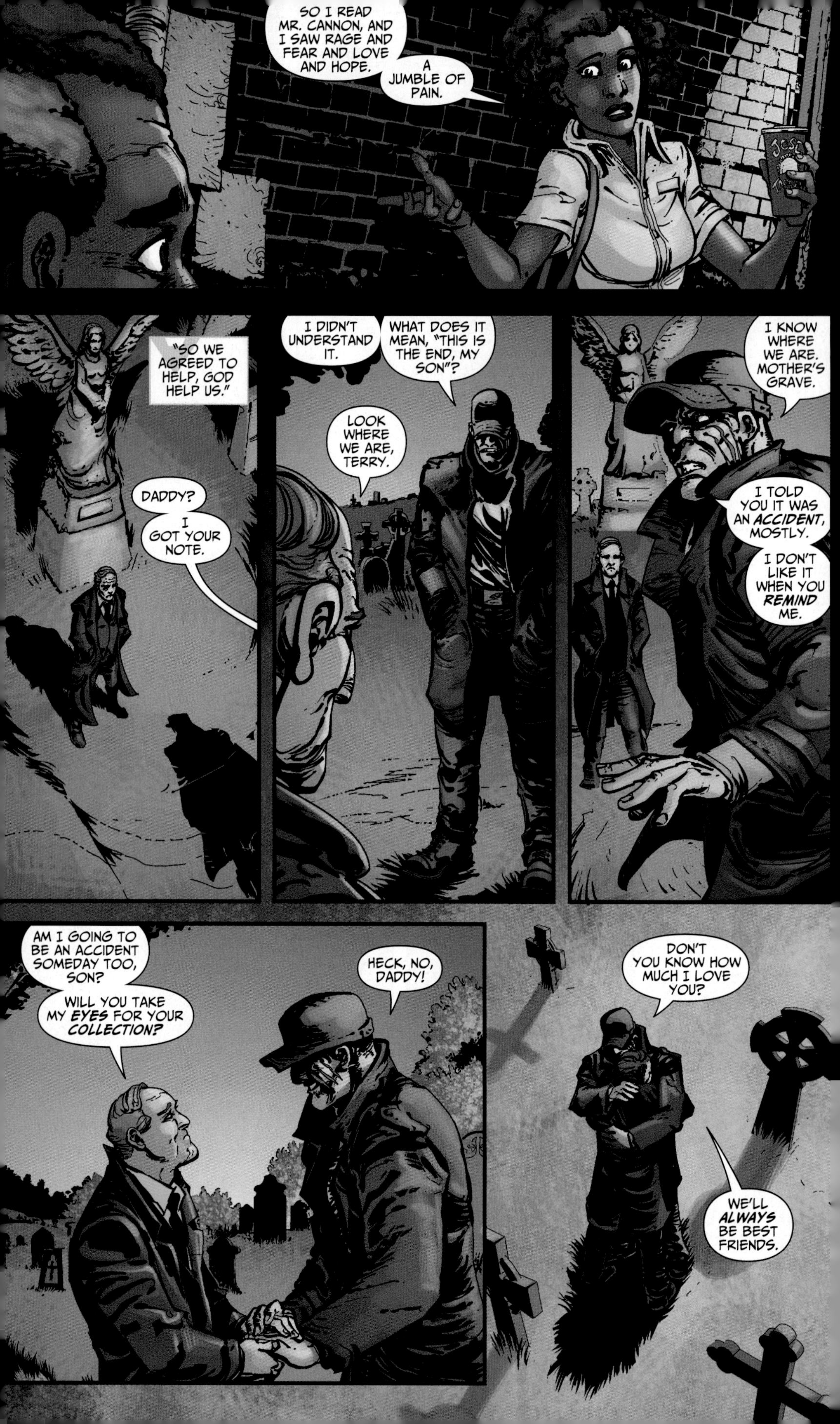
SO I READ MR. CANNON, AND I SAW RAGE AND FEAR AND LOVE AND HOPE.
A JUMBLE OF PAIN.
"SO WE AGREED TO HELP, GOD HELP US."
DADDY?
I GOT YOUR NOTE.
I DIDN'T UNDERSTAND IT.
WHAT DOES IT MEAN, "THIS IS THE END, MY SON"?
LOOK WHERE WE ARE, TERRY.
I KNOW WHERE WE ARE. MOTHER'S GRAVE.
I TOLD YOU IT WAS AN ACCIDENT, MOSTLY.
I DON'T LIKE IT WHEN YOU REMIND ME.
AM I GOING TO BE AN ACCIDENT SOMEDAY TOO, SON?
WILL YOU TAKE MY EYES FOR YOUR COLLECTION?
HECK, NO, DADDY!
DON'T YOU KNOW HOW MUCH I LOVE YOU?
WE'LL ALWAYS BE BEST FRIENDS.

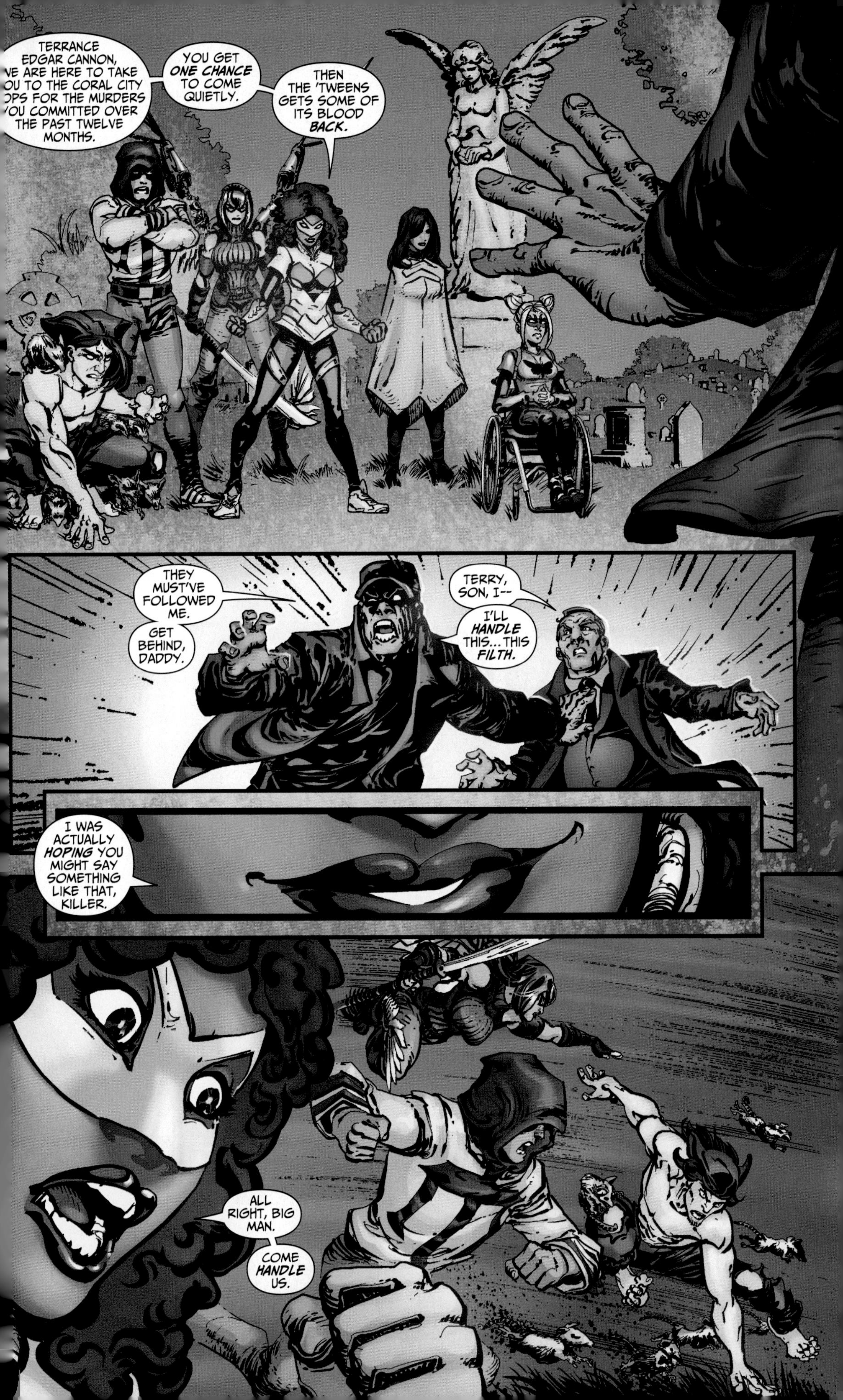

TERRANCE EDGAR CANNON, WE ARE HERE TO TAKE YOU TO THE CORAL CITY COPS FOR THE MURDERS YOU COMMITTED OVER THE PAST TWELVE MONTHS.
YOU GET ONE CHANCE TO COME QUIETLY.
THEN THE 'TWEENS GETS SOME OF ITS BLOOD BACK.
THEY MUST'VE FOLLOWED ME.
GET BEHIND, DADDY.
TERRY, SON, I--
I'LL HANDLE THIS...THIS FILTH.
I WAS ACTUALLY HOPING YOU MIGHT SAY SOMETHING LIKE THAT, KILLER.
ALL RIGHT, BIG MAN.
COME HANDLE US.

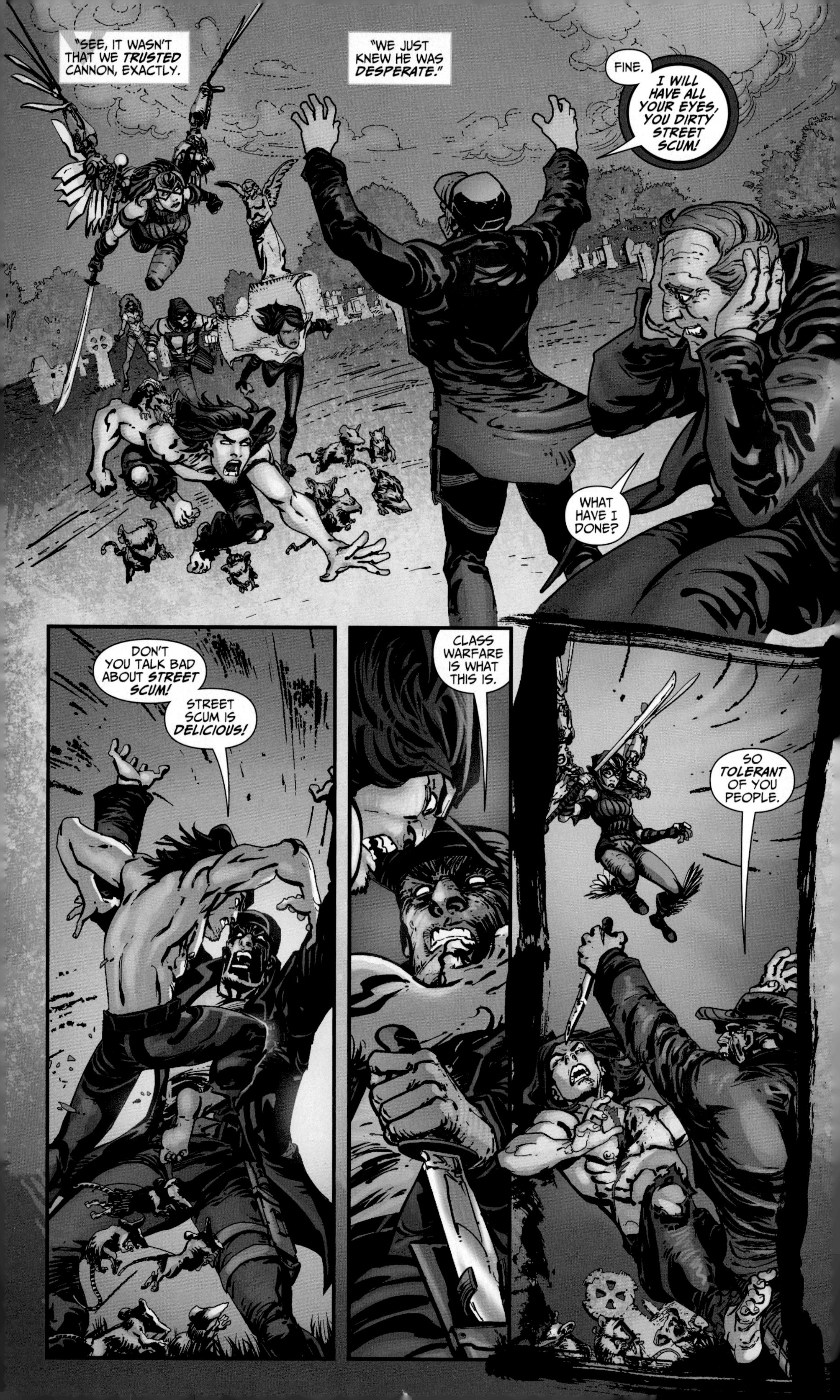
"SEE, IT WASN'T THAT WE TRUSTED CANNON, EXACTLY.
"WE JUST KNEW HE WAS DESPERATE."
FINE.
I WILL HAVE ALL YOUR EYES, YOU DIRTY STREET SCUM!
WHAT HAVE I DONE?
DON'T YOU TALK BAD ABOUT STREET SCUM!
STREET SCUM IS DELICIOUS!
CLASS WARFARE IS WHAT THIS IS.
SO TOLERANT OF YOU PEOPLE.

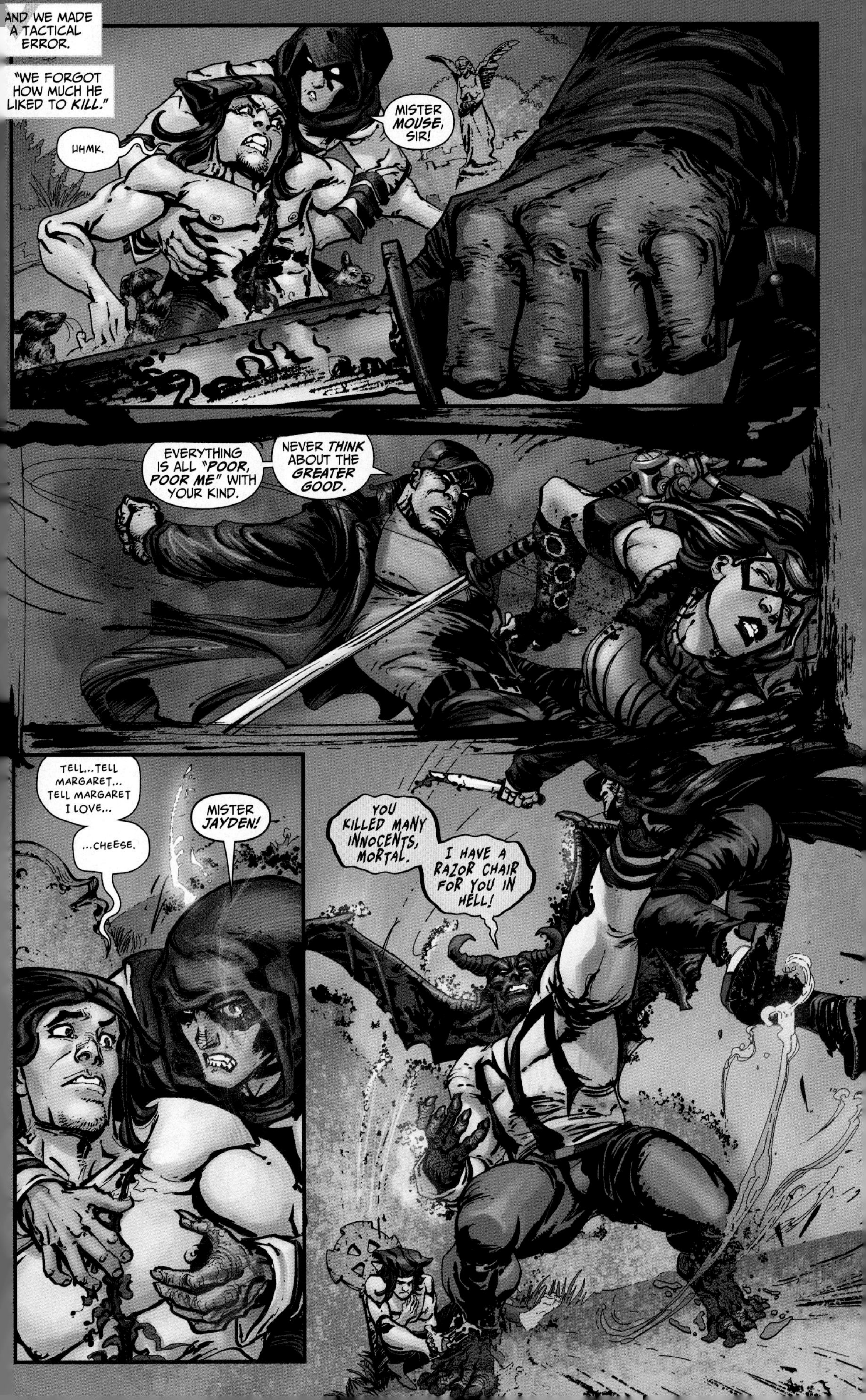
AND WE MADE A TACTICAL ERROR.
"WE FORGOT HOW MUCH HE LIKED TO KILL."
UHMK.
MISTER MOUSE, SIR!
EVERYTHING IS ALL "POOR, POOR ME" WITH YOUR KIND.
NEVER THINK ABOUT THE GREATER GOOD.
TELL...TELL MARGARET... TELL MARGARET I LOVE...
...CHEESE.
MISTER JAYDEN!
YOU KILLED MANY INNOCENTS, MORTAL.
I HAVE A RAZOR CHAIR FOR YOU IN HELL!

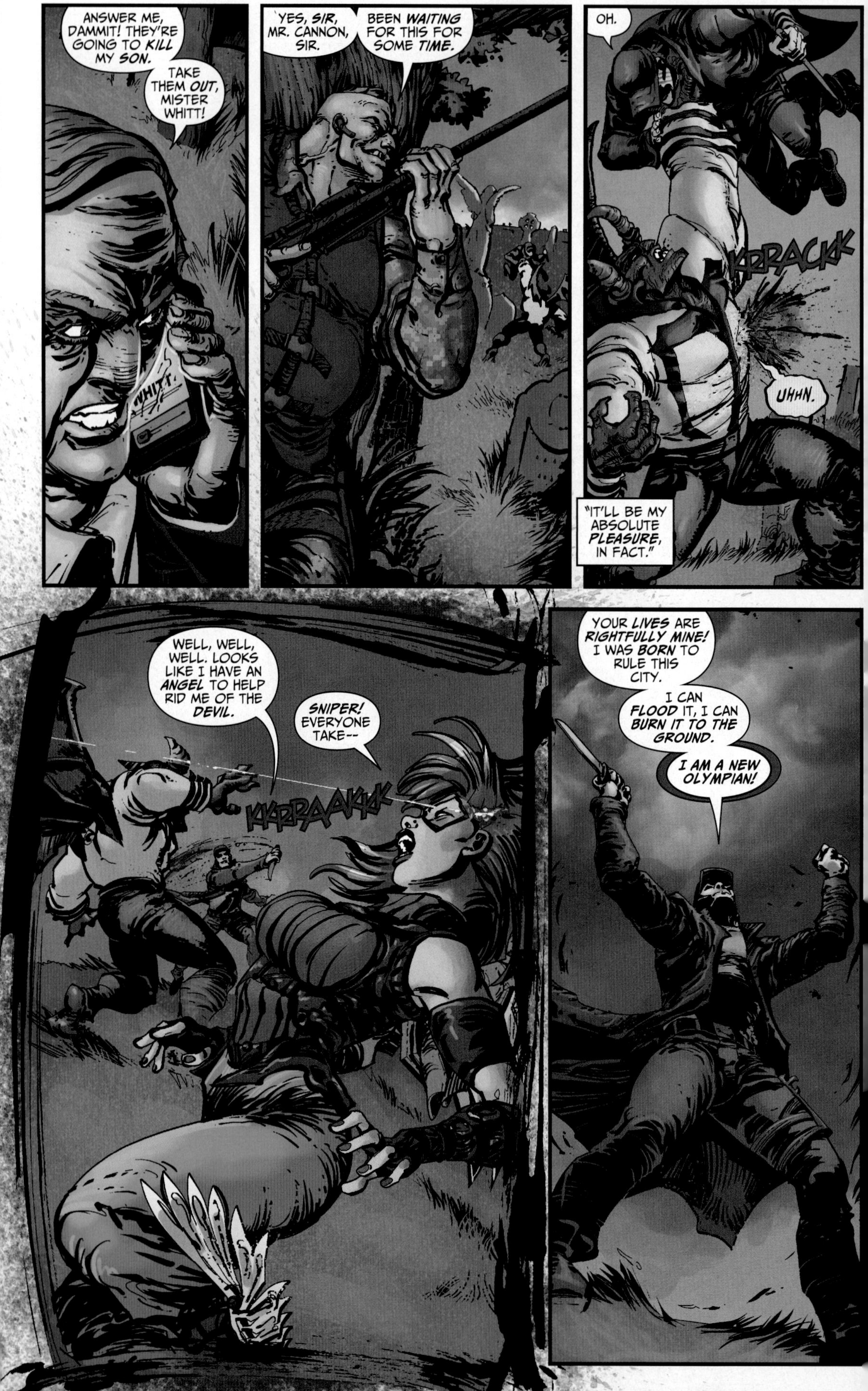

ANSWER ME, DAMMIT! THEY'RE GOING TO KILL MY SON.
TAKE THEM OUT, MISTER WHITT!
WHITT
YES, SIR, MR. CANNON, SIR.
BEEN WAITING FOR THIS FOR SOME TIME.
OH.
KRRACKK
UHHN.
"IT'LL BE MY ABSOLUTE PLEASURE, IN FACT."
WELL, WELL, WELL. LOOKS LIKE I HAVE AN ANGEL TO HELP RID ME OF THE DEVIL.
SNIPER! EVERYONE TAKE--
KKRRAAKKK
YOUR LIVES ARE RIGHTFULLY MINE! I WAS BORN TO RULE THIS CITY.
I CAN FLOOD IT, I CAN BURN IT TO THE GROUND.
I AM A NEW OLYMPIAN!

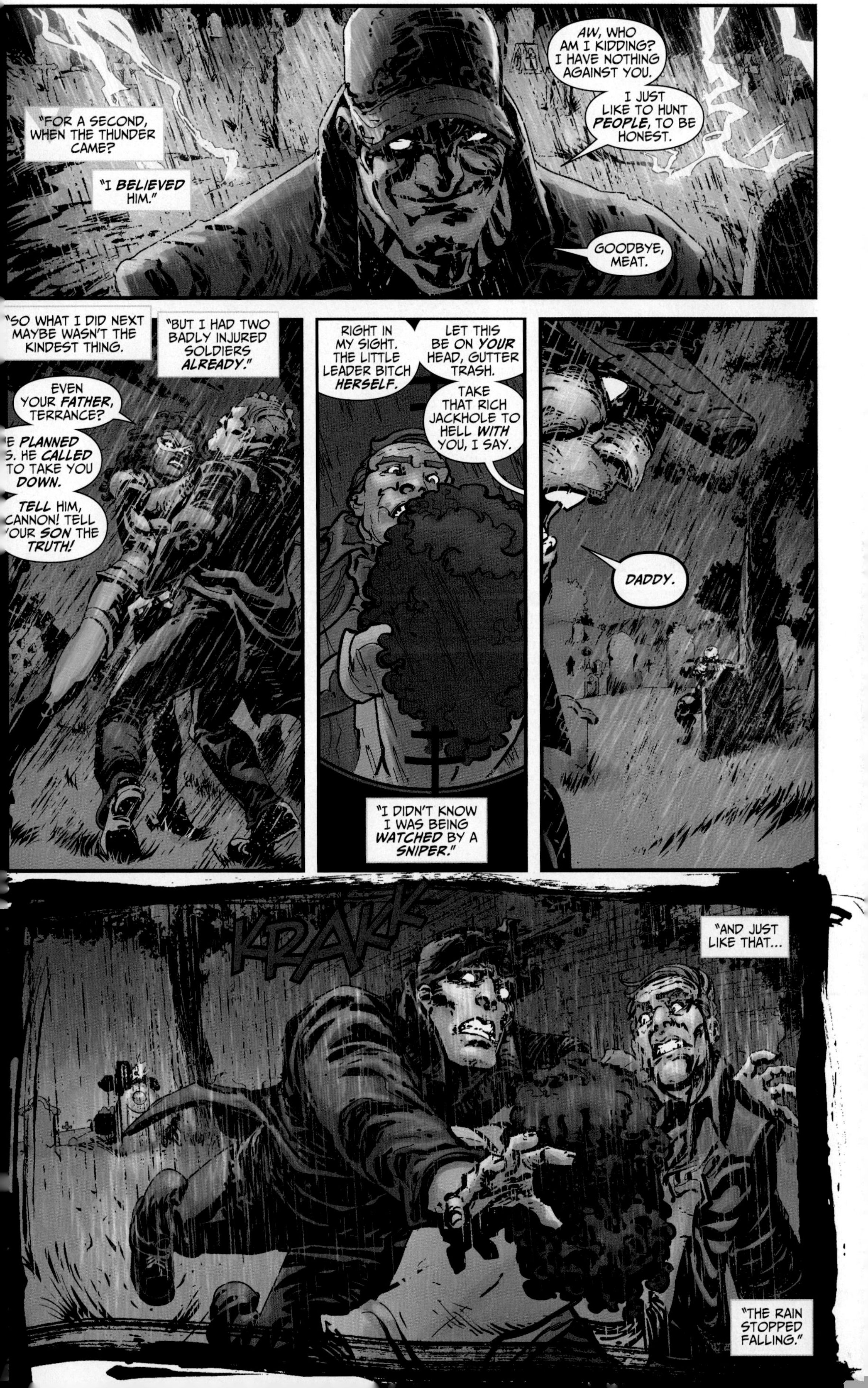
"FOR A SECOND, WHEN THE THUNDER CAME?
"I BELIEVED HIM."
AW, WHO AM I KIDDING? I HAVE NOTHING AGAINST YOU.
I JUST LIKE TO HUNT PEOPLE, TO BE HONEST.
GOODBYE, MEAT.
"SO WHAT I DID NEXT MAYBE WASN'T THE KINDEST THING.
"BUT I HAD TWO BADLY INJURED SOLDIERS ALREADY."
EVEN YOUR FATHER, TERRANCE?
E PLANNED S. HE CALLED TO TAKE YOU DOWN.
TELL HIM, CANNON! TELL OUR SON THE TRUTH!
RIGHT IN MY SIGHT. THE LITTLE LEADER BITCH HERSELF.
LET THIS BE ON YOUR HEAD, GUTTER TRASH.
TAKE THAT RICH JACKHOLE TO HELL WITH YOU, I SAY.
"I DIDN'T KNOW I WAS BEING WATCHED BY A SNIPER."
DADDY.
KRAKK
"AND JUST LIKE THAT...
"THE RAIN STOPPED FALLING."

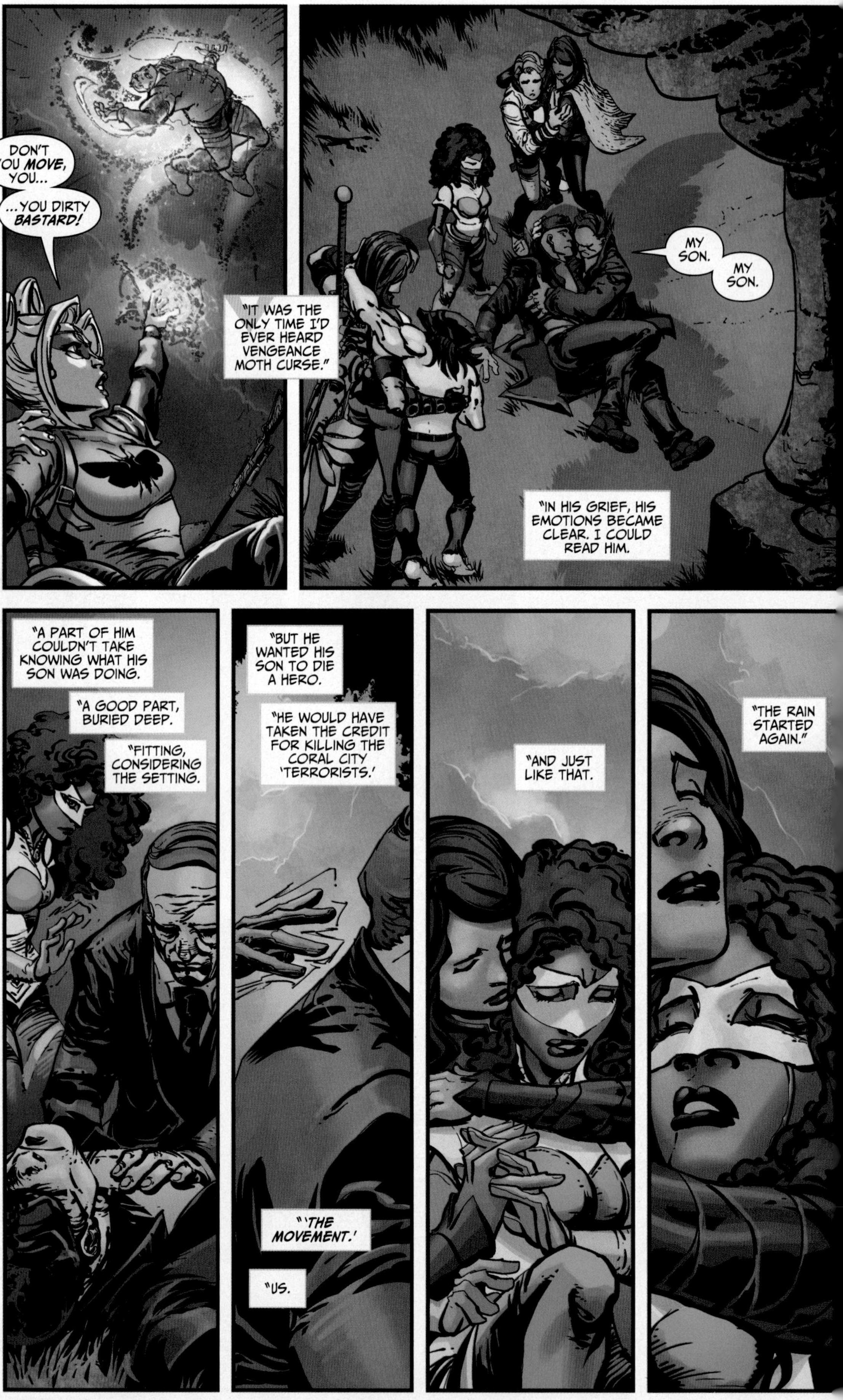
DON'T YOU *MOVE*, YOU...
...YOU DIRTY *BASTARD!*
"IT WAS THE ONLY TIME I'D EVER HEARD VENGEANCE MOTH CURSE."
MY SON.
MY SON.
"IN HIS GRIEF, HIS EMOTIONS BECAME CLEAR. I COULD READ HIM.
"A PART OF HIM COULDN'T TAKE KNOWING WHAT HIS SON WAS DOING.
"A GOOD PART, BURIED DEEP.
"FITTING, CONSIDERING THE SETTING.
"BUT HE WANTED HIS SON TO DIE A HERO.
"HE WOULD HAVE TAKEN THE CREDIT FOR KILLING THE CORAL CITY 'TERRORISTS.'
"'*THE MOVEMENT.*'
"US.
"AND JUST LIKE THAT.
"THE RAIN STARTED AGAIN."

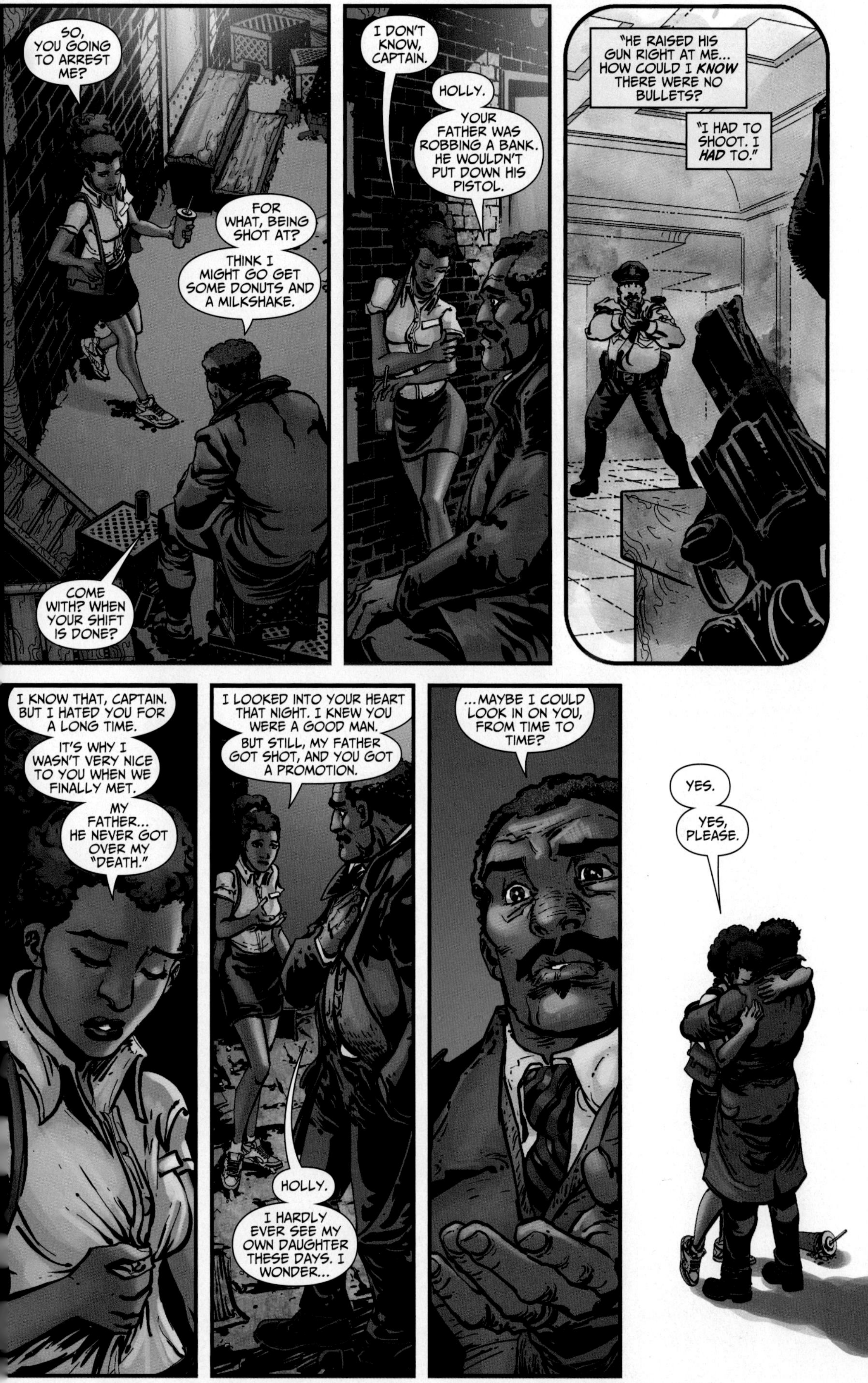
SO, YOU GOING TO ARREST ME?
FOR WHAT, BEING SHOT AT?
THINK I MIGHT GO GET SOME DONUTS AND A MILKSHAKE.
COME WITH? WHEN YOUR SHIFT IS DONE?
I DON'T KNOW, CAPTAIN.
HOLLY.
YOUR FATHER WAS ROBBING A BANK. HE WOULDN'T PUT DOWN HIS PISTOL.
"HE RAISED HIS GUN RIGHT AT ME... HOW COULD I KNOW THERE WERE NO BULLETS?
"I HAD TO SHOOT. I HAD TO."
I KNOW THAT, CAPTAIN. BUT I HATED YOU FOR A LONG TIME.
IT'S WHY I WASN'T VERY NICE TO YOU WHEN WE FINALLY MET.
MY FATHER... HE NEVER GOT OVER MY "DEATH."
I LOOKED INTO YOUR HEART THAT NIGHT. I KNEW YOU WERE A GOOD MAN.
BUT STILL, MY FATHER GOT SHOT, AND YOU GOT A PROMOTION.
HOLLY.
I HARDLY EVER SEE MY OWN DAUGHTER THESE DAYS. I WONDER...
...MAYBE I COULD LOOK IN ON YOU, FROM TIME TO TIME?
YES.
YES, PLEASE.

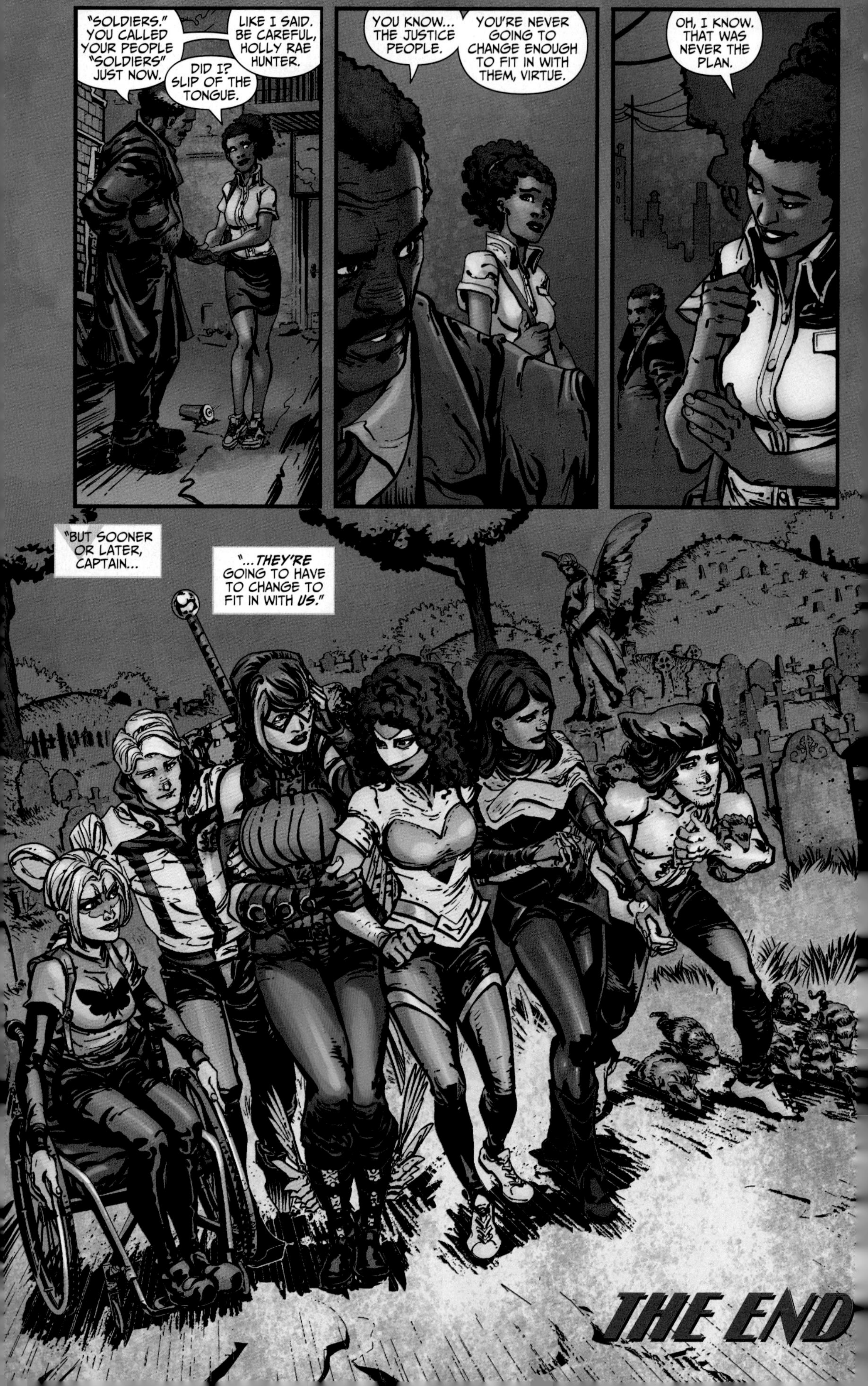
"SOLDIERS." YOU CALLED YOUR PEOPLE "SOLDIERS" JUST NOW.
LIKE I SAID. BE CAREFUL, HOLLY RAE HUNTER.
DID I? SLIP OF THE TONGUE.
YOU KNOW... THE JUSTICE PEOPLE.
YOU'RE NEVER GOING TO CHANGE ENOUGH TO FIT IN WITH THEM, VIRTUE.
OH, I KNOW. THAT WAS NEVER THE PLAN.
"BUT SOONER OR LATER, CAPTAIN...
"...*THEY'RE* GOING TO HAVE TO CHANGE TO FIT IN WITH *US*."
THE END

THE MOVEMENT
SKETCHBOOK BY FREDDIE WILLIAMS II

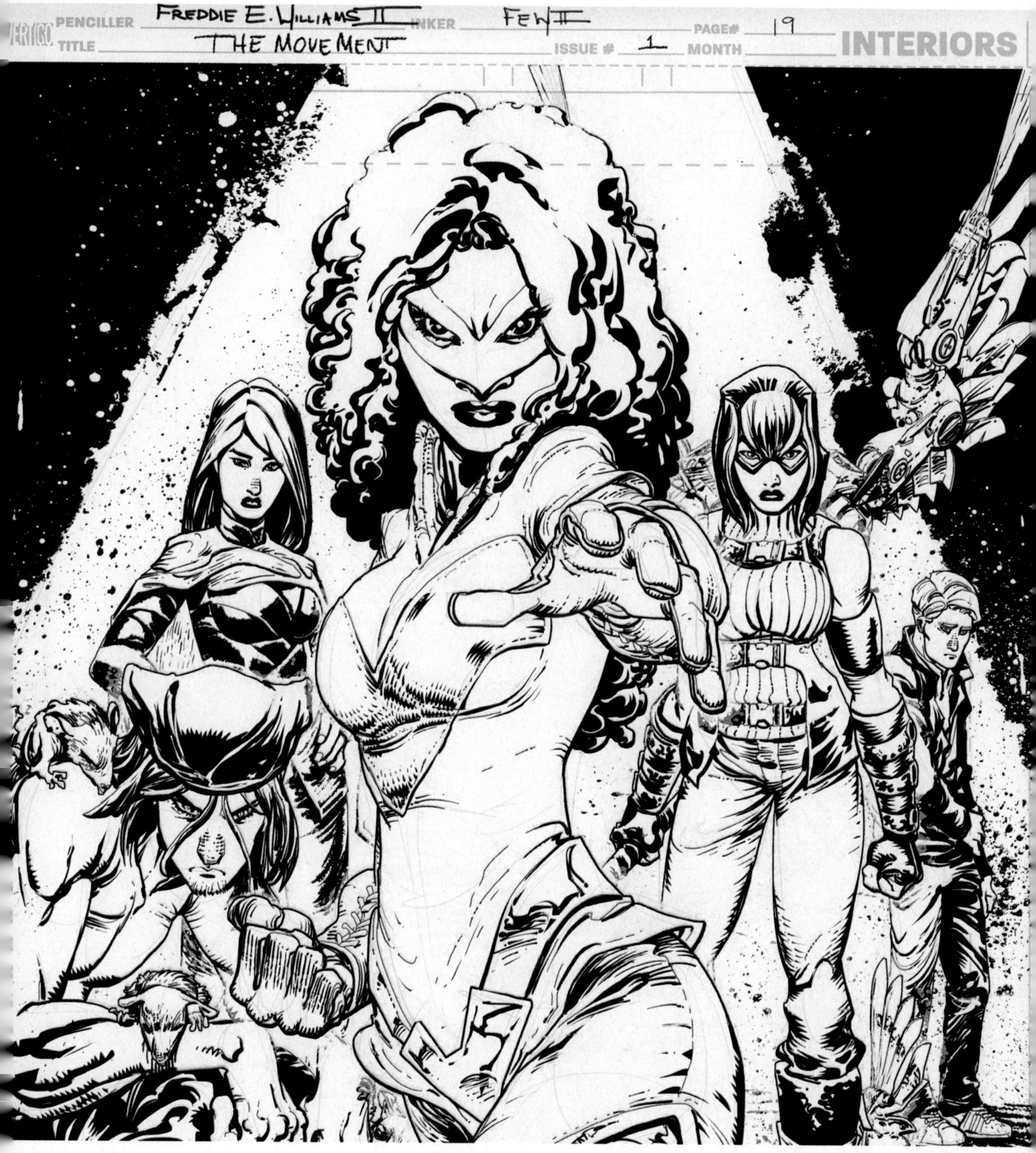

PENCILLER FREDDIE E. WILLIAMS II INKER FEW II PAGE# 19
TITLE THE MOVEMENT ISSUE # 1 MONTH
INTERIORS

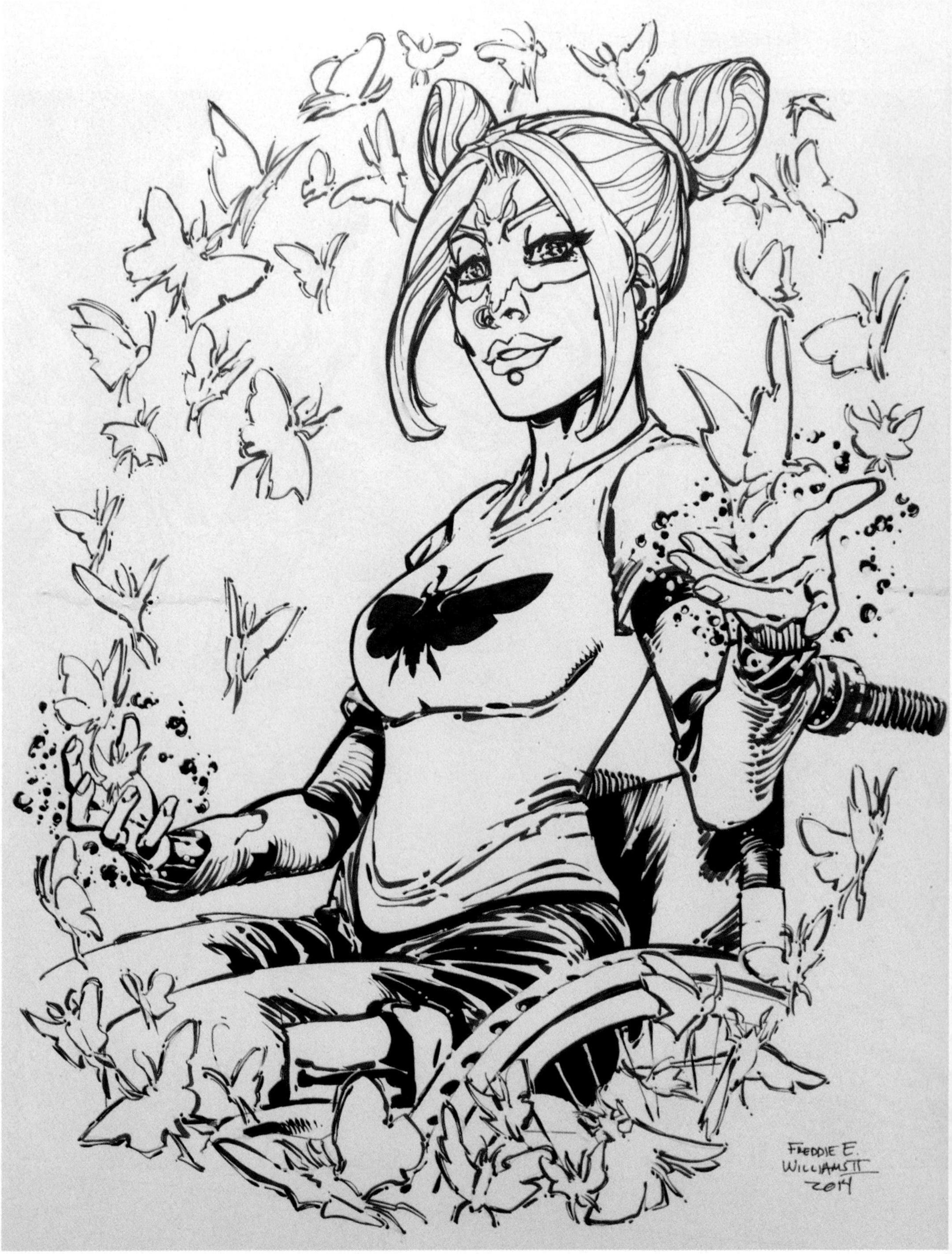
FREDDIE E.
WILLIAMS II
2014

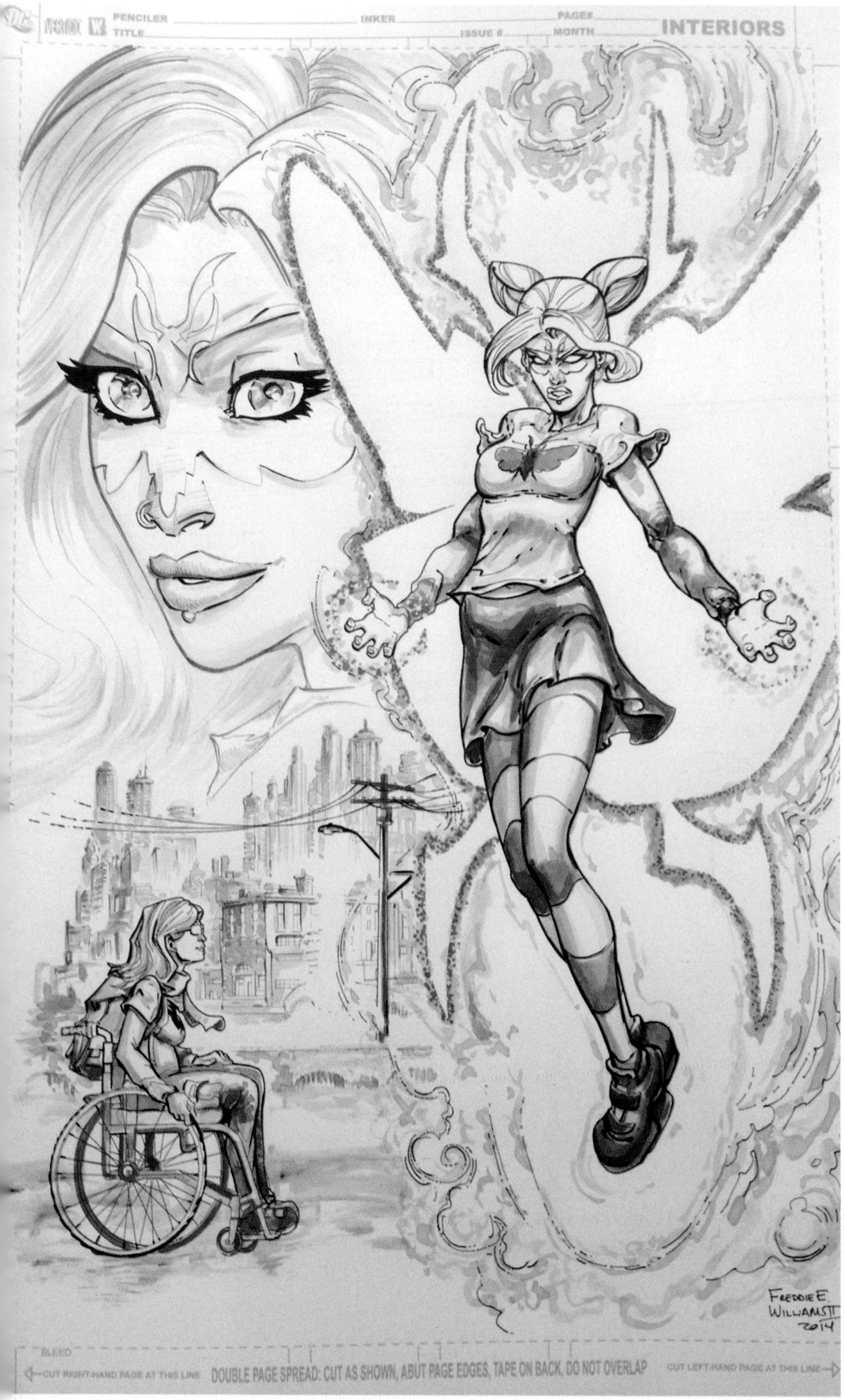
PENCILER
INKER
PAGE#
TITLE
ISSUE #
MONTH
INTERIORS
FREDDIE E. WILLIAMS II 2014
BLEED
CUT RIGHT-HAND PAGE AT THIS LINE
DOUBLE PAGE SPREAD: CUT AS SHOWN, ABUT PAGE EDGES, TAPE ON BACK, DO NOT OVERLAP
CUT LEFT-HAND PAGE AT THIS LINE

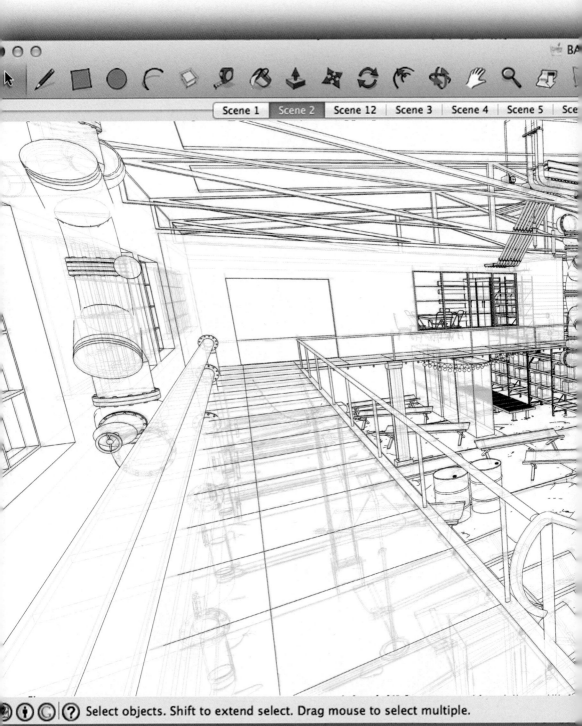

Scene 1   Scene 2   Scene 12   Scene 3   Scene 4   Scene 5   Sce

Select objects. Shift to extend select. Drag mouse to select multiple.

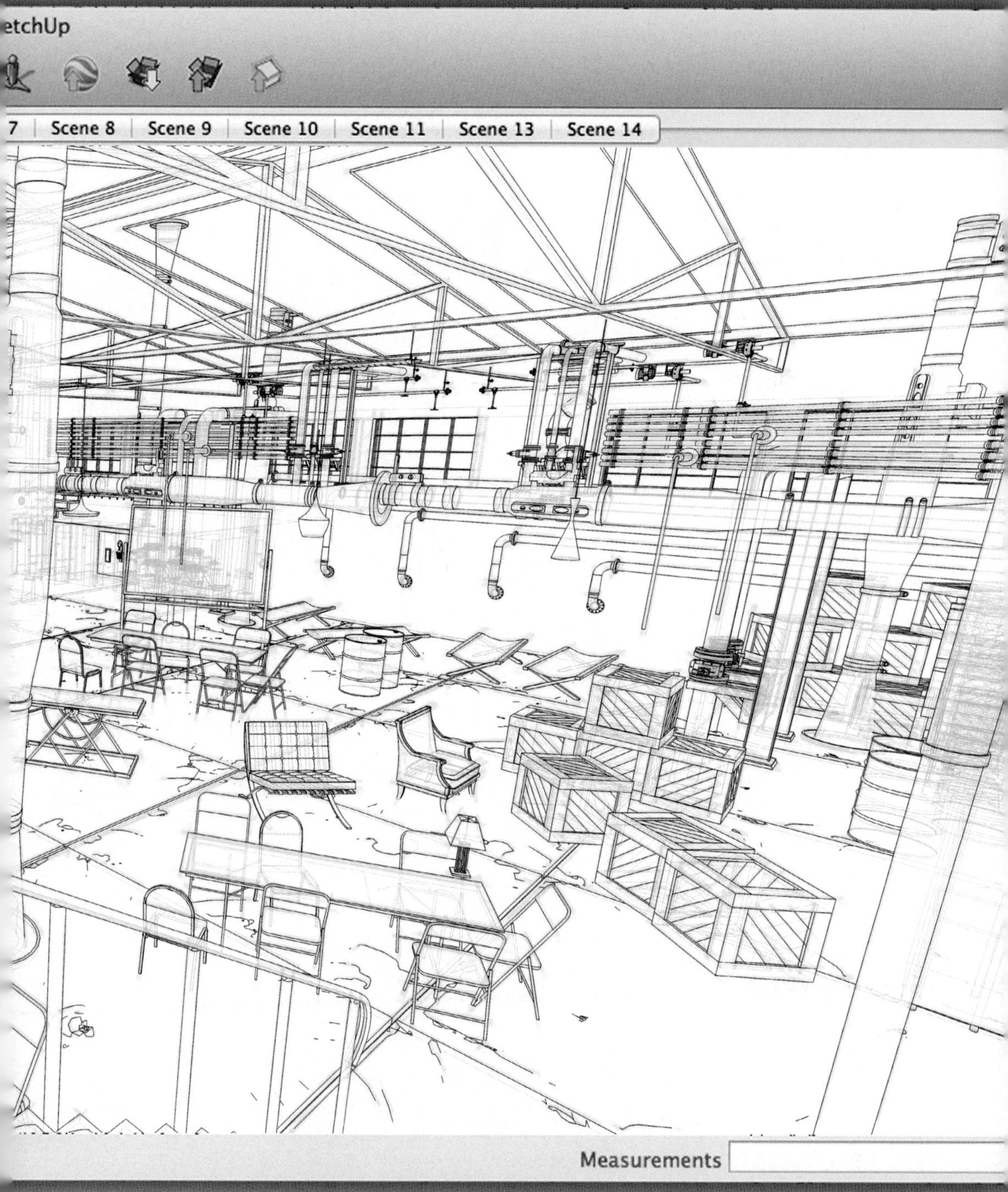
etchUp
7
Scene 8
Scene 9
Scene 10
Scene 11
Scene 13
Scene 14
Measurements

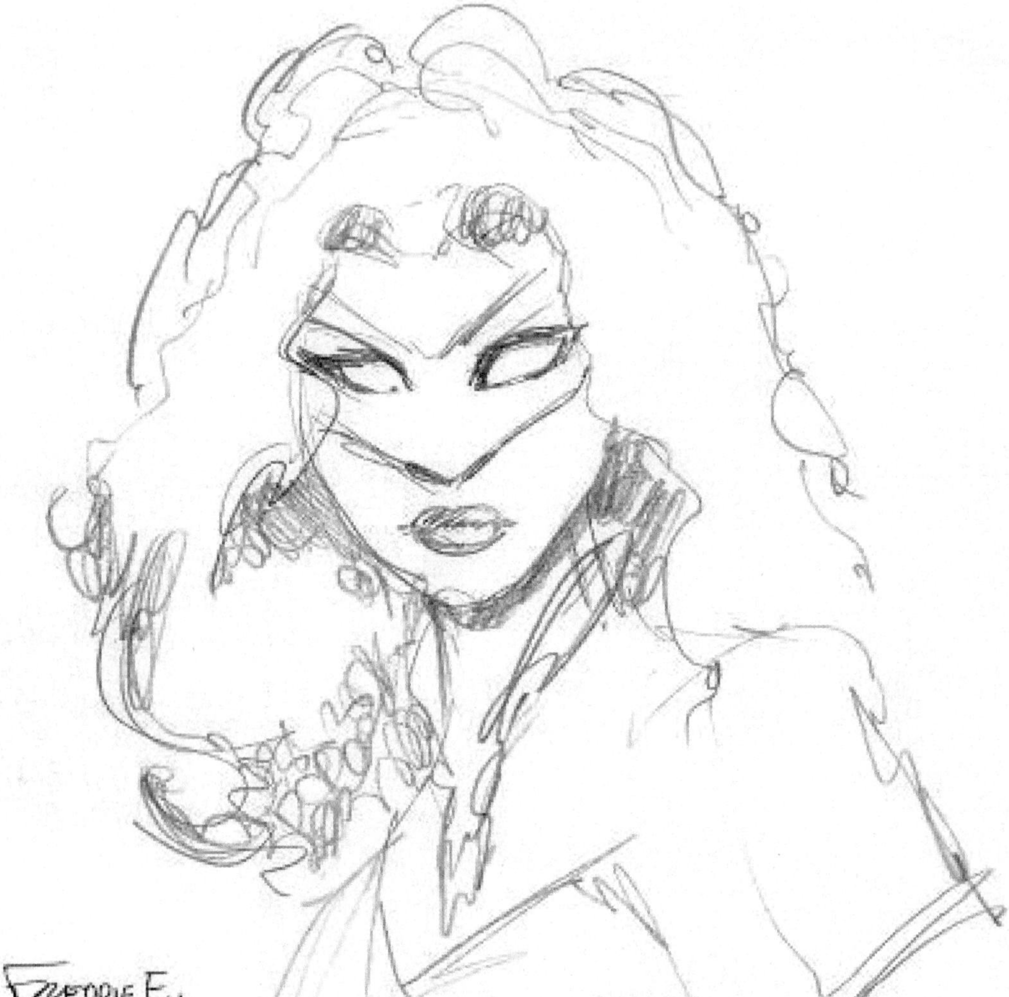
FREDDIE E.
WILLIAMS II
2013

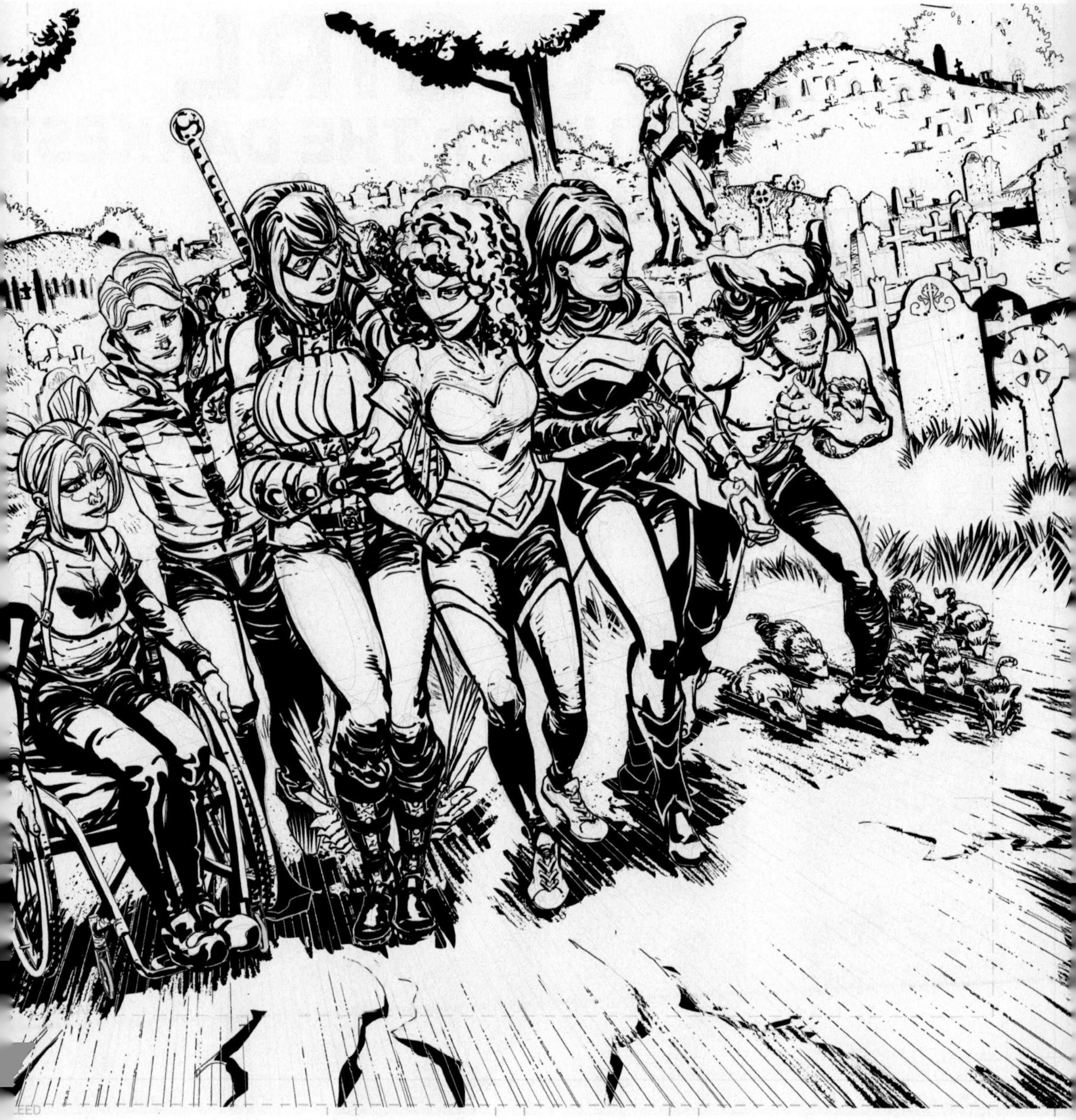

DC COMICS™

"Simone and artist Ardian Syaf not only do justice to Babs' legacy, but build in a new complexity that is the starting point for a future full of new storytelling possibilities. A hell of a ride."—IGN

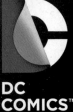

START AT THE BEGINNING!

BATGIRL

VOLUME 1: THE DARKEST REFLECTION

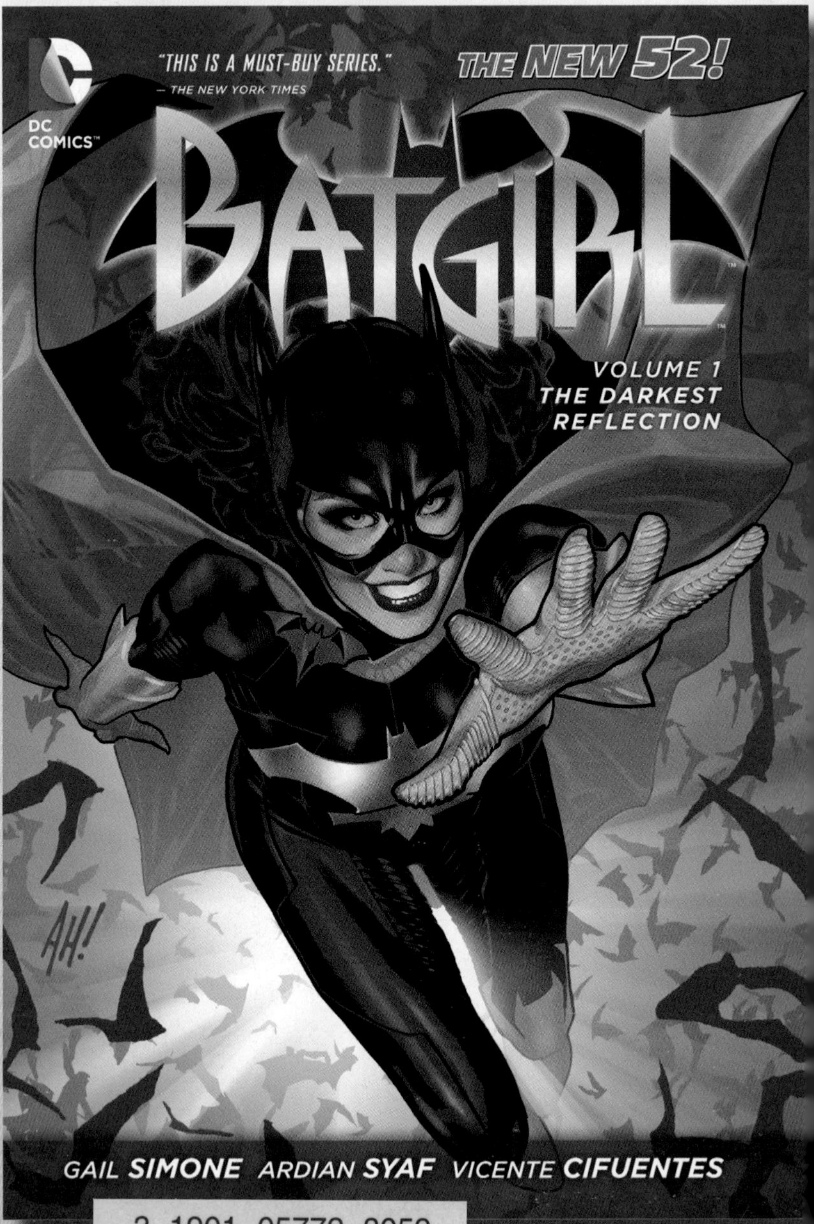
DC COMICS
"THIS IS A MUST-BUY SERIES."
— THE NEW YORK TIMES
THE NEW 52!
BATGIRL
VOLUME 1
THE DARKEST
REFLECTION
AH!
GAIL SIMONE ARDIAN SYAF VICENTE CIFUENTES

BATGIRL VOL. 2:
KNIGHTFALL
DESCENDS

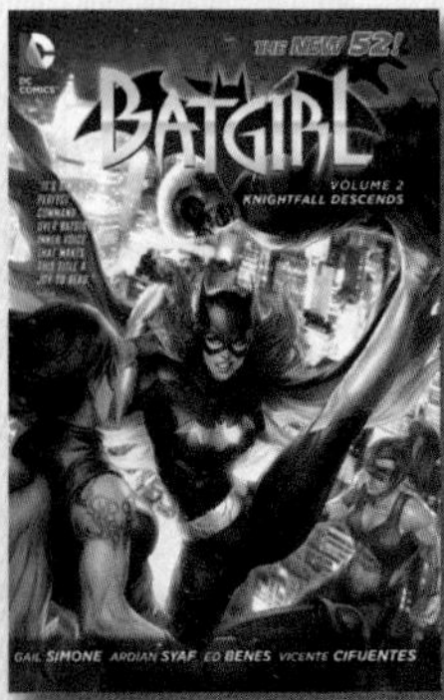
THE NEW 52!
BATGIRL
VOLUME 2
KNIGHTFALL DESCENDS
GAIL SIMONE ARDIAN SYAF ED BENES VICENTE CIFUENTES

BATGIRL VOL. 3:
DEATH OF THE FAMILY

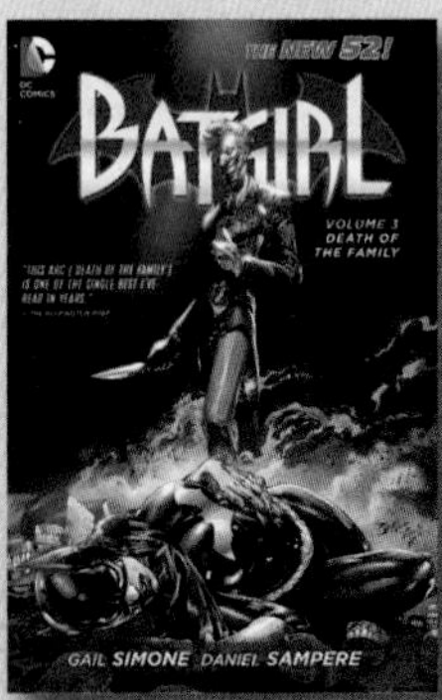
THE NEW 52!
BATGIRL
VOLUME 3
DEATH OF
THE FAMILY
GAIL SIMONE DANIEL SAMPERE

BATWOMAN VOL. 1:
HYDROLOGY

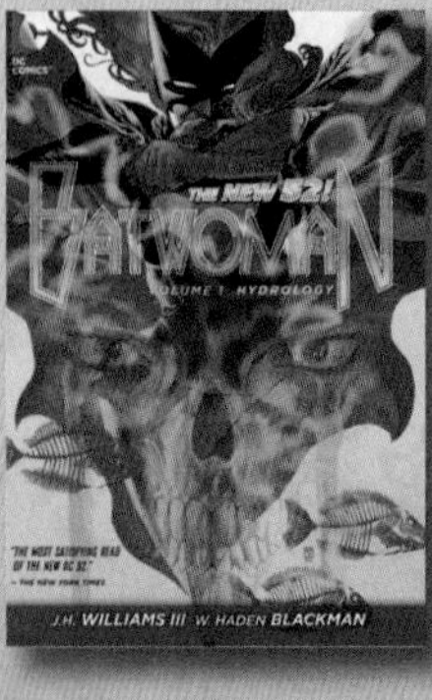
THE NEW 52!
BATWOMAN
VOLUME 1 HYDROLOGY
J.H. WILLIAMS III W. HADEN BLACKMAN